T0369247

We are the ANGELS

We are the
ANGELS

by LEROY WHITFIELD

Order this book online at www.trafford.com
or email orders@trafford.com

Most Trafford titles are also available at major online book retailers.

© Copyright 2010, 2011 Leroy Whitfield.
All rights reserved. No part of this publication may be reproduced, stored in a retrieval
system, or transmitted, in any form or by any means, electronic, mechanical, photocopying,
recording, or otherwise, without the written prior permission of the author.

The views expressed in this work are solely those of the author and do not necessarily reflect
the views of the publisher, and the publisher hereby disclaims any responsibility for them.

Printed in the United States of America.

ISBN: 978-1-4269-3407-0 (sc)
ISBN: 978-1-4269-3408-7 (hc)
ISBN: 978-1-4269-3409-4 (e)

Library of Congress Control Number: 2011902952

Trafford rev. 02/22/2011

 www.trafford.com

North America & international
toll-free: 1 888 232 4444 (USA & Canada)
phone: 250 383 6864 ✦ fax: 812 355 4082

CONTENTS

INTRODUCTION

If you have received this book and are interested in what it has to say, may God bless you for being spiritually aware and hungry enough to seek a greater understanding of God's Word. With God's help, this book will make the attempt to explain some of the hidden mysteries of God that have eluded humankind's understanding for thousands of years. You may ask, "Why has this understanding escaped mankind for so long?" The answer is that it was part of God's plan to hide it until the appointed time. I am confident thought that God has not revealed this plan to me alone; there are others in the world who know this truth and will recognize it when they read it, but I know that most will reject this message and that is simply because this book has to be spiritually discerned. I understand this, and it cannot be helped. Nevertheless, I know that there will be those who will accept it, and for that reason alone I believe I should share this understanding with those who have a thirst for a spiritual understanding of God Word.

These revelations are extremely difficult to explain, because they concern heavenly things and as humans, we are limited to explaining these heavenly things in earthly terms. In most cases, there are no accurate earthly words, so I must use words that can only come close to the spiritual meaning. There are many spiritual things I would love to reveal to you but these things are mostly felt and cannot be explained. Understanding spiritual things, however, is one of the main reasons God placed us on this earth: not just for the purpose of saving us, but to also teach us to have understanding. Most of us who believe think that salvation is God's only objective, but what we don't understand is that along with salvation, that it must be accompanied knowledge of spiritual things, or God's will. This is our final objective.

God has made this difficult by hiding his will within the words of the Bible. One way to hide meaning with words is to speak in the form of parables. This way, man would be forced to seek God's help in the attempt to understand his word. This in turn is supposed to make the man humble. The other way to hide things within the Bible is to write some things in a natural way, some in a spiritual way, and some symbolically. If a person cannot tell what to take literally and what to take spiritually, he or she will never truly understand what is written within the Bible. These are but a few ways he has hidden things that most do not understand.

This book will attempt to unlock the symbolic language for the average reader so that he or she might understand the methods God uses to preserve the truth and some of his hidden truths that are within the Bible. If it had been written for all to see and know, in some simple form, people would have changed it by now to suit their own needs, but no one can change what they cannot understand. Furthermore, those who would have sought to change the Bible would have to have been offended by what was written, but if they could not understood what was written, then they would have no reason to change it since they would not know it was referring to them.

Now, with no further delay, I will get to the core meaning of this book, which is encompassed in the title of the chapter itself, "The Doctrine of the Election."

Chapter One

The Doctrine of the Election

The doctrine of the election is part of a much larger plan called predestination. Predestination means to predetermine and outcome by manipulating the circumstances. Simply put God operates invisibly, unseen by the most, expect those whom he chooses to reveal his plan to. Because God operates in secret, most people don't think He is doing anything or is the type of God that just sits back and watches while twit tiling his thumbs. This understanding is to me is an inactive unjust God who does not care about the affairs of man, this is not the God I have come to understand. The God I have come to understand is a very active God who is actively involved in the affairs of man. This is why he has chosen this time for me to share the understanding that has been given to as to just how active he is and has been, since the beginning of time. The way in which I hope to show all that read this book is by explaining just a small portion of his plan called the Doctrine of Election. This is a plan put in place in order to bring about the salvation by perfecting man's love towards God and his fellow man. Most people are completely unaware of God's plan which involves predetermining certain things. In fact most people believe that everything in this universe is based on choice, even the salvation of God. Choice does play a it's part, but let me ask you this question, if you eventually made a choice that was influence by some else it that choice completely yours? Most people believe that these two things oppose one other. This book makes the attempt at showing how choice and predestation, which really means God's choice, as to how they can both work together as one. Before I go any further into the explanation of the Doctrine of Election, let me address the most burning question that anyone would have concerning predestation or election. The question is what is the purpose of it? The answer is love. Love is God's ultimate goal, love is perfection. Love fulfills of God's law, and his will. The problem is that love can't be forced upon anyone. God can't make anyone love him or for that matter anyone else, including one's self. So in order to cause this love to manifest itself in almost all men towards Him, his fellow man, as well as himself, God has to come up with and elaborate plan in order to achieve this. This plan has to be kept secret, no one can know what you are doing behind the scenes, because that would spoil the plan. How would knowing what is going on affect God's plan? When scientist, or doctors are conducting an experiment in order to find an answer by using different group of people they always have a control group. The control group in this case are God's chosen people the other groups are unaware just as they are in any earthy experiment. What is God trying to find out? Who will love Him. By predestation he caused his control group to love him, but they are few. The majority, however, he wants' them to love him by choice. If you told them how to pass the test, how would you know if you have arrived at a true answer? For that matter, does anyone give a test and hand out the answers to the test at the same time, no because that wouldn't be a test.

This plan was put in place before the world was even created. This was a plan put in motion by God and his Son from the very beginning in order to save man, their most precious creation. This is because God knew the nature of man before man knew his own nature which is destructive in and of itself, in which the man is mostly unaware of. What was wrong with the nature of man that he is aware of? We are not born with love in our hearts. Love has to learned and this is something that God cannot make and so this is why we could not be made perfect upon our creation; time would be needed to perfect it. This means that the Father and the Son knew what it would take to save most people from themselves, because they lacked the ability to love like him even before they were created. They also knew that this meant that not all of their creations would return, and so to ensure that at least 95 percent of men would return to him, they put a plan in motion. That plan in it's entirety is called the Doctrine of Predestination, but that plan is so large even I cannot completely understand it. The reason is it so large is because it involves everybody and everything, and so I chose to write only about a small portion of that plan. This in and of itself will still prove to be very difficult.

What we need to understand about the Doctrine of Election is that this plan have to have been put in place before the foundation of the world. Yes this means that God the Father and God the Son had to have discussed everything that they were going to do before they did it. This means that they had to plan everything if they were going to be successful. The part that I want to focus on is how they decided whom out of their creations they were going to predestinate first, before the world began. You might ask what does it mean to predestinate someone? It means to predetermine their life as to how it will turn out. This is achieved by directing them on a path that they will at first feel like they chose for themselves, but later on realize that they were being directed. Who directs them, the Holy Spirit. You also might ask why did God predestinate them and for what purpose. Those who are predestinated are called chosen, and the answer to that question is found in Romans 8:29.

> For whom he did foreknow, he also did predestinate to be conformed to the image of his Son, that he might be the firstborn among many brethren. Moreover whom he did predestinate, them he also called: and whom he called, them he also justified: and whom he justified, them he also glorified.

Many people think that these scriptures means that they way in which God foreknew people is by going through time and seeing what they would choose. They problem with that understanding is that it means that God chose the person because of what the man did. This means that the person was chosen because of his works and the Bible has concluded that works are unto debt and that works are not of faith. That is the problem with God making a choice by what the man does in his or her lifetime. What most people have not considered is that these scriptures point towards another way that God decided who would be chosen. Before I explain the how though, I would like to point out one more detail about these scriptures and that is the answer to the question of what are they being predestined for. The answer to that question is to be conformed in the image of his Son. What this means is that there are people in this world today who are being made to going through trials and tribulations for the purposes of teaching how to be like Christ. One might say, isn't that what all Christians are learning, and the answer would be yes, except for there is one difference, who's teaching them. In this case, it is the God in the form of the Holy Spirit teaching these select few. This is so that their won't be any mistakes and that these few will learn his perfect will.

This doctrine was conceived out of the very thought of how he was going to perfect his first creations, the angels. You might ask, "I thought we were talking about man?" The answer is yes and no. Man was the Lord's second greatest creation, but before he created man he first created the angels. What most people don't realize is that they were in need of salvation long before Adam was. How could I conceive the thought that an angel was in need of salvation? The answer is this, I have come to understand love and for love God you need your soul. Angels do not have souls because a soul is an earthly thing. This is what they lacked, and without a soul you cannot love with your heart. The angels were in need of a soul. A soul has two very important functions, first and foremost it is connected to the heart and it is what makes it possible for us to love. Without a soul we would not be capable of love. This love can then be used to love the one who created it, which is God, as well as his or her fellow man. The second function a soul helps us to achieve is to experience things spiritually. Things such as joy, happiness, sadness and regret which in-turn teach us the next most important thing God wants us to know is the difference between good and evil.

Man as we know it is a combination of earth and heaven. We all know the part that is of the earth, but what we don't know is the part that is from heaven. The part that is from heaven is our spirit. The spirit that God put's into our body does not come from out of thin air it comes from that of an angel. This way God ultimately teaches that angel how to love him as well as how to love his counterparts. Why do I believe that God did this? This is because I understand love, and that it cannot be forced, it cannot be made, it can only be learned overtime, therefore it cannot be programmed into the angels upon their creations. This would even explain why some of his angels turned against him, they didn't understand him.

Whether we know it or not, man's destiny and that of the angels are tied together more than anyone can ever imagine. This is why I answered the question with yes and no. What we need to understand is that sin began in heaven long before Adam ate off the wrong tree. Another reason for why an angel would be in need of salvation, the answer lies in the fact that a war took place in heaven. If a war in heaven does not strike you as a big problem for God, this is why you are oblivious to the angels being

4

in need of salvation long before man. If you are curious, you would have to ask yourself, "How could a war have occurred in heaven in the first place?" The answer to that question will amaze you: they could not receive the Holy Spirit because they were in need of a soul which is necessary for salvation.

Before I explain why a soul is necessary, let us first consider the traditional story about Lucifer, who was an angel. Iniquity was found in him. The questions are: what was that iniquity, and how was it even possible for iniquity to be found within an angel? I am trying to tell you about his iniquity, which led to the doctrine of election. Most people think that the angels were made perfect, but, in fact, they were not. The evidence is in the fact that there was a war in heaven. If we can conclude that one angel was bad, we can conclude that it was also possible for many more angels to be capable of going against the will of God. If one could be disobedient, then more than one could be disobedient. If more than one could be disobedient, where does is stop? Just how many could turn against their creator? Either God made all of them perfect, or he made none of them perfect. The answer is that he made none of them perfect, if not all. How do we know this? We know because God is fair. He would have never made some angels perfect and others imperfect. God would have made them all the same. Is there evidence that he did not make them perfect? Yes, there is evidence found in the book of Job.

The Origins of the Plan

The last question prompted me to see where the origins of the plan of predestination comes from. I was asked by none other than Job himself, a man who couldn't understand why God would allow the things that happened. Especially since he felt that he had been doing right in the sight of God.

Job 4:17–20 (KJV), it says,

> Shall mortal man be more just than God? shall a man be more pure than his maker? Behold, he put no trust in his servants; and his angels he charged with folly: How much less in them that dwell in houses of clay, whose foundation is in the dust, which are crushed before the moth?

Job ask this question because he did not feel trusted by God, and as he later found out from God, that he didn't even trust his angels, This is why God charged them with folly, and just so no one thinks that folly is a good word, let me show you how God feels about folly, which means to have a lack of understanding. This is what God said in the book of Proverbs about anyone found with folly. Proverbs 14:18 (KJV) says, "The simple inherit folly: but the prudent are crowned with knowledge."

You might ask how his angels can be found to be without understanding. The short answer is that they were newly created beings and did not know any better. What does anyone know on the day he or she is born? This is the only logical explanation as to why the angel Lucifer said what he said to God, which led to God having to kick him out of heaven. Now, read about the folly God charged to his angel Lucifer.

In Ezekiel 28:13–18 (KJV), it says,

Thou hast been in Eden the garden of God; every precious stone was thy covering, the sardius, topaz, and the diamond, the beryl, the onyx, and the jasper, the sapphire, the emerald, and the carbuncle, and gold: the workmanship of thy tabrets and of thy pipes was prepared in thee in the day that thou wast created. Thou art the anointed cherub that covereth; and I have set thee so: thou wast upon the holy mountain of God; thou hast walked up and down in the midst of the stones of fire. Thou wast perfect in thy ways from the day that thou wast created, till iniquity was found in thee. By the multitude of thy merchandise they have filled the midst of thee with violence, and thou hast sinned: therefore I will cast thee as profane out of the mountain of God: and I will destroy thee, O covering cherub, from the midst of the stones of fire. Thine heart was lifted up because of thy beauty, thou hast corrupted thy wisdom by reason of thy brightness: I will cast thee to the ground, I will lay thee before kings, that they may behold thee. Thou hast defiled thy sanctuaries by the multitude of thine iniquities, by the iniquity of thy traffick; therefore will I bring forth a fire from the midst of thee, it shall devour thee, and I will bring thee to ashes upon the earth in the sight of all them that behold thee.

This is the first sin, which took place long before Adam sinned, and this was the problem in heaven with God's angels. It was based on what

Lucifer did. This is why God needed this plan, not just to save us, but to save his angels first. With the help of the Holy Spirit, I will try to show you this using the Bible as my only reference and evidence of what I have said so far. Let us read more about what Lucifer said to himself that God calls folly. In Isaiah 14:12–15 (KJV), it says,

> How art thou fallen from heaven, O Lucifer, son of the morning! how art thou cut down to the ground, which didst weaken the nations! For thou hast said in thine heart, I will ascend into heaven, I will exalt my throne above the stars of God: I will sit also upon the mount of the congregation, in the sides of the north: I will ascend above the heights of the clouds; I will be like the most High. Yet thou shalt be brought down to hell, to the sides of the pit.

This is the folly; this comes from the lack of understanding. The point that I am making here is that this folly was the cause of the war in heaven. That war was started by an angel, who led other angels into this rebellion. These angels belonged to God and saw God face-to-face, and yet they still rebelled against him. Lucifer, who was an angel, decided to turn against his creator. "How was this even possible in the first place?" Many Christians believe that angels do not have free will, but these scriptures tell us otherwise.

Free will is a basic right of all of God's creations, and free will is the only way God will ever receive the love he seeks from all his creations. However, before God can receive that love, he had to stop his angels from rebelling against him, and the solution to that problem is directly connected to the destiny of man. The destiny of the angels and man are connected, whether we know it or not. One of the reasons why they are connected is that the angels had just found out that they would not be the heirs to the kingdom of God and that man would be the heir. This put them in direct conflict with each other, and this I truly believe led to the iniquity found in Lucifer. This prompted a question found in the Bible that I believe a man could not have asked but could only have come from an angel. That question is, "What is man?" found in Hebrews 2:9–11:

> But one in a certain place testified, saying, What is man, that thou art mindful of him? or the son of man that thou visitest him? Thou madest him a little lower than the angels; thou crownedst him

with glory and honour, and didst set him over the works of thy hands: Thou hast put all things in subjection under his feet. For in that he put all in subjection under him, he left nothing that is not put under him. But now we see not yet all things put under him.

I believe this angel is asking this question, because he just found out that the angels will neither inherit the kingdom of God nor will they be part of it. The answer to his question, I believe, is found in Hebrews 2:5 (KJV): "For unto the angels hath he not put in subjection the world to come, whereof we speak."

Not only did God exclude the angels from the world to come, he also told them that they would always be servants and that a servant could not inherit the kingdom of God.

Hebrews 1:13–14 (KJV) says,

But to which of the angels said he at any time, Sit on my right hand, until I make thine enemies thy footstool? Are they not all ministering spirits, sent forth to minister for them who shall be heirs of salvation?

Focus on the fact that this scripture reveals that an angel was to minister to those who are called heirs. In other words, they were not called heirs. This is additional confirmation of the fact that heirs are also called firstfruits, and firstfruits are chosen by God.

James 1:17–18 says,

Every good gift and every perfect gift is from above, and cometh down from the Father of lights, with whom is no variableness, neither shadow of turning. Of his own will begat he us with the word of truth, that we should be a kind of firstfruits of his creatures.

God knew the angels would rebel against him, based on the fact that they lacked understanding. What was that lack of understanding? It was a lack of understanding of who he was, why he created them, and what their destiny was. As a result of this, he created the plan known as the election, without telling them. How can I make such a bold statement? The answer is found in the book of Romans.

Romans 8:19–25 says,

> For the earnest expectation of the creature waiteth for the manifestation of the sons of God. For the creature was made subject to vanity, not willingly, but by reason of him who hath subjected the same in hope, Because the creature itself also shall be delivered from the bondage of corruption into the glorious liberty of the children of God. For we know that the whole creation groaneth and travaileth in pain together until now. And not only they, but ourselves also, which have the firstfruits of the Spirit, even we ourselves groan within ourselves, waiting for the adoption, to wit, the redemption of our body. For we are saved by hope: but hope that is seen is not hope: for what a man seeth, why doth he yet hope for? But if we hope for that we see not, then do we with patience wait for it.

Who are the "creatures" that were made "subject to vanity" and were "not willing" participants of this plan? Why, none other than the angels themselves, and the being responsible for making them subject to this vanity is God himself. What was this hope that he had for them? That hope was based on the hope that if he did this to them, they would learn to love him and return to him greater than they were when he first made them. This would be accomplished by remaking them in human form; this would be the first act of this plan, which would mark the beginning of the plan of salvation of men, who were formerly angels. If he had not done this, they would not able to be part of the new world that God was going to create. Why? Because iniquity or folly was found in them. Does the Bible tell us this? Yes, this answer is found in the book of Hebrews, something I mentioned a little earlier in this chapter.

Hebrews 2:5 (KJV) says, "For unto the angels hath he not put in subjection the world to come, whereof we speak."

Why would this scripture be found in the Bible? Why would the Bible say that an angel is not subject to the world to come? "Not subject" means not having a role to play, unless the answer is what I have been hinting at all along, and that is that an angel is only at the first stage of the evolutionary process that will ultimately lead to perfection. During this stage, only the spirit was created, but the problem with just being a spirit is that you don't have a soul. What is the problem with just being a spirit? First of all, God is a spirit but not just a spirit only. God also has a soul. What is a soul useful for? A soul gives you the ability to love; without it, you can never learn from mistakes.

The second stage of that process is that of man. This is where God combines heaven and earth, by putting a spirit with a soul. How did God perform this act? He did it by putting the spirit of that angel in the man. Putting the spirit of the former angel into the man gives both a chance to learn the difference between good and evil at the same time. That is where our spirits come from. The funny thing is that if you asked any Christian today where he or she comes from, he or she would say without hesitation, "From heaven." Christians will also say that when they die, they are going home, but for some reason, they do not fully understand why they say this. Why do we somehow feel that heaven is home, unless it somehow was?

There are three stages altogether in this evolutionary process; the third stage will be when we are resurrected by God. We will shed the flesh and receive a new body, an incorruptible body, that will be combined with a soul and spirit. Then we will truly be like God, having a trinity of our own. What do I mean by this? God is a trinity, having a soul, a spirit, and a body. Their names are the Father, the Holy Spirit, and the Son. These are the three that are one. When He is finished making us, we will have a soul, a spirit, and a body like his, therefore completing the process.

This was done so that God could beget us again, three times in all. The first is when we were created as angels, the second when we were men, and the last time upon our resurrection. Christ followed this same path, and he became the first to return to his father; the rest are still asleep. The reason that God would not bestow this inheritance upon the angels was because he had not finished making them. This is why Christ is called his only begotten son. What is a begotten son? First, let me establish that Christ was the first begotten and the only begotten at that time.

John 3:16 (KJV) says, "For God so loved the world, that he gave his only begotten Son, that whosoever believeth in him should not perish, but have everlasting life."

Begotten means fathered through training and chastising. Anyone who is not chastened does not become a son of God. This is why these scriptures are found in the book of Hebrews.

10

Hebrews 12:5–11 (KJV) says,

> And ye have forgotten the exhortation which speaketh unto you as unto children, My son, despise not thou the chastening of the Lord, nor faint when thou art rebuked of him: For whom the Lord loveth he chasteneth, and scourgeth every son whom he receiveth. If ye endure chastening, God dealeth with you as with sons; for what son is he whom the father chasteneth not? But if ye be without chastisement, whereof all are partakers, then are ye bastards, and not sons. Furthermore we have had fathers of our flesh which corrected us, and we gave them reverence: shall we not much rather be in subjection unto the Father of spirits, and live? For they verily for a few days chastened us after their own pleasure; but he for our profit, that we might be partakers of his holiness. Now no chastening for the present seemeth to be joyous, but grievous: nevertheless afterward it yieldeth the peaceable fruit of righteousness unto them which are exercised thereby.

This is what God wants to do to us all, and this is what he could not do to the angels. This is also one of the reasons why Christ returned to his father greater than was before he left heaven. This is also reflected in scriptures found in the book of Hebrews.

Hebrews 1:4–6 (KJV) says,

> Being made so much better than the angels, as he hath by inheritance obtained a more excellent name than they. For unto which of the angels said he at any time, Thou art my Son, this day have I begotten thee? And again, I will be to him a Father, and he shall be to me a Son? And again, when he bringeth in the firstbegotten into the world, he saith, And let all the angels of God worship him.

This is why being begotten is so important; it enables us to receive the inheritance that God has waiting for us, just as he did for Christ. We receive this inheritance by becoming sons, and we become sons by becoming like Christ.

1 John 3:1–2:

Behold, what manner of love the Father hath bestowed upon us, that we should be called the sons of God: therefore the world knoweth us not, because it knew him not. Beloved, now are we the sons of God, and it doth not yet appear what we shall be: but we know that, when he shall appear, we shall be like him; for we shall see him as he is.

This is the answer to the question that was presented in the Bible that could only have come from an angel, and that question was "What is man?" Man was to become like Christ if he received him. This is what it means when Christ said he had the ability to make you a son of God. This is found in the book of 1 John.

John 1:12 says, "But as many as received him, to them gave he power to become the sons of God, even to them that believe on his name ..." This "power to become the sons of God" is our destiny, a destiny that the angels did not share, and this ultimately caused the war in heaven. There is another cause for the angels' initiation of the war in heaven. That other cause once again is based on man's destiny, which is to judge the world. Consider the following scriptures found in the book of Corinthians.

In 1 Corinthians 6:2–3 (KJV)

"Do ye not know that the saints shall judge the world? and if the world shall be judged by you, are ye unworthy to judge the smallest matters? Know ye not that we shall judge angels? how much more things that pertain to this life?"

Why does this scripture tell us that we will be judging angels? We will be judging them; we are them, and they are us. We will be judging our brothers and our sisters, and God has made a logical decision to plan such a judgment. We are the perfect choices for this job, because we are the peers of our brothers. Who else would understand what our brothers have gone through? Who better to judge a peer than someone who endured the same challenges and made some of the same mistakes and the same decisions? Up to this point, I have been talking about the doctrine of election from its origins to its final stages, but I have yet to discuss it from the standpoint of those who knew that they were elected in the Bible. Now I must digress and talk about this plan once again from its origins, from others who have known this plan in the past and how it pertains to what they have said in the Bible.

Who Are the Elects?

Now that I have discussed the origin as well as the end result of God's plan of election and the necessity of it, let's discuss how this doctrine relates to those who were the elects from times past and what they did. Remember, this doctrine involved people who were chosen to carry out specific missions for God; these people from the past are people, such as the prophets and apostles, as well as many others we may never know about until Christ returns. This doctrine is the center of all discussion throughout this book but is the main focus of this chapter. Those who were able to come into the understanding of this plan are called God's elects. An elect is a person who was chosen before the world began to know God's plan for salvation for all men through the receiving of his Holy Spirit. This is the meaning of the promised son, who would receive the promised seed. This means that at the appointed time for each of God's chosen, the Holy Spirit will teach him or her and that no man would teach these people to know the things about the Father and his son, Jesus Christ. I have understood this plan for the last ten years of my life and have tried repeatedly to share it with others to no avail. In fact, I have found it impossible to share with others, and I was confounded as to why until now. The short answer was that it simply was not time yet for anyone to know, and so God would not allow it to be known. However, I now believe that I have received the order to share it with you by means of this book. Therefore, I pray that you are able to receive it and not reject it before you have completely read this book.

Today, the biggest concern of most Christians in this world—or for that matter, any person of any religion—is whether or not they are saved by their God. Some will believe that they are saved, without a doubt, but most will live in doubt of that for the rest of their lives. The elect do not live in doubt or fear of their salvation, because God has assured them. He has assured them by the many revelations they have received from him. You might ask these questions, "If there are such people in the world, why haven't they made themselves known? Why haven't they come forth with all of these revelations to edify the church?" The answer is that no one is willing to listen to them, because what they have to say will seem to be different from what the church has told them. In fact, most Christians would accuse them of blasphemy against the church. The chosen of the past who have come forth because it was their appointed time to do so have been killed for what they know. Have you forgotten that Israel killed all of its prophets and the apostles? They were chosen by God, but did Israel listen to them? The answer is no, and neither will anyone listen to them today, because their message does not sit well with mainstream religion. This is based solely on the fact that the law still exists; it is their choice to remain under it. The only way you can understand what a chosen of God is trying to say is first to be willing to accept the true freedom that is in Christ and come out from under law or the first covenant.

Another problem mankind has with those who have been chosen is that other people will never accept a person who insists that God really talks to him or her; this world includes the church ironically. This is because there have been so many false prophets in the past and so it is easy to think that this person is not of God as well. Nevertheless, there has always been an election or hidden ones. When Isaiah the prophet thought that he was the only person left in Israel who still believed in God, what did God tell him?

In 1 Kings 19:18 (KJV)

"Yet I have left me seven thousand in Israel, all the knees which have not bowed unto Baal, and every mouth which hath not kissed him."

Even Isaiah didn't know about these hidden ones, because God hides them from the world. As to the why, I will discuss that in another chapter. The election can be summed up in the book of Romans.

How Do They Know They Are Elect?

The elect are the people who God chose to carry out specific parts of his plan. They are people that he says he foreknew, which means that either he went down through time and knew that they would do as he asked, or he gave them the will to do what he asked from the beginning of their lives. The evidence of this can be found in the book of Romans.

Romans 8:29–30 says,

For whom he did foreknow, he also did predestinate to be conformed to the image of his Son, that he might be the firstborn

14

among many brethren. Moreover whom he did predestinate, them he also called: and whom he called, them he also justified: and whom he justified, them he also glorified.

Those who were predestinated are called the elect or children of promise; they are the first to be conformed into the image of Christ. They are the first to become aware of the doctrine of election; even though they did not know it, they were chosen before they were born, and they were not chosen at random. God chose the elects for a particular reason. That reason will be addressed later on in this chapter; for now, we will focus on examining who these elects are. Remember, the purpose of this plan is so that the election will stand or come to pass, meaning the elects will accomplish what God intended for them to accomplish. In the book of Romans, God demonstrates the fact that he can favor or dislike people even before they are born. The notion that God judges a person before he or she has had the opportunity to live and make decisions may seem unfair and some may even say ungodly. However, the following passages confirm the accuracy of this statement.

Romans 9:8–14 (KJV) says,

That is, They which are the children of the flesh, these are not the children of God: but the children of the promise are counted for the seed. For this is the word of promise, At this time will I come, and Sarah shall have a son. And not only this; but when Rebecca also had conceived by one, even by our father Isaac; (For the children being not yet born, neither having done any good or evil, that the purpose of God according to election might stand, not of works, but of him that calleth; It was said unto her, The elder shall serve the younger. As it is written, Jacob have I loved, but Esau have I hated. What shall we say then? Is there unrighteousness with God? God forbid.

Romans 9:11 says, "(For the children being not yet born, neither having done any good or evil, that the purpose of God according to election might stand, not of works, but of him that calleth ..."

How can God make such a decision unless he knew you more intimately than you realize at this time? These passages demonstrate that

God can like or dislike a person before he or she is born at the same time these scriptures do not address the reason why. The reason, however, goes far beyond a man's ability to understand. A man can understand these things only with the help of the Holy Spirit. This is what the Lord said in the book of John to his apostles.

John 15:16 says, "Ye have not chosen me, but I have chosen you, and ordained you, that ye should go and bring forth fruit, and that your fruit should remain: that whatsoever ye shall ask of the Father in my name, he may give it you."

This is what the Lord has said to all those who have been chosen in the book of 2 Thessalonians.

2 Thessalonians 2:13–14, it says,

But we are bound to give thanks alway to God for you, brethren beloved of the Lord, because God hath from the beginning chosen you to salvation through sanctification of the Spirit and belief of the truth: Whereunto he called you by our gospel, to the obtaining of the glory of our Lord Jesus Christ.

In John 15:16, the Bible tells us that he chose us; this contradicts how most think they receive their salvation. They believe it is simply by their choice alone. While this is true for some, it is not true for all. Despite all of the clear answers in the Bible, a person may or may not be able to completely understand what he or she is without the Holy Spirit. Most have not gotten to know him yet.

Most of us know Christ, but what we do not know is who the Holy Spirit is. His job is to teach us. This is because God does not want man to come into an understanding without his help. If we figured this out on our own, we would most likely become vain in our own understanding. In order to prevent this, God hid this wisdom within parables, so that we would need him to achieve the understanding that is hidden from most. This is so that no one will be able to boast, and most important, so that we may all agree. This is God's method of bringing us into one understanding and as well as overcoming our many different interpretations of his word. We will all need his Holy Spirit to properly interpret his word. Then we will all be on one accord. Without it, we are just guessing and in

16

disagreement. The understanding, however, is given to the elects, not without studying, but not by studying alone. This is why the apostle Paul said in 1 Corinthians 2:6–7 (KJV):

> Howbeit we speak wisdom among them that are perfect: yet not the wisdom of this world, nor of the princes of this world, that come to nought: But we speak the wisdom of God in a mystery, even the hidden wisdom, which God ordained before the world unto our glory …

The doctrine of election is also called hidden manna or hidden wisdom, known only by the elects. This hidden manna teaches us that people will be saved in a particular order and will be raised in this same order. Most people do not realize that not all people will be saved at the same time but in a particular order. The first to be saved, as stated previously, are called the elects, and then those who have been called, because they have believed in Christ also before they have seen him. The last group of people to be saved are those who were previously lost and only came to believe after they had seen him. This is why Christ told Thomas, "You believe because you see me, but blessed are the ones who believe in me without seeing me." This was an indication that Christ would save some who only believed after they saw him, just as Thomas did. However, this will be during the thousand years of the reign of Christ on earth. This order is mentioned in the book of Corinthians.

1 Corinthians 15:20–23 (KJV), it says,

> But now is Christ risen from the dead, and become the firstfruits of them that slept. For since by man came death, by man came also the resurrection of the dead. For as in Adam all die, even so in Christ shall all be made alive. But every man in his own order: Christ the firstfruits; afterward they that are Christ's at his coming.

The first fruits are predestined, but not everyone is predestined by God, only the first fruits. This still means, however, that there are second and third fruits or those who answered the call before they saw him and those who answered the call after they saw him. Being predestined does not mean that God makes the person's everyday choices; being predestined only determines where a person will end up despite what they have gone through. Within context, those whom God predestined in the Bible will end up with him no matter what. Even though God sent us out into the wilderness that is this world, he has ensured that all the predestined would return to him no matter what. In the beginning, none of us knows who we are or where we come from, but this will not always be so.

God's Word, whom we know as Christ, was born saved, because God had to ensure that those who didn't know him would come to know him and to ensure his Word would be spread. God had to ensure that his Word was spread by causing some to be born saved. When God gives a person this type of salvation, he also imparts another gift, a small faint understanding of how they received their salvation. Knowing this ensures that they will return first ahead of others. Those who understand God first, in time help their fellow brethren to understand God and they in-turn find salvation. Those who have been chosen or called have been used this way since the beginning in order to save others. We know them as the prophets and the apostles. When we take a closer look at what these prophets and apostles have said about themselves, they reveal that they were aware of their chosen status before they were even born. Read what Job, Isaiah, and Jeremiah had to say about themselves.

They Knew They Were Chosen

To answer this question let us first look in the book of Job.

Job 31:14–16

"Did not he that made me in the womb make him? and did not one fashion us in the womb?"

This same question puzzled Job. In other words, Job wants to know, when did he become like he was and for what purpose. The same question was asked later by Isaiah the prophet. These men of God seemed to want to know how they were chosen and from when they were chosen.

Isaiah 49:4–6 says,

"And now, saith the LORD that formed me from the womb to be his servant, to bring Jacob again to him, Though Israel be not gathered, yet shall I be glorious in the eyes of the LORD, and my God shall be my strength."

God Knew Whom He Would Choose

The question that Job, and Isaiah raised came about because they did not fully understand exactly how God was working in their lives, but according to these scriptures, God shows that he knows.

Jeremiah 1:4–6 says,

"Before I formed thee in the belly I knew thee; and before thou camest forth out of the womb I sanctified thee, and I ordained thee a prophet unto the nations."

There are many examples of those whom God has used throughout the Bible. They were used by God to physically lay the foundation of his plan of salvation. Some elects have a larger part to play, and some have a smaller role to play in this plan. One thing is certain, however, and that is that all of us are part of this plan in one way or another, whether we are saved or not.

Anyone can be used by God to carry out what has already been written in the Bible, because it has been prophesized. The Father knows who will be saved and who will not based on whether or not they will believe in him. Still, those who have come to believe and know that they are saved are still lacking something. That something is the maturing of their faith. This is what God ultimately wants us to achieve. The elects are simply those who will achieve this before the other two groups will. What most Christians don't understand is that even though salvation is a good thing, salvation alone does not please God. The Bible states that faith is the only thing that pleases God. This is found in the book of Hebrews.

Hebrews 11:6 says, "But without faith it is impossible to please him: for he that cometh to God must believe that he is, and that he is a rewarder of them that diligently seek him."

Faith is what God wants to increase in us. Salvation is a free gift and was not meant to be for a reward for our works. God's intent was that we first come into the understanding that we are saved and then seek out his wisdom as to how he made it possible. In this seeking, we would find our way back to him. Unfortunately, most Christians are not seeking the maturity of their faith and have fallen asleep spiritually. In other words, they have become satisfied with their limited knowledge of salvation. What the elects understand, by faith, is that they have been given the seed of promise, that being the Holy Spirit, and they have become baptized by fire, not by the hands of man, but by the hands of God himself, and are not under law, but grace.

They Are the Children of Promise

The children of promise is another name for the elects. For God to make a promise to someone means that it definitely will come true. This promise is that these children would not be under the law. This means that they will be free, and this freedom can only be achieved in Christ.

Romans 4:13–14 says,

"For the promise, that he should be the heir of the world, was not to Abraham, or to his seed, through the law, but through the righteousness of faith. For if they which are of the law be heirs, faith is made void, and the promise made of none effect ..."

Romans 9:7 says,

"That is, They which are the children of the flesh, these are not the children of God: but the children of the promise are counted for the seed."

The children of promise are those who were predestined to receive the Holy Spirit. This is the promise God gave to Abraham. Not every believer has the faith necessary to receive the seed, which is the Holy Spirit. The Holy Spirit is that which allows one to be counted among the first fruits.

Romans 4:5–8 says,

"But to him that worketh not, but believeth on him that justifieth the ungodly, his faith is counted for righteousness. Even as David also describeth the blessedness of the man, unto whom God imputeth righteousness without works, Saying, Blessed are they whose iniquities are forgiven, and whose sins are covered. Blessed is the man to whom the Lord will not impute sin."

Many of the people I have encountered have never read this scripture in the Bible, and even if they have, most have misunderstand it. Most think that this scripture is only made possible after a person has repented of his or her sins. What they don't realize is that with God, it is possible to have never even been born with sin. This because they have all heard the scripture found in Rom 3:23, that says, "For all have sinned and fell short of the glory." However, what they do not know is that there is another scripture that precedes this one and makes it null and void to a certain group of people. Now let us read both of these contradicting scriptures.

Romans 3:23–25 (KJV) says,

"For all have sinned, and come short of the glory of God; Being justified freely by his grace through the redemption that is in Christ Jesus: Whom God hath set forth to be a propitiation through faith in his blood, to declare his righteousness for the remission of sins that are past, through the forbearance of God ..."

When most Christians read this scripture, they only see the first part of it and conclude that they all are lost, what they fell to see is that following that same scripture is says that even they who have fallen short are set free and justified by grace. This means they have no longer fallen short. However is that does not make it clear that God makes exceptions these the next verses should found in the book of Romans.

Romans 4:4–8 (KJV),

"Now to him that worketh is the reward not reckoned of grace, but of debt. But to him that worketh not, but believeth on him that justifieth the ungodly, his faith is counted for righteousness. Even as David also describeth the blessedness of the man, unto whom God imputeth righteousness without works, Saying, Blessed are they whose iniquities are forgiven, and whose sins are covered. Blessed is the man to whom the Lord will not impute sin."

This is what makes an elect an elect; whenever God does not impute the sin of Adam to a person at birth this means they are born with sin.

People forget that they were born dead to God, not that they become dead after they have grown up in this world and commit a sin at some point in their lifetime. God did this for his elects because he knew that they would sin or transgress the law before they came into the understanding that he had chosen them. Sin by definition means to transgress the law, and if one transgress the law he or she is separated from God. An elect of God cannot be separated from him, therefore He must not impute sin to them, not that they have never committed a sin, but that He would not charge it to them. God has the power to do this. He can forgive a person before they are born. Simply put, God will not impute sin against them, even though they have sinned. This is also reflected in the book of 1 John.

1 John 3:9, it says,

"Whosoever is born of God doth not commit sin; for his seed remaineth in him: and he cannot sin, because he is born of God."

This is a very hard thing for those who are babes in Christ to understand. Most will simply not want to accept the scripture for what it is or try to change it in some type of way in their minds so that it does not mean what it says. I have also discovered that different translations of the Bible change the wording of different passages in order to accomplish this also. By the different translations, scriptures can be changed to fit the meaning of what men think they should sound like, but in effect, they are changing the Word of God. This is one scripture in particular that this has happened to. This is one of the most critical scriptures in the Bible for ever having a chance to understand the true potential of a person who is born of God. I believe that the new translations of the Bible changed this because it was too difficult to prove. So instead of us trying to figure out how this scripture, found in the King James Version, is true, it was easier to just change the wording.

Indeed, it would be problematic for anyone to accept that some people are born without sin even though they will undoubtedly commit sin at some point in time. An apparent contradiction, the statement does not make sense to those without this deeper understanding. This apparent contradiction is exemplified by the scripture I have stated earlier that states, "All are under sin." I've considered this conflict many times, but what we need to understand is that with God all things are possible. Let us consider the following passages from the Bible, concerning this conflict. Listen to what God has to say to us about it in the book of Romans.

Romans 9:18–23 says,

"Therefore hath he mercy on whom he will have mercy, and whom he will he hardeneth. Thou wilt say then unto me, Why doth he yet find fault? For who hath resisted his will? Nay but, O man, who art thou that repliest against God? Shall the thing formed say to him that formed it, Why hast thou made me thus? Hath not the potter power over the clay, of the same lump to make one vessel unto honour, and another unto dishonour? What if God, willing to shew his wrath, and to make his power known, endured with much longsuffering the vessels of wrath fitted to destruction: And that he might make known the riches of his glory on the vessels of mercy, which he had afore prepared unto glory,"

What these verses support is that God has the power to choose some before they were born to do his will and to deem them blameless or not blameless, honorable or not honorable. What can we do about it if he chooses to do this or not? Concomitantly, he has the power to proscribe others from doing his will. In the end, it is God's decision to make, and we have no choice in the matter. This is God's will, and it is not subject to our ability to understand it or agree with it. We are simply at his mercy. There are also other scriptures that support this.

Titus 3:3–7 (KJV) says,

For we ourselves also were sometimes foolish, disobedient, deceived, serving divers lusts and pleasures, living in malice and envy, hateful, and hating one another. But after that the kindness and love of God our Saviour toward man appeared, Not by works of righteousness which we have done, but according to his mercy he saved us, by the washing of regeneration, and renewing of the Holy Ghost; Which he shed on us abundantly through Jesus Christ our Saviour; That being justified by his grace, we should be made heirs according to the hope of eternal life.

This scripture acknowledges the fact that we all did foolish things before we knew God, but it verifies that salvation was never based on our acts. This is how God's grace actually saves us from ourselves. The following scriptures tell us that it is not by our works of righteousness that we are saved but through his mercy and grace. It is also telling us that he made these decisions before the foundations of the world.

Ephesians 1:3–14 (KJV) says,

Blessed be the God and Father of our Lord Jesus Christ, who hath blessed us with all spiritual blessings in heavenly places in Christ: According as he hath chosen us in him before the foundation of the world, that we should be holy and without blame before him in love: Having predestinated us unto the adoption of children by Jesus Christ to himself, according to the good pleasure of his will, To the praise of the glory of his grace, wherein he hath made us accepted in the beloved. In whom we have redemption through his blood, the forgiveness of sins, according to the riches of his grace; Wherein he hath abounded toward us in all wisdom and prudence; Having made known unto us the mystery of his will, according to his good pleasure which he hath purposed in himself: That in the dispensation of the fulness of times he might gather together in one all things in Christ, both which are in heaven, and which are on earth; even in him: In whom also we have obtained an inheritance, being predestinated according to the purpose of him who worketh all things after the counsel of his own will: That we should be to the praise of his glory, who first trusted in Christ. In whom ye also trusted, after that ye heard the word of truth, the gospel of your salvation: in whom also after that ye believed, ye were sealed with that holy Spirit of promise, Which is the earnest of our inheritance until the redemption of the purchased possession, unto the praise of his glory.

In 2 Thessalonians 2:13–17 (KJV), it says,

But we are bound to give thanks always to God for you, brethren beloved of the Lord, because God hath from the beginning chosen you to salvation through sanctification of the Spirit and belief of the truth: Where unto he called you by our gospel, to the obtaining of the glory of our Lord Jesus Christ. Therefore, brethren, stand fast, and hold the traditions which ye have been taught, whether by word, or our epistle. Now our Lord Jesus Christ himself, and God, even our Father, which hath loved us, and hath given us everlasting consolation and good hope through grace, Comfort your hearts, and establish you in every good word and work.

2 Timothy 1:6–10 (KJV) says,

Wherefore I put thee in remembrance that thou stir up the gift of God, which is in thee by the putting on of my hands. For God hath not given us the spirit of fear; but of power, and of love, and of a sound mind. Be not thou therefore ashamed of the testimony of our Lord, nor of me his prisoner: but be thou partaker of the afflictions of the gospel according to the power of God; Who hath saved us, and called us with an holy calling, not according to our works, but according to his own purpose and grace, which was given us in Christ Jesus before the world began, But is now made manifest by the appearing of our Saviour Jesus Christ, who hath abolished death, and hath brought life and immortality to light through the gospel …

Verse six of these scriptures tells us that this gift is stirred up in the chosen when God is ready for them to do what he needs them to do, by the laying on of his hands. They will be placed first in the kingdom of God, not because of anything that they have done to deserve it but because of the heart that God has given them, which is full of love for their fellow man. Through this love, the Spirit of God, who gave us the ability to understand the way God thinks and the way Christ thinks, also gave us the understanding of the suffering that he still endures to this day. This understanding, however, is important to comprehending the order in which men will enter into the kingdom. Every believer will eventually receive the Holy Spirit, but there is an order as to how and when that will occur.

The Order in which People Will Be Saved
(Spiritual virgins, forgiveness of sins from birth)

Whether we understand it or not, the Bible does inform us of an order that men will be saved in. What we need to understand is why this order exist, and in order to do that let us look at scriptures that tell us about this order.

1 Corinthians 15:20–23, it says,

But now is Christ risen from the dead, and become the firstfruits of them that slept. For since by man came death, by man came also the resurrection of the dead. For as in Adam all die, even so in Christ shall all be made alive. But every man in his own order: Christ the firstfruits; afterward they that are Christ's at his coming.

The previous passage is the most notable one in the Bible that discusses this order. This order is important to God, because it will determine the type of reward that each believer will receive. One of the main reasons that they are first is that God chose them and he trained them. This is reflected in these next scriptures found in the book of Matthew.

Matthew 19:11–13 says,

For there are some eunuchs, which were so born from their mother's womb: and there are some eunuchs, which were made eunuchs of men: and there be eunuchs, which have made themselves eunuchs for the kingdom of heaven's sake. He that is able to receive it, let him receive it.

Most people who read this scripture don't understand that it is referring to how different people come to know Christ. The word *eunuch* in this scripture means virgin, but not in the natural sense. These are spiritual virgins, which means in God's eyes, they have never been defiled, and to be undefiled means that you have never been corrupted by this world. The eunuch, or the virgins, in the previous scripture are in the order in which they will be saved, and this is where the Bible first mentions the beginning of that order, just like in 1 Corinthians 15:20–23.

There are three ways according to this scripture that one becomes a eunuch. The first eunuch was made a eunuch, or spiritual virgin, from birth, by God himself. The second eunuch was made a eunuch by other men. The last eunuch believed and made himself a virgin on his own. How did the last eunuch achieve this? This will happen in the millennium, when all will see Christ and come to believe in him. This salvation is not by faith but by sight. This salvation that will come though the millennium is the subject of another chapter. For now, just know that it is possible for God to make the decision to forgive a person's sins even before he or she is born. Whether one is living, has yet to be born, or has been resurrected, God can decide to give a person a second chance. Does the Bible support this statement? It does, and the evidence is found in the book of Hebrews.

Hebrews 11:35 (KJV) says, "Women received their dead raised to life again: and others were tortured, not accepting deliverance; that they might obtain a better resurrection …"

What else could "a better resurrection" mean, except a second chance, and who is this scripture referring to when it says "they"? I believe that the "they" refers to those who, at first, would not accept deliverance by believing in Christ while they were alive the first time. I believe God is saying that these people will have a second chance. I do not completely understand why God will do this, but I do know that he will do this, because it is written. Another reference to this order is found in Luke 12:36–38 (KJV):

And ye yourselves like unto men that wait for their lord, when he will return from the wedding; that when he cometh and knocketh, they may open unto him immediately. Blessed are those servants, whom the lord when he cometh shall find watching: verily I say unto you, that he shall gird himself, and make them to sit down to meat, and will come forth and serve them. And if he shall come in the second watch, or come in the third watch, and find them so, blessed are those servants.

These scriptures also refer to the different times the Lord will come and receive his people, and all he is asking here is that you wait faithfully for him. If you will pay close attention, you will see in verse 36 that this takes place only after the wedding. This is one way in which we know that the salvation of all who are saved doesn't take place at the same time. This means that the resurrections cannot take place at the same times also.

The book of Revelation explains the different resurrections. How does this relate to the order of salvation? If we are brought into the body at different times, we would certainly have to be raised at different times. The fact that the book of Revelation talks about a first resurrection means that there are others.

Revelation 20:6 (KJV) says, "Blessed and holy is he that hath part in the first resurrection: on such the second death hath no power, but they shall be priests of God and of Christ, and shall reign with him a thousand years."

The Order in which People Will Be Resurrected

Those who take part in the first are the chosen; they are the first to be saved, and they are the first to rise, because they are the first fruits. The Bible sometimes refers to the order as the harvest or the reaping of the earth. When the word harvest is used, it usually refers to the plants that men cultivate in a field and collect as food or fruits.

Luke 10:2 (KJV) says,

"Therefore said he unto them, The harvest truly is great, but the labourers are few: pray ye therefore the Lord of the harvest, that he would send forth labourers into   his harvest."

Matthew 13:36–43 (KJV) says,

Then Jesus sent the multitude away, and went into the house: and his disciples came unto him, saying, Declare unto us the parable of the tares of the field. He answered and said unto them, He that soweth the good seed is the Son of man; The field is the world; the good seed are the children of the kingdom; but the tares are the children of the wicked one; The enemy that sowed them is the devil; the harvest is the end of the world; and the reapers are the angels. As therefore the tares are gathered and burned in the fire; so shall it be in the end of this world. The Son of man shall send forth his angels, and they shall gather out of his kingdom all things that offend, and them which do iniquity; And shall cast them into a furnace of fire: there shall be wailing and gnashing of teeth. Then shall the righteous shine forth as the sun in the kingdom of their Father. Who hath ears to hear, let him hear.

The Bible uses the word *harvest* to refer to people and how they will be harvested. Most Christians are familiar with this term but think the harvest is a one-time event, when in fact, the Bible states that it will happen four times. This can be found in the book of Revelation. According to this book, the first is done by Christ himself when he collects his elects; the next three are done by three different angels.

Revelation 14:14–20 says,

And I looked, and behold a white cloud, and upon the cloud one sat like unto the Son of man, having on his head a golden crown, and in his hand a sharp sickle. And another angel came out of the temple, crying with a loud voice to him that sat on the cloud, Thrust in thy sickle, and reap: for the time is come for thee to reap; for the harvest of the earth is ripe. And he that sat on the cloud thrust in his sickle on the earth; and the earth was reaped. And another angel came out of the temple which is in heaven, he also having a sharp sickle. And another angel came out from the altar, which had power over fire; and cried with a loud cry to him that had the sharp sickle, saying, Thrust in thy sharp sickle, and gather the clusters of the vine of the earth; for her grapes are fully ripe. And the angel thrust in his sickle into the earth, and gathered the vine of the earth, and cast it into the great winepress of the wrath of God. And the winepress was trodden without the city, and blood came out of the winepress, even unto the horse bridles, by the space of a thousand and six hundred furlongs.

This means that three groups will be saved at different times, which can be called the first, second, and third harvest, or they could also be called the first fruits, second fruits, and third fruits. The last angel that reaps is reaping those who will be thrown into the lake of fire. This is what the punishment is for those who receive the wrath of God in the great "winepress."

Those who reign with him are of the first harvest. They are the elects, the chosen, those who were predestined to be conformed into his image. When it says in this scripture that they will reign with him for a thousand years, it is referring to the time in which the chosen will be teaching people who Christ really is. This is one of the reasons they were chosen, and this teaching is part of their mission during Christ's rule on earth.

To Those Who Will Stick to Traditional Teaching

All of us who are Christian and have grown up in the church have been told that we will go to heaven and be like the angels. What we have not yet realized is that there are two problems associated with this way of thinking. The first problem is that an angel is an incomplete being. The angel was perfect in body but not judgment; the angel lacked understanding, as previously stated. Their understanding is being perfected here on earth as we go through trials and tribulations.

The second problem associated with maintaining this idea that angels are perfect is that if it is true, the same conflict that began in heaven in the beginning will happen again. If it is true, God would not have accomplished anything. Consider the problem in the form of a question. Ask yourself, "Would this be fair to an angel? Would it be fair to an angel, who has been with God from the beginning, to end up serving someone who has only known God for a short time? Would it be fair to that angel if all that time he was greater than you and all of a sudden, you became greater than he? The answer is no, that would not be fair. If you agree, then you have to search the scriptures meticulously in order to find out what the true destiny of an angel is, as I have done and am telling you.

After studying and finding clues the Holy Spirit later confirmed, this was what I was hearing in my spirit. I found it hard to accept, as it probably will be for you or anyone. Not many people are ready to accept the truth behind God's plan for the salvation of man. In order for God, however, to compel anyone to accept what he is telling them, he has to prepare them for the truth. Because the nature of man is contrary to God, it is not able to receive the truth easily. The nature of man does not allow for truth without hard evidence.

In our natural state, we say that if something cannot be explained naturally or tested scientifically, then it cannot be true. Anything that does not conform to this method, we reject as nonsense and quickly dismiss. Most of us consider ourselves very smart, and in the natural sense, we are. However, when it comes to spiritual things, most of us are severely lacking. Nevertheless, do not be offended if you do not understand this spiritual deficiency. What we need to remember is that God said he would use foolish things to confound the wise. Then it should not be surprising if these things seem a little foolish. I would like to point out the scripture that says this, which can be found in 1 Corinthians 1:26–27 (KJV):

> For ye see your calling, brethren, how that not many wise men after the flesh, not many mighty, not many noble, are called: But God hath chosen the foolish things of the world to confound

the wise; and God hath chosen the weak things of the world to confound the things which are mighty ...

It is easy to have difficulty understanding something that is new and seems to be contrary to the natural way of thinking. I had the same difficulty at first; we all have to have a starting point. However, when I began to understand what God was revealing to me, I had an overwhelming desire to share what I had just discovered, which was confirmed to me by the Bible, with others. I had to tell someone about the thoughts that were overwhelming my mind and spirit, because I was overjoyed at the good news. I couldn't wait to tell someone this good news, especially what I had learned about how easy God had made his free gift of salvation. This is how I learned the hard way how a chosen must suffer for the things that God is teaching him through the Spirit. As I attempted to share this information with others, I faced repeated rejections, and my joy quickly turned to disappointment. I had inadvertently stumbled upon the same obstacle Christ came across; when he wanted to share the good news with all men, they rejected him. I discovered that other people lacked faith to hear from God through his Holy Spirit. I found that the majority of men tended to follow whatever the majority believed in and that they would never be willing to step out on their faith when it comes to believing in spiritual things. Then, I remembered the definition of faith, which is the belief in the things that are not seen.

Hebrews 11:1–3 (KJV) says,

Now faith is the substance of things hoped for, the evidence of things not seen. For by it the elders obtained a good report. Through faith we understand that the worlds were framed by the word of God, so that things which are seen were not made of things which do appear.

From this point on, you will need this faith to comprehend this book. It will be a test of your faith and ability to see beyond common religious thoughts and practices. The war in heaven was initiated because the angels found out that they were not going to inherit the kingdom. As previously stated, if we stick to our conventional thinking, this would not be fair to an angel who has been with God from the beginning. Why should he have to take a backseat to man? I hope we can agree that this should not be the case. Fortunately, God, in his wisdom, created the solution to this problem. The answer, however, is complex. I will do my best with the help of the Spirit to explain it.

To begin to answer this question, let us start by using logic to figure out what took place just before the war. By putting together the facts we have in the Bible, we know that Lucifer managed to convince a third of all the angels to follow him. This must mean that the angels, as well as Lucifer, must not have completely known who God was.

The rebellion they were planning was impossible. So, either God didn't give them intelligence when he made them, or he simply did not tell them everything about himself. Understand that Lucifer's plan was to defeat God. How could he have conceived such a thought? He either lacked intelligence, or he didn't know any better. We have to come to a rational conclusion he must not have known any better. So if Lucifer didn't know better, what does that say about the rest? It is just not logical that God would make some angels with intelligence and some without. I believe he made them all the same.

So it seems Lucifer was able to talk these other angels into following him because they didn't know any better. It was easy to recruit them, especially since Lucifer promised them a higher position than they initially had and a kingdom of their own. It was the angels' ignorance that got them in trouble with God.

As the angels sided with Lucifer, this caused a division in heaven. During this war, as in any war, the participants had to choose sides. The division between the angels and men began here, as some have already made their choice and some have not. There were three choices an angel could have made. They could have chosen to fight with God, to fight against God, or to remain neutral.

Those who chose to fight on God's side are now called the firstfruits; those who fought against God are your fallen angels or demons. The last group refers to the majority of the angels. They are the ones who chose to remain neutral and are now called lukewarm. They did not make a choice; for their sakes, all angels must come to earth. This is so that they can finally make their decision. In order for the angels to make their choices, they must be given a chance to make both choices. This is accomplished by letting them experience both good and evil. Without both options to choose from, their free will would have been violated, and God will not do that.

How is it possible for an angel to not have known God? The answer to this question is that the angel had just been created, so he would have known very little. Look at it this way, at some point in time, God spoke the angels into existence. Their creation would have been instantaneous when they appeared in their original form, not as children, but as they are even until this day. If they were given free will, then they were not created as robots, and therefore, they had to learn, just as we do today. This is a fundamental rule that cannot be changed. Nothing that is created knows everything the moment it is created. This was even true for the Word of God. He had to come to earth and learn "obedience unto death.", found in,

Hebrews 5:7–10 (KJV)

Who in the days of his flesh, when he had offered up prayers and supplications with strong crying and tears unto him that was able to save him from death, and was heard in that he feared; Though he were a Son, yet learned he obedience by the things which he suffered; And being made perfect, he became the author of eternal salvation unto all them that obey him; Called of God an high priest after the order of Melchisedec.

This is what we all have to learn, so that we can be made perfect. This is one of the reasons why God even allowed the war to take place in heaven. He knew that it would eventually lead to salvation and the perfection of all. This is also why he let Adam eat of the wrong tree and why he allows bad things to happen to all of us. He knows that it will eventually make us stronger. Without understanding, war was inevitable, on earth and even in heaven, anywhere where there are at least two people or beings who are not in agreement. He gave all creatures free will; however, the problem with free will is that it compels one to desire independence. This independence leads one to try to exist without God, and this is an impossible task which some angels were willing to try, even as people continue to try today. Though they have the right to try to live without him, they do not know that this choice is foolish, just as the angels didn't know when they tried it; nevertheless, this is free will in action. This is why you and I were given a second chance to get to know him. He knows of our ignorance. Is there evidence of the angels' lack of understanding?.

Job 4:17–20 says,

Shall mortal man be more just than God? shall a man be more pure than his maker? Behold, he put no trust in his servants; and his angels he charged with folly: How much less in them that dwell in houses of clay, whose foundation is in the dust, which are crushed before the moth? They are destroyed from morning to evening: they perish for ever without any regarding it. Doth not their excellency which is in them go away? they die, even without wisdom.

Can anyone see the connection between man and the angels? I hope it is beginning to become clearer. The connection is that neither men nor angels knew God. So how does God fix this problem? Only those to whom God has revealed this can see it. God put the angel and the man together by combining them. This is where our spirits come from, and this is where man comes into the picture. Man is the second stage in the evolutionary process that God is taking us though. This is the same process Christ went through. This is what makes Christ greater than the angels.

Hebrews 1:4–6 (KJV)

Being made so much better than the angels, as he hath by inheritance obtained a more excellent name than they. For unto which of the angels said he at any time, Thou art my Son, this day have I begotten thee? And again, I will be to him a Father, and he shall be to me a Son? And again, when he bringeth in the firstbegotten into the world, he saith, And let all the angels of God worship him.

The previous scripture is discussing Jesus Christ, whom God made a little lower than an angel, an angel being the equivalent of man. The perfection that God wants for us can only be attained in a weaker form, the form of the angels. His purpose of making this requirement is so that we can pay the price for our sins. If you remember correctly, the Bible states that our sins can only be covered by death. We could not have paid for our sins in the spirit, fulfilling the requirement of death, yet still live. This is why Paul said in the book of John that he was made perfect in weakness.

In 2 Corinthians 12:9, it says, "And he said unto me, My grace is sufficient for thee: for my strength is made perfect in weakness. Most gladly therefore will I rather glory in my infirmities, that the power of Christ may rest upon me."

What we really need to comprehend is that if Jesus, who is the head of the body, had to come to earth and humble himself, why wouldn't we believe that all the angels have to follow the same route? Wouldn't this be a good way to simultaneously learn about their father in heaven and learn the difference between right and wrong? All the while, one could still learn any other thing God wanted one to learn. Isn't this the best way to obtain an even greater inheritance? This is why we have to suffer, because it brings us into perfection. The word *perfection* is a stumbling block for most Christians today. What they don't understand is that this is what God wants us to achieve in the end. The process has already begun, and those who come the closest to perfection in the flesh obtain a higher degree of sonship, which is what Christ has obtained. He was the Son of God before he came to earth, yet he was greater after he returned. This is the same thing God wants for us; this perfection means that you will no longer be a servant. God did not develop such an intricate plan for us to simply remain servants. The angels were already servants, but it is obvious that he is not satisfied with that. He wants heirs. Christ obtained the higher degree of sonship through his suffering and because of his sacrifice; this is the same thing we must accomplish. This is what Christ wants for you and me.

John 15:14–15 (KJV) says, "Ye are my friends, if ye do whatsoever I command you. Henceforth I call you not servants; for the servant knoweth not what his lord doeth: but I have called you friends; for all things that I have heard of my Father I have made known unto you."

God will not share his secrets or his throne with a servant, whether in the form of an angel or a man. He will, however, share his kingdom as he has already done with his angels. There is a difference between his throne and his kingdom. He will only share his throne with those who have the potential to be true sons or heirs. This again can be found in the book of Hebrews.

Hebrews 1:13–14 (KJV) says, "But to which of the angels said he at any time, Sit on my right hand, until I make thine enemies thy footstool? Are they not all ministering spirits, sent forth to minister for them who shall be heirs of salvation?"

Heirs of salvation are those who have lived and died on earth. How did they achieve this salvation through belief in Christ? God even said that angels did not even know these things.

1 Peter 1:10–12 (KJV)

Of which salvation the prophets have enquired and searched diligently, who prophesied of the grace that should come unto you: Searching what, or what manner of time the Spirit of Christ which was in them did signify, when it testified beforehand the sufferings of Christ, and the glory that should follow. Unto whom it was revealed, that not unto themselves, but unto us they did minister the things, which are now reported unto you by them that have preached the gospel unto you with the Holy Ghost sent down from heaven; which things the angels desire to look into.

This passage explains what angels desired to know from God, which means God did not tell them. This reinforces the previous scriptures and the interpretation that had been given to me by the Holy Spirit. Let us not stop there though; more evidence can be found in the book of Galatians.

Galatians 4:3–7 (KJV) says,

Even so we, when we were children, were in bondage under the elements of the world: But when the fulness of the time was come, God sent forth his Son, made of a woman, made under the law, To redeem them that were under the law, that we might receive the adoption of sons. And because ye are sons, God hath sent forth the Spirit of his Son into your hearts, crying, Abba, Father. Wherefore thou art no more a servant, but a son; and if a son, then an heir of God through Christ.

This is what the Father and the Son want for you and me. The Father and the Son want us to stop being servant sons and become heirs. This is our true destiny. If we achieve this, we have reached our potential. How can you truly determine that someone loves you, if that person only does so because he or she is instructed to? This is not the kind of love that either the Father or the Son wants from us. The only way to receive the kind of love that God seeks from us is to bring us into oneness with God by making us free sons and heirs.

The Biblical Evidence of Men Having Passed through the Earth Who Are Now in Heaven

The following is a passage providing evidence as to why it was necessary for the angels to become men.

Luke 20:34–38 (KJV)

The children of this world marry, and are given in marriage: But they which shall be accounted worthy to obtain that world, and the resurrection from the dead, neither marry, nor are given in marriage: Neither can they die any more: for they are equal unto the angels; and are the children of God, being the children of the resurrection. Now that the dead are raised, even Moses shewed at the bush, when he calleth the Lord the God of Abraham, and the God of Isaac, and the God of Jacob. For he is not a God of the dead, but of the living: for all live unto him.

I would like to call attention to verse 36 and the fact that Christ said that his children would be equal to the angels and the fact that he called them the children of the resurrection. What does he mean by "equal to the angels"? Is he implying that they are one in the same? You can read into it as you see fit, but these verses do not give us strong enough evidence of that. In fact, there is not one scripture that can explain that, such a scripture would make it too easy to see and would defeat the fact that the Father wants us to search hard for the truth. This information is only clear through piecing together myriad scriptures.

Now the next confirmation of this is found in the book of Revelation. In this scripture, John is standing in front of an angel, and as he begins to bow to the angel, the angel tells him not to bow to him. The reason he says this might surprise you. The angel says that he is his fellow servant and brother. What exactly does that mean?

Revelation 22:8–9(KJV)

And I John saw these things, and heard them. And when I had heard and seen, I fell down to worship before the feet of the angel which shewed me these things. Then saith he unto me, See thou do it not: for I am thy fellowservant, and of thy brethren the prophets, and of them which keep the sayings of this book: worship God.

According to the Webster's dictionary, the term *fellow servant* is defined as a group of people under a common law. If this is true, how could an angel find himself under the same law as a man unless he had been a man and suffered under the same law? Another point I would like to make here is that toward the end of verse 8, the angel said that he was of a particular group of his brethren, the prophets. Here, not only is the angel saying he is a brother but exactly how he is related to him. There is another account of this happening in the book of Revelation.

Revelation 6:9–11 (KJV)

And when he had opened the fifth seal, I saw under the altar the souls of them that were slain for the word of God, and for the testimony which they held: And they cried with a loud voice, saying, How long, O Lord, holy and true, dost thou not judge and avenge our blood on them that dwell on the earth? And white robes were given unto every one of them; and it was said unto them, that they should rest yet for a little season, until their fellowservants also and their brethren, that should be killed as they were, should be fulfilled.

This group, the group that were given the white robes and told to wait on their brothers, were they angels or men? The way this was written suggests that they are men without a doubt. If that is true, then some men that die on earth, go back to their Father, and talk with him. Who were these men? They are those that Christ rescued from hell. This is why Christ went to hell to preach for the three days while he was in his grave. Evidence of this can be found in the book of 1 Peter.

1 Peter 3:18–20 (KJV)

For Christ also hath once suffered for sins, the just for the unjust, that he might bring us to God, being put to death in the flesh, but quickened by the Spirit: By which also he went and preached unto the spirits in prison; Which sometime were disobedient, when once the longsuffering of God waited in the days of Noah, while the ark was a preparing, wherein few, that is, eight souls were saved by water.

Maybe this is one of those men that John met when he was allowed to see into heaven. If that is true also, notice that John did not recognize him as a former man, but as an angel. This is why he fell down and worshiped him. This may be why the angel said, "Don't do it. I am like you, a fellow servant and brethren." The word *brethren* was explained to us by Jesus in the book of Matthew.

Matthew 12:47–50 (KJV) says,

Then one said unto him, Behold, thy mother and thy brethren stand without, desiring to speak with thee. But he answered and said unto him that told him, Who is my mother? and who are my brethren? And he stretched forth his hand toward his disciples, and said, Behold my mother and my brethren! For whosoever shall do the will of my Father which is in heaven, the same is my brother, and sister, and mother.

Now that we have defined the words *fellow servant* and the word *brethren*, let us look at one more account of John talking to an angel and mistaking him for something else.

Revelation 19:9–10 (KJV) says,

And he saith unto me, Write, Blessed are they which are called unto the marriage supper of the Lamb. And he saith unto me, These are the true sayings of God. And I fell at his feet to worship him. And he said unto me, See thou do it not: I am thy fellowservant, and of thy brethren that have the testimony of Jesus: worship God: for the testimony of Jesus is the spirit of prophecy.

Now the angel is telling John that he has the testimony of Jesus. What does it mean to have the same testimony as John did? Well, we know what John's testimony was; his testimony was that he was a witness for Christ. God wanted John to write about the last days concerning Christ and the Father. Traditional thinking says that angels could only be witnesses of these things from afar, not participants. So, is the angel telling John he has the same testimony because he watched, or is he telling John this because he participated? The answer is in what he said last. The angel in Revelation 22:9 said that he was of his brethren, the prophets. The angel in Revelation 19:10 said that he was of his brethren that had the testimony of Jesus. These are two different periods of time on the earth. One is during the time frame of the prophets, and the other came afterward, during the time frame that Jesus existed on the earth. These two different angels are saying that they are his brethren from two different times on the earth. This could only mean that these two angels had been men at different points in time and had experienced some of the same things that John had experienced. Particularly, in Revelation 22:9, the angel said the he was of his brothers, the prophets. Even John, the apostle, did not realize this at first. How do we know this? We know because he bowed to this being. Why? Because he didn't know what kind of being was approaching him. I imagine he was very shocked when he heard the angel say that he was his fellow servant. There is another scripture that seems to support that angels and man are the same.

In 2 Corinthians 5:4–6, it says,

For we that are in this tabernacle do groan, being burdened: not for that we would be unclothed, but clothed upon, that mortality might be swallowed up of life. Now he that hath wrought us for the selfsame thing is God, who also hath given unto us the earnest of the Spirit. Therefore we are always confident, knowing that, whilst we are at home in the body, we are absent from the Lord: (For we walk by faith, not by sight:) …

While in the flesh, our spirit is absent from God. This is one of the revelations God has kept hidden from men. This is what God intended whenever he said "seal" up the "book" until the "appointed time." This means that God is keeping something hidden until a certain time. This is also why God allowed the apostles to write books, such as the book of Revelation, with so much symbolism in them. Either the apostles or the prophets wrote exactly what they saw in heaven or God only showed them what he wanted them to see; either way, it was done in order to hide the true meaning of it until the appointed time.

The truth is that angels were only the first stage in the process of making God's creation perfect. At the first stage, we were new creations, not knowing who God was. We'd just been created, and it took time to learn. God could have told them all about himself, but experience is the best teacher. Besides, God wanted to test his angels to see who really loved him, just as he is continuing to do with man. A fundamental law applies; God knew that his angels would rebel against him in advance, so he prepared a way to save them. The fundamental fact is that most of us do not realize that if an angel sins in his spiritual form, there is no way to repay the punishment for his sins. This is because death is the punishment. God invented flesh in order that they could pay that price for forgiveness. If death is the punishment, then all can die and yet live on in spiritual form.

Man is the second stage in this process. During this stage, man learns the difference between good and evil. We also learn who the Father and the Son are, as well as how much they love us. There is a third stage, when heaven and earth are combined. It was first done in Christ. We have an example of this written in our Bibles. It happened after Jesus rose from the dead, when he was in his resurrected body, a body that was both earthly and spiritual. This is found in the book of Luke.

Luke 24:36–40 says,

And as they thus spake, Jesus himself stood in the midst of them, and saith unto them, Peace be unto you. But they were terrified and affrighted, and supposed that they had seen a spirit. And he said unto them, Why are ye troubled? and why do thoughts arise in your hearts? Behold my hands and my feet, that it is I myself: handle me, and see; for a spirit hath not flesh and bones, as ye see me have. And when he had thus spoken, he shewed them his hands and his feet. And while they yet believed not for joy, and wondered, he said unto them, Have ye here any meat? And they gave him a piece of a broiled fish, and of an honeycomb. And he took it, and did eat before them.

Christ had risen, and he had obtained his new body, a body that was both heavenly and earthly at the same time. This is how he was able to suddenly appear before his apostles, as only a spirit can do, and at the same time, he became solid enough to be touched, as well as to eat something.

As in Christ, the heavenly part of him was his spirit and the earthly part of him was his soul. This is the same thing that has happened to man. Our spirit is the heavenly part of us that came from God, and the earthly part of us is our soul, that was born on earth. Man does not know how important his soul is; he doesn't know that without it, salvation would not be possible. This is what Christ was willing to die for. This is his goal: to gain our souls. Satan wants the same thing: the souls of men, and not the spirit. Why the soul and not the spirit of a man? The answer is that a soul is capable of loving something, but a spirit is not. You must realize that an angel does not have a soul and therefore is not capable of loving God with the kind of love he desires. This is their one weakness, and this weakness made them imperfect. God is making them perfect by adding a soul to a spirit, therefore making what he started with greater than before. Perfection is achieved through the gaining of a soul. How does a soul help us to achieve this?

The soul is connected to our heart; in one sense, they are one and the same. It is through our soul that we learn the difference between what is right and what is wrong. It is with our souls that we learn how to love or hate. Haven't you ever said you learned something by heart, or "I got it deep down in my soul"? This is because they are the same and are the part of you that records things. It is the only part of you that is capable of loving God. Most of us are not in touch with our spirits. So how could you love God though your spirit when you do not even know your spirit? You do, however, know who you are, deep down in your soul, and so this is how you first learn to love God. This is what the grave was made for, the soul and not the spirit, and this is why the following scripture is found in the book of Psalms.

Psalms 49:14–15 (KJV),

Like sheep they are laid in the grave; death shall feed on them; and the upright shall have dominion over them in the morning; and their beauty shall consume in the grave from their dwelling. But God will redeem my soul from the power of the grave: for he shall receive me.

Now, let us get back to something I said earlier: the angels did not have souls, so they were never able to truly love God. This is what angels gain by being born in this world. This is how they will be greater when they return. A heart or a soul that will not love him is doomed. Before people are born, they exist with the Father in the form of a spirit, an angel that is. When they are born, that spirit becomes united with a soul. When that person dies, the soul and the spirit become temporarily separated again. This is how it is possible for the following scripture to be true.

The Book of 2 Corinthians 5:6, it says,

"Therefore we are always confident, knowing that, whilst we are at home in the body, we are absent from the Lord ..."

Another explanation appears in Hebrews 4:12, "For the word of God is quick, and powerful, and sharper than any twoedged sword, piercing even to the dividing asunder of soul and spirit, and of the joints and marrow, and is a discerner of the thoughts and intents of the heart."

The soul and the spirit can be divided or put together; this is how a man can be separated from his spirit. This is how when a man dies, his soul remains in the grave, while his spirit returns to the Father, from where it came. The chosen have been made whole, meaning they have come into an understanding of the trinity based first on understanding how they are made whole. What I mean by this is that we are all trinities just like God; we have a soul, a spirit, and a body. This is exactly how the trinity of God works. The Godhead is composed of the Father, the Holy Spirit, and the Son. These are three in one, because they share the same Spirit. They can also function separately even while still being connected by their spirit. This means that at all times, they are one.

What makes the trinity possible is that God can separate his soul from his spirit, and his body. The soul is different from the spirit, and the spirit is different from the soul as well as the body. We cannot do this, and therefore, we think God is limited like we are, but he is not. This is what God said about Christ concerning his soul in the book of Isaiah.

Isaiah 42:1 (KJV) says, "Behold my servant, whom I uphold; mine elect, in whom my soul delighteth; I have put my spirit upon him: he shall bring forth judgment to the Gentiles." This is none other than Christ himself that God is talking about here. In this scripture, God is saying that his soul delights in Christ, and at the same time, he says that he would put his spirit upon him. This is what I meant by God being able to separate himself. This is how they can be one and yet be the same. When God is whole, he is one; when he is separate, he is a trinity.

When people are not whole, that means they cannot get their spirit to agree with their body and soul. Their bodies do not do what their spirits want them to do, because they will not agree. In other words, they cannot control themselves; they cannot do what they wish to do, but find themselves doing what they do not wish to do. This is the conflict within the body of man. It is between his soul and spirit. When a person is able to get the soul and spirit to agree, that person is made whole. Another way to put this is to say my heart and mind will agree, and then my body or flesh will follow. On the other hand, if the soul and spirit do not agree, then the body or flesh will do what it pleases. This is what Paul meant when he said that we have two wills present in us.

Romans 7:14–21 (KJV) says,

For we know that the law is spiritual: but I am carnal, sold under sin. For that which I do I allow not: for what I would, that do I not; but what I hate, that do I. If then I do that which I would not, I consent unto the law that it is good. Now then it is no more I that do it, but sin that dwelleth in me. For I know that in me (that is, in my flesh,) dwelleth no good thing: for to will is present with me; but how to perform that which is good I find not. For the good that I would I do not: but the evil which I would not, that I do. Now if I do that I would not, it is no more I that do it, but sin that dwelleth in me. I find then a law, that, when I would do good, evil is present with me.

This is an example of what we are like when our spirit does not agree with our soul. We cannot get ourselves to do what our minds want us to do. This is because each has its own will—the will of the flesh and the will of the spirit, which is connected to the Spirit of God. Christ heals us from this problem; this is what the Bible meant by Christ making people whole again, and this is the healing of Christ that only he can perform. Being made whole is done today with the help of the Bible; it makes us whole when we agree on the Word of God, by making our soul agree with the spirit that is in us. If they agree on the Word of God, then the flesh will follow. This happens to a person as his or her faith matures through the understanding of God's Word. This is also called being conformed into the image of Christ. This was how God accomplished the predestination of those whom he chose. This is how he conformed them to the image of Christ, the first and second 144,000, that is.

Who Are the First and Second 144,000?

We all know who the first 144,000 are because the Bible clearly says who they are in the book of Revelation. They were 12,000 from each of the tribes of Israel, but what most people have never even thought of is that there is a second 144,000. The Bible distinguishes between these two, but for now, let me start with the first group.

Revelation 7:4 (KJV) says, "And I heard the number of them which were sealed: and there were sealed an hundred and forty and four thousand of all the tribes of the children of Israel."

The first 144,000 were the first group whom God elected. They also go by many names—chosen, firstfruits, the sealed, or those who are predestined. What we need to understand is that the first group comes from Israel only; this group is not of the Gentiles. The Gentiles make up the second 144,000, but before I tell you who they are, I would like to address two big misunderstandings about this 144,000. Many Christian religions believe that this number represents the finite number of people who will be saved from among all the people in the entire world. This is not true; this number only represents the first group of God's elects. They were chosen under the law and carried out missions for God under the law. This made them part of the first group. They came from the twelve tribes of Israel, which the Bible clearly states. We know that this is not the only group of people who will be saved because of what is later said in the same chapter of the book of Revelation, chapter seven, that is. John the apostle asked who the large number of people surrounding God were. The angel answered him by saying what is found in these next scriptures from Revelation.

Revelation 7:13–17 says,

And one of the elders answered, saying unto me, What are these which are arrayed in white robes? and whence came they? And I said unto him, Sir, thou knowest. And he said to me, These are they which came out of great tribulation, and have washed their robes, and made them white in the blood of the Lamb. Therefore are they before the throne of God, and serve him day and night in his temple: and he that sitteth on the throne shall dwell among them. They shall hunger no more, neither thirst any more; neither shall the sun light on them, nor any heat. For the Lamb which is in the midst of the throne shall feed them, and shall lead them unto living fountains of waters: and God shall wipe away all tears from their eyes.

This is the rest of humankind that will be saved. This is why other religions have gotten it wrong; they failed to understand the people who followed the first 144,000. They even failed to notice the second 144,000 found in chapter fourteen of the book of Revelations.

Revelation 14:1–5 says,

And I looked, and, lo, a Lamb stood on the mount Sion, and with him an hundred forty and four thousand, having his Father's name written in their foreheads. And I heard a voice from heaven, as the voice of many waters, and as the voice of a great thunder: and I heard the voice of harpers harping with their harps: And they sung as it were a new song before the throne, and before the four beasts, and the elders: and no man could learn that song but the hundred and forty and four thousand, which were redeemed from the earth. These are they which were not defiled with women; for they are virgins. These are they which follow the Lamb whithersoever he goeth. These were redeemed from among men, being the firstfruits unto God and to the Lamb. And in their mouth was found no guile: for they are without fault before the throne of God.

This is the second 144,000. They are of the Gentiles, and they are also called the chosen, elected, or firstfruits. Most people have never heard of a second group. This is because there is very little distinction between the two and most don't know what their differences are. The most obvious though is the fact that the first group was under law and the second was not. Because of this, the first group belonged to the Father and the second to the Son. For this reason, these groups have two different names; the first is called Zion, and the second is called Sion. I know that the words *Zion* and *Sion* also refer to a place. God sometimes uses these words in a way that they mean the same thing, a place and a people. Zion is not just a place; it is also the name of the first group of people who are from Israel. The same goes for Sion; they are from a group of people called the Gentiles, and they are a people and a place as well. Let me start by pointing out the scriptures that tell us Zion is a place and a people, meaning one is a physical place and the other is a spiritual place. Let us start with the physical place.

In 1 Kings 8:1 (KJV), it says,

Then Solomon assembled the elders of Israel, and all the heads of the tribes, the chief of the fathers of the children of Israel, unto king Solomon in Jerusalem, that they might bring up the ark of the covenant of the LORD out of the city of David, which is Zion.

This is the physical Zion, the city of Jerusalem that is earthly, located in the Middle East. These next scriptures tell us that salvation will come out of Israel, the spiritual Israel, that is.

Psalm 53:6 (KJV) says, "Oh that the salvation of Israel were come out of Zion! When God bringeth back the captivity of his people, Jacob shall rejoice, and Israel shall be glad."

This is where the physical Zion's salvation will come from; it will come from those who are of Israel that God will chose. The same will happen to the Gentiles in this same way. God speaks about the second group that will be first in the book of Psalms.

Psalm 65:1–4 says,

Praise waiteth for thee, O God, in Sion: and unto thee shall the vow be performed. O thou that hearest prayer, unto thee shall all flesh come. Iniquities prevail against me: as for our transgressions, thou shalt purge them away. Blessed is the man whom thou choosest, and causest to approach unto thee, that he may dwell in thy courts: we shall be satisfied with the goodness of thy house, even of thy holy temple.

Sion in these verses refers to a people, because a vow will be performed unto them. These are those people whose sins were purged away, and it continues to say that they will dwell in his holy temple. This group is greater than the first because they were redeemed by the Son and not the Father. We know they are greater because the Bible tells us so in the book of Matthew.

Matthew 20:16 says, "So the last shall be first, and the first last: for many be called, but few chosen."

These are the two groups these scriptures are talking about, and this is why these scriptures are widely misunderstood. Not many people know that there are two groups. Most Christians think this scripture is only referring to Jews and Christians. This is because all Christians know where they get their religion from: the Jews. Both groups believe in God, and those who are Christians believe that the Jews lost their place with God because they rejected Christ. This, however, is not the answer; this scripture is referring to the first and the second 144,000. The main reason why the first group is last is because they were born under the law, and they have not yet received Christ. The law cannot be greater than grace. God has ordained it to be this way. Those who were chosen under grace have already received Christ and are ready for the kingdom, but those who have died without receiving Christ, even though they were chosen first, cannot come before those who are in Christ. This is the difference between the Old and New Testament, even though the law came first. This is because the law was only a shadow of things to come, which was grace. One covenant is greater than the other.

Chapter Two

The Sons of God

The Introduction of the Chosen, the Servant, and the Faithful Sons of God

What I hope to achieve by this chapter is to promote unity within the body of Christ among the different sons of God. I pray that no one will be offended by the words that are written within this chapter but that we all come into a greater understanding as to why the body of Christ has been divided. I will be discussing who the different types of sons are and the reasons as to why there are divisions between them. The names of the four types of sons, as found in the Bible, are chosen sons, servant sons, faithful sons, and the lost sons of God. Another name for these same four is the elect, the called, the lost, and the unbelieving sons of God. The body of Christ or the church as we know it is divided. What has caused this division? Something that even until this day Christians are unaware of, and that is that they are divided between bond sons, free sons and those who are lost. Bonds sons are the same as those who are called, elect sons are the few who are chosen, unbelieving sons are those who later come to believe, and the lost sons are those who never come to believe in God. These four groups live in the world together and often share the same church. This division is one of the reasons why there are so many different interpretations of the Bible. This is because each type of son sees God differently, or in other words from their own perspective. Each son can

49

find instances within the Bible to support their version of God, and so they often reach a stalemate, and because of this they ultimately try to find some way to just accept each other. Even though there are four different groups, technically they fall into two main categories according to the Bible and that either bond or free.

There are several places that are found within the Bible that speaks about the four groups and about bond and free. One good reference to the four types are can be found in Luke 12:41-53. There are many more places that can be found where the Bible refers to them by there division. There are only a few places that can be found within the Bible as to when it talks about the all four types of sons and these scriptures can be found in Matthew 21:28 and Gal 4:22-31. The Bible mainly talks about these different types of sons as either bond or free since this is the main reason they are different. How does a son become bond or free? According to the Bible they are born this way, because this is where predestination come in to the picture. According to the Bible those who are born bond are born by the will of the flesh, and those who are born by predestination or by the promise of God are born by the will of God.

John 3:6 (KJV)
That which is born of the flesh is flesh; and that which is born of the Spirit is spirit.

Gal 4:23-24 (KJV)
But he *who was* of the bondwoman was born after the flesh; but he of the freewoman *was* by promise. 24 Which things are an allegory: for these are the two covenants;

The main reason why God allows some of His sons to born in bondage and some not centers around his law, the commandments of God. This is what this bondage mainly pertains to, this is because some sons are not very obedient to God and therefore need to be reminded of the punishment or the wrath of God in order to keep them in line. Those who are free do not need to be told by law to do what is right because they have love in their hearts and therefore do not need to be reminded of God's punishments for not doing what he ask. They are free from the law, because they have fulfilled the law simply by loving their heavenly father and by loving his or her neighbors. God has to place this love in their hearts at the birth, otherwise the world would take it away. This is because the world does not teach love, it only teaches survival. Those who are born this way are the chosen of God, they eventually become the bride of Christ.

Who Is the Bride of Christ?

Those who become the bride are those who are born free, meaning not under the bondage of this world. Now I would like to explain the differences between those that are born free and those who are born in bondage. Let's start by dealing with some of the misconception about being called or chosen which is the same as saying bond of free. Most Christians believe that to be called or chosen means to do work in the ministry, and for the most part, that is correct. However, it is not the full meaning of the words *called* and *chosen*. What this scripture is truly referring to is the marriage. We are being called to a wedding, and some have been chosen to be the bride. Those who have been chosen are the ones getting married, and those who were called are the wedding guests. I know from being in the church many years that the church thinks that it will be the bride of Christ, but in fact, it will only be those who have been chosen, who will be the bride. This is reflected in two places in the Bible.

In Matthew 22:1–14 (KJV), it says,

And Jesus answered and spake unto them again by parables, and said, The kingdom of heaven is like unto a certain king, which made a marriage for his son, And sent forth his servants to call them that were bidden to the wedding: and they would not come. Again, he sent forth other servants, saying, Tell them which are bidden, Behold, I have prepared my dinner: my oxen and my fatlings are killed, and all things are ready: come unto the marriage. But they made light of it, and went their ways, one to his farm, another to his merchandise: And the remnant took his servants, and entreated them spitefully, and slew them. But when the king heard thereof, he was wroth: and he sent forth his armies, and destroyed those murderers, and burned up their city. Then saith he to his servants, The wedding is ready, but they which were bidden were not worthy. Go ye therefore into the highways, and as many as ye shall find, bid to the marriage. So those servants went out into the highways, and gathered together all as many as they found, both bad and good: and the wedding was furnished with guests. And when the king came in to see the guests, he saw there a man which had not on a wedding garment: And he saith unto him, Friend, how camest thou in hither not having a wedding garment? And he was speechless. Then said the king to the servants, Bind him hand and foot, and take him away, and cast him into outer darkness; there shall be weeping and gnashing of teeth. For many are called, but few are chosen.

Many people who repeat this verse misquote it by saying all are called. Not all are called because God knows that not all people will answer his call. So instead, it reads many are called, and many of them answered that call. Those who did became believers; they are also known as the servant sons of God. They have a specific mission from God as well as those who were chosen. However, there is a difference between these two missions. For the servant son who is a believer, his job is to help save others by preaching the Gospel of Christ; this causes nonbelievers to come into the fold of God. The chosen's mission was to bring them into a greater understanding of God's word because they have been instructed by the Spirit and not another person. An example of this is found the book of Acts.

Acts 18:24–26 (KJV) says,

And a certain Jew named Apollos, born at Alexandria, an eloquent man, and mighty in the scriptures, came to Ephesus. This man was instructed in the way of the Lord; and being fervent in the spirit, he spake and taught diligently the things of the Lord, knowing only the baptism of John. And he began to speak boldly in the synagogue: whom when Aquila and Priscilla had heard, they took him unto them, and expounded unto him the way of God more perfectly.

In other words, no one can give more than what they are themselves or more than what they have been taught. This is why Jesus said this in Matthew 10:40–41 (KJV):

He that receiveth you receiveth me, and he that receiveth me receiveth him that sent me. He that receiveth a prophet in the name of a prophet shall receive a prophet's reward; and he that receiveth a righteous man in the name of a righteous man shall receive a righteous man's reward.

For those who are chosen, their specific mission is mainly composed of edifying the body of Christ spiritually. It is not that they cannot witness to others, but they are given more in order to do more. What the church does not know at this time is that the chosen were not given the mission to bring others to the cross but to take them beyond the cross. This mission cannot start until they that are called have finished their mission and the Gospel has been preached around the world. This often makes the chosen appear to have forsaken the church, because of this, the chosen are scolded and misunderstood by the majority. While the church is busy saving others, the chosen are hearing and learning from the Spirit of God. You might ask, "Well, why can't they do both at the same time?" The answer is that the church teaches only the milk of the Word, which will bring a person into salvation, but the spirit teaches the meat of the Word. This is something you will see throughout this book. The church has rejected the meat and settled on the milk and has therefore kicked the chosen out. This is part of the reason why there is a division among the believing sons of God. The chosen seem to be renegades and are often accused of leaning toward their own understanding. Another reason for the division is that the servant son believes that they must still fall under the law, even though the Bible has told them that they are no longer under the law. This can be found in the book of Romans

The Difference between Law and Grace as It Pertains to the Sons

Let's begin with the main difference between the sons of God. You will know those who are servants by what they believe in, one will say the he is under law, the other will say he is not, and finally there is one that would say, the he is both under law and grace.

Romans 6:14 (KJV)

"For sin shall not have dominion over you: for ye are not under the law, but under grace"

The servant son of God has chosen to remain under law because he does not fully understand why Christ died on the cross to bring in the grace of God, which is the New Testament. This is one of the main differences between the two believing sons of God. Having a full understanding of grace is the only way, according to Romans 6:14, that we can not allow sin to have dominion over us and keep us in bondage. Grace is mercy, meaning God will forgive you of your sins and remember them no more. This forgiveness is not just for a person's past sins but for his or her future sins also. Nevertheless, since Paul the apostle first preached this, this issue has been the wall that keeps these two sons apart. Both sons have the right to choose which covenant they would like to live under, and believe it or not, there is a third choice. Some people try to live under both covenants by combining the Old and New Testament. They do this by saying they live under the law and grace at the same time. What they don't know is that Paul spoke of the dangers of this a long time ago.

2 Corinthians 3:6–15 (KJV),

Who also hath made us able ministers of the new testament; not of the letter, but of the spirit: for the letter killeth, but the spirit giveth life. But if the ministration of death, written and engraven in stones, was glorious, so that the children of Israel could not stedfastly behold the face of Moses for the glory of his countenance; which glory was to be done away: How shall not the ministration of the spirit be rather glorious? For if the ministration of condemnation be glory, much more doth the ministration of righteousness exceed in glory. For even that which was made glorious had no glory in this respect, by reason of the glory that excelleth. For if that which is done away was glorious, much more that which remaineth is glorious. Seeing then that we have such hope, we use great plainness of speech: And not as Moses, which put a vail over his face, that the children of Israel could not stedfastly look to the end of that which is abolished: But their minds were blinded: for until this day remaineth the same vail untaken away in the reading of the old testament; which vail is done away in Christ. But even unto this day, when Moses is read, the vail is upon their heart.

In verse six, Paul says that the letter, which is the law, kills. He also said in verse six that the spirit, which comes from the belief in

Christ, gives life. Why would anyone want to try to keep something that they know is impossible to keep, especially when the penalty is death? Nevertheless, this is what the two believing sons of God seem to be hopelessly locked in battle over. Those under law tend to see the world in a natural way, and those under grace see things in a spiritual way. The two cannot agree. Let us read what Paul in the book of Romans said about this.

Romans 8:1–5 (KJV) says,

There is therefore now no condemnation to them which are in Christ Jesus, who walk not after the flesh, but after the Spirit. For the law of the Spirit of life in Christ Jesus hath made me free from the law of sin and death. For what the law could not do, in that it was weak through the flesh, God sending his own Son in the likeness of sinful flesh, and for sin, condemned sin in the flesh: That the righteousness of the law might be fulfilled in us, who walk not after the flesh, but after the Spirit. For they that are after the flesh do mind the things of the flesh; but they that are after the Spirit the things of the Spirit.

According to these scriptures, the freedom that is in Christ can only be enjoyed under grace, through the spirit, not the law. The law blinds people to this fact, and they cannot see spiritually. So if one puts himself under the law, he or she sees things in a natural way, while the other sees things in a spiritual way. Both are correct, because the Bible was written in a natural and a spiritual way. This was unavoidable because God had to use natural things that we could understand to explain heavenly things. This was done so that we would have a chance at understanding. This, however, was only supposed to be the beginning of our understanding, not the end result. All of us who believe start with a lack of understanding and cannot see spiritually, but in order to do so, all one has to do is keep looking harder. This will cause our faith to mature over time. If God had not started from the beginning using natural things, how would we have ever understood him or had a chance to understand spiritual things? The disagreement between the two believing sons is so great that the Bible says the servant or bond son will persecute the chosen or free son. This is what Paul said in the book of Galatians.

Galatians 4:21–24 (KJV) says,

Tell me, ye that desire to be under the law, do ye not hear the law? For it is written, that Abraham had two sons, the one by a bondmaid, the other by a freewoman. But he who was of the bondwoman was born after the flesh; but he of the freewoman was by promise. Which things are an allegory: for these are the two covenants ...

The bond children and the children of promise are the two covenants, meaning the Old and the New Testaments. Now listen to what is said just a few verses down about these two sons.

Galatians 4:28–31 (KJV):

Now we, brethren, as Isaac was, are the children of promise. But as then he that was born after the flesh persecuted him that was born after the Spirit, even so it is now. Nevertheless what saith the scripture? Cast out the bondwoman and her son: for the son of the bondwoman shall not be heir with the son of the freewoman. So then, brethren, we are not children of the bondwoman, but of the free.

We who believe in Christ are supposed to live apart from the law, because the body of Christ was always meant to be whole, not split in two, composed of all who believe in Christ. The members of that body regardless of race, nationality, color, or what church they go to are supposed to be one body. This is how the son who was born free sees the body of Christ with his spiritual eyes. However, the division within the body shows up every Sunday or Saturday in this nation. It shows its presence within the different denominations, teachings, and baptisms we have within our churches today. I am not saying that anyone is wrong; I am only saying that since there is only one God, one Spirit, and one Christ, we should therefore have one understanding.

Isn't it apparent that Christ will not prefer one religion over the other? Haven't we discovered by now that Christ does not have a religion, because that would mean he would have to show favoritism? The fact that God does not show favoritism is addressed in Romans 2:10–11 (KJV): "But glory, honour, and peace, to every man that worketh good, to the Jew first, and also to the Gentile: For there is no respect of persons with God."

He is only interested in those who believe in him, and that is the bottom line. It does not matter what religion we belong to. If this is the case, then it also doesn't matter if we belong to any religion at all. We are saved based on the fact that we believe. This is found in Mark 16:16 (KJV): "He that believeth and is baptized shall be saved; but he that believeth not shall be damned."

If we all could just agree on this, there would not be so much division in the body, since we have one Bible and one God. The sons of God seem not to be able to find any common ground or worship together. There are many more issues that keep the sons from coming together, but this is one of the main reasons.

What people do not realize is that this division did not start on earth. It started in heaven and resulted in a war. (This is the war that I addressed in the first chapter.) We have the same problem in today's society because of these differences. Men become divided, and when they become divided, this often leads to war. In our everyday lives, this division gets played out on a smaller scale. For example, if two people cannot agree on something, it can lead to a dispute, which in turn could lead to a fight and ultimately could escalate into someone's death. This is why God wants to bring us all into oneness, so that there will be no division or differences among us. This is what Jesus meant when he said that the body is one, meaning that those who are within the body of Christ are in agreement and become one, just as he and the Father are.

In 1 Corinthians 12:12–18 (KJV), it says,

For as the body is one, and hath many members, and all the members of that one body, being many, are one body: so also is Christ. For by one Spirit are we all baptized into one body, whether we be Jews or Gentiles, whether we be bond or free; and have been all made to drink into one Spirit. For the body is not one member, but many. If the foot shall say, Because I am not the hand, I am not of the body; is it therefore not of the body? And if the ear shall say, Because I am not the eye, I am not of the body; is it therefore not of the body? If the whole body were an eye, where were the hearing? If the whole were hearing, where were the smelling? But now hath God set the members every one of them in the body, as it hath pleased him.

Disagreement amongst the believing sons of God has existed since the church was established, and the angels were no different. After all, they were closer to God than we are, and they still fought. It seems that only God can remove this division and bring us all together into one understanding. In the first chapter, I told you that because of the war, angels had to choose sides and they either chose to fight for God, fight against God, or they remained undecided. This is how the division first manifested among the sons of God. Lucifer, on one hand, expressed his disagreement with God by telling the other angels he could show them a better way. On the other hand, we have Christ who says that he is the way, the only way.

There were three divisions of angels in heaven, the same as there are three divisions of men on earth. In heaven, there were the angels chosen from amongst the seraphim, known as the archangels, and the angels called cherubim, known as guardian angels who engage in battle. Finally, regular angels are the messenger servants of God.

On earth, they are the elect or chosen of God, the servant son or the called, and the unbelieving son. Both the servant son and the unbelieving son were previously undecided. From amongst the group of unbelievers, God sometimes chooses a faithful son. The faithful son is someone who does not believe at the present but will come to believe before it's too late. They are those who decide at the last minute, just before their death, to believe in Christ. The Bible refers to them as those who believe in his name only. This is because they waited until it was almost too late and have no works to speak of. In John 1:12 (KJV), it says, "But as many as received him, to them gave he power to become the sons of God, even to them that believe on his name ..."

They become the faithful, because of that one faithful act; however, most of these become sons during the tribulations, which is something I will talk about later on in this chapter. For now though, I must give you an example of the faithful as found in the Bible. The man known as the thief on the cross is a good example. He had no works to speak of, was a thief all his life, and was not deserving of any kind of salvation. However, because he showed one act of faith at the last minute, Christ told him, "This day, you shall be with me in the kingdom." He was saved because he fulfilled this scripture found in Romans 10:9 (KJV): "That if thou shalt confess with thy mouth the Lord Jesus, and shalt believe in thine heart that God hath raised him from the dead, thou shalt be saved."

You might ask, "How could the thief on the cross be saved without a baptism?" How could Jesus grant him access to the kingdom of God if he said in Mark 16:16 that a person must be baptized? If Jesus allowed this man into the kingdom, then he must have received a baptism. The baptism that he received, however, was not a baptism by water, which is by the hands of man. He received the baptism by fire, which is by the hands of God. This is the only way the faithful can enter into the kingdom, since they were not among the believers and were not baptized unto repentance. I will go further in depth about the two baptisms later on in this book, but for now, I will give you a brief understanding of it. First, let me show you the place in the Bible where it talks about this baptism by fire, also known as the baptism by the Holy Ghost. This is what John the Baptist was talking about in the book of Matthew.

Matthew 3:11 (KJV) says, "I indeed baptize you with water unto repentance: but he that cometh after me is mightier than I, whose shoes I am not worthy to bear: he shall baptize you with the Holy Ghost, and with fire ..."

No man can give another man the baptism by fire; God gives this baptism to whomever he chooses to give it to. I know this may not seem fair to those who have been with Jesus a long time and have done many things in his name, but this is God's choice. I know that if it were up to the servant son, this man would never enter into the kingdom of God based on the fact that he has no works to speak of. What most Christians don't understand is that it only requires one work of faith to enter into the kingdom of God and that work of faith is just to believe. An example of a servant becoming angry when another received the same reward as he did though he did not put in the same amount of time is found in the parable of the vineyard.

Matthew 20:1–16 (KJV) says,

For the kingdom of heaven is like unto a man that is an householder, which went out early in the morning to hire labourers into his vineyard. And when he had agreed with the labourers for a penny a day, he sent them into his vineyard. And he went out about the third hour, and saw others standing idle in the marketplace, And said unto them; Go ye also into the vineyard, and whatsoever is right I will give you. And they went their way. Again he went out about the sixth and ninth hour, and did likewise. And about the eleventh hour he went out, and found others standing idle, and saith unto them, Why stand ye here all the day idle? They say unto him, Because no man hath hired us. He saith unto them, Go ye also into the vineyard; and whatsoever is right, that shall ye receive. So when even was come, the lord of the vineyard saith unto his steward, Call the labourers, and give them their hire, beginning from the last unto the first. And when they came that were hired about the eleventh hour, they received every man a penny. But when the first came, they supposed that they should have received more; and they likewise received every man a penny. And when they had received it, they murmured against the goodman of the house, These last have wrought but one hour, and thou hast made them equal unto us, which have borne the burden and heat of the day. But he answered one of them, and said, Friend, I do thee no wrong: didst not thou agree with me for a penny? Take that thine is, and go thy way: I will give unto this last, even as unto thee. Is it not lawful for me to do what I will with mine own? Is thine eye evil, because I am good? So the last shall be first, and the first last: for many be called, but few chosen.

The laborers or the servant sons will be very angry when they find out that some of the people that they would not have allowed into the kingdom are there. They didn't see them attend church or do any of the works that they did or spend the time with the Lord they think they should have spent to be deserving of the kingdom of God. What we all need to remember is that at one point in time, we were all unbelievers. We are born that way. When we are children, we simply do not know. We have to come into that understanding, but God called us into the body while we were unbelievers. This shows the true mercy of God, the same mercy we should show toward unbelievers, because we were once where they are now. This is perfectly illustrated in these scriptures found in the book of Romans.

Romans 11:30–32 (KJV) says,

For as ye in times past have not believed God, yet have now obtained mercy through their unbelief: Even so have these also now not believed, that through your mercy they also may obtain mercy. For God hath concluded them all in unbelief, that he might have mercy upon all.

Those who do not believe at this time still have the opportunity to become faithful sons of God. One thing that I want to make clear is why I have called them the faithful sons. It is because the Bible calls them the faithful. These are the only three groups of people who will be with Lord when He returns to earth. Revelation 17:14 (KJV) says, "These shall make war with the Lamb, and the Lamb shall overcome them: for he is Lord of lords, and King of kings: and they that are with him are called, and chosen, and faithful."

In this scripture, we see the called, the chosen, and the faithful will be with the Lord when he returns. If these are the only groups that will be with him when he returns, then we all must fit in these groups somewhere. The called in scripture is referring to the servant son, and we know who the chosen are. The main difference between these three types of sons is that the servant son of God has done many things in God's name and has many works that can be seen by anyone. The chosen son's works are seen by hardly anyone, and the faithful son has only one work of faith but has fulfilled the requirement. The servant son will have more works, and there is nothing wrong with that in and of itself. The problem is that the servant son believes that he has to do these works for his salvation or reward. This means that all the works they do are for themselves and not entirely for the body of Christ. The reason they do this is so that they might keep their salvation, not knowing that it is not necessary. The work that they do should not be toward their salvation, since it is a free gift, given to all who believe. All their work should be directed toward their fellow man, those who are saved and also those who are not saved. The servant sons need to understand that if they believe and are baptized, they are saved. The only work that needs to be done from that point is to be a witness for others in the body of Christ and to those who are not yet come into the body of Christ. They also lack faith in that they still believe their salvation can be lost. Because they don't believe their salvation is assured through the baptism of repentance, which is their first work, then all other works are not of faith. The Bible has concluded that a man should not be justified by works; if people do this, they have tripped over the stumbling stone. This mistake has already been made by Israel.

Romans 9:30–32 (KJV)

What shall we say then? That the Gentiles, which followed not after righteousness, have attained to righteousness, even the righteousness which is of faith. But Israel, which followed after the law of righteousness, hath not attained to the law of righteousness. Wherefore? Because they sought it not by faith, but as it were by the works of the law. For they stumbled at that stumbling stone ...

If the work is done out of debt, debt they think they owe, then it is not of faith. It should be done by faith, because we cannot hope to ever pay this debt. This is why Christ paid the price for their sins. This can be found in the book of Romans.

Romans 4:2–6 (KJV) says,

For if Abraham were justified by works, he hath whereof to glory; but not before God. For what saith the scripture? Abraham believed God, and it was counted unto him for righteousness. Now to him that worketh is the reward not reckoned of grace, but of debt. But to him that worketh not, but believeth on him that justifieth the ungodly, his faith is counted for righteousness.

This is how the chosen son has obtained righteousness without the same works as the servant son. Even though the chosen sons were saved before they came into that understanding, they were being used by God long before they knew they were chosen. This can be found in the book of Galatians.

Galatians 4:1–7 (KJV) says,

Now I say, That the heir, as long as he is a child, differeth nothing from a servant, though he be lord of all; But is under tutors and governors until the time appointed of the father. Even so we, when we were children, were in bondage under the elements of the world: But when the fulness of the time was come, God sent forth his Son, made of a woman, made under the law, To redeem them that were under the law, that we might receive the adoption of sons. And because ye are sons, God hath sent forth the Spirit of his Son into your hearts, crying, Abba, Father. Wherefore thou art no more a servant, but a son; and if a son, then an heir of God through Christ.

A child is what a chosen is called when he or she doesn't know what it means to be chosen, but when he or she does come into the understanding, he or she is no longer a servant. Until that time comes, he or she acts like a servant of God until his or her appointed time. If these people do bad things, or even sin, God has made a way for them to not receive his punishment. This is found in the book of Romans.

Romans 4:8 (KJV) says, "Blessed is the man to whom the Lord will not impute sin."

Those who are chosen have come into the knowledge of salvation, not by reading only, but by having been taught by God in addition to reading. When each of the believing sons comes into this knowledge of salvation, one remains unsure, while the other approaches God boldly. This scripture shows how this has come to be in the second book of Corinthians.

2 Corinthians 3:1–3 (KJV)

Do we begin again to commend ourselves? or need we, as some others, epistles of commendation to you, or letters of commendation from you? Ye are our epistle written in our hearts, known and read of all men: Forasmuch as ye are manifestly declared to be the epistle of Christ ministered by us, written not with ink, but with the Spirit of the living God; not in tables of stone, but in fleshy tables of the heart.

This is what Jesus said to the chosen who were with him. Matthew 13:11–12 (KJV) says, "Because it is given unto you to know the mysteries of the kingdom of heaven, but to them it is not given. For whosoever hath, to him shall be given, and he shall have more abundance …" This is also what Paul meant by what he said in the book of Romans.

Romans 1:19–20 (KJV) says,

Because that which may be known of God is manifest in them; for God hath shewed it unto them. For the invisible things of him from the creation of the world are clearly seen, being understood by the things that are made, even his eternal power and Godhead.

God has showed it unto them through the type of baptism they have received. This type of baptism is a with fire, meaning the Holy Spirit. The type of baptism that most have received is the water baptism. This type of baptism is done for the repentance of sins, or in other words, it is a type of confession that says that you are worthy of death, but "please save me, Lord." This type of baptism was never meant to wash a person's sins completely away; only the fire baptism can do this. This can be found in many different places in the Bible. This is what John the Baptist said in the book of Matthew.

Matthew 3:11(KJV) says, "I indeed baptize you with water unto repentance, but he that cometh after me is mightier than I, whose shoes I am not worthy to bear: he shall baptize you with the Holy Ghost, and with fire." Read also what Paul had to say about the water baptism.

I Pet 3:20 (KJV)

Which sometime were disobedient, when once the longsuffering of God waited in the days of Noah, while the ark was a preparing, wherein few, that is, eight souls were saved by water. The like figure whereunto even baptism doth also now save us (not the putting away of the filth of the flesh, but the answer of a good conscience toward God,) by the resurrection of Jesus Christ ...

The Meaning of the Baptism of Fire and Who Receives It

Do not misunderstand me, I am not saying that the water baptism is not needed; it is just that alone it is not enough. We all need the baptism by fire, which is from the Holy Spirit. The fire the Bible refers to is the method of teaching. The word *fire* refers to the Holy Spirit who helps us through hardships, and it is through these hardships that we learn of spiritual things. It is through the spiritual fire or fiery trials that we burn away any unnecessary thoughts, feelings, hatred, ignorance, or anything that is contrary to God from our minds. Another way God refers to this process is when he calls us precious gold. The process that gold goes through while being refined is called purification. This is the same process that God uses on us. When gold goes through this refining process, all impurities are melted away, and nothing is left but pure gold. No one likes to go through trials. In fact, while we are going through these trials, it would be easy for some to think that God has abandoned them, but he hasn't. Trials teach us not to rely on ourselves and to turn to God. They are absolutely necessary in the training process. This is why we must go through them. This is so that we will be ready when Christ appears. This is found in 1 Peter 1:6–9 (KJV):

Wherein ye greatly rejoice, though now for a season, if need be, ye are in heaviness through manifold temptations: That the trial of your faith, being much more precious than of gold that perisheth, though it be tried with fire, might be found unto praise and honour and glory at the appearing of Jesus Christ: Whom having not seen, ye love; in whom, though now ye see him not, yet believing, ye rejoice with joy unspeakable and full of glory: Receiving the end of your faith, even the salvation of your souls.

Here is another good reason, the Bible says, trials are a necessity.

1 Peter 4:12–13 (KJV), it says,

Beloved, think it not strange concerning the fiery trial which is to try you, as though some strange thing happened unto you: But rejoice, inasmuch as ye are partakers of Christ's sufferings; that, when his glory shall be revealed, ye may be glad also with exceeding joy.

After a person has been through the fire, he or she has been remade into the image of Christ. This is the first group of people Christ will be looking for when he returns. These are the people who have received the baptism by fire. Where can this be found in the Bible?

Luke 12:49–51 (KJV)

I am come to send fire on the earth; and what will I, if it be already kindled? But I have a baptism to be baptized with; and how am I straitened till it be accomplished! Suppose ye that I am come to give peace on earth? I tell you, Nay; but rather division …

If this person has already been kindled, or burned with this fire, he or she is ready to be used by Christ immediately and does not need to go through the tribulations, which is another trial by fire. However, we need to understand that only God decides who will receive this baptism, which is by his hand only, so that these people may be ready when Christ comes as a thief in the night. The reason God sent fire on the earth is because of our ignorance. He knows that most of the sins that people commit are because they are unaware of what they are doing. This is why God said in Ezekiel 20:22–26 (KJV), "And I polluted them in their own gifts, in that they caused to pass through the fire all that openeth the womb, that I might make them desolate, to the end that they might know that I am the Lord."

If you are having trouble understanding what I am saying, let me ask you a question. If you think a person chose God and still think it was the person's choice alone,. Whom would you rather have in control of your salvation, God or yourself? As for me, I would rather God be in control of my destiny, because I have made too many mistakes in my lifetime to count myself worthy of the claim that I caused my own salvation by my own righteousness. Even by just believing, I did not cause by own salvation, even that was given to me, because he chose me first.

John 6:37 (KJV) says, "All that the Father giveth me shall come to me; and him that cometh to me I will in no wise cast out." I know that for some, this might be hard to accept, but it is the truth; we do not even belong to ourselves. This is found in the book of Corinthians.

1 Corinthians 6:14–20 (KJV)

And God hath both raised up the Lord, and will also raise up us by his own power. Know ye not that your bodies are the members of Christ? shall I then take the members of Christ, and make them the members of an harlot? God forbid. What? know ye not that he which is joined to an harlot is one body? for two, saith he, shall be one flesh. But he that is joined unto the Lord is one spirit. Flee fornication. Every sin that a man doeth is without the body; but he that committeth fornication sinneth against his own body. What? know ye not that your body is the temple of the Holy Ghost which is in you, which ye have of God, and ye are not your own? For ye are bought with a price: therefore glorify God in your body, and in your spirit, which are God's.

The Three Spiritual Women of the Bible

The next topic of discussion that I would like to share with you is the three spiritual women of the Bible and how they relate to the different sons of God. To achieve this, I would like to go further in depth about the bondswoman and the free woman, spoken of in the book of Galatians.

Galatians 4:21–24 (KJV) says,

Tell me, ye that desire to be under the law, do ye not hear the law? For it is written, that Abraham had two sons, the one by a bondmaid, the other by a freewoman. But he who was of the bondwoman was born after the flesh; but he of the freewoman was by promise. Which things are an allegory: for these are the two covenants ...

Later on in verses 28 and 29, it speaks about the fact that they that are born after the flesh persecuted him that was born after the Spirit. And just to remind you, here are the scriptures.

Galatians 4:28–29 (KJV) says, "Now we, brethren, as Isaac was, are the children of promise. But as then he that was born after the flesh persecuted him that was born after the Spirit, even so it is now."

The bondmaid and her children and the free woman and the children of promise are the two covenants, meaning law and grace, or Old and New Testaments. Now listen to what was written in verse 28 of Galatians 4, the one born after the flesh persecuted him that was born after the spirit. There are several things here that have been hidden from many people's understanding for a long time. The first is that there are two types of spiritual women and their children and the fact that they are born this way, even though in these scriptures, Paul is speaking of the two natural women by whom Abraham had children. The first hint is in verse 24 of chapter 4 of Galatians, where it is said that these were the two covenants. God made only two covenants with man; the first was the law in which a man or woman has to work to achieve salvation, and the second was grace in which a man or woman does not have to work in order to receive salvation, because it is a free gift to those who believe in Christ. One brings you into debt and the other freedom, depending on which covenant or woman you are born under, you are either free or bond.

You might ask, "How can the covenants be women?" The spiritual word for women is anything that can reproduce, and these covenants can reproduce. If you place yourself under the law, you hear the voice of the bondwoman, and if you hear the voice of the free woman, then you are free, freed from the law of bondage which will kill you because no one can keep it. This is the spiritual way the Bible sometimes talks, in order to hide the meaning from those to whom God does not want reveal the meaning. These women are two of the three great spirits of this world. I have already given you the names of two of those spiritual women who give birth to children. The third woman God calls the beast. She is also known in the Bible as the spirit of the Antichrist, and she also reproduces children. The children of the first two women are saved, but the children of the beast will be thrown into the lake of fire.

The children of the woman known as the beast are called tares. The children of the free woman are called wheat, and the children of the bondwoman are mixed with both tare and wheat. Let us now examine the parable of the tare and wheat.

Matthew 13:24–30 (KJV) says,

Another parable put he forth unto them, saying, The kingdom of heaven is likened unto a man which sowed good seed in his field: But while men slept, his enemy came and sowed tares among the wheat, and went his way. But when the blade was sprung up, and brought forth fruit, then appeared the tares also. So the servants of the householder came and said unto him, Sir, didst not thou sow good seed in thy field? from whence then hath it tares? He said unto them, An enemy hath done this. The servants said unto him, Wilt thou then that we go and gather them up? But he said, Nay; lest while ye gather up the tares, ye root up also the wheat with them. Let both grow together until the harvest: and in the time of harvest I will say to the reapers, Gather ye together first the tares, and bind them in bundles to burn them: but gather the wheat into my barn.

The tares have the spirit of Satan within them; the wheat have the Spirit of God within them, but there are those with both in them. God allowed this, so that we could all learn from each other and to also give those who have both spirits within time to decide which one they are going to follow. How do we know this? Within this parable, God planted seed. The seed he planted was wheat not tare. The enemy planted tares. This means that the tares never belonged to God. The same question was asked of Jesus, and this was his answer.

Matthew 13:37–40 (KJV)

He answered and said unto them, He that soweth the good seed is the Son of man; The field is the world; the good seed are the children of the kingdom; but the tares are the children of the wicked one; The enemy that sowed them is the devil; the harvest is the end of the world; and the reapers are the angels. As therefore the tares are gathered and burned in the fire; so shall it be in the end of this world.

This is also found in Romans 9:6–9 (KJV):

For they are not all Israel, which are of Israel: Neither, because they are the seed of Abraham, are they all children: but, In Isaac shall thy seed be called. That is, They which are the children of the flesh, these are not the children of God: but the children of the promise are counted for the seed. For this is the word of promise, At this time will I come, and Sarah shall have a son.

The children born to the bondwoman are born after the flesh and are not counted for the seed, meaning the inheritors of the throne of God; only the children of promise are counted for as seed. This does not mean the children of the bondwoman are not saved; they are, and they do have an inheritance. That inheritance will be the kingdom of God, in which we will all dwell together. The reason they do not inherit the throne of God and become joint heirs with Christ is because of how they receive the Word of God in their hearts and what they did with the Word after they had received it. This can be found in

Luke 8:11–15 (KJV):

Now the parable is this: The seed is the word of God. Those by the way side are they that hear; then cometh the devil, and taketh away the word out of their hearts, lest they should believe and be saved. They on the rock are they, which, when they hear, receive the word with joy; and these have no root, which for a while believe, and in time of temptation fall away. And that which fell among thorns are they, which, when they have heard, go forth, and are choked with cares and riches and pleasures of this life, and bring no fruit to perfection. But that on the good ground are they, which in an honest and good heart, having heard the word, keep it, and bring forth fruit with patience.

These are the four types of sons. Some cannot be saved because they belong to Satan, and Satan ensures that the word never grows within them. They are those by the wayside. The next two sons are those whom God is trying to save, because of the weakness of their hearts and their inability to endure the temptations of this world and Satan. They can be saved, if they strengthen themselves and hold to the Word of God. The last group of sons is the group that God uses to teach the others. They are the chosen sons of God. They are the good ground that the seed can grow in. They are the children of promise, chosen by God.

These sons all have spiritual mothers that are over the sons of God. These are the same three spiritual women to which this chapter has been referring. As this chapter has said earlier, they are called women because they produce sons, and anything that produces sons is feminine in nature. This also means that God has a feminine side as well, because he produces sons that have his nature through the Holy Spirit. What most of us don't know is that there are other spirits that can produce sons, and they are feminine in nature also. The Bible calls these spirits or women by their spiritual names. They go by many names in the Bible, but the names that are the most recognized names are the free woman, the bondwoman, and the adulterous woman. These are other ways in which the Bible refers to these women, and as this chapter goes through the different scriptures that refer to these women, the understanding will come.

The first thing we need to understand is that even though the word *woman* is being used to describe a single person, it really refers to a group of people. The next thing we need to know in order to be able to see who these women truly are is to first understand what God means by the words *adultery* and *fornication*. The spiritual meaning of these words will reveal to you who these women are spiritually and why God gives them the names that he gives them. We all know what fornication and adultery in the natural sense mean, and the spiritual meaning is not that much different.

Fornication in the spiritual sense is the same as idol worshiping, putting something before God. God does not like this, but he will forgive you if you learn the error of your ways. He knows that most people are ignorant of this sin and are not aware that they are fornicating in the spiritual sense. Adultery to God in the spiritual sense is different; it is unforgivable, because it means that a person has turned his or her back on God. The person actually hates him and does not want to follow him. He or she has turned against him so he gives up on them and turns them over to a reprobated mind. What I am saying that spiritual adultery is can be verified in Jeremiah 3:6–9. I will talk more about spiritual adultery later in this chapter; for now though, I will continue explaining spiritual fornication.

You might be asking yourself by now, "How is it that a person can commit spiritual fornication without knowing it?" There are many ways. The first is with money; it is easy to put one's trust in money rather than God. The second is with engraved images of heavenly things. Many religions do this. I will not name them all, but I will name the one that has caused all of us at one time to commit this type of fornication without knowing it. It is religion itself. I know this is a very bold statement, but bear with me and I will show you the scriptures that tell us this. Religion is not of God, because it divides and the body of Christ must not be divided; it is one body. Anything that tries to divide the body of Christ must not be of God, and therefore, he is not the author of it. God, however, has allowed it for now because it in and of itself does make an attempt to do what is right; it simply falls short. It also is allowed because at the present time, it is the only means by which a person will come even to know of God. No one will listen to a person who is not certified or ordained in some kind of way. So in this sense, God has no choice but to use it in order to try to save his people, but it will not always be this way.

Religion is called a woman because it reproduces many children. She is also called the desolate women. This is because she is not married. Married in the spiritual sense means joined with Christ. The people are joined with Christ but not the religion that they are joined with. This is found in the book of Isaiah.

Isaiah 54:1 (KJV) says, "Sing, O barren, thou that didst not bear; break forth into singing, and cry aloud, thou that didst not travail with child: for more are the children of the desolate than the children of the married wife, saith the LORD."

People who are desolate are people with whom God is angry and whom he punishes by withdrawing himself from them. God first did this to Israel when he was angry with them. This is found in Ezekiel 20:22–26 (KJV):

Nevertheless I withdrew mine hand, and wrought for my name's sake, that it should not be polluted in the sight of the heathen, in whose sight I brought them forth. I lifted up mine hand unto them also in the wilderness, that I would scatter them among the heathen, and disperse them through the countries; Because they had not executed my judgments, but had despised my statutes, and had polluted my sabbaths, and their eyes were after their fathers' idols. Wherefore I gave them also statutes that were not good, and judgments whereby they should not live; And I polluted them in their own gifts, in that they caused to pass through the fire all that openeth the womb, that I might make them desolate, to the end that they might know that I am the LORD.

The fact that God does not intend to destroy them as a people is repeated in the book of first Timothy. He also emphasizes the fact that they are widows, with a husband.

1 Timothy 5:3–6 (KJV)

Honour widows that are widows indeed. But if any widow have children or nephews, let them learn first to shew piety at home, and to requite their parents: for that is good and acceptable before God. Now she that is a widow indeed, and desolate, trusteth in God, and continueth in supplications and prayers night and day. But she that liveth in pleasure is dead while she liveth.

I am aware that these scriptures are referring to natural widows, but I am using them because God feels the same way spiritually. God does not destroy the people who do this, but he will punish them. This is done in order to give them a chance to get back in his good graces. This is because he is merciful in his judgments. He is always willing to give his creations a second chance.

Isaiah 54:1 also revealed another name of one of these women to us. She was called the barren woman, meaning she doesn't have children. The barren woman is also known as the married woman. Why doesn't she reproduce and have children? Because her number is set and she cannot increase. She is the chosen woman, and all of her children are the elects. Another reason why this woman cannot increase her numbers at this time is because no one will listen to the children of this woman. Whenever they speak, the children of the bondwoman will kill them, because to them they speak blasphemy. This is why these scriptures are found in the book of Galatians.

Galatians 4:28–31 (KJV) says, "Now we, brethren, as Isaac was, are the children of promise. But as then he that was born after the flesh persecuted him that was born after the Spirit, even so it is now."

This is why all the prophets, apostles, and even Christ were killed. Why? Because of the way they spoke. They spoke too boldly and with authority, as if they knew something that the others did not know, which happens to be the case. Is there more evidence found in the Bible as to different groups of people being called a type of woman? Before we talk about that, let me further expound on the word *barren*.

2 Peter 1:2–9 (KJV)

Grace and peace be multiplied unto you through the knowledge of God, and of Jesus our Lord, According as his divine power hath given unto us all things that pertain unto life and godliness, through the knowledge of him that hath called us to glory and virtue: Whereby are given unto us exceeding great and precious promises: that by these ye might be partakers of the divine nature, having escaped the corruption that is in the world through lust. And beside this, giving all diligence, add to your faith virtue; and to virtue knowledge; And to knowledge temperance; and to temperance patience; and to patience godliness; And to godliness brotherly kindness; and to brotherly kindness charity. For if these things be in you, and abound, they make you that ye shall neither be barren nor unfruitful in the knowledge of our Lord Jesus Christ. But he that lacketh these things is blind, and cannot see afar off, and hath forgotten that he was purged from his old sins.

I used these scriptures here, because even though the barren woman cannot reproduce children, the children themselves are not barren. They have received these eight things in abundance from God. The only reason their numbers do not increase is because no one will listen to them, and therefore they cannot pass these gifts along to someone else. These are not the ways of the world. They are the virtues of God and cannot be passed along. They are given in abundance only to those who have been chosen by the Holy Spirit to receive them.

The spirit of this woman and her children will not be manifested until the appointed time of God. This is something I will discuss later in this book; for now, I will continue expounding on the other two women.

The Three Resurrections and the Types of Seed within the Resurrection

This is also how it will be in the resurrection of man. God is going to give each man a new body according to the type of person that he is. This can be found in the book of first Corinthians.

1 Corinthians 15:35–38 (KJV)

But some man will say, How are the dead raised up? and with what body do they come? Thou fool, that which thou sowest is not quickened, except it die: And that which thou sowest, thou sowest not that body that shall be, but bare grain, it may chance of wheat, or of some other grain: But God giveth it a body as it hath pleased him, and to every seed his own body.

This is God's choice not ours. If we do not like the choice that God made for us, he gave an answer to this Romans 9:18–24 (KJV):

Therefore hath he mercy on whom he will have mercy, and whom he will he hardeneth. Thou wilt say then unto me, Why doth he yet find fault? For who hath resisted his will? Nay but, O man, who art thou that repliest against God? Shall the thing formed say to him that formed it, Why hast thou made me thus? Hath not the potter power over the clay, of the same lump to make one vessel unto honour, and another unto dishonour? What if God, willing to shew his wrath, and to make his power known, endured with much longsuffering the vessels of wrath fitted to destruction: And that he might make known the riches of his glory on the vessels of mercy, which he had afore prepared unto glory, Even us, whom he hath called, not of the Jews only, but also of the Gentiles?

This is what God has to say to those who have objections to his will and what he is doing. In these scriptures, God is telling us part of his plan of election. In verse 23, he is telling us that this is how he will show his glory or power to his creations. He is also telling us that he prepared some ahead of time, the chosen, not just of the Jews, but of the Gentiles also.

Israel, the Fornicating and Adulterous Women

Israel, to God, is a woman. In fact, she was his bride, and her children are the bond sons. He had married her but had to give her a letter of divorce because she committed adultery—spiritual adultery, that is. How can someone commit spiritual adultery? A person commits spiritual adultery when he or she stops believing in God; by turning his or her back on God and never repenting, he or she becomes lost. Israel did this at one time during the reign of King Ahab and Queen Jezebel, when they decided to follow Baal instead of God. This is what Jeremiah was writing about.

Jeremiah 3:6–9 (KJV)

Hast thou seen that which backsliding Israel hath done? she is gone up upon every high mountain and under every green tree, and there hath played the harlot. And I said after she had done all these things, Turn thou unto me. But she returned not. And her treacherous sister Judah saw it. And I saw, when for all the causes whereby backsliding Israel committed adultery I had put her away, and given her a bill of divorce; yet her treacherous sister Judah feared not, but went and played the harlot also. And it came to pass through the lightness of her whoredom, that she defiled the land, and committed adultery with stones and with stocks.

Here in these scriptures, it is unmistakable that Israel is referred to as a woman. We know, however, that Israel is composed of many different people, so why does God refer to it as if he is talking to a single woman? Because they were supposed to be single-minded in their pursuit of him; if they had continued to do that, he would have continued to bless them and would have caused them to reproduce more and more children who also followed him. Instead, they rebelled against him, and as a result of this, he eventually turned to the Gentiles and blessed them through his son. This is one of the main reasons why the Bible says, "The first shall be last and the last shall be first." The Gentiles will be placed ahead of the Jews, who first received his Word, because they are now in bondage, and those who are in Christ are free. This is what God said about Israel to Isaiah. In Isaiah 57:3–6 (KJV), it says,

> But draw near hither, ye sons of the sorceress, the seed of the adulterer and the whore. Against whom do ye sport yourselves? against whom make ye a wide mouth, and draw out the tongue? are ye not children of transgression, a seed of falsehood, Enflaming yourselves with idols under every green tree, slaying the children in the valleys under the clifts of the rocks?

God calls them the seed of the adulterer and the whore. It is not that they are lost, because in verse 4, he says to them that they are not the children of transgression, because they belong to him. They are supposed to be his; they are wheat, acting like tares.

The Woman Who Sits on Top of the Beast

The next woman I would like to talk about is the woman who is mixed with both tare and wheat. She is those who love God but are controlled unknowingly by the beast. The beast is a woman also, and she is the power behind the other woman. The beast is Satan's bride. She is spiritual in nature, and her children are brutal, love power, and will do anything to have that power. They are the ones who are in control of this world at this time. This is found in Revelation 17:3–6 (KJV):

> So he carried me away in the spirit into the wilderness: and I saw a woman sit upon a scarlet coloured beast, full of names of blasphemy, having seven heads and ten horns. And the woman was arrayed in purple and scarlet colour, and decked with gold and precious stones and pearls, having a golden cup in her hand full of abominations and filthiness of her fornication: And upon her forehead was a name written, MYSTERY, BABYLON THE GREAT, THE MOTHER OF HARLOTS AND ABOMINATIONS OF THE EARTH. And I saw the woman drunken with the blood of the saints, and with the blood of the martyrs of Jesus: and when I saw her, I wondered with great admiration.

Many people have wondered who this woman is. Until now, the meaning of this has been hidden from most. The identity of this woman has been revealed to me, and I will now share that with you. She is the people who believe in God but are full of religion and are being controlled by the beast. They have become blinded by their religion and have killed saints without realizing it. The book of Revelation describes her as being arrayed in purple and scarlet. These colors show her connection with divine things. These colors represent the priesthood and royalty, and this is how she massacres herself as royalty. She kills the saints unknowingly because they seem to be a threat to the church as she knows it. These people think they are doing the will of God, but in fact, they are doing the will of Satan. This is why she is described as riding on the beast; they are together.

The beasts are the children of the woman who is destined to be thrown into the lake of fire. She is the bride of Satan. She is filled with the spirit of the Antichrist. Her seed or children are known as tares, and these tares are people whom Satan controls. They are his seed, and they seek to control God's people. This is what Satan has wanted since the beginning of time, and he has obtained it through religion, which kills or condemns anyone who opposes it. This is how he controls the people of God. They are mentioned in Ezekiel 34:7–8 (KJV).

> Therefore, ye shepherds, hear the word of the LORD; As I live, saith the Lord GOD, surely because my flock became a prey, and my flock became meat to every beast of the field, because there was no shepherd, neither did my shepherds search for my flock, but the shepherds fed themselves, and fed not my flock …

The shepherds are those who are supposed to lead God's people to him but who are instead gone astray, the people with them. This is why God says in these scriptures they are meat for every beast of the field. The children of the beast cause people in this world to worship them. The is found in Revelation 13:11–15 (KJV).

> And I beheld another beast coming up out of the earth; and he had two horns like a lamb, and he spake as a dragon. And he exerciseth all the power of the first beast before him, and causeth the earth and them which dwell therein to worship the first beast, whose deadly wound was healed. And he doeth great wonders, so that he maketh fire come down from heaven on the earth in the sight of men, And deceiveth them that dwell on the earth by the means of those miracles which he had power to do in the sight of the beast;

saying to them that dwell on the earth, that they should make an image to the beast, which had the wound by a sword, and did live. And he had power to give life unto the image of the beast, that the image of the beast should both speak, and cause that as many as would not worship the image of the beast should be killed.

There are many things in these scriptures I would like to discuss, but for now, I will focus on the beast and her children. This is the second great beast, because the first one almost died when it received a deathblow from Christ. The reason that the second beast lived is because of the spirit of the beast, which Christ did not destroy; it later revived the first beast. They come in two forms. There is the beast, and there is the image of the beast. The first are the actual people in the form of governments and people of great power, and the second is the spirit of this woman who influences these people to do what they do. It is by the spirit of the woman that the beast controls them, and they force people to worship them or be killed. This is the way it has always been, and this is what God is trying to rid the earth of.

The beast, however, will be destroyed, along with Satan. This can be found in Revelation 20:10 (KJV): "And the devil that deceived them was cast into the lake of fire and brimstone, where the beast and the false prophet are, and shall be tormented day and night for ever and ever."

What will happen to the woman who rides on the beast? This is what the Bible said in the book of Revelation,

Revelation 17:16–18 (KJV).

And the ten horns which thou sawest upon the beast, these shall hate the whore, and shall make her desolate and naked, and shall eat her flesh, and burn her with fire. For God hath put in their hearts to fulfil his will, and to agree, and give their kingdom unto the beast, until the words of God shall be fulfilled. And the woman which thou sawest is that great city, which reigneth over the kings of the earth.

That great city is Babylon, the city that first opposed God, the opposite of the other great city, New Jerusalem. This is what will happen to those who become joined with the beast even until today. The answer can be found also in the book of Revelation.

WE ARE THE ANGELS

Revelation 18:1–7 (KJV) says,

And after these things I saw another angel come down from heaven, having great power; and the earth was lightened with his glory. And he cried mightily with a strong voice, saying, Babylon the great is fallen, is fallen, and is become the habitation of devils, and the hold of every foul spirit, and a cage of every unclean and hateful bird. For all nations have drunk of the wine of the wrath of her fornication, and the kings of the earth have committed fornication with her, and the merchants of the earth are waxed rich through the abundance of her delicacies. And I heard another voice from heaven, saying, Come out of her, my people, that ye be not partakers of her sins, and that ye receive not of her plagues. For her sins have reached unto heaven, and God hath remembered her iniquities. Reward her even as she rewarded you, and double unto her double according to her works: in the cup which she hath filled fill to her double. How much she hath glorified herself, and lived deliciously, so much torment and sorrow give her: for she saith in her heart, I sit a queen, and am no widow, and shall see no sorrow.

The woman, who is also called Babylon the Great, is a people, a city, and controls people through her spirit. She will be given double the punishment that she gave to the people she punished. The verse I would like to focus on that tells us the fate of the people who were blinded is in verse four, where God essentially says, "Come out of her, my people. I will not punish you with her." This is because God is merciful and understands that they do love him but that they were blinded.

The Chosen Woman
She is also known as the bride of Christ and was chosen even before the world began. The next scriptures that I would like to show you do pertain to an earthly marriage. The reason I am using them is that the same laws that govern a natural marriage govern a spiritual marriage and the spiritual bride.

In Romans 7:1–4 (KJV), it says,

Know ye not, brethren, (for I speak to them that know the law,) how that the law hath dominion over a man as long as he liveth?

For the woman which hath an husband is bound by the law to her husband so long as he liveth; but if the husband be dead, she is loosed from the law of her husband. So then if, while her husband liveth, she be married to another man, she shall be called an adulteress: but if her husband be dead, she is free from that law; so that she is no adulteress, though she be married to another man. Wherefore, my brethren, ye also are become dead to the law by the body of Christ; that ye should be married to another, even to him who is raised from the dead, that we should bring forth fruit unto God.

Those who are married to Christ were able to marry him because they have no other husband. The law was our former husband; we were at one time married to it. But God caused this husband to die to us, and if we accept this death, we are free to marry another. The law, however, is still alive to others, and therefore, these people cannot have a new husband, which is Christ. So for the chosen, the law is dead to them. This is what Christ died for, and because we died with him to the law, we shall live with him. There have only been a few who have understood this and will by faith not live under the law even though they believe in God. For this, God prepared them to become the bride of Christ. This is the woman who is spoken of in the book of Revelation in a singular sense because they are one. However, they are really composed of many more. When she is spoken of in this book, she has already been married.

Revelation 12:1–2 (KJV) says, "And there appeared a great wonder in heaven; a woman clothed with the sun, and the moon under her feet, and upon her head a crown of twelve stars: And she being with child cried, travailing in birth, and pained to be delivered."

She is a she because she can reproduce other sons like them and she herself was reproduced from the Spirit of God who impregnated them with the Word of God. These are people, both men and women, of whom the Bible speaks as those who have overcome the world. This is before they become married. They have already been given the victory of having overcome the world, because they were predestined to do so. The first place this is mentioned is in 1 John 5:4–5 (KJV), "For whatsoever is born of God overcometh the world: and this is the victory that overcometh the world, even our faith. Who is he that overcometh the world, but he that believeth that Jesus is the Son of God?"

These are the rewards that are given to those who overcome the world, and there are seven in all. These are the rewards that the Bible said that the eye of man has not seen nor the ear of man heard, but God has shown it to his elects by the Spirit.

Revelation 2:7 (KJV) says, "He that hath an ear, let him hear what the Spirit saith unto the churches; To him that overcometh will I give to eat of the tree of life, which is in the midst of the paradise of God."

Revelation 2:11 (KJV) says, "He that hath an ear, let him hear what the Spirit saith unto the churches; He that overcometh shall not be hurt of the second death."

Revelation 2:17 (KJV) says, "He that hath an ear, let him hear what the Spirit saith unto the churches; To him that overcometh will I give to eat of the hidden manna, and will give him a white stone, and in the stone a new name written, which no man knoweth saving he that receiveth it."

Revelation 2:26–28 (KJV) said, "And he that overcometh, and keepeth my works unto the end, to him will I give power over the nations: And he shall rule them with a rod of iron; as the vessels of a potter shall they be broken to shivers: even as I received of my Father. And I will give him the morning star."

Revelation 3:5 (KJV) says, "He that overcometh, the same shall be clothed in white raiment; and I will not blot out his name out of the book of life, but I will confess his name before my Father, and before his angels."

Revelation 3:12 (KJV) says,

Him that overcometh will I make a pillar in the temple of my God, and he shall go no more out: and I will write upon him the name of my God, and the name of the city of my God, which is new Jerusalem, which cometh down out of heaven from my God: and I will write upon him my new name."

Revelation 21:7 (KJV) says, "He that overcometh shall inherit all things; and I will be his God, and he shall be my son."

Chapter Three

The Precious Trees of God

I know the title of this chapter sounds very strange, but by the time this chapter is finished, the meaning of the trees will be understood and found to be very fruitful to your understanding. The first question you might ask is, "What are the trees of God?" However, the question you should be asking is, "Who are the trees of God?" That's right, I said *who*. What few realize is that the Bible uses trees as a symbolic representation of people, as well as all other spiritual beings, including God himself. I am sure that if you are a Christian, you have heard of the tree of life and the opposing tree, the tree of the knowledge of good and evil. These two trees represent God and Satan. This, however, is well known to most Christians. But what is not known is that God refers to his creations, meaning man and the angels, as trees also. What has been hidden from most is that God judges people by the kind of tree they are. We are all trees of one kind or another, depending on the type of fruit we produce or, on the other hand, do not produce. The parable of the fig tree is one of the most well-kept secrets in the Bible. The Bible talks in this symbolic language in order to hide the true meaning of whatever God is not ready to reveal. Why? Because it was not meant for all to know until the time was right, and furthermore, God wanted to reveal it to his elects first. However, it is his will now that I tell you, so that your understanding can be increased, increased in a way that you may understand what God is telling all men about themselves in the symbolic language.

As trees, we are all supposed to produce fruit, fruit that pleases God. So in this chapter, I will be explaining the meaning of who the trees are, the fruit they produce, whether good or bad, and how our own fruit will be used to judge us. The first tree I would like to start with is the tree of life. All Christians know that the tree of life is God, but what most don't know is that there is a tree that opposes this tree called the tree of the knowledge. Whether we know it or not, we all have to choose between these two trees. Choose the right one and you live; choose the wrong one and you die the second death. So God calls himself the tree of life, simply because you get to live if you choose to eat from this tree.

Before I get into the explanation of the tree of life, you must know that I will be talking about spiritual things. While explaining the meaning of the trees, certain words and concepts are going to come up that are very spiritual in nature and must be explained first in order for you to get the full understanding of the trees. These are words and concepts, such as *fruit*, the *eating* of these fruits, the *leaves*, and the *branches*, as well as how we *produce* fruit ourselves—not only that, but also how we ourselves are fruit and how our fruit can be seen or not seen by others.

Who and what are the trees and the fruits of God? Let me start by talking about the most important tree of all, the tree of life. It is first found in the book of Genesis.

The Forbidden Fruit
Genesis 2:8–9 (KJV) says,

> And the LORD God planted a garden eastward in Eden; and there he put the man whom he had formed. And out of the ground made the LORD God to grow every tree that is pleasant to the sight, and good for food; the tree of life also in the midst of the garden, and the tree of knowledge of good and evil.

We've all heard the story of Adam and Eve eating off of the wrong tree, and we think that this is a very cut-and-dry story but not really. The reason is that most of us think we know what it means to eat. Most of us think that Adam and Eve literally ate a natural fruit, but they did not. The trees in this garden are spiritual trees, and therefore, the word *tree* is used only as a symbolic representation of who was actually there in the garden. Adam and Eve ate spiritual fruit, which means they made a choice between these two trees as to whom they would follow. To be fed from God is to listen to him and follow his word; this is how we eat spiritually. This is what Adam and Eve did wrong. They made a decision to follow the words of Satan, and therefore, they ate from the wrong tree. A description of the fruit of this tree can be found Galatians 5:17–21 (KJV):

> For the flesh lusteth against the Spirit, and the Spirit against the flesh: and these are contrary the one to the other: so that ye cannot do the things that ye would. But if ye be led of the Spirit, ye are not under the law. Now the works of the flesh are manifest, which are these; Adultery, fornication, uncleanness, lasciviousness, Idolatry, witchcraft, hatred, variance, emulations, wrath, strife, seditions, heresies, Envyings, murders, drunkenness, revellings, and such like: of the which I tell you before, as I have also told you in time past, that they which do such things shall not inherit the kingdom of God.

These are the fruits of Satan, and these fruits are being eaten every day. Every time people do these things, they are listening to the spirit that is in them. It tells them to do these things. Most people who either don't commit these acts or stop doing these acts stop because their conscience bothers them. What they don't realize is that what they think of as their conscience is really the Spirit of God, urging them to stop. This is the spiritual way in which both God and Satan influence the believers or the nonbelievers. We all are subject to both. We all hear both, and it is up to us to make up our minds to do whatever pleases us. This is the way in which God allows us to exercise our free will. We choose which fruit we want to eat at any given time. This means that old saying found in the Bible will take effect: "You reap what you sow." This means that depending on the type of fruit you are eating, at the time, there will be consequences or rewards. The disadvantage of God's fruit, as opposed to Satan's fruit though, is in which one will manifest itself first. Satan has the advantage. Why? Because the difference between these fruits is that one has an immediate reward and the other you may not get until you die. This is the trade-off; it is because of this that Satan's fruit seems more appealing, because you can see the immediate results. Another difference between these fruits is that none of Satan's fruits are spiritual in nature. They are all done with the body, and the reward is physical in nature. The rewards of Satan's fruit are all for the self-satisfaction of the individual's needs.

This means that the ability to resist or not resist his fruit is based on how great the need is of the individual. If his or her needs are great, they will not be able to resist.

God's fruits are these, found in Galatians 5:22–26 (KJV):

But the fruit of the Spirit is love, joy, peace, longsuffering, gentleness, goodness, faith, Meekness, temperance: against such there is no law. And they that are Christ's have crucified the flesh with the affections and lusts. If we live in the Spirit, let us also walk in the Spirit. Let us not be desirous of vain glory, provoking one another, envying one another.

God's fruits are spiritual in nature and are very unselfish, meaning there may or may not be an immediate reward so that they can be seen or felt. This is why it requires faith to eat them. One must trust in him in order to eat his fruit, because his fruit requires sacrifice. God's fruits are contrary to this world, meaning they require a person to do the opposite of what it otherwise would have been natural for him or her to do. The spiritual fruits of God are eaten only by faith; the eating of them is accomplished by practicing the Word of God found in the Bible. They are eaten by faith because by doing these things to your neighbors, you might not be rewarded by the same kindness that you show to them. This would make anyone unwilling to keep practicing this; in fact, it would be easy to say that it doesn't pay. This is why people who practice this way of life are considered weak, foolish, and naive. At first, the people who practice this way of life will feel betrayed by God, because of the ridicule they receive from other people, but as they mature, they will find out more and more why this is happening to them. This is the price all who follow Christ must pay for eating God's fruit in this world. This is why there are more people who eat the fruit of Satan than the fruit of God. They are not willing to pay the price. Lastly, what they don't realize is that Satan's fruit leads a person to his or her death. This is found in Romans 7:5 (KJV): "For when we were in the flesh, the motions of sins, which were by the law, did work in our members to bring forth fruit unto death."

This is why the Bible talks so much about fruit. Depending on which one you eat or follow, you will either live or die. Listen to what God had to say to those who eat from the tree of life, meaning they listen to him.

The Good Fruit

Proverbs 11:30 (KJV) says, "The fruit of the righteous is a tree of life; and he that winneth souls is wise."

The Bible calls you a wise person if you eat from this tree. Reading the Bible is also another form of eating; after all, they are his words, and we can either accept them or reject them. If you accept them, your soul and spirit will be fed, but if you reject them, you will starve spiritually. The Bible says that you will know a tree by its fruit and then makes the statement that it is impossible for either of these trees to be mistaken for the other. Matthew 7:17–20 (KJV) says,

> Even so every good tree bringeth forth good fruit; but a corrupt tree bringeth forth evil fruit. A good tree cannot bring forth evil fruit, neither can a corrupt tree bring forth good fruit. Every tree that bringeth not forth good fruit is hewn down, and cast into the fire. Wherefore by their fruits ye shall know them.

To see someone's fruit, all we have to do is look at his or her life. Do they cause trouble everywhere they go, or do they try to bring peace? Do they kill and destroy or build and unite? Lastly, do they try to promote love or hatred? It is that simple and easy to see their fruits. Now, does that mean that just because a person is showing bad fruit at the moment that he or she is condemned by God? No. A person can make mistakes and do things contrary to who he or she is, or in other words, he or she will come back to being the kind of tree that God originally made him or her. Sooner or later, the person will.

Jesus the Vine

Jesus is a tree of life like his father, because he has life in himself and this makes it possible for him to give life to those who eat of his fruit. The Bible gives us several symbolic tree names that Jesus goes by. The first tree that describes Christ is the vine tree. John 15:1–8 (KJV) says,

> I am the true vine, and my Father is the husbandman. Every branch in me that beareth not fruit he taketh away: and every branch that beareth fruit, he purgeth it, that it may bring forth more fruit. Now ye are clean through the word which I have spoken unto you. Abide in me, and I in you. As the branch cannot bear fruit of itself, except it abide in the vine; no more can ye,

except ye abide in me. I am the vine, ye are the branches: He that abideth in me, and I in him, the same bringeth forth much fruit: for without me ye can do nothing. If a man abide not in me, he is cast forth as a branch, and is withered; and men gather them, and cast them into the fire, and they are burned. If ye abide in me, and my words abide in you, ye shall ask what ye will, and it shall be done unto you. Herein is my Father glorified, that ye bear much fruit; so shall ye be my disciples.

Here in these scriptures, in which Christ calls himself the true vine and those who believe in him the branches. He also points out the fact that no one can bear fruit without him. This is the mistake that Israel made and why Christ could find no fruit when he went to Jerusalem. Israel goes by the names of three trees. First, it is called the olive tree. Second, it is called the fig tree, and third, the cedars of Lebanon. I will use these names in context as they are found, and I will expound on them as this chapter goes on. However, here in the next scriptures though, the Lord is calling Israel evil because they are supposed to bring forth fruit meant for him, but instead, they make offerings of their fruit to another god named Baal.

The Olive Trees

The two olive trees are the two groups of people under the two different covenants. One tree is that if the Jews, while the other is that of the Gentiles. This is reflected in the book of Jeremiah.

Jeremiah 11:15–19 (KJV)

The LORD called thy name, A green olive tree, fair, and of goodly fruit: with the noise of a great tumult he hath kindled fire upon it, and the branches of it are broken. For the LORD of hosts, that planted thee, hath pronounced evil against thee, for the evil of the house of Israel and of the house of Judah, which they have done against themselves to provoke me to anger in offering incense unto Baal. And the LORD hath given me knowledge of it, and I know it: then thou shewedst me their doings. But I was like a lamb or an ox that is brought to the slaughter; and I knew not that they had devised devices against me, saying, Let us destroy the tree with the fruit thereof, and let us cut him off from the land of the living, that his name may be no more remembered.

When Israel did this evil in his sight, he went out and planted another olive tree, called the Gentiles in order to raise them up to bring forth fruit unto him. They are known as the wild olive branches, which were grafted into the vine to replace the original olive branch because they rejected the Son of God. This is found in Romans 11:14–25 (KJV):

> If by any means I may provoke to emulation them which are my flesh, and might save some of them. For if the casting away of them be the reconciling of the world, what shall the receiving of them be, but life from the dead? For if the firstfruit be holy, the lump is also holy: and if the root be holy, so are the branches. And if some of the branches be broken off, and thou, being a wild olive tree, wert graffed in among them, and with them partakest of the root and fatness of the olive tree; Boast not against the branches. But if thou boast, thou bearest not the root, but the root thee. Thou wilt say then, The branches were broken off, that I might be graffed in. Well; because of unbelief they were broken off, and thou standest by faith. Be not highminded, but fear: For if God spared not the natural branches, take heed lest he also spare not thee. Behold therefore the goodness and severity of God: on them which fell, severity; but toward thee, goodness, if thou continue in his goodness: otherwise thou also shalt be cut off. And they also, if they abide not still in unbelief, shall be graffed in: for God is able to graff them in again. For if thou wert cut out of the olive tree which is wild by nature, and wert graffed contrary to nature into a good olive tree: how much more shall these, which be the natural branches, be graffed into their own olive tree? For I would not, brethren, that ye should be ignorant of this mystery, lest ye should be wise in your own conceits; that blindness in part is happened to Israel, until the fulness of the Gentiles be come in.

So once again, we are the wild olive branches that were grafted into the vine, or the family of God, and the only reason we were even given this opportunity is because the natural olive tree rejected Christ. Therefore, we are not to boast, after being given this chance against the original olive tree, because this would not please God. We are supposed to be thankful to him that gave us this opportunity.

Israel and the Gentiles, now known as Christians, are called by two other names in the Bible. These names are more precious to God than any other names by which he calls them. The name by which he calls them is the fig tree. The fig tree and the vine are husband and wife, the bride and the bridegroom. The fig tree must produce fruit that pleases her husband. If she does not, then the husband will divorce his bride. This is exactly what God did to Israel. Jeremiah 3:6–9 (KJV) says,

> The LORD said also unto me in the days of Josiah the king, Hast thou seen that which backsliding Israel hath done? she is gone up upon every high mountain and under every green tree, and there hath played the harlot. And I said after she had done all these things, Turn thou unto me. But she returned not. And her treacherous sister Judah saw it. And I saw, when for all the causes whereby backsliding Israel committed adultery I had put her away, and given her a bill of divorce; yet her treacherous sister Judah feared not, but went and played the harlot also. And it came to pass through the lightness of her whoredom, that she defiled the land, and committed adultery with stones and with stocks.

This was the whole nation of Israel that God was referring to when he said that they had turned their back to him and would not return to him. So God had no choice but to write a letter of divorce to them. They committed adultery by worshiping Baal, who is not even a real god, only a figment of someone's imagination made of stones and rock. This is why the fig tree had no fruit on it, and this is why Jesus on his journey to Israel cursed the fig tree. The tree that Jesus cursed because it had no fruit on it was a real tree, but it represented the same condition in which he found the real Jerusalem. He cursed the tree, which was a symbolic representation of what he was going to do to the real nation. Nevertheless, until this day, they are still known as a fig tree, and so is the new bride or new nation called by the same name. His new bride is represented by the parable of the fig tree, found in the book of Matthew.

The Fig Tree

?????????????
Matthew 24:32–36 (KJV) says,

> Now learn a parable of the fig tree; When his branch is yet tender, and putteth forth leaves, ye know that summer is nigh: So likewise

ye, when ye shall see all these things, know that it is near, even at the doors. Verily I say unto you, This generation shall not pass, till all these things be fulfilled. Heaven and earth shall pass away, but my words shall not pass away. But of that day and hour knoweth no man, no, not the angels of heaven, but my Father only.

The meaning of this parable is one of the most well-kept secrets in the Bible. The reason it has been kept secret is because this parable tells the time of when we all can expect the next coming of Christ. That is what this parable is telling us, and this is how. The fig tree are the chosen people of God. When they put forth their branches, this means that they are coming into the knowledge that they were meant to understand since the beginning of time. They now know who they are, and when they come into this understanding, it means that their fruit is mature and is ready to be picked. To be picked off the tree is to be taken away by the one who planted them. This means the he will come soon after. They do not know the exact time, but they do know it is near. This is the meaning of the word *summer*. Summer is a natural time when all trees put forth their fruit, and so it is in the spiritual sense as well. Summer is a time of newness, revival, joy, and happiness. Winter is a time when the earth appears old, dead, and sad, and so it is in the spiritual sense also. To God, the earth is going through a long period of winter, meaning all the trees, which are people, appear to be dead and do not bear fruit. It was only summer for a short time, while Christ was on the earth. Since that time, it has been winter, but this is why this parable says "know that summer is near." The tender branches are about to put forth their leaves. This is everything that God and his son have been waiting for, according to Romans 8:17–19 (KJV):

And if children, then heirs; heirs of God, and joint-heirs with Christ; if so be that we suffer with him, that we may be also glorified together. For I reckon that the sufferings of this present time are not worthy to be compared with the glory which shall be revealed in us. For the earnest expectation of the creature waiteth for the manifestation of the sons of God.

This is the revealing of the fig tree. They are the fruit that the Father and the Son have been growing in their garden, meaning the world. This is repeated also in 1 John 3:1–2 (KJV):

Behold, what manner of love the Father hath bestowed upon us, that we should be called the sons of God: therefore the world knoweth us not, because it knew him not. Beloved, now are we the sons of God, and it doth not yet appear what we shall be: but we know that, when he shall appear, we shall be like him; for we shall see him as he is.

The true sons of God will be like Christ; this is what this scripture is telling those who have been chosen. This is the true manifestation of the sons of God.

Now that I have revealed to you a future thing that will happen upon the return of Christ, let me go backward for a moment to tell you about a story of the trees talking to one another. Yes, that is what I said. Within the Bible, there is a story of certain trees asking other trees to reign over them, and a particular tree telling them in a sense that no he will not. This found in the book of Judges.

Trees Fighting for Power
Judges 9:8–15 (KJV) says,

The trees went forth on a time to anoint a king over them; and they said unto the olive tree, Reign thou over us. But the olive tree said unto them, Should I leave my fatness, wherewith by me they honour God and man, and go to be promoted over the trees? And the trees said to the fig tree, Come thou, and reign over us. But the fig tree said unto them, Should I forsake my sweetness, and my good fruit, and go to be promoted over the trees? Then said the trees unto the vine, Come thou, and reign over us. And the vine said unto them, Should I leave my wine, which cheereth God and man, and go to be promoted over the trees? Then said all the trees unto the bramble, Come thou, and reign over us. And the bramble said unto the trees, If in truth ye anoint me king over you, then come and put your trust in my shadow: and if not, let fire come out of the bramble, and devour the cedars of Lebanon.

The trees in this parable are the angels. The olive tree is the family of God. They would not do as the other trees asked. Then these trees asked the fig tree, which is the bride of Christ to reign over them, but the bride refused. Then these trees asked the vine to reign over them, and he said he would not do it. Then these trees, which are angels, asked the bramble tree, which is Lucifer, to reign over them, and he accepted. He then asked these angels to put their trust in him and come under his authority, and he further promised them that no fire would ever hurt them, meaning that they who are made of wood would never burn. This fire that he is telling them will not hurt them is the fire of God in the form of the Holy Spirit. We know this because this is what Christ said in the book of Luke.

Luke 12:49–50 (KJV) says, "I am come to send fire on the earth; and what will I, if it be already kindled? But I have a baptism to be baptized with; and how am I straitened till it be accomplished!"

This fire is the Holy Spirit, and it was sent to the earth to baptize those who would become the sons of God. This type of baptism can only be given by the Father and the Son, and this is how the sons, being made of wood, spiritually that is, are kindled or burned. This burning purges them of any evil thoughts, sins, or bad works. This is what this parable means when it says, "What will I if it is already kindled." What he means by this is what do you think he will do with those who have already been burned by his fire and are ready to receive him? The answer is that he will make them heirs. This is that fire that the bramble tree told the other trees that he would protect them from, and for the most part, he was correct because the bramble tree told this to the trees called the cedars of Lebanon. Who are these trees that are called the cedars of Lebanon? None other than Israel, the ones who kept the law. By keeping the law, they prevented themselves from receiving the baptism of fire or receiving grace, known as Christ. Therefore, until this day, they remain under the law, and the law prevents them from receiving Christ. You might ask, "Where in the Bible does God call them the cedars of Lebanon?" This is first found in the book of Psalms.

The Cedars of Lebanon
Psalm 29:4–11 (KJV) says,

> The voice of the LORD is powerful; the voice of the LORD is full of majesty. The voice of the LORD breaketh the cedars; yea, the LORD breaketh the cedars of Lebanon. He maketh them also to skip like a calf; Lebanon and Sirion like a young unicorn. The voice of the LORD divideth the flames of fire. The voice of the LORD shaketh the wilderness; the LORD shaketh the wilderness of Kadesh. The voice of the LORD maketh the hinds

to calve, and discovereth the forests: and in his temple doth every one speak of his glory. The LORD sitteth upon the flood; yea, the LORD sitteth King for ever. The LORD will give strength unto his people; the LORD will bless his people with peace.

The Lord wanted to bless Israel and give strength to his people, and he did for a while, but in the book of Ezekiel, it describes how he cut down the trees of Lebanon because of their sins. Ezekiel 19:10–14 (KJV) says,

Thy mother is like a vine in thy blood, planted by the waters: she was fruitful and full of branches by reason of many waters. And she had strong rods for the sceptres of them that bare rule, and her stature was exalted among the thick branches, and she appeared in her height with the multitude of her branches. But she was plucked up in fury, she was cast down to the ground, and the east wind dried up her fruit: her strong rods were broken and withered; the fire consumed them. And now she is planted in the wilderness, in a dry and thirsty ground. And fire is gone out of a rod of her branches, which hath devoured her fruit, so that she hath no strong rod to be a sceptre to rule. This is a lamentation, and shall be for a lamentation.

This is what God did to Israel in a spiritual sense, meaning he put out the fire, or since he is that fire, he withdrew himself. She would have been the strongest nation in the world, but because she rejected Christ, she became weak. Thirsty ground means ground that lacks water or the Holy Spirit who gives strength. This strength is power.

That his people were the inhabitants of Israel is repeated in Jeremiah 22:23–25 (KJV):

O inhabitant of Lebanon, that makest thy nest in the cedars, how gracious shalt thou be when pangs come upon thee, the pain as of a woman in travail! As I live, saith the LORD, though Coniah the son of Jehoiakim king of Judah were the signet upon my right hand, yet would I pluck thee thence; And I will give thee into the hand of them that seek thy life, and into the hand of them whose face thou fearest, even into the hand of Nebuchadrezzar king of Babylon, and into the hand of the Chaldeans.

This is the punishment that God placed upon his people when he led them into captivity, under the king of Babylon, King Nebuchadnezzar. This is how *cut down* in the spiritual sense translated into the real thing that happened to Israel. Since God loved Israel, though, he would never completely give up on them. So God sent a prophet named Jeremiah to warn them. Before he sent his son, he sent a prophet to warn them of their evil ways, and when they would not listen, this prophet gave them a warning that a seed would come out of the branches of David. That seed or that branch would become known as Christ.

The *Branch* and the Branches

Jesus is a branch also, a branch off the tree of life, that came through the branches that came from King David. The Bible tells us this in Jeremiah 23:5–7 (KJV):

> Behold, the days come, saith the LORD, that I will raise unto David a righteous Branch, and a King shall reign and prosper, and shall execute judgment and justice in the earth. In his days Judah shall be saved, and Israel shall dwell safely: and this is his name whereby he shall be called, THE LORD OUR RIGHTEOUSNESS. Therefore, behold, the days come, saith the LORD, that they shall no more say, The LORD liveth, which brought up the children of Israel out of the land of Egypt …

He was cut off, burned with fire, and grafted in again upon his return to his father, just as it has been done to us. This is the method that the Father uses in order to train his sons. By the casting off of his sons, he allows them to experience hardships. This teaches them to rely on him and not themselves. These hardships are called trials and tribulations. Casting off spiritually means to cut down a tree or cut off the branches of that tree so that it may dry up or die. He will not leave them in this state permanently, but nevertheless, it is necessary. This is told to us in Job 14:7–9 (KJV):

> For there is hope of a tree, if it be cut down, that it will sprout again, and that the tender branch thereof will not cease. Though the root thereof wax old in the earth, and the stock thereof die in the ground; Yet through the scent of water it will bud, and bring forth boughs like a plant.

Cutting down the tree means that he must allow us to die, so that we may live again and be better than we were before. He did the same thing to his son as told in Ezekiel 15:1–8 (KJV):

And the word of the LORD came unto me, saying, Son of man, What is the vine tree more than any tree, or than a branch which is among the trees of the forest? Shall wood be taken thereof to do any work? or will men take a pin of it to hang any vessel thereon? Behold, it is cast into the fire for fuel; the fire devoureth both the ends of it, and the midst of it is burned. Is it meet for any work? Behold, when it was whole, it was meet for no work: how much less shall it be meet yet for any work, when the fire hath devoured it, and it is burned? Therefore thus saith the Lord GOD; As the vine tree among the trees of the forest, which I have given to the fire for fuel, so will I give the inhabitants of Jerusalem. And I will set my face against them; they shall go out from one fire, and another fire shall devour them; and ye shall know that I am the LORD, when I set my face against them. And I will make the land desolate, because they have committed a trespass, saith the Lord GOD.

Even Christ himself was cut down and used for fuel in the fire, and even though this was meant to be, God the Father is still angry with Israel for cutting down his Son. If they do not repent of this sin, He will throw them in another fire, called the lake of fire, according to these scriptures.

Lucifer, a Tree in the Garden that Did Not Want to Be Cut Down

There is a story in the Bible that gives us a better sense of what happened in the Garden of Eden than the one found in the book of Genesis, but because it is written in the symbolic language, most don't realize who the Bible is talking about. I hope that by showing you this account found in the Bible and using the gift of interpretation that God has given me, I can reveal it to you. It is found in Ezekiel 31:3–18 (KJV):

Behold, the Assyrian was a cedar in Lebanon with fair branches, and with a shadowing shroud, and of an high stature; and his top was among the thick boughs. The waters made him great, the deep set him up on high with her rivers running round about his plants, and sent her little rivers unto all the trees of the field.

Therefore his height was exalted above all the trees of the field, and his boughs were multiplied, and his branches became long because of the multitude of waters, when he shot forth. All the fowls of heaven made their nests in his boughs, and under his branches did all the beasts of the field bring forth their young, and under his shadow dwelt all great nations. Thus was he fair in his greatness, in the length of his branches: for his root was by great waters. The cedars in the garden of God could not hide him: the fir trees were not like his boughs, and the chestnut trees were not like his branches; nor any tree in the garden of God was like unto him in his beauty. I have made him fair by the multitude of his branches: so that all the trees of Eden, that were in the garden of God, envied him. Therefore thus saith the Lord GOD; Because thou hast lifted up thyself in height, and he hath shot up his top among the thick boughs, and his heart is lifted up in his height; I have therefore delivered him into the hand of the mighty one of the heathen; he shall surely deal with him: I have driven him out for his wickedness. And strangers, the terrible of the nations, have cut him off, and have left him: upon the mountains and in all the valleys his branches are fallen, and his boughs are broken by all the rivers of the land; and all the people of the earth are gone down from his shadow, and have left him. Upon his ruin shall all the fowls of the heaven remain, and all the beasts of the field shall be upon his branches: To the end that none of all the trees by the waters exalt themselves for their height, neither shoot up their top among the thick boughs, neither their trees stand up in their height, all that drink water: for they are all delivered unto death, to the nether parts of the earth, in the midst of the children of men, with them that go down to the pit. Thus saith the Lord GOD; In the day when he went down to the grave I caused a mourning: I covered the deep for him, and I restrained the floods thereof, and the great waters were stayed: and I caused Lebanon to mourn for him, and all the trees of the field fainted for him. I made the nations to shake at the sound of his fall, when I cast him down to hell with them that descend into the pit: and all the trees of Eden, the choice and best of Lebanon, all that drink water, shall be comforted in the nether parts of the earth. They also went down into hell with him unto them that be slain with the sword; and they that were his arm, that dwelt under his shadow in the midst of the heathen. To whom art thou thus like in glory and in greatness among the trees of Eden? yet shalt thou be brought down with the trees of Eden unto the nether parts of the earth: thou shalt lie in the midst of the uncircumcised with them that be slain by the sword.

The tree that God is talking to in these scriptures is none other than Satan himself, even though he is referred to as the Assyrian and a cedar in Lebanon. Lebanon is a symbolic name for the Garden of Eden and is sometimes used to describe Israel. Those are just the different names, among many others, Satan goes by. The other trees are the other angels who envied him and were sad when he was cut down. This is the meaning of these scriptures found in the book of Ezekiel. Why does God talk this way? As I have told you before, the reason for the symbolic language is he wants to hide the true meaning of who he's talking about from those he does not want to know.

What a Tree Needs in order to Grow

Naturally speaking, a tree only needs a few things in order to grow naturally. It needs first and foremost sunlight from the sun. The two next most important things it needs are water and soil. Lastly, it needs air, carbon dioxide, to be exact, to complete the process of making air, the thing that brings life to this planet. Coincidently, spiritual trees need the exact same things. The sunlight that the natural tree needs is replaced by the light of the Son, Jesus Christ. The water a natural tree needs is replaced by spiritual water, otherwise known as the Holy Spirit. The soil a natural trees needs to get its nutrients from is replaced by the words of God. They are our sustenance. Lastly, the air a natural tree needs in order to complete the process of photosynthesis is called carbon dioxide. It is deadly to us but life to the tree. This carbon dioxide is used to produce the nutrients it needs, or in other words, a tree can turn death into life. This is exactly what God does for us spiritually. Carbon dioxide is sin and too much of it will kill us.

Why does God call himself a tree in the first place? Why does he use this analogy? The answer is because a tree is the perfect way to describe God. Let us review some of the things a natural tree does for the earth and man. A tree provides life-giving oxygen to the world. A tree provides shelter by providing the wood needed to build dwelling places. A tree provides shelter for animals and a home for birds. A tree cools the earth by providing shade, which keeps the earth cool while protecting it from the sun. A tree can be used to keep us warm by burning it. A tree helps hold the soil together, and lastly, a tree can provide food. Basically, a tree can provide all the things we need in order to survive in this world. These are all the things God does for us, so this why he calls himself the tree of life.

The Parable of the Forest

The revealing of the mystery of the parable of the forest. There are forests all over the world, both naturally and spiritually. Forest are what God calls people, because in his eyes, we are all trees, because he calls himself a tree; therefore, we are all branches off of this tree. So God planted trees all over the world, and he calls them forests. The Lord told Ezekiel a parable about the forest in the south. It is found in Ezekiel 20:45–49 (KJV):

> Moreover the word of the LORD came unto me, saying, Son of man, set thy face toward the south, and drop thy word toward the south, and prophesy against the forest of the south field; And say to the forest of the south, Hear the word of the LORD; Thus saith the Lord GOD; Behold, I will kindle a fire in thee, and it shall devour every green tree in thee, and every dry tree: the flaming flame shall not be quenched, and all faces from the south to the north shall be burned therein. And all flesh shall see that I the LORD have kindled it: it shall not be quenched. Then said I, Ah Lord GOD! they say of me, Doth he not speak parables?

The south forests are the nations of the Gentiles, and the flaming fire that will not be quenched is the coming of the Holy Spirit, which will happen after the death of Christ and will be offered to anyone who believes in the Son. The cutting down of a tree means that the tree must die. This symbolizes the spiritual death of a person after he or she has found out that without Christ, he or she is lost and that the baptism he or she has is not enough. Now read what the book of Matthew has to say about this. Matthew 3:7–11 (KJV) says,

> But when he saw many of the Pharisees and Sadducees come to his baptism, he said unto them, O generation of vipers, who hath warned you to flee from the wrath to come? Bring forth therefore fruits meet for repentance: And think not to say within yourselves, We have Abraham to our father: for I say unto you, that God is

able of these stones to raise up children unto Abraham. And now also the axe is laid unto the root of the trees: therefore every tree which bringeth not forth good fruit is hewn down, and cast into the fire. I indeed baptize you with water unto repentance: but he that cometh after me is mightier than I, whose shoes I am not worthy to bear: he shall baptize you with the Holy Ghost, and with fire ...

The Pharisees and Sadducees were indeed believers of God the Father, but John the Baptist knew that they would not accept the Son who was coming. This is why he said that they would be cut down to produce fruit and cast into the fire. This is also why Paul the apostle said the following in 1 Corinthians 1:17–18 (KJV):

For Christ sent me not to baptize, but to preach the gospel: not with wisdom of words, lest the cross of Christ should be made of none effect. For the preaching of the cross is to them that perish foolishness; but unto us which are saved it is the power of God.

What these are referring to is who the cross should be preached to and they are those who don't know Christ and are therefore in need of salvation. The way in which salvation is achieved is by explaining to a person why Christ died for him or her and subsequently that person accepts this, repents of their sins and becomes a believer in Christ. This is what it means to bring someone to the cross and this is what these scriptures mean by the preaching of the cross is to them that perish, the problem is that after a person is saved. Because of a lack of understanding that all servant sons of God suffer from is that they never move on for the cross. If they knew that by only preaching the message of the cross, which is to say the death of Christ, they are only concentrating on repentance. What has cause those who have become free to be free is the life of Christ, which means that they have moved on from the death of Christ into the life of Christ. This means that they have moved passed the cross. The preaching of the cross, however is a very necessary first step in moving towards the perfection of a person's love, it alone is not enough to bring a person into perfection, which is what God really wants. This is accomplished by meditating on the resurrection of Christ. Why is it more important to focus on the resurrection of Christ? This is how you move beyond the cross and into perfection, not that you would achieve it in the flesh but spiritually you can, by looking forward and not backward, meaning God wants us to stop worrying about death, know that we are saved, and look forward to the day when we will see him. This is why Paul said the following in Hebrews 6:1–6 (KJV):

> Therefore leaving the principles of the doctrine of Christ, let us go on unto perfection; not laying again the foundation of repentance from dead works, and of faith toward God, Of the doctrine of baptisms, and of laying on of hands, and of resurrection of the dead, and of eternal judgment. And this will we do, if God permit. For it is impossible for those who were once enlightened, and have tasted of the heavenly gift, and were made partakers of the Holy Ghost, And have tasted the good word of God, and the powers of the world to come, If they shall fall away, to renew them again unto repentance; seeing they crucify to themselves the Son of God afresh, and put him to an open shame.

This is what Paul is telling us, to look forward, not backward, because if we were made partakers or have become part of God, it is impossible for us to be lost. If you do not know this and continue to repent of the sins that Christ has already forgiven you for, you will put Christ to shame. You accomplish this by not having enough faith in his ability to forgive you of you sins the first time you asked him, even if you commit that same sin again. This is because Christ has died for all sins, one time; therefore, any sin that you commit, except the sin of unbelief, can and will be forgiven. This is the mercy of God. This is the why he sent his son, because he knew that we would fall short and miss the mark.

The Third of the Trees that Were Burnt

There is a scripture found in the book of revelations that talks about the trees being burnt. The meaning of this has puzzled many people for a very long time.

> Revelation 8:7 (KJV)
> "The first angel sounded, and there followed hail and fire mingled with blood, and they were cast upon the earth: and the third part of trees was burnt up, and all green grass was burnt up."

I saved these scriptures for last, because I knew it would be hard to convince anyone that these scriptures are really referring to a third part of man and to be more precise, a particular type of tree. The word *tree* used in this verse is a symbolic word for man, a particular group of men, and they are the firstfruits. We know this because they are the only ones who will be burnt with this fire, and that fire is the Holy Spirit. Another key to know that these are men is in the fact that the Bible uses the word *third*. This word has been used many times in the Bible and has always referred to the three types of sons that God has. The three types of sons I have mentioned before are the chosen sons, the servant sons, and the faithful sons. These are the three types of sons that God will save. They are all thirds, and the three make one. This is exactly how God is made up, three that are one. A third, a third, and a third make up a whole but can be broken down into three different parts, just as God can be. The first third is the chosen son, who goes by different names, gold, fruit trees, firstfruits, and so on and so forth. The second group is the servant son, who can go by different names also, such as silver, trees without fruit, second fruits, and so on and so forth. The last third are men redeemed from the sons of God that were previously lost because they were nonbelievers. When they come to believe, God calls them brass, dry tree, and fruitless.

The fire that burns these trees is a spiritual fire, not a natural fire. The only trees that get to be burned by this fire are the fruit trees, who are God's chosen. This burning simply means that they will be filled with the Holy Spirit. This is the third that is mentioned in the book of Revelation. The other thirds that the book of Revelation talks about as being in the sea and earth, I will expound on in chapter 4 when I talk about the metals of God.

Chapter Four

The Spiritual Names
of the Sons of God

The Refining Process

God uses the symbolic language when he calls his sons different types of metals. They become different types of metals, based on how long they were in the fire. The longer they are in, the greater their value. The refining process uses fire. This fire burns away impurities, and at that point, whatever metal remains is the final product, whether it will be gold, silver, iron, or some other metal. What is the fire or this refining process that the sons of God must go through: They are the trials and tribulations we all must go through in this world whether we want to or not. It is also called chastisement from the Father. The ones who have been chastised the most stay in the fire for less time than those who have been chastised less. Why does chastisement have this effect? The Bible says that God chastises those whom he loves. This means that he wants these people to know his will. Therefore, they receive more information from him than the others, in order to pull them from the fire sooner. The orders of the rest of the metals by rank are silver, bronze, iron, and tin. The temperature of the fire needed to make these metals more precious depends on the type of metal they were originally. The fire needed to remove the impurities from the other metals other than gold, since gold has the lowest melting point, must be hotter, because they are harder. The temperature does not need to be so hot for gold because it is the softest metal of all. In other words, the softer the metal is to begin with, the faster it turns into a more pure version of what it was in the beginning, and the harder the metal was to begin with, the longer it takes to make it more precious. They also receive less chastisement from the Father, simply because everything must happen in order. Silver is precious but less precious than gold and so on and so forth for the other metals. Now let me reveal to you the metals that are in the Father's house from the book of 2 Timothy.

2 Timothy 2:19–21 (KJV),

Nevertheless the foundation of God standeth sure, having this seal, The Lord knoweth them that are his. And, Let every one that nameth the name of Christ depart from iniquity. But in a great house there are not only vessels of gold and of silver, but also of wood and of earth; and some to honour, and some to dishonour. If a man therefore purge himself from these, he shall be a vessel unto honour, sanctified, and meet for the master's use, and prepared unto every good work.

In these scriptures, God is telling us what will be in his kingdom. These are people who have been through the refining process. How do we know this? God has no need for material things. He is simply referring to people by their value. Also within these same scriptures though, he refers to wood and earth. He is really talking about the same thing but using a different type of symbolism. Wood and earth refer to the symbolic language I used in chapter 3, when men were called trees. The word *earth* is used to describe a type of soil, and the types of soils are found in the parable of the sower found in Mathew 13:1. In short, the types of soil are called good ground, in which the seed grows well; stony ground; thorny ground; and the wayside, which means really, really bad soil, unfit for growing anything. This is the symbolic language that God is using in these scriptures to disguise what he is truly saying to the world in the parable of the sower and in the parable about the metals in his house. Earlier, I told you about the fire used in the refining process being our trials. This is found in 1 Peter 1:6–9 (KJV):

Wherein ye greatly rejoice, though now for a season, if need be, ye are in heaviness through manifold temptations: That the trial of your faith, being much more precious than of gold that perisheth, though it be tried with fire, might be found unto praise and honour and glory at the appearing of Jesus Christ: Whom having not seen, ye love; in whom, though now ye see him not, yet believing, ye rejoice with joy unspeakable and full of glory: Receiving the end of your faith, even the salvation of your souls.

These scriptures tell us of the reward for having gone through these trials, which are tried by fire, which is the Holy Spirit. This is the goal and the end result that God wants for us. This is why he puts us through the things he puts us through. Listen to what God has to say about this in Haggai 2:5–9 (KJV):

According to the word that I covenanted with you when ye came out of Egypt, so my spirit remaineth among you: fear ye not. For thus saith the LORD of hosts; Yet once, it is a little while, and I will shake the heavens, and the earth, and the sea, and the dry land; And I will shake all nations, and the desire of all nations shall come: and I will fill this house with glory, saith the LORD of hosts. The silver is mine, and the gold is mine, saith the LORD of hosts. The glory of this latter house shall be greater than of the former, saith the LORD of hosts: and in this place will I give peace, saith the LORD of hosts.

The gold and the silver always belonged to the Father, meaning we have always belonged to God. We are just here on earth for training. This is why Jesus said this in the book of Revelation. Remember the parable of the ten virgins found in Matthew 25:1, where five of the virgins' lamps had oil and five did not? The oil is referring to the Holy Spirit and the lights the fire. This is why here in the following scriptures, Jesus counsels everyone to become gold tried by fire. This is the same thing he told the five virgins when he told them to go and buy oil. The oil and the gold are essentially the same thing.

The Sons of Gold
Revelation 3:18–22 (KJV) says,

I counsel thee to buy of me gold tried in the fire, that thou mayest be rich; and white raiment, that thou mayest be clothed, and that the shame of thy nakedness do not appear; and anoint thine eyes with eyesalve, that thou mayest see. As many as I love, I rebuke and chasten: be zealous therefore, and repent. Behold, I stand at the door, and knock: if any man hear my voice, and open the door, I will come in to him, and will sup with him, and he with me. To him that overcometh will I grant to sit with me in my throne, even as I also overcame, and am set down with my Father in his throne. He that hath an ear, let him hear what the Spirit saith unto the churches.

We are the spiritual gold that Jesus is talking about purchasing; the only way to purchase this gold is to pay the price. What is the price? The price is your suffering, or in other words, what it will cost you to behave like Christ. What will you have to give up? What sacrifices are you willing to make? This is a cost you must pay, and this is the only thing that you give that is of value to God. Your value is shown in your love, if you are willing to be Christ like. This is the same way that Christ paid the price for our sins, with his love. His love cost him his life. He of course is not asking us to go as far as Christ. He will only ask of you what he knows you are perfectly able to pay.

Zechariah 13:7–9 (KJV)

Awake, O sword, against my shepherd, and against the man that is my fellow, saith the LORD of hosts: smite the shepherd, and the sheep shall be scattered: and I will turn mine hand upon the little ones. And it shall come to pass, that in all the land, saith the LORD, two parts therein shall be cut off and die; but the third shall be left therein. And I will bring the third part through the fire, and will refine them as silver is refined, and will try them as gold is tried: they shall call on my name, and I will hear them: I will say, It is my people: and they shall say, The LORD is my God.

This is the refining process that I mentioned earlier, and this is also a perfect example of who the gold and the silver are. They are the Lord's people. There is one other thing here that I mentioned in chapter 3, and that is the number of them that are gold and silver. It is mentioned in verses 8 and 9. This is the number of people who will be redeemed and become as silver and gold to God out of the whole earth. A third part of these people will be the gold and a third part will be the silver. This corresponds with what is also found in Revelation 8:7 where it talks about a third part of the trees being burnt, something I expounded on in chapter 3 of this book.

The Sons of Silver

Silver is a precious metal, and it belongs to God as well. All who remain under the law will be refined as silver. However, if God is angry with people, he calls them a type of worthless metal. This is found in Ezekiel 22:17–22 (KJV):

> And the word of the LORD came unto me, saying, Son of man, the house of Israel is to me become dross: all they are brass, and tin, and iron, and lead, in the midst of the furnace; they are even the dross of silver. Therefore thus saith the Lord GOD; Because ye are all become dross, behold, therefore I will gather you into the midst of Jerusalem. As they gather silver, and brass, and iron, and lead, and tin, into the midst of the furnace, to blow the fire upon it, to melt it; so will I gather you in mine anger and in my fury, and I will leave you there, and melt you. Yea, I will gather you, and blow upon you in the fire of my wrath, and ye shall be melted in the midst thereof. As silver is melted in the midst of the furnace, so shall ye be melted in the midst thereof; and ye shall know that I the LORD have poured out my fury upon you.

If, however, God has mercy upon men, he will blow upon them and melt them, because they are metal. This is how God speaks symbolically. In these next scriptures, Jesus is called a refiner. A refiner is someone who purifies something. This is exactly what Christ was born to do. This is found in Malachi 3:1–3 (KJV):

> Behold, I will send my messenger, and he shall prepare the way before me: and the Lord, whom ye seek, shall suddenly come to his temple, even the messenger of the covenant, whom ye delight in: behold, he shall come, saith the LORD of hosts. But who may abide the day of his coming? and who shall stand when he appeareth? for he is like a refiner's fire, and like fullers' soap: And he shall sit as a refiner and purifier of silver: and he shall purify

the sons of Levi, and purge them as gold and silver, that they may offer unto the LORD an offering in righteousness.

If this fire has come upon you and you still refuse to do the will of the Father or the Son, God will call you reprobated silver. Reprobated silver is someone whom God has abandoned. God no longer has any interest in this person or group of people, because they will not listen to him.

Reprobated Silver and Brass

What a lot of people are not willing to accept is that God will give up on certain people. These are people who refuse time and time again to come to know and love God. In other words they will not repent. God called these people reprobated, or unusable. They are spoken of in the book of Jeremiah.

Jeremiah 6:26–30 (KJV)

O daughter of my people, gird thee with sackcloth, and wallow thyself in ashes: make thee mourning, as for an only son, most bitter lamentation: for the spoiler shall suddenly come upon us. I have set thee for a tower and a fortress among my people, that thou mayest know and try their way. They are all grievous revolters, walking with slanders: they are brass and iron; they are all corrupters. The bellows are burned, the lead is consumed of the fire; the founder melteth in vain: for the wicked are not plucked away. Reprobate silver shall men call them, because the LORD hath rejected them.

God is saying here in verse 29 that he melted in vain, and all his efforts were wasted. This is why he calls them reprobated metal. Another point I would like to make about this scripture is that when God calls a person corrupt, he refers to them as brass and iron, which are your non-precious metals.

The Vision of the Statue with the Head of Gold

King Nebuchadnezzar had a vision and in that vision he saw a statue which had a head of Gold. The head of gold was his kingdom, and it was gold because God had just converted King Nebuchadnezzar as well as his kingdom into a nation of people who believed and feared him.

Daniel 2:31–35 (KJV) says,

Thou, O king, sawest, and behold a great image. This great image, whose brightness was excellent, stood before thee; and the form thereof was terrible. This image's head was of fine gold, his breast and his arms of silver, his belly and his thighs of brass, His legs of iron, his feet part of iron and part of clay. Thou sawest till that a stone was cut out without hands, which smote the image upon his feet that were of iron and clay, and brake them to pieces. Then was the iron, the clay, the brass, the silver, and the gold, broken to pieces together, and became like the chaff of the summer threshingfloors; and the wind carried them away, that no place was found for them: and the stone that smote the image became a great mountain, and filled the whole earth.

The image the King Nebuchadnezzar had was a vision about nations that would follow his kingdom; they would be more and more inferior to his kingdom. Notice that these inferior kingdoms are represented by different kinds of metals, starting with gold and ending with clay. These are the symbolic representations of men, and these metals represent how God values them. This means that at this time, according to this vision, we are at the feet of that statue. The only thing left to happen is for the stone to break it into pieces. Most men have no value to God at this time. This is not because God hates them, but because they hate God, and no amount of refining will change that.

The second meaning to this statue is that the metals, starting with gold, represent the conditions of men's hearts. That means that since the first kingdom, men have slipped further and further away from God, from gold to dirt. The reason that the statue started with a head of gold is that God directly intervened. He had to first punish the king of Babylon so severely that he would become a believer who was without any doubt that God existed. This king in turn convinced everyone else in his kingdom that God the Father did indeed exist and not only that, but also that he was the true ruler of this world. This ensured that the people at that time would be gold, because of their faith. Then God sat back and watched as time went on. He watched that faith disappear with each passing kingdom, one after another—until today. We have arrived at the feet of that statue. It was like a kind of countdown to the arrival of the stone. This is what that vision is telling us. It is also telling us that the stone that will break that statue into pieces is Christ upon his return. He is the stone that will fall from heaven and take over this world. He is the stone that was cut without hands—without man's hands, that is.

The Beasts of the Sea and Earth

You might ask yourself, "What does the sea have to do with the coming of Christ?" The logical answer is that the natural sea has nothing to do with the return of Christ, but a spiritual sea does. Because if it is a spiritual sea, then this means that the sea in the book of Revelation is really talking about people. The sea is a spiritual place of origin, and those who are in the sea are called fish, spiritual fish, because they are in need of being caught in a spiritual net. Both God and Satan have a sea. The Bible uses the word *sea* as a symbolic representation of where life comes from. Things that come to life out of the sea can become men or beasts, depending on which sea they came from. The sea that is God's sea is called a crystal sea because it shines like light. This sea is mentioned in Revelation 4:6 (KJV): "And before the throne there was a sea of glass like unto crystal: and in the midst of the throne, and round about the throne."

This sea is different from Satan's sea. Only good things come out of God's sea. The sea I am about to talk about next is a sea from which things come out to kill and destroy the things that come out of God's sea.

Revelation 13:1 (KJV) says, "And I stood upon the sand of the sea, and saw a beast rise up out of the sea, having seven heads and ten horns, and upon his horns ten crowns, and upon his heads the name of blasphemy."

This particular beast with the seven heads and ten horns has been on the earth since the beginning and plays a significant role in accomplishing what God wants this beast to accomplish. This beast is spiritual in nature, but it is not a man. It is a spiritual beast called the image of the beast. It is where the beast which rises from the earth gets its power. This spiritual beast cannot be seen with human eyes, unlike the beast that rises from the earth. This beast is directly connected to Satan and his attempt to spiritually control God's people. This beast occupies people spiritually in order to get them to do his will. If this beast occupies a person, it is because he or she has voluntarily given himself or herself over to Satan in mind, body, and spirit. They seek power, authority, riches, and fame, as well as the power of life and death over the people of the earth. This is how the beast that rises out of the earth, which is the Antichrist, gets its power from the beast that rises out of the sea, which is Satan.

The beasts that have come out of the earth at different times in earth's history always make history by trying to rule the world. This is because they are men. This is exactly what this next scripture will tell us. Revelation 13:11–14 (KJV) says,

> And I beheld another beast coming up out of the earth; and he had two horns like a lamb, and he spake as a dragon. And he exerciseth all the power of the first beast before him, and causeth the earth and them which dwell therein to worship the first beast, whose deadly wound was healed. And he doeth great wonders, so that he maketh fire come down from heaven on the earth in the sight of men, And deceiveth them that dwell on the earth by the means of those miracles which he had power to do in the sight of the beast; saying to them that dwell on the earth, that they should make an image to the beast, which had the wound by a sword, and did live.

The only way this beast could do this in the sight of men is that he himself has to be a man, since his wonders were done in the sight of men and they were able to see it.

The Third that Will Be Saved out of the Earth

Even though there have been particular places on earth that the beasts of the earth have come from time and time again, the Lord will still show mercy upon the people of these particular parts of the world. Egypt is one of those places. It is even where the nation of Israel was held captive for four hundred years and is the birthplace of all the pharaohs. This is the mercy that the Lord will have on different people who once were the enemy of his people. Egypt has always been known as the enemy of his people throughout the Bible, but look at the third that the Lord will save out of Egypt in Isaiah 19:22–25 (KJV):

> And the LORD shall smite Egypt: he shall smite and heal it: and they shall return even to the LORD, and he shall be intreated of them, and shall heal them. In that day shall there be a highway out of Egypt to Assyria, and the Assyrian shall come into Egypt, and the Egyptian into Assyria, and the Egyptians shall serve with the Assyrians. In that day shall Israel be the third with Egypt and with Assyria, even a blessing in the midst of the land:

Whom the LORD of hosts shall bless, saying, Blessed be Egypt my people, and Assyria the work of my hands, and Israel mine inheritance.

This type of smiting means to chastise, and if the Lord chastises you, he will eventually heal you, not destroy you. This is the same thing the book of Revelation is trying to reveal to us. Many people who have read the book of Revelation have come to the conclusion that this book is talking about total destruction by natural fire and therefore become afraid of this book. The book of Revelation is only talking about destroying those who hate God not naturally by spiritually. If you do not hate God, you will not be destroyed. Those who love God, but find themselves in tribulations will be smiting of God, which means to chastise them in order to make you realize your mistakes they have made in order to cause them to come back to him. This is the purpose of the tribulations, revealed to us in the book of Revelation. Listen to what the Bible say's the Lord will be doing to the different spiritual parts of the world in Revelation 8:7–9 (KJV):

The first angel sounded, and there followed hail and fire mingled with blood, and they were cast upon the earth: and the third part of trees was burnt up, and all green grass was burnt up. And the second angel sounded, and as it were a great mountain burning with fire was cast into the sea: and the third part of the sea became blood; And the third part of the creatures which were in the sea, and had life, died; and the third part of the ships were destroyed.

What does this mean? It means good things will be happening to these groups of people. The fire mingled with blood, which is cast upon the earth, means the Holy Spirit and the blood of Christ cause men to become saved. The trees that are burnt up are men who become burnt with the fire that is the Holy Spirit; they receive the fire baptism, so that they know the Lord's will and they can complete their mission. This is what God will destroy, and these are spiritual things that cannot be seen by the eyes of man. God will destroy Satan's sea and the ships that deceive the people. This is the meaning of the thirds that become burned in this fire. These are not natural disasters.

The River of God

The next group of people God talks about come out of the river, his river, the river of life. They are the river. Lastly, the opposite of the people who come out of the river—or him, because the river flows from the throne—is the flood. The flood comes from Satan, and they are called the flood because this is exactly what they act like. To expound on this further, a flood destroys anything and everything in its path. This is why God calls them a flood. The other reason God calls them a flood is based on their sheer numbers. They are many, as opposed to the river people, who are few.

The river is calm. It is slow moving and does not overwhelm anything wheresoever it goes. It nourishes the earth and causes things to grow, because a river is peaceful. This is the same thing that God wants to happen to people, and this is why he calls those that he has trained to do this a river or a tree. The book of Psalms reflects this in the first chapter. Psalm 1:1–3 (KJV) says,

> Blessed is the man that walketh not in the counsel of the ungodly, nor standeth in the way of sinners, nor sitteth in the seat of the scornful. But his delight is in the law of the LORD; and in his law doth he meditate day and night. And he shall be like a tree planted by the rivers of water, that bringeth forth his fruit in his season; his leaf also shall not wither; and whatsoever he doeth shall prosper.

The river causes those who love God to produce fruit. Just like a natural tree that is planted by a natural river, a spiritual river will cause a spiritual tree to grow. This river is a combination of two things, the Holy Spirit and the chosen of God. This is mentioned in Revelation 22:1–2 (KJV):

> And he shewed me a pure river of water of life, clear as crystal, proceeding out of the throne of God and of the Lamb. In the midst of the street of it, and on either side of the river, was there the tree of life, which bare twelve manner of fruits, and yielded her fruit every month: and the leaves of the tree were for the healing of the nations.

I went to the book of Revelation to show you, the reader, where the origin of this river is, which is the throne of God, and as I said earlier, this river, which is the Holy Spirit, causes people to produce fruit. There are twelve manner of fruit, meaning people can be broken down into twelve different categories, according to the type of heart they have or in other words, how much love they possess. Remember, this tree is the tree of life. This tree is God, and the fruit on this tree is people. The river that flows are people mixed with the Holy Spirit, who will be used for the healing of the nations of the world.

Ezekiel 47:6–12 (KJV) says,

And he said unto me, Son of man, hast thou seen this? Then he brought me, and caused me to return to the brink of the river. Now when I had returned, behold, at the bank of the river were very many trees on the one side and on the other. Then said he unto me, These waters issue out toward the east country, and go down into the desert, and go into the sea: which being brought forth into the sea, the waters shall be healed. And it shall come to pass, that every thing that liveth, which moveth, whithersoever the rivers shall come, shall live: and there shall be a very great multitude of fish, because these waters shall come thither: for they shall be healed; and every thing shall live whither the river cometh. And it shall come to pass, that the fishers shall stand upon it from Engedi even unto Eneglaim; they shall be a place to spread forth nets; their fish shall be according to their kinds, as the fish of the great sea, exceeding many. But the miry places thereof and the marishes thereof shall not be healed; they shall be given to salt. And by the river upon the bank thereof, on this side and on that side, shall grow all trees for meat, whose leaf shall not fade, neither shall the fruit thereof be consumed: it shall bring forth new fruit according to his months, because their waters they issued out of the sanctuary: and the fruit thereof shall be for meat, and the leaf thereof for medicine.

These scriptures tell us of what is to come, which is found in the book of Revelation. This is something that Paul spoke about in John 7:37–39.

In the last day, that great day of the feast, Jesus stood and cried, saying, If any man thirst, let him come unto me, and drink. He that believeth on me, as the scripture hath said, out of his belly shall flow rivers of living water. (But this spake he of the Spirit, which they that believe on him should receive: for the Holy Ghost was not yet given; because that Jesus was not yet glorified.)

This is the same river of water; this water comes from the mouth of those who are filled with the Holy Spirit. This water will heal anyone who suffers from a lack of understanding of their Father in heaven. This is what the water heals you from. If you suffer from a lack of understanding, you are an enemy to God. Why? The same reason Adam ate off the wrong tree, He didn't know any better, and you will sin against God out of your ignorance. Therefore, ignorance is sin, in and of itself, and out of it, we have all done things that were contrary to the Word of God. The chosen have already received this water, and rivers of water already flow from them. It is just that the ground is so dry that this water is quickly dried up. This is the same water that Jesus spoke about to the woman at the well, when he said he had water to drink that she knew not of. John 4:9–11 (KJV), says,

Then saith the woman of Samaria unto him, How is it that thou, being a Jew, askest drink of me, which am a woman of Samaria? for the Jews have no dealings with the Samaritans. Jesus answered and said unto her, If thou knewest the gift of God, and who it is that saith to thee, Give me to drink; thou wouldest have asked of him, and he would have given thee living water. The woman saith unto him, Sir, thou hast nothing to draw with, and the well is deep: from whence then hast thou that living water? Art thou greater than our father Jacob, which gave us the well, and drank thereof himself, and his children, and his cattle? Jesus answered and said unto her, Whosoever drinketh of this water shall thirst again: But whosoever drinketh of the water that I shall give him shall never thirst; but the water that I shall give him shall be in him a well of water springing up into everlasting life.

This is where Jesus first mentions this living water. He says that if a man drinks, he will never thirst again. This is a spiritual thirst, a thirst caused by a lack of understanding of the Word of God. The Word of God is life to the spirit of a person. Without it, we will die. The life we have right now is only temporary and is not self–sustaining, but the water of God can give it eternal life and make it self–sustaining. Those who were chosen will receive this gift when Christ returns, and he will give them the power to give this water to anyone else who is willing to receive it. This is how the river or those who flow from this river will heal the nations. This next scripture is a symbolic representation of how the chosen received this gift, but most people when they read this think that it is a very bad thing happening to the natural rivers of the earth. This will only happen to a third of man, the chosen, that is.

In Revelation 8:10–13, it says, "And the third angel sounded, and there fell a great star from heaven, burning as it were a lamp, and it fell upon the third part of the rivers, and upon the fountains of waters ..."

The lamp that fell upon the third part of the rivers is none other than Christ himself, coming to receive his chosen, which are also called fountains of water.

The Woman Clothed in the Sun, Moon, and Stars

This is where I would like to start the explanation of the sun, the moon, and the stars, because Joseph was the first to mention them. God gave Joseph this dream in order to tell him about the future which was to come. Most think that this has already occurred because Joseph's brothers did bow to him while he was in Egypt. This, however, was not what God was referring to when he gave Joseph this dream. God was referring to Joseph in his spiritual form not his earthly form. Joseph was a chosen of God, meaning he was elected to be one of the firstfruits. His light was to be as bright as the sun, while his brothers' were not. Their light was destined to be a lesser light, that of the moon. This is what the dream of Joseph really meant. In Joseph's dream, he was the sun, his brothers were the moon, and each tribe was the star, and one day, they will all indeed bow to him. That day will come when the kingdom of God has come to this earth. In Matthew 13:41–43(KJV), it says,

> The Son of man shall send forth his angels, and they shall gather out of his kingdom all things that offend, and them which do iniquity; And shall cast them into a furnace of fire: there shall be wailing and gnashing of teeth. Then shall the righteous shine forth as the sun in the kingdom of their Father. Who hath ears to hear, let him hear.

This is the destiny of all that God calls his righteous ones; they will shine like the sun. Why? Because this will be an indication of how much the Father and the Son will glorify them. There will be other groups that the Father and Son will glorify, such as the group of people who will become the moon and the stars. However, none are greater than the third that will become a representation of the sun. This is based solely on the fact that he first predestined them, and because he did this to them, they had to suffer more than those who are of the moon and stars. The is why the Bible says that there is one glory of the sun, another of the moon, and yet another of the stars. This is found in 1 Corinthians 15:40–44 (KJV).

> There are also celestial bodies, and bodies terrestrial: but the glory of the celestial is one, and the glory of the terrestrial is another. There is one glory of the sun, and another glory of the moon, and another glory of the stars: for one star differeth from another star in glory. So also is the resurrection of the dead. It is sown in corruption; it is raised in incorruption: It is sown in dishonour; it is raised in glory: it is sown in weakness; it is raised in power: It is sown a natural body; it is raised a spiritual body. There is a natural body, and there is a spiritual body.

The resurrection of the sons of God will occur according to this format. Some will be like the sun, some like the moon, and some like the stars. Each one will have a different amount of light, and this light comes from the Father, because the Father is light. This light reflects the amount of righteousness the Father has bestowed upon a person. These three groups of lights will make up the kingdom, the city, and the bride of Christ all at the same time. This is mentioned in the book of Revelation.

The Sons Who Are the Sun

Revelation 12:1–2 (KJV) says, "And there appeared a great wonder in heaven; a woman clothed with the sun, and the moon under her feet, and upon her head a crown of twelve stars: And she being with child cried, travailing in birth, and pained to be delivered."

Who is this woman? Well, to start with, she is not an individual. She is a spiritual representation of the whole kingdom of God. She is composed of all who will be saved in the form of the sun, the moon, and the stars. She is primarily the bride of Christ, whom all people will see who are of the moon and stars. Christ will only be married to the part of her that is the sun, because they are the best of what came out of the world. They are the most worthy, and once again, it is because they have suffered like Christ. This is why this parable says that she is clothed with the sun, and the moon is under her feet, meaning they are beneath her. The stars are not part of the woman either but are a crown upon her head. This crown is a group of people with a slightly lesser light than the moon. Who are these people? They are those whom the Father elected to be chosen from the remnants of Israel. How do we know this? Listen to what God told Israel in Isaiah 62:1–2 (KJV):

> For Zion's sake will I not hold my peace, and for Jerusalem's sake I will not rest, until the righteousness thereof go forth as brightness, and the salvation thereof as a lamp that burneth. And the Gentiles shall see thy righteousness, and all kings thy glory: and thou shalt be called by a new name, which the mouth of the LORD shall name.

First of all, this is God's promise to Israel. Even though he has been very angry with them for a long time, he still promised to show their righteousness to the Gentiles. Then later on, he promised something else to them that shows their rightful place among the sons of God. This is found in the book of Isaiah.

The Sons Who Become the Crown of Twelve Stars
Isaiah 62:3–4 (KJV) says,

> Thou shalt also be a crown of glory in the hand of the LORD, and a royal diadem in the hand of thy God. Thou shalt no more be termed Forsaken; neither shall thy land any more be termed Desolate: but thou shalt be called Hephzibah, and thy land Beulah: for the LORD delighteth in thee, and thy land shall be married.

These twelve stars are the twelve tribes of Israel, the first 144,000, and they will be a symbolic representation of the crown that will be placed on the bride of Christ. This will not happen until a certain time comes upon the earth, such as the world has never seen before, a time mentioned in the book of Daniel 12:1–4:

> And at that time shall Michael stand up, the great prince which standeth for the children of thy people: and there shall be a time of trouble, such as never was since there was a nation even to that same time: and at that time thy people shall be delivered, every one that shall be found written in the book. And many of them

that sleep in the dust of the earth shall awake, some to everlasting life, and some to shame and everlasting contempt. And they that be wise shall shine as the brightness of the firmament; and they that turn many to righteousness as the stars for ever and ever. But thou, O Daniel, shut up the words, and seal the book, even to the time of the end: many shall run to and fro, and knowledge shall be increased.

That time is very near, because knowledge on the earth has increased, but I will not get into predictions. I will only say that the time is near. Those who are of the group that will shine like the sun are told in the book of Revelation that Christ will shine like the sun also. Revelation 1:14–16 (KJV) says,

His head and his hairs were white like wool, as white as snow; and his eyes were as a flame of fire; And his feet like unto fine brass, as if they burned in a furnace; and his voice as the sound of many waters. And he had in his right hand seven stars: and out of his mouth went a sharp twoedged sword: and his countenance was as the sun shineth in his strength.

The next scripture tells us that those who are of the sun will shine like him and this is how he shows his love for them. In 1 John 3:2–3 (KJV), it says,

Behold, what manner of love the Father hath bestowed upon us, that we should be called the sons of God: therefore the world knoweth us not, because it knew him not. Beloved, now are we the sons of God, and it doth not yet appear what we shall be: but we know that, when he shall appear, we shall be like him; for we shall see him as he is. And every man that hath this hope in him purifieth himself, even as he is pure.

Then the Bible gives us a future look at what God will tell the sun, the moon, and the stars to do when all the kingdom is assembled, which is to praise his son. In Psalm 148:1–5 (KJV), it says,

Praise ye the LORD. Praise ye the LORD from the heavens: praise him in the heights. Praise ye him, all his angels: praise ye him, all his hosts. Praise ye him, sun and moon: praise him, all ye stars of light. Praise him, ye heavens of heavens, and ye waters that be above the heavens. Let them praise the name of the LORD: for he commanded, and they were created.

After the praising of the Lord, the Lord tells a group of people to bring out the bones of the kings, princes, priests, prophets, and inhabitants of Jerusalem to stand before the sun, moon, and stars to be judged. Jeremiah 8:1–3 says,

> At that time, saith the LORD, they shall bring out the bones of the kings of Judah, and the bones of his princes, and the bones of the priests, and the bones of the prophets, and the bones of the inhabitants of Jerusalem, out of their graves: And they shall spread them before the sun, and the moon, and all the host of heaven, whom they have loved, and whom they have served, and after whom they have walked, and whom they have sought, and whom they have worshipped: they shall not be gathered, nor be buried; they shall be for dung upon the face of the earth. And death shall be chosen rather than life by all the residue of them that remain of this evil family, which remain in all the places whither I have driven them, saith the LORD of hosts.

These are the people who did evil in the sight of God. They are the evil kings, evil princes, and false prophets. They are the evil family, and they are to be judged and thrown into the lake of fire.

Now let me back up just a little, to just before the tribulations take place on the earth, and talk a little bit about what happens to the sun, moon, and stars, before they receive their reward. The Bible tells us that they will become darkened and they will not give their light. What this means is that they will be taken out of the world and not have to go through the tribulation. This is the darkness that the Lord is talking about. This darkness is a spiritual darkness, because this is a time when those who know what is happening on the earth will not be there to help guide the rest through, because God does not want to punish them with the same punishment as he will give the world. Now this punishment is not to destroy those who have to go through it. It will be given to save them also. This is found in many places throughout the Bible, but I would like to start with what is found in Ezekiel 32:7–10 (KJV),

And when I shall put thee out, I will cover the heaven, and make the stars thereof dark; I will cover the sun with a cloud, and the moon shall not give her light. All the bright lights of heaven will I make dark over thee, and set darkness upon thy land, saith the Lord GOD. I will also vex the hearts of many people, when I shall bring thy destruction among the nations, into the countries which thou hast not known. Yea, I will make many people amazed at thee, and their kings shall be horribly afraid for thee, when I shall brandish my sword before them; and they shall tremble at every moment, every man for his own life, in the day of thy fall.

Next, I would like to show you how the book of Revelation says the same thing, but it sounds even more terrible. Revelation 8:12 (KJV) says,

And the fourth angel sounded, and the third part of the sun was smitten, and the third part of the moon, and the third part of the stars; so as the third part of them was darkened, and the day shone not for a third part of it, and the night likewise.

This is the short period of time that will occur when they who are chosen and come from the groups of people who are of the sun, moon, and stars will disappear and be with Christ. They are composed of only a third of each of these groups and not the whole amount. They are the third, a third, and a third. The first two groups are the first and second 144,000. The third in the middle come from the moon. They are people who were redeemed from the servant sons of God. These are the people who will not have to go through the tribulations. This is what it means by darkened, which means to take away for a third part of the day.

Those Who Make It through the Tribulations

Most people think that the tribulations are for those people who hate God and all who go through it will be destroyed. They could not be more wrong. The purpose of the tribulations is to teach the rest of humanity to love the Father and the Son. This is why these scriptures are found in Revelation 7:13–17 (KJV):

And one of the elders answered, saying unto me, What are these which are arrayed in white robes? and whence came they? And I

120

said unto him, Sir, thou knowest. And he said to me, These are they which came out of great tribulation, and have washed their robes, and made them white in the blood of the Lamb. Therefore are they before the throne of God, and serve him day and night in his temple: and he that sitteth on the throne shall dwell among them. They shall hunger no more, neither thirst any more; neither shall the sun light on them, nor any heat. For the Lamb which is in the midst of the throne shall feed them, and shall lead them unto living fountains of waters: and God shall wipe away all tears from their eyes.

This is the number of people that no man could count, of all races, and of all nations, who have now become of one mind toward the Father, Son, and Holy Spirit.

The Sons Who Are the Fishes in the Sea

The next analogy I would like to discuss is another example of the symbolic language that God uses to describe people: he describes them as fish. He uses this term because there are two types of nets that are used to snare the souls of men. Of course, God has a net, but Satan has a net also. Nets both naturally and spiritually are made to catch things, mainly fish, but they can be made to catch anything, even wild beasts. Using the analogy of fish, birds, and nets, God successfully hid things from the world that it desperately needed to know. Why did God do this? Because you have free will and therefore have the right to choose. This is how he gives Satan a chance to catch you in his net. Once again, why would God give Satan a chance to catch you in his net? Because this is the only way to give you a free choice to make. Habakkuk 1:14–17 (KJV) says,

And makest men as the fishes of the sea, as the creeping things, that have no ruler over them? They take up all of them with the angle, they catch them in their net, and gather them in their drag: therefore they rejoice and are glad. Therefore they sacrifice unto their net, and burn incense unto their drag; because by them their portion is fat, and their meat plenteous. Shall they therefore empty their net, and not spare continually to slay the nations?

These are the spirits under Satan's command that use the people of this world to catch people and make them do their will, These scriptures are saying that their nets will always be full because the people lack understanding. This is why the Father and his Son said that they would make his disciples fishers of men. They could catch people in their nets and set them free, so that they would not be caught by the enemy's net and be eaten. Matthew 4:17–20 (KJV) says,

> From that time Jesus began to preach, and to say, Repent: for the kingdom of heaven is at hand. And Jesus, walking by the sea of Galilee, saw two brethren, Simon called Peter, and Andrew his brother, casting a net into the sea: for they were fishers. And he saith unto them, Follow me, and I will make you fishers of men. And they straightway left their nets, and followed him.

In these next scriptures, God showed Ezekiel the great numbers of fish that he caught in his net and showed him the trees that are the people he used to catch them. Ezekiel 47:6–12 (KJV) says,

> And he said unto me, Son of man, hast thou seen this? Then he brought me, and caused me to return to the brink of the river. Now when I had returned, behold, at the bank of the river were very many trees on the one side and on the other. Then said he unto me, These waters issue out toward the east country, and go down into the desert, and go into the sea: which being brought forth into the sea, the waters shall be healed. And it shall come to pass, that every thing that liveth, which moveth, whithersoever the rivers shall come, shall live: and there shall be a very great multitude of fish, because these waters shall come thither: for they shall be healed; and every thing shall live whither the river cometh. And it shall come to pass, that the fishers shall stand upon it from Engedi even unto Eneglaim; they shall be a place to spread forth nets; their fish shall be according to their kinds, as the fish of the great sea, exceeding many.

In verse 10 of these scriptures, it says, "the fish shall be according to their kinds." What it is referring to is that these people are of different ethnicities, races, and backgrounds. These scriptures are also telling us that they will be healed by the water that flows from the river that is of God.

Chapter Five

The Trinity and Oneness of God

The question that many believers have about God is whether God is one being or three beings, or a trinity. Christianity has long been divided over this question. In the past, one side would argue that God is one, because the Bible clearly says so, which made for a very strong argument. This, however, would be followed by another strong argument that God was composed of three individuals, which the Bible strongly suggests also. The Bible supports the theory of God being one by what it says in 1 John 5:7: "These Three are one." No one can argue against this, except when someone brings up what is found in Matthew 28:19, which says, "... be baptized in the name of the Father, Son, and Spirit," which suggests that there are three.

So what is going on here? Is the Bible contradicting itself? If evidence is found in the Bible that supports both sides, which side is right? The answer is both sides are right. Then the next question you might ask is, "How this is possible?" The answer to that question is what I will be discussing in this chapter, which is how the trinity and the oneness of God are both possible at the same time.

I will also be discussing something most people have never heard of, and that is the trinity of man. Yes, I know we have all heard of the trinity of God but not the trinity of man. Why would I say a thing like the trinity of man? This is because God said in the book of Genesis, "Let us make man in our own image." Since God is a trinity, he made man operate this way as well, because he made man in his image. The only question is how and in what way did he do this? The next question should be, "Is there evidence in the Bible to support the statements I just made, concerning the trinity of God and man?" The answer is yes, and I will do my best to walk you through the answers found in the Bible and expound on the meaning of each scripture, so that you can see the trinity and oneness of both God and man.

I am sure that most people who are Christians have heard the two main differences of opinion as to whether or not God is one or three persons. Each side is pitted against the other, as if locked in battle, with strong arguments for the trinity and for the oneness of God, not knowing that both have been right all along. The only reason why neither side knows that both are right is because God has not chosen to reveal it to them yet, because it can only be revealed by the Spirit of God. I myself can only point out the scriptures that brought me to my conclusions, and even after that, it is still between you and the Spirit of God to make a final conclusion. When the Spirit does help you to see it, it will make perfect sense. The difficulty in explaining this is that it is an attempt to explain a spiritual thing with only natural words. This is especially true for something as unique as the trinity of God.

The first thing I would like to share is that everything we need to know about God is found in the Bible, because this is one of the things God freely wants those who believe in him to know. If anything is hidden from you about God, it is hidden for a reason, and mostly because he did not want those who hate him to know. This in turn created a problem for those who do love him, because his hiding himself from those who hate him makes it difficult for those who love him to know everything they need to know about him. The Bible first mentions this in the book of 2 Corinthians.

In 2 Corinthians 4:3–4 (KJV), it says, "But if our gospel be hid, it is hid to them that are lost: In whom the god of this world hath blinded the minds of them which believe not, lest the light of the glorious gospel of Christ, who is the image of God, should shine unto them."

What do we know about God? First of all, the word *God*, is a generic term. This is not the name of God. The word *God* simply means a being that is all-knowing and all-powerful. This in no way describes who God really is. However, when the Bible uses the word *God*, it is also referring to him as our father in heaven. Therefore, when we refer to him as God, we are acknowledging that he is our father. At the same time, people who call him God, when referring to him, are people who have yet developed a more intimate relationship with him. What do I mean by this? The way in which we are to develop a more intimate relationship with God is by spending more and more time reading the Bible, which is his word. After this, we come to know him as our heavenly father. This pleases him, because this is how he wants us to acknowledge him. The Bible tells us this in the book of John.

John 1:12 (KJV) says, "But as many as received him, to them gave he power to become the sons of God, even to them that believe on his name ..."

Even though this scripture is really referring to the receiving of Christ, remember that God is one with Christ, and therefore when we receive Christ, he becomes our heavenly father through our having belief in the Son. God is our spiritual father because he is the maker and giver of our spirits, which is where life comes from. Life comes from the spirit that is in us, which originally came from the Spirit that is in God.

Heb 12:7–9 (KJV) says,

If ye endure chastening, God dealeth with you as with sons; for what son is he whom the father chasteneth not? But if ye be without chastisement, whereof all are partakers, then are ye bastards, and not sons. Furthermore we have had fathers of our flesh which corrected us, and we gave them reverence: shall we not much rather be in subjection unto the Father of spirits, and live?

Those who do not believe in God think that we have life simply because we have beating hearts in our chests. However, the Bible tells us where life comes from, which is from our Father in heaven. It tells us this by explaining to us that the body without the spirit is dead. In James 2:26 (KJV), it says, "For as the body without the spirit is dead, so faith without works is dead also."

Where does this spirit come from? It comes from our Father in heaven. This is the same as our Father in heaven because he is a spirit. The Bible tells us this in the book of John. John 4:24 (KJV) says, "God is a Spirit: and they that worship him must worship him in spirit and in truth."

I referred to this scripture so that I could show the relationship between God and man. What I mean by that is that by our spirit, God communicates with us through his spirit; in other words, communication is from spirit to Spirit. The Bible refers to this in the book of first Corinthians. In 1 Corinthians 2:9–11 (KJV), it says,

> But as it is written, Eye hath not seen, nor ear heard, neither have entered into the heart of man, the things which God hath prepared for them that love him. But God hath revealed them unto us by his Spirit: for the Spirit searcheth all things, yea, the deep things of God. For what man knoweth the things of a man, save the spirit of man which is in him? even so the things of God knoweth no man, but the Spirit of God.

This is the method God uses to communicate with man, and in this way, we who are in communication with him know him. This is also how we know that he is a trinity, as well as one with all things. As to the how, I will explain as this chapter goes on.

In the beginning of our relationship with God, we only know of God; we do not know Christ or the Holy Spirit. We only learn of them as time goes on. This is why it is better that we first get to know God as our father, because this is the correct order in which we must learn of them. I believe this is because God wants us to see his oneness first and not the trinity, because it is the simplest and easiest way to get to know him in the beginning. In the beginning of our walk with God, we are very limited in our understanding. We need to know first that God is one, and this in turn might help us to act as one. In learning of the oneness first, we might want to become like him and operate as a family or one as he does. God is one, meaning one family with no division in it. If man could have achieved this oneness with his neighbors, meaning the entire world, we would not have had the wars that we have had in this world. We would have achieved the oneness that he was trying to show us. If we cannot understand the oneness, how can we even hope to understand the trinity that is also within God? Whether we know it or not, the oneness and the trinity work together. How is this possible? How can I explain it like this? Understand that the end goal of God is to make all men understand that they are part of one big family that is within his family. By this, I mean millions upon millions of people act as one family, composed of all races and all nations of the world. How can millions act as one? Let us look at the smallest unit of one, the individual. A person is one and yet three at the same time, because people have a soul, a spirit, and a body. If we can not get ourselves to agree in these three areas, we become conflicted in many ways, such as indecisiveness and discontentment. We develop a sense of uneasiness, and in the worst-case scenario, this leads to depression. The sad thing is that most people don't even know about these three areas of their lives so they do not know how important they are.

The Oneness or Family of God

The second smallest unit that I would like to discuss is the family. This is a better example to use in the understanding of the oneness and the trinity of God. Let me start with the following example. Let's say a certain family had a family business, and the eldest son took over that business after the father passed away. The new head of that family wants to take that business in a new direction, which seems risky. After discussing it as a family, they decide to take that risk and also decide what each family member must do in order to make that new venture profitable for their business. Since they are all dependant upon one another, they either fail or succeed based on each individual effort. If one individual within that family acts selfishly, they fail. On the other hand, if all act unselfishly, they succeed. Therefore, the actions of one individual affect the whole, and the whole either benefits or suffers. Using this scenario, an individual's actions can be viewed both as an individual effort and as part of a group effort. Individual efforts are a part of the oneness and part of what we call the trinity. Because as long as the individual is acting within the will of the family, all his or her actions are for the whole, or the family, but if more than one person is acting on behalf of the family, it becomes a trinity.

Another name for the trinity, or family, is the body of Christ, known to the Christian community as the church. The body of Christ represents the oneness of God, because even though it is composed of many different people, one day, they will all act on one accord. This will cause them to be one, and this is the how the oneness and the trinity work together at the same time. This can be found in the book of John.

John 17:20–23 (KJV) says,

Neither pray I for these alone, but for them also which shall believe on me through their word; That they all may be one; as thou, Father, art in me, and I in thee, that they also may be one in us:

that the world may believe that thou hast sent me. And the glory which thou gavest me I have given them; that they may be one, even as we are one: I in them, and thou in me, that they may be made perfect in one; and that the world may know that thou hast sent me, and hast loved them, as thou hast loved me.

This is the prayer that Jesus prayed to his father that "They may be one, as we are." This is an example of the many that he wants to act as one, as he does with his Father. When the time comes that God will bring us into his family, his family will no longer be composed of just three individuals anymore; it will be many—meaning it will no longer be just a trinity; it will be much more than that because the Father will have many more sons than the one he has now. This is why the Bible says that the greatest expectation of God's plan is the manifestations of his new sons. Romans 8:17–19 (KJV) says,

And if children, then heirs; heirs of God, and joint-heirs with Christ; if so be that we suffer with him, that we may be also glorified together. For I reckon that the sufferings of this present time are not worthy to be compared with the glory which shall be revealed in us. For the earnest expectation of the creature waiteth for the manifestation of the sons of God.

The bottom line is that we can operate as an individual within the family as long as our actions support the family; this is a representation of the trinity of God, meaning more than one individual with the same goal. If we follow the examples that God has already provided for us in the Bible, we do not divide the oneness or the trinity, which is the family of God. This is also another way of proving that we are his children. We can prove this by our coming together as a family, starting first with our immediate family and expanding this out into the world. Whether we like it or not, this is what God is going to do eventually, with or without us. Although he allowed it to start with us, if we fail, he will cause it to happen without fail. However, we know that this task was given to those who believe in God, and we know that we have fallen short many times over, but this should not stop us. The being to be blame for the failure when it comes to the efforts of the believers in the attempt to unite the world, is Satan. This is because Satan does not want the world to unite, because if that happened, then he would have no place in it. He is the cause of the division of God's family, meaning the oneness on earth and in heaven. Revelation 12:9–10 (KJV) says,

> And the great dragon was cast out, that old serpent, called the Devil, and Satan, which deceiveth the whole world: he was cast out into the earth, and his angels were cast out with him. And I heard a loud voice saying in heaven, Now is come salvation, and strength, and the kingdom of our God, and the power of his Christ: for the accuser of our brethren is cast down, which accused them before our God day and night.

Satan is the first son of God to cause a division within the family of God. He did this by acting selfishly and not in unity with the plan of God. I know now that he reacted this way because he did not understand God's plan. As I stated in chapter 1, the plan I am referring to is the doctrine of election. This is the reason for that plan; this plan would eventually lead to the salvation of both the angels and man. This is why the angel Lucifer could have been the only one who could have asked this question found in Hebrews 2:5–8 (KJV),

> For unto the angels hath he not put in subjection the world to come, whereof we speak. But one in a certain place testified, saying, What is man, that thou art mindful of him? or the son of man, that thou visitest him? Thou madest him a little lower than the angels; thou crownedst him with glory and honour, and didst set him over the works of thy hands: Thou hast put all things in subjection under his feet. For in that he put all in subjection under him, he left nothing that is not put under him.

These words are words of anger, which could have only been spoken by someone who is worried about his or her future, as opposed to man's future. This person is really asking, "What is in this for me? Why should I continue to follow you, if I have no place in the world to come?" This is why I believe Satan rebelled against God, and this is why I believe this is directly related to the plan that God put in place called the doctrine of election. He put it in place before the beginning of the world. Once again, Satan split from this family. He wanted nothing else to do with it because of this. This tore apart the oneness of God. What Satan did not know is that the oneness is a part of everything and cannot really be torn apart. This is what the Bible tells us in Ephesians 4:4–6 (KJV)

"There is one body, and one Spirit, even as ye are called in one hope of your calling; One Lord, one faith, one baptism, One God and Father of all, who is above all, and through all, and in you all."

This is the summation of the oneness of God that is within all things, whether man knows it or not. This is also true even if a person does not believe that there is a God. This means that God is even spiritually within the nonbeliever. The person who does not believe this, simply doesn't not know it. The next scripture I will show you is about the oneness that exists between the Father and the Son in heaven, where Jesus says that he and his Father are one. This type of oneness also means that they are always in agreement.

John 10:29–30 (KJV) says, "My Father, which gave them me, is greater than all; and no man is able to pluck them out of my Father's hand. I and my Father are one."

These scriptures without a doubt provide all the proof a person needs to believe in the oneness of God. There would be nothing wrong with their conclusion if that was all there was to it. If one concluded one's studies of this matter on this one scripture, that person would only be half right.

The Trinity of Individuals within God

From this point on, I will be focusing on the trinity of God, which is the other part of God most people do not understand. At the end of this chapter, I will show how both the trinity and oneness work together. I would like to start this discussion with 1 John 5:7 (KJV): "For there are three that bear record in heaven, the Father, the Word, and the Holy Ghost: and these three are one."

This scripture provides clear evidence that there are three in heaven, and at the same time, it says that they are one. This is because within this one scripture, it shows the trinity and the oneness at the same time. The key to understanding this is in the fact that the purpose of the three is to bear record, meaning to witness something. What does this mean? Well, the Bible sometimes tries to tell us something from a legalistic point of view. This means that by law, you must have more than one witness for something in order for it to be declared true. The explanation of this can be found in Deuteronomy 19:15 (KJV): "One witness shall not rise up against a man for any iniquity, or for any sin, in any sin that he sinneth: at the mouth of two witnesses, or at the mouth of three witnesses, shall the matter be established."

The Lord does, after all, have to follow the same rules he laid down for us, because he is the example we should follow. This is the first evidence of the need for there to be a trinity. Yes, there is a need for a trinity, and that is to provide a true witness. If God is going to judge the world, he will need witnesses, not only to his actions but the actions of the whole world. Why would God need a witness? Because of the unbelief that exists in the world. Believe it or not, those who will be convicted and thrown into the lake of fire will need to be convinced that they are guilty and deserve to be put there. For this reason, the trinity of God and man exists. This is why the following scripture appears in the Bible in 1 John 5:7–9 (KJV):

> For there are three that bear record in heaven, the Father, the Word, and the Holy Ghost: and these three are one. And there are three that bear witness in earth, the Spirit, and the water, and the blood: and these three agree in one. If we receive the witness of men, the witness of God is greater: for this is the witness of God which he hath testified of his Son.

These scriptures provide us with the evidence of both the trinities of God and man, as well as the need for them. Notice that in verse 7, it says that there are three that bear record "in" heaven and in verse 8, it says that there are three that bear record "in" the earth. The "in earth" instead of "on earth" shows that there is a difference between the two. The distinction shows the reader that there are differences and that they are not the same things in the same places. These same scriptures give us the reason for the trinity, and that is for the purposes of making a testimony true, by providing a witness. This means that God needs a witness whose witness is true, and man needs a witness whose witness is true. The next scripture I would like to use in order to show that there are three distinct individuals within the Godhead are from the words of Jesus Christ himself found in John 5:31–34 (KJV):

> If I bear witness of myself, my witness is not true. There is another that beareth witness of me; and I know that the witness which he witnesseth of me is true. Ye sent unto John, and he bare witness

unto the truth. But I receive not testimony from man: but these things I say, that ye might be saved.

In reading these scriptures, we see how Jesus needs his father to bear witness of him. This is one way in which the trinity works, from the standpoint of needing a witness. By this, we can see that there is a legal way. There needs to be more than one in order to prove something is true. Jesus also has another witness besides his father, who will bear witness for him. This is what Jesus said in John 15:26 (KJV): "But when the Comforter is come, whom I will send unto you from the Father, even the Spirit of truth, which proceedeth from the Father, he shall testify of me ..."

From these scriptures, a person can see why both sides have a point. The greatest argument against those who believe that Jesus and God are the same person is found in John 10:30, where Jesus said, "I and my Father are one." Neither side should be arguing this point, because, as I have said, both sides are right; it is a simple matter of finding out how.

Most of us who believe in the trinity of God know who the witness is for the Father and the Son: the Holy Spirit. For that matter, they all witness for each other. On the other hand, most of us do not know who the three witnesses are in the earth. According to 1 John 5:7–9, the names that were given are the Spirit, the water, and the blood. How do these relate to a man? The first thing that God named was the Spirit. This is the Holy Spirit, who witnesses things in both heaven and earth. The second was the water; this is none other than the water baptism, which is unto repentance. The last and final witness is the blood; this carries a twofold meaning. This is both the blood of the lamb and the blood of the man. Yes, our blood is a witness for us. This is because our life is in our blood, and this is true both naturally and spiritually. This was said in the book of Leviticus 17:11 (KJV), "For the life of the flesh is in the blood: and I have given it to you upon the altar to make an atonement for your souls: for it is the blood that maketh an atonement for the soul."

Even though this scripture is referring to the blood of animals, listen to what God said just a few verses down from this one. In Leviticus 17:14 (KJV), it says, "For it is the life of all flesh; the blood of it is for the life thereof ..."

Blood is one of the most important things to God; it is by blood that everything is established.

Hebrews 9:20–22 (KJV) says,

Saying, This is the blood of the testament which God hath enjoined unto you. Moreover, he sprinkled with blood both the tabernacle, and all the vessels of the ministry. And almost all things are by the law purged with blood; and without shedding of blood is no remission.

If it had not been for the shedding of Christ's blood, God would have required our blood, meaning the blood of every person, for the remission of our sins. This is what these scriptures tell us. Because our life is in our blood, by offering it back to God, you could not offer any greater thing. Our life is the greatest possession that we have and is the only thing that is of any value to God. Now, let us look at how precious God has made the blood of Jesus as it relates to us. John 6:53–56 (KJV) says,

Then Jesus said unto them, Verily, verily, I say unto you, Except ye eat the flesh of the Son of man, and drink his blood, ye have no life in you. Whoso eateth my flesh, and drinketh my blood, hath eternal life; and I will raise him up at the last day. For my flesh is meat indeed, and my blood is drink indeed. He that eateth my flesh, and drinketh my blood, dwelleth in me, and I in him.

This is how precious the blood of Jesus Christ is to us; without it, we will no have eternal life. The question is how do we drink this blood? This, of course, is a spiritual saying, and we can only accomplish this by the Spirit of God. The spiritual way to drink is to listen; by this, I mean to listen to the Holy Spirit. Why do I say this? Because our spirits, like our natural bodies, require nourishment. We eat and drink in order to live naturally. This is the same thing we must do for our spirits in order to live eternally. If we do not drink natural water, our bodies will eventually die; if we do not drink spiritually, we will die the second death, which means to not have eternal life with the Father. Therefore, this type of drinking can only be accomplished by reading the Word of God and finding the answer to why he died for us. By trying to model your life after Christ's, you would be spiritually drinking his blood. If a man does this, he in turn will suffer like Christ; therefore, he will have accomplished the drinking of the blood, which really means to try to follow in the footsteps of Christ.

This next scripture shows the power of the blood of Christ, as well as what the shedding of it accomplished. Ephesians 2:12–19 (KJV) says,

But now in Christ Jesus ye who sometimes were far off are made nigh by the blood of Christ. For he is our peace, who hath made both one, and hath broken down the middle wall of partition between us; Having abolished in his flesh the enmity, even the law of commandments contained in ordinances; for to make in himself of twain one new man, so making peace; And that he might reconcile both unto God in one body by the cross, having slain the enmity thereby: And came and preached peace to you which were afar off, and to them that were nigh. For through him we both have access by one Spirit unto the Father. Now therefore ye are no more strangers and foreigners, but fellowcitizens with the saints, and of the household of God ...

This is how we are brought into the body of Christ, and this is how we are made fellow citizens in the kingdom of God.

The Trinity or Different Parts of Man

The answer to the question of the trinity of man is found in the understanding of how God first made man, when he said, "Let us make man in our own image." If we were able to figure out just what he meant when he said this, we would know exactly what the trinity of God is. Let us now examine how God made man by starting with the scripture found in the book of Genesis. Genesis 1:26 (KJV) says, "And God said, Let us make man in our image, after our likeness ..."

Most people do not interpret this scripture properly. Those who don't think it only means that God created man in his image by giving him awareness, or intellect. While others think that we have arms, legs, and a face like his, and thus we are made in his image. The truth is that all of the above are true. We are made like God in every way, in body, soul, and spirit. This is exactly what God meant when he said, "Let us make man in our own image."

I am sure you have heard many interpretations of this scripture, but not the one I just gave you. You might ask, "How can this be? We are flesh, and he is Spirit." Well, most people think that God is invisible, and this is true for the most part, that is unless God wants to reveal himself to you, as he did to Moses. God did this because he wanted to prove to Moses that he existed and because he loved Moses to the extent that he fulfilled Moses's request, which was to reveal himself. This can be found in the book of Exodus.

Exodus 33:18–23 (KJV) says,

And he said, I beseech thee, shew me thy glory. And he said, I will make all my goodness pass before thee, and I will proclaim the name of the LORD before thee; and will be gracious to whom I will be gracious, and will shew mercy on whom I will shew mercy. And he said, Thou canst not see my face: for there shall no man see me, and live. And the LORD said, Behold, there is a place by me, and thou shalt stand upon a rock: And it shall come to pass, while my glory passeth by, that I will put thee in a clift of the rock, and will cover thee with my hand while I pass by: And I will take away mine hand, and thou shalt see my back parts: but my face shall not be seen.

In these scriptures, God describes himself as having a face, arms, legs, hands, and back parts. This is proof that God not only has a body, but it is shaped like that of a man. Isn't this exactly how we look? This is what God meant when he said, "Let us make man in our likeness." The way in which we should interpret what God meant by likeness is that he meant in bodily form only. This is because image is an entirely different thing in and of itself.

The image of God is something that is a little harder to understand. The key to understanding what God meant by his image are the words, "Let us." God is referring to himself in a plural sense, not in the singular sense. By this, he is letting us know that within him, there is more than one. In fact, there are three, and these three all agree in one, which is the oneness, but the fact still remains that there are three. He made man in this same way. He put within our bodies a spirit and a soul. That means that there is more than one of us. One of us is a spirit, one of us is a soul, and the last one is our body. All three are us, and these three are one. When we look at each other in person, all we see is one individual, but the fact is that we have a spirit and a soul that exist within the same body. This is exactly how the trinity of God works; the only difference is that he can talk with his different parts, because he has given them life in themselves. Can God do this? Yes, he can, without a doubt.

We have these same three parts that make up a whole within us. Can we talk to them? Yes, we can. I know that we can at least talk with our soul and spirit. They don't always obey, but this is how we try to get them to obey. The body, soul, and spirit are brought together when we are born and separated upon our deaths. The soul remains with our bodies in the grave when we die, but the spirit, which belongs to God, returns to him. We remain in that state until God resurrects us and brings the soul and spirit back together in a new body, a body not made of flesh. If we know that we are made up of these three things, why can't God be the same? Haven't we all heard that God consists of the Father, the Son, and the Holy Spirit?

God simply has the power to separate himself from his other parts, which make up the whole, which is called the Godhead. The Godhead is composed of his body, spirit, and soul. God the Father is the soul; the Holy Spirit is the spirit that the Father and the Son share equally; and the body is that of Jesus Christ and the church. Christ is the head of that body, and the church fulfils the rest of that embodiment, spiritually, that is.

The Bible tells us that Christ embodied the fullness that is God. This is found in Colossians 2:9–11 (KJV):

> For in him dwelleth all the fulness of the Godhead bodily. And ye are complete in him, which is the head of all principality and power: In whom also ye are circumcised with the circumcision made without hands, in putting off the body of the sins of the flesh by the circumcision of Christ ...

We as children of God have a lot of trouble understanding this, since it cannot be explained naturally. This is the only way God can say, "Let us make man"; there is more than one of them. God in at least one instance in the Bible referred to men in their plural form when he said that we should fear the one who has the power to separate the soul and the spirit and not man. If he can do it to us, why shouldn't he be able to do it to himself? The account of God saying this can be found in the book of Hebrews. Hebrews 4:12 (KJV) says, "For the word of God is quick, and powerful, and sharper than any twoedged sword, piercing even to the dividing asunder of soul and spirit, and of the joints and marrow, and is a discerner of the thoughts and intents of the heart."

Christ and his Father share the same spirit and the same body, and this is the destiny that he wishes for us as well. We will share in this body through the Holy Spirit, which is how God shares the Godhead with Christ. This will be the end result of God's plan, which is found Ephesians 1:10 (KJV): "That in the dispensation of the fulness of times he might gather together in one all things in Christ, both which are in heaven, and which are on earth; even in him ..."

136

Christ became the first to represent both heaven and earth in bodily form. He accomplished this by having the Spirit of God and an earthly soul in one body. This is exactly the way man was made, with one exception: the spirit he gave us in the beginning was not his spirit but our own spirit. This means that we will not be complete until we have combined our spirit with his spirit, as Jesus Christ has done. We were still created in his image by having a spirit and a soul in one body, but God wants us to have a new body and a new spirit, so that our maturity will be complete. We will always bear the image of heaven and earth, just as Christ did when he rose from the grave. After Jesus rose from the grave with his new body, he met with the apostles and asked them to touch him and to give him something to eat so that they would know that he was still a man and yet not a man. This is found in the book of Luke.

Luke 24:36–43 (KJV) says,

And as they thus spake, Jesus himself stood in the midst of them, and saith unto them, Peace be unto you. But they were terrified and affrighted, and supposed that they had seen a spirit. And he said unto them, Why are ye troubled? and why do thoughts arise in your hearts? Behold my hands and my feet, that it is I myself: handle me, and see; for a spirit hath not flesh and bones, as ye see me have. And when he had thus spoken, he shewed them his hands and his feet. And while they yet believed not for joy, and wondered, he said unto them, Have ye here any meat? And they gave him a piece of a broiled fish, and of an honeycomb. And he took it, and did eat before them.

This is the example of what the new body will be like. This is the combination of heaven and earth that we who believe will receive. The evidence that this body is not limited to the natural laws of this world is in the fact that out of nowhere he just appeared, which suggests that the physical laws of this world have no effect on this body, because it does not always have to be physical. However, that he was touched and did eat lets us know that this body can be physical at the same time, if he so desires.

Even though we will be within the body of Christ and all will be as one, we will still have individuality within the body. God ensured this by giving us a soul. The soul is unique to each individual, because each soul has unique characteristics, but not our spirits; they were all made the same. A soul is unique because each person was exposed to different circumstances that made one either stronger or weaker. Our spirits, which came from God, did not receive this opportunity, because we interact in this world with our souls. We feel with our souls, we love with our souls, and we hate with our souls, because a soul was made for the world. A spirit was made for heaven, to experience things in heaven, and since we were only there for a short time, we cannot remember them directly; nevertheless, it is our spirit along with the Spirit that will bring us into oneness, and it will be with our souls that we will remain an individual and still operate as one.

Let us go a little deeper into what the purpose of the soul is. The soul gives the spirit within us a personality. It brings character to the individual, which is what make us different from one another. God delights in the differences in his creation; otherwise, we would be boring. Since a soul gives us character, our character in turn helps to guide us. If we have no character, then we have no personality. Who do you think Jesus got his character and personality from? The answer is his Father; this is how the soul part of God, which is his Father, acts within the Godhead. It gives them character, the same as our soul gives us character.

The next question you might ask yourself is if the soul gives us character, then what does our spirit do for us? The spirit that is within us acts as our conscience and warns us if we are about to do or have done something wrong.

It is also through our spirits that the Spirit, which is the Holy Spirit, communicates with us. The spirit is mainly connected to what we think, not what we feel; this is what our souls are connected to. If something does not feel right, it probably isn't. On the same hand, if this does feel right, it probably is. Either way, our soul will let us know. If we understood the purpose for having a soul and a spirit, we would know how to operate between the two. This is how our conscience or our spirits warn us. If we ignore both our spirits and our souls, then we are truly on our own, and if the outcome is bad, we cannot say God didn't warn us. We can't say this because he put these early warning devices within us, and if we still choose to ignore them, we cannot blame God. This is how God remains neutral. He did not make us do anything either way. He did, however, send us strong signals, and in this way, he is not interfering with our free will. By the way, just to let you know, this is the way the devil works. He does not make us do anything; he only sends strong urges for us to do something that he wants us to do, and if we do it, he can say he didn't make us do it.

He simply tries to override the urges of the Father, which come through our spirits, with stronger urges that come through our flesh. The problem is that most of us are not aware of our spirits and do not have a clue as to what is going on inside us, and in this way, Satan has the advantage over God. This is why God had to predestine some people so that they would be beyond the control of Satan. They are beyond his control, because God made them able to listen to the Spirit. This is what the Bible meant in Romans 8:5–9 (KJV):

> For they that are after the flesh do mind the things of the flesh; but they that are after the Spirit the things of the Spirit. For to be carnally minded is death; but to be spiritually minded is life and peace. Because the carnal mind is enmity against God: for it is not subject to the law of God, neither indeed can be. So then they that are in the flesh cannot please God. But ye are not in the flesh, but in the Spirit, if so be that the Spirit of God dwell in you. Now if any man have not the Spirit of Christ, he is none of his.

This means that some people were born with the ability to hear spiritually, and some people were not. They must learn how to do this. Before a person can learn to do this, Satan has the upper hand and takes advantage of this time. If not for God choosing the time that he wants a person to stop listening to his or her flesh instead of his or her spirits, then most would be lost. Almost none of us could have been saved, because without God, we are incapable of overriding the desires of the flesh.

The Meaning of the Spiritual Words *Male* and *Female* within the Godhead

When we use each name individually—the Father, the Son, and the Holy Spirit—we are dividing the Godhead into three parts. When God uses the word *man*, he is talking to us in our plural form. In our plural form, we are both male and female in the spiritual sense. When he refers to a man in his singular form, he calls him by his given name, just as we do when we know which of the Godhead is doing the talking while reading a particular passage in the Bible. Is there evidence in the Bible of this? Yes, and it can be found in Genesis 1:27 (KJV), "So God created man in his own image, in the image of God created he him; male and female created he them."

A hidden secret about the creation of man is contained within this very scripture, but most people cannot catch it. It is in the fact that God said that when he made man in his own image, he made the man both a male and a female, at the same time. Most of us don't realize that Eve, Adam's wife, does not get created until Genesis 2:21, yet these scriptures tell us that he made them at the same time. Did the Bible make a mistake? No, it is simply showing us that man was born a dual being. Further proof of this is in the fact that Eve came from Adam. Adam was created by God, but Eve came from Adam or rather out of Adam.

Genesis 2:21–23 (KJV) says,

> And the LORD God caused a deep sleep to fall upon Adam, and he slept: and he took one of his ribs, and closed up the flesh instead thereof; And the rib, which the LORD God had taken from man, made he a woman, and brought her unto the man. And Adam said, This is now bone of my bones, and flesh of my flesh: she shall be called Woman, because she was taken out of Man.

Even though God made Eve's flesh from Adam's rib, her spirit is what came out of Adam. This is what chapter 1 of Genesis meant when God said he made man both male and female. Eve came from the man. This is the same way Christ came from God; he came out of God, meaning God gave birth to him, a spiritual birth, that is. When he came into existence, his name was the Word. By understanding who the Word was, we can understand the trinity a little better. The scripture I am referring to from which we can gain an understanding of who the Word is can be found in the book of John. John 1:1 (KJV), "In the beginning was the Word, and the Word was with God, and the Word was God."

Within this scripture, there are two mysteries. What has escaped most is that within these scriptures, the Bible gives us the birth of the Word of God. Most people think this scripture is pertaining to the spoken Word of God, not the being known as the Word, who later became known as Christ. Many don't even know Christ existed before he came to earth, which is what this scripture tells us later on. The two mysteries that this scripture is telling us about is who the Word was and where he came from.

Let us analyze this scripture a little more closely. In this scripture, we find that John is saying that in the beginning was the Word. This part of the scripture lets us know that the Word was the first thing that the Father created. The next part of this scripture says that the Word was with God, letting us know that the Word is not God, because he is with God or beside him. The very next part of this scripture shows that the Word was God, letting us know he is part of the Godhead and that they are one. This is another example of the trinity and the oneness at the same time. The Word also spoke about his Father training him in the book of Proverbs.

Proverbs 8:22–36 (KJV) says,

> The LORD possessed me in the beginning of his way, before his works of old. I was set up from everlasting, from the beginning, or ever the earth was. When there were no depths, I was brought forth; when there were no fountains abounding with water. Before the mountains were settled, before the hills was I brought forth: While as yet he had not made the earth, nor the fields, nor the highest part of the dust of the world. When he prepared the heavens, I was there: when he set a compass upon the face of the depth: When he established the clouds above: when he strengthened the fountains of the deep: When he gave to the sea his decree, that the waters should not pass his commandment: when he appointed the foundations of the earth: Then I was by him, as one brought up with him: and I was daily his delight, rejoicing always before him; Rejoicing in the habitable part of his earth; and my delights were with the sons of men. Now therefore hearken unto me, O ye children: for blessed are they that keep my ways. Hear instruction, and be wise, and refuse it not. Blessed is the man that heareth me, watching daily at my gates, waiting at the posts of my doors. For whoso findeth me findeth life, and shall obtain favour of the LORD. But he that sinneth against me wrongeth his own soul: all they that hate me love death.

This is the Holy Spirit who has also been with the Lord since the beginning. Verse 22 says that the "Lord possessed me," and in verse 30, it says that they were "as one brought up with Him." This is suggesting that they are separate. This is very strong evidence that the Bible is telling us that God is a trinity, but there is even stronger evidence in the fact that Jesus said many times, "My Father in heaven." How many times did he say, "I will pray to the Father"? How many times did he say, "I do not come to do my will, but the will of the one that sent me?" I will ask you this question: if Jesus and God were the same individual, why would he talk or pray to himself? If we were to talk to ourselves like this, other people would think that we were crazy.

Having said all this, I hope that I have shown you how the oneness and trinity of God, as well as the oneness and the trinity of man, works. You and I have one spirit, one soul, and one body, the same as the trinity of God.

Chapter Six

The Daily Lives of the Sons of God

This chapter is written in the following format: circumstances that each of the sons of God face are presented, followed by how each of them reacts to the situation. These experiences are based on how I have interacted with the different sons of God. Once again, I do not think that all people think this way, but some do, and if it the shoe fits, wear it. However, if the shoe does not fit, and you do not agree, I am certain that you know someone that it does fit. Please do not be offended if you do not agree with anything I have written in this chapter. If you can relate to these life experiences, I hope that it will lead you to think about how you choose to react in these given situations.

This chapter is written with a two or three-line description of each of the sons of God. I will be using the following abbreviations to discuss the different sons of God: free son (FS) or chosen son (CS), servant son (SS) or bond son (BS), and the lost sons (LS) or unbelieving son (UBS). We can all learn something by examining each son's perspective. These experiences include church, religion, the Holy Spirit, love, faith, family, and many other aspects of life. I will also try to capture how each son thinks about these different aspects of life and how they react to them. Whether we know it or not, we are what we think we are, based on how we interpret the world. How a person thinks about the world defines him or her spiritually. Therefore, based on the way you think, you are a free son, a servant son, or a lost son.

One of the hardest things Christians must do in this world is judge themselves, because they do not want to face themselves in the mirror. I wrote this in the hopes that if people read this, it will help them accomplish that task. Please do not be offended if you find that you might be one of the sons you might not want to be; remember, it is the Spirit of God that convicts us all, not I.

The Holy Spirit

- The FS has within him the Father and the Son.
- The SS has only the Father.
- The LS does not know who his Father is.
- The FS has the Holy Spirit within him, and it stays with him at all times.
- The SS has the Holy Ghost, and it comes and goes at certain times.
- The LS does not know the Father or the Son.
- The FS is taught by the Holy Spirit and Christ.
- The SS is taught by the Father and the law.
- The LS is taught by no one.
- The FS is assured of his salvation by the Holy Spirit.
- The SS is never sure of his because he breaks the laws of God.
- The LS does not care about any natural or spiritual laws.
- The FS converses with the Holy Spirit daily.
- The SS converses with God in prayer daily.
- The LS converses with himself daily.

The Anointing

- The FS knows that the anointing is the Holy Spirit, which gives all gifts.
- The SS thinks that each of his gifts is a different anointing.
- The LS thinks that his ability to manipulate others is an anointing.
- The FS has the anointing, which means the Holy Spirit lives in him. This gives him both salvation and the understanding of that salvation, which teaches him how to use faith.

144

- The SS has only salvation and limited understanding of his salvation, which does not lead to the power of faith.
- The UBS has neither.
- The FS understands that righteousness was given to him.
- The SS thinks that he has to work for righteousness.
- The UBS says to himself, "Righteousness is in the eyes of the beholder."
- The FS has received the seal of God already.
- The SS has not yet received the seal of God.
- The UBS will never receive the seal of God.

Love

- The FS learns to love unconditionally.
- The SS learns to love conditionally.
- The UBS never learns to love.
- The FS is a son who is very close to achieving unconditional love toward his brethren.
- The SS is a son who loves only those who love him.
- The UBS is a son who loves only himself.
- Love to the FS is an expression of his character toward others, without favoritism.
- Love to the SS is an expression of his character toward others, with favoritism.
- Love to the LS is an expression of his physical nature, for physical gain.
- The FS knows that love is his ultimate goal.
- The SS thinks that salvation is his ultimate goal.
- The LS thinks love is a weakness, and only those who are weak love.

Faith

- The FS knows that faith means to act on one's belief.
- The SS thinks that faith means to have stronger belief than anyone else does.
- The LS thinks that faith is only for fools.
- The FS knows how to use his faith, by taking an action on what he believes God is for and then praying about that action to his Father.

- The SS prays about everything before an action, which does not put faith into action.
- The LS puts faith in himself and puts only himself into action.
- The FS will live by faith daily and not rely on his own strength for anything.
- The SS will live by faith only when he thinks he needs it, because he relies partially on his own strength.
- The UBS will not live by faith, because he trusts solely in himself.
- The FS has complete faith in the Father's word, because he understands it.
- The SS does not have complete faith in the Father's word because he does not completely understand it.
- The UBS has faith only in what he knows and that is only worldly things.
- The SS will not continue in faith if the thing failed they were having faith for.
- The FS will continue in faith even when he fails many times, until the thing he was having faith for happens.
- The UBS doesn't even know what faith is.

Peace

- The FS will use words skillfully in all situations, in order to keep the peace.
- The SS will not use words skillfully in all situations and therefore may not always keep the peace.
- The UBS will use words skillfully to deceive for personal gain and does not care for peace.
- The FS does not mind being wrong, if it keeps the peace.
- The SS hates being wrong at any time, even if it means not keeping the peace.
- The UBS doesn't even care if he is wrong, because peace is boring to him.

Money

- When it comes to money, the FS is satisfied with having just enough to meet his needs, because he will not fear what will happen.

- When it comes to money, the SS is not satisfied with just having enough, because he fears what might happen if he doesn't one day.
- When it comes to money, the UBS is not satisfied with his own, he wants yours, mine, and everyone else's money.
- The FS will save money for tomorrow because his conscience tells him to be prepared for anything.
- The SS will not save money because his conscience says, "The Lord will provide."
- The UBS will not save any money because his conscience says, "I do not know if I will live or die tomorrow, so let me live for today."
- The LS will not leave an inheritance to his children, because he will say to himself, "No one else will spend what I worked hard to achieve."
- The SS will not leave an inheritance because he says, "We can't take it with us."
- The FS will leave an inheritance to his children, of all that he has.
- The inheritance of the FS is his wisdom.
- The inheritance of the SS is his religion.
- The inheritance of the LS is destruction.
- The FS will never be rich with earthly riches.
- The SS thinks that his earthly riches reflect his favor with God.
- The LS thinks he is entitled to earthly riches, and woe to anyone who gets in his way.
- The FS will store treasure in heaven with his heavenly works of faith.
- The SS will store treasure on earth, with his earthly works.
- The LS will not store anything.
- The SS will desire to be physically rich in order to flaunt his blessings.
- The FS will only desire to be spiritually rich, in order to show his blessings.
- The LS will also only desire to be physically rich to show off.
- The FS will save money for the future, in case of a rainy day, because the Lord teaches a person to prepare himself.

- The SS will save a little money and then say to himself, "The Lord will provide the rest."
- The UBS will not save anything and say to himself, "You only live once."
- The FS will help someone in need and will say to himself, "The Lord will repay me."
- The SS will help someone in need and will say to another, "Donate to me in the name of the Lord."
- The UBS will help someone in need and will say, "Do you think that was for free?"

Strengths and Weaknesses

- The SS will not speak of his faults, because it might show weakness on his part and he hopes to avoid showing weakness to others.
- The FS will speak of his faults and weaknesses often, because in his understanding of his faults and weaknesses he shows his strength.
- The UBS hides his faults as well but not out of guilt or weakness, but because he suffers from denial. He denies everything in order to avoid guilt.
- The FS will take action when it is needed to help someone.
- The SS will not take action but will say, "I will pray about it."
- The UBS will only take action if he can see a personal gain in it.
- The FS will enter into a new situation or circumstance boldly, expecting to conquer it, in the name of God.
- The SS will enter into a new situation or circumstance very cautiously, trying to predict the outcome, not knowing if he will conquer it.
- The UBS will enter into a new situation or circumstance very boldly, expecting to conquer in his own name.
- The FS will fight his battles with the Word of God, his spirit, and the Holy Spirit.
- The SS fights his battles with the Word of God and his flesh.
- The UBS fights all his battles with his flesh.
- The FS knows that he cannot lose his salvation.
- The SS still believes that he can lose his salvation.

- The UBS could care less.
- The FS will stand up for the falsely accused, even if it means losing his reputation as well.
- The SS will not stand up for the falsely accused, because it might mean losing his reputation as well.
- The UBS will only stand for himself.
- The SS thinks that the power of God is in how well he can quote scripture, which gives an outward show of strength.
- The FS knows that the power of God lies in the understanding of scripture, which is an inward show of strength that comes from the heart.
- The LS knows that power comes from knowledge but not the knowledge of God.
- The UBS will fight his battles with his flesh.
- The SS will fight his battles with the Word of God and flesh.
- The FS will fight his battles with the Word of God, his spirit, and with the Holy Spirit.
- The conscience of the FS is free and clear.
- The conscience of the SS is mixed between freedom and guilt.
- The conscience of a UBS is full of guilt, but he ignores it.
- The FS has overcome the world.
- The SS is still struggling with the world.
- The UBS enjoys all worldly things.

Prayer

- The FS knows that there is power in prayer, but only if it is accompanied by an action.
- The SS knows that there is power in prayer, but it may not always be accompanied by an action.
- The UBS does not pray.
- The FS knows that faith without works is dead, which is the same as prayer without an action.
- The SS does not know that this applies to prayer.
- The LS does not know to pray for himself or for others.
- The FS knows to pray when something is out of his control, but when something is within his control, he will act and then pray.

- The SS thinks that everything is out of his control and will not always act.
- The LS thinks prayer is foolishness.
- The SS only knows to pray about something but not act himself; he does not put faith into action.
- The FS will not only pray but act on it, therefore, putting faith into action.
- The LS puts his or her faith in himself and puts himself into action; if it is not accomplished, he says to himself, "It cannot be done."
- The FS tells his father what he wants, because he knows what is in his will and does not ask for what is outside of his will.
- The SS only asks for what he wants from the Father, because he is not sure it is within his will.
- The UBS does not ask for anything from anyone; he only takes.
- The FS will not ask anyone to pray for him, because he does not lack faith, and he knows that the Bible has said, "The prayers of a righteous man availeth much."
- The SS will always ask others to pray for him, because he lacks faith and thinks that with the combination of the prayers of many others, God will grant him what he is asking for because he says to himself, "The more the better; there is power in numbers."
- The UBS will not pray, because he says to himself, "What I don't have, I will take."
- The FS will pray only to the Father in the name of Jesus.
- The SS is not sure if he should pray to the Father or Jesus.
- The UBS prays to no one.
- Ask the UBS for help, and he will say, "No, I will not."
- Ask the SS for help, and he will say, "I will pray for you."
- Ask the FS for help, and he will say, "What do you need me to do for you?"
- The FS walks and talks with his Father all day long in spirit.
- The SS walks and talks with his Father for only part of the day in prayer.
- The UBS walks and talks with another UBS.

Church

- The SS will look for Christ in a particular church or building.
- The FS will look in the right place for Christ, which is inside the heart, where God said he placed his kingdom.
- The UBS will never look for Christ, only another of his kind.
- The FS will carry the church around with him in his heart every day.
- The SS will only carry the church in his heart during the time he is in church service.
- The UBS will not have anything to do with church.
- The SS will live through the Bible in addition to an earthly doctrine.
- The FS will live through the Bible and no other earthly doctrine.
- The UBS will not live by any Bible or doctrine.
- The SS thinks that the entire body of Christ consists of his church only.
- The FS knows that the entire body of Christ consists of all the churches.
- The UBS thinks that the entire body of Christ consists of nothing but hypocrites.
- The SS thinks that the body of Christ is within his church building.
- The FS knows that the body of Christ is every person who believes in Christ.
- The body of Christ is foolish talk to the UBS.

Religion

- The FS does not have a religion but understands why others need it.
- The SS will always have a religion and cannot do without it.
- The UBS's religion is the worship of himself.
- The FS will also not worry about the future, because he knows it's in God's hands.

- The SS will worry about the future, because he does not always wait upon the Lord, and so he sometimes takes matters into his own hands.
- The UBS will try to predict the future or have it predicted for him by someone else and leave matters in someone else's hands.
- The FS will worship the Father in spirit, body, and soul.
- The SS will worship the Father in body and soul.
- The UBS will not worship the Father at all.
- The FS eats the meat of the Word.
- The SS drinks the milk of the Word.
- The UBS eats only forbidden fruits.
- The FS knows that he cannot lose his salvation.
- The SS still believes that he can lose his salvation.
- The UBS could care less.
- The FS does the will of the Father.
- The SS does the will of another, who says he is from the Father.
- The UBS does his own will.
- The FS will have fellowship with anyone of any race or religion, or for that matter, of no religion.
- The SS will have fellowship with only his own kind, within his own religion.
- The UBS will only have fellowship with his own kind.
- The FS will not always avoid temptation because he knows he will overcome and learn from it with the help of the Holy Spirit.
- The SS will always avoid temptation because he is not sure that he will always overcome it and learn from it, so it is simpler to just try to avoid it and learn nothing.
- The UBS will not avoid temptation at all; on the contrary, he will seek it out, so that he can enjoy indulging himself in it.
- The FS looks at the inner spirit of a person in order to draw his conclusions about him or her.
- The SS will only look at a person's works in the church to draw conclusions.
- The UBS will only look at work outside the church in order to draw his conclusions about a person.
- The soul of the FS is easily satisfied.

- The soul of the SS is hard to satisfy.
- The soul of the UBS can never be satisfied.
- The FS knows that nothing happens by coincidence or chance.
- The SS always wonders which of the two has occurred.
- The UBS thinks that everything is by coincidence.
- The FS does not need a sign from God in order to believe.
- The SS needs a sign from God in order to believe.
- The UBS does not pay attention to signs.
- When it comes to his walk with Christ, the SS thinks that these changes occur overnight. He does not have much patience with himself.
- When it comes to his walk with Christ, the FS knows that change in his walk with Christ does not happen overnight and will have patience with himself. He knows it will take many trials and tribulations to grow into what he will be.
- The LS does not walk with Christ.
- The SS will commit scripture to memory, and when he quotes scripture to a babe in Christ, it is not as effective. The listener may not understand it.
- The FS will remember scripture by heart and may not quote scripture exactly as it is written. When he relates scripture to a person, he will make sure the person understands it. He relates scripture to a person in relation to the person's ability to understand; therefore, he will be more successful.

Teaching

- The FS is taught by the Holy Spirit and the Bible.
- The SS is taught by another man and the Bible.
- The LS is taught by himself and by others of his kind.
- The FS does not need anyone to teach him about the Father and the Son, because he has learned through diligent searching of the Bible.
- The SS does need someone to teach him about the Father and the Son, because he will not do it for himself. He will not search the scriptures hard enough.
- The UBS does not like being taught by anyone. He rejects any teachings, except what the world teaches him.

- The FS reads the Bible looking forward to the good things it will say to him next.
- The SS reads the Bible in fear of conviction.
- The LS will not read the Bible at all.
- The FS will read the Bible and understand the natural and spiritual.
- The SS will read the Bible and understand only the natural meaning.
- The LS will not read the Bible.

Sin and Law

- The FS is not under the letter of the law but under the spirit of the law.
- The SS will try to keep the letter of the law but not be unable to do so; therefore, he will condemn himself as well as others.
- The UBS has a law of his own: "Do unto others before they do to it to you."
- The FS knows that all sins are forgiven, except unbelief, because he walks in the Spirit and knows that the blood of Jesus keeps on forgiving him indefinitely.
- The SS does not know that all sins are forgiven by Christ but believes that sin is still present in his life. This is because he does not walk in the Spirit, which makes us walk boldly. He walks in fear, because he does not fully believe that Jesus will repeatedly forgive him, especially for the same mistakes.
- The UBS does not even care about any of this.
- The FS cannot be condemned for his faults, because of his love for the Son of God.
- The SS still believes that he can be condemned for his faults, even though he cannot be condemned, because he believes also.
- The UBS does not care.
- The FS is no longer under the law and is therefore dead to sin.
- The SS still believes he is under the law. He does know he is dead to sin, and therefore, sin is alive to him through the law.
- The UBS could care less about how man's or God's law operates.

- The FS will "do unto others" as he would like things to done unto him.
- The SS will not always follow this rule of God.
- The LS will never follow this rule but will break it, just for the fun of doing so.

Fear

- The FS does not follow the commandments of God out of fear; he follows them out of love.
- The SS follows the commandments of God out of fear and hopes that God still loves him.
- The UBS follows no one out of fear or love.
- The SS uses fear to recruit new believers into the kingdom of God.
- The FS uses love to recruit new believers into the kingdom of God.
- Neither fear nor love will cause the UBS to hear the words of God.
- The FS appears to be reckless because he leaps into a project without fear.
- The SS thinks that he is being more cautious by keeping fear in mind during any project.
- To the UBS, fear is excitement and an adrenaline rush.
- Fear of the Lord to the FS simply means respect.
- Fear of the Lord to the SS means fear.
- Fear of the Lord to the UBS means nothing.
- Ask the SS what he fears, and he will tell you, "I fear only the Lord."
- Ask the FS what he fears, and he will tell you, "I fear myself."
- Ask the UBS what he fears, and he will tell you, "I fear nothing."
- The FS knows that the fear of the Lord is only the beginning of knowledge, but when he has found the love of God, his training is near completion.
- The SS thinks that fear is the beginning and ending of knowledge.
- The UBS uses fear in order to make people do his will.

- The SS will not speak in terms of reality if the reality he is speaking of is negative.
- The FS will speak in terms of reality, even if that reality is negative.
- The LS always speaks in terms of reality, whether positive or negative.
- The FS does not fear death, because he knows what awaits.
- The SS fears death, because he does not know what will happen.
- The LS fears death dreadfully, because in his heart, he knows he is condemned.
- The FS does not have fear during a trial or tribulation, because he will accept the outcome because he believes it is the Lord's will.
- The SS will have fear because he may not be ready for the outcome.
- The UBS will have fear of anything and everyone all his life.

Failure
- The SS thinks that God is not with him when he fails and tries to forget his failures.
- The FS knows that God is with him, even in failure, because he knows that even in failure something good can come, such as the building of character, patience, and even stronger faith.
- When the UBS fails, he also tries to forget, in order to maintain the image of success and to prove that he does not need God.
- Failure to the SS is just another misfortune, something caused by the devil, and is only an attempt to draw him away from the Lord.
- Failure to the FS is just another opportunity from God to overcome an unfortunate situation and draw closer to the Lord.
- Failure to a UBS is just something to be forgotten.

Family
- The FS will raise his children in the church as well as teach them the ways of the Lord from his own experience.

- The SS will raise his children in the church also and continue to let someone else teach them the ways of the Lord.
- The UBS will not raise his children period and will not be concerned with who teaches them anything or even whether they are taught.
- The FS of the Father will be given a mate because he waits on the Lord.
- The SS will try to wait on the Lord to send him a mate, but if it takes too long, he will give up waiting and choose for himself.
- The UBS never waits and therefore marries and divorces many times.
- The FS will treat his spouse as his own flesh.
- The SS will treat his spouse as only a helpmate.
- The UBS will treat his spouse as a servant.
- The FS will treat his children as his own flesh.
- The SS will treat his children as his helpmates.
- The UBS will treat his children with contempt.
- The FS will leave an inheritance for his children.
- The SS will not always do so.
- The UBS will never do so but say to himself, "I will spend all I can while I'm alive. I only live once."

Humility

- The FS will always keep his humility, because he or she has learned from his trials and tribulations and found out that humility is one of his strengths.
- The SS will not always stay in his or her humility, because he has not learned from his trials and tribulations and uses humility only in the beginning.
- The UBS thinks humility is for those who are weak.
- Insult the FS, and he will not retaliate; he will say nothing and walk away.
- Insult the SS, and he might retaliate with equal words.
- Insult a UBS, and violence will be the most likely outcome.
- The FS will hide his godliness with humility.
- The SS will proudly show off his godliness, with a sense of pride.

- The UBS will proudly show of his ungodliness with even more pride and arrogance.
- Meet the FS for the first time, and he will show his humility, not boldness in the Lord.
- Meet the SS for the first time, and he will show his boldness, not humility in the Lord.
- Meet the UBS for the first time, and he will show his arrogance.
- Meet the FS for the first time, and he will seem naive and weak.
- Meet the SS for the first time, and he will seem wise and bold.
- Meet the LS for the first time, and he will seem arrogant and strong.

Friendships and Disagreements

- The FS builds with his hands.
- The UBS only destroys with his hands.
- The SS's hands both build and destroy.
- The FS knows he cannot win a disagreement with a UBS or the SS, so the FS wins by walking away and allowing each to think that he has won, because the FS knows that the strongest person is willing to give in to the other and allow the other to learn from his own mistakes.
- The UBS wonders why his weapons of destruction do not work on the SS or the FS, since they have never failed on his kind. What he doesn't know is that God is with both of them.
- The FS is his brother's keeper.
- The SS keeps to himself.
- The UBS does not even keep himself.

Knowledge, Understanding, and Love

- The FS knows how to use the armor of God.
- The SS only knows about the armor of God.
- The UBS uses money for his armor.
- The FS understands the gifts that have been given to him and operates within them.
- The SS has gifts also but does not know fully how to use them and often operates outside the gifts that he has been given.

- The UBS uses his gifts as well, but he uses them to take from others.
- The FS has been given the understanding of the mysteries of the kingdom of God.
- The SS has not been given the ability to understand these things, so he discredits the free son.
- The UBS discredits them both.
- The FS has found out that he has been made righteous by the blood of Christ.
- The SS still thinks that he has to work to maintain his righteousness.
- The UBS says, "Righteousness is in the eye of the beholder."
- The FS understands the trinity of God.
- The SS only understands the oneness of God.
- The UBS says to himself, "There is no God; only a fool would believe in that."
- The FS has learned to have patience with many things.
- The SS has learned to have patience with a few things.
- The UBS has no patience with anything.
- The FS has found the truth hidden in the Gospel.
- The SS still searches for the truth of the Gospel.
- For the UBS, truth is whatever is real to him at the time.
- The FS has the knowledge and wisdom of God's Word.
- The SS only has the knowledge of God's Word.
- The UBS only has knowledge of the world.
- The FS no longer thirsts for the knowledge, because he has drunk the water that causes him to never thirst again.
- The SS still thirsts for knowledge, because the water he drank did not cure his thirst forever.
- The UBS only knows of natural water, and he will thirst again.
- The FS trusts his heavenly Father completely.
- The SS does not know how to completely trust his heavenly Father.
- The UBS hates his earthly father and much more his heavenly Father.
- The FS calls God, "my Father."
- The SS calls God, "God."
- The UBS doesn't even call him.

- The FS knows that he has the victory at present, because he is an overcomer of the world.
- The SS will not know that he has the victory until the Lord returns.
- The UBS will not know that he has lost all until the Lord returns.
- The SS will think that the FS is an unbeliever, because he does not agree with him.
- The UBS will think the SS is normal, because he knows him and that the FS is not normal because he does not know him.
- The FS will be misunderstood by both.
- The FS will lay down his life for a friend, or in other words, another son of God.
- No other kind of son will do this.
- The FS seeks to love, heal, and build.
- The UBS seeks to kill, steal, and destroy.
- The SS will do a little of each.
- The FS will not need to experience all things that are against God in order to learn.
- The SS will only learn by experience and so has to experience all things, even the things that God hates.
- The UBS never learns, period.
- The SS will use knowledge like a cloak to mask his ignorance.
- The FS will use knowledge like a weapon to unmask ignorance.
- The UBS will use knowledge like a weapon to kill, steal, and destroy.

Misfortune

- If the FS should fall into harm's way, he will stay and fight the battle with the Lord.
- If the SS should fall into harm's way, he will run away and say, "The Lord will fight my battles."
- If the UBS should fall into harm's way, he will try to fight his battles on his own.

Faults and Mistakes

- The FS will receive chastisement positively from the Father and still know that he is loved.
- The SS will receive chastisement negatively and come to the conclusion that he might have fallen out of grace with the Father.
- The UBS hates any form of discipline or chastisement, and anyone who tries to give it to him might be met with harsh words.
- The FS will tell the truth even if it hurts his reputation.
- The SS will tell the truth only when it will not hurt his reputation.
- The UBS will never tell the truth.
- The FS will see beyond another person's faults.
- The UBS will exploit the faults of other people.
- The SS may do either depending on the circumstances.
- Even if the FS makes a mistake and experiences a bad outcome, he will learn from it and be a stronger and better person for the Lord.
- If the SS makes a mistake and experiences a bad outcome, he will not always learn from it and may not become stronger for the Lord.
- If the UBS makes a mistake and experiences a bad outcome, he will just call it bad luck and try to forget about it.

Jealousy and Envy

- Sometimes, a UBS pretends to be the SS or the FS in order to get the things that he sees others, who have been blessed by God, have.
- The UBS wants to receive the same blessings given by God to the SS and the FS but is not willing to believe and make the necessary sacrifices in order to receive them.
- The UBS really believes that when the time comes, he will be able to manipulate himself into heaven, just as he has manipulated others on earth.
- The heart of the UBS cannot hear the Lord's voice, so he hates the other sons of God for saying they can.

- Even though the UBS is jealous of the SS and the FS, the SS is also jealous of the freedom of both the UBS and the FS, but the FS is jealous of neither.

Suffering

- The FS will suffer more in the spirit and body, because these are the things the Father wants him to know. Suffering in the spirit and body brings the heart and mind closer to God.
- The SS will suffer more in the flesh, because these are the things the Father wants him to know. Suffering in the flesh brings the body closer to God.
- The UBS will not suffer much, because God does not chastise this son.
- If the FS suffers loss, he will carry himself as if nothing happened.
- If the SS suffers loss, he will let everyone know and ask for prayers and donations.
- If a UBS suffers loss, he will take from the other two sons of God and recover his losses quickly.
- If the FS sees another suffering, he will say to him, "How can I help you?"
- If the SS sees another suffering, he will say to him, "You need Jesus."
- If a UBS sees another suffering, he will say to him, "You're out of luck."
- Suffering to the FS tells him that he is being brought a step closer to the Lord.
- Suffering makes the SS feel like he is being pushed away from the Lord.
- Suffering makes the UBS feel like he may be losing his touch.

Spirituality

- The FS is predestined to be what he is, because he has already made the choice and his fate is sealed.
- The SS is not predestined to be what he is, because God waits for him to make the choice.
- The UBS will not make the choice, so his fate sealed, because of his unbelief.

- The FS is chosen by Christ, and there are only a few.
- The SS is called by God, and there are many.
- The UBS ignores the call from both God and Christ and chooses his own path.
- The FS will ask questions directly to the Father and expect an answer.
- The SS will not ask questions directly to the Father but indirectly through another man.
- The UBS will not ask God anything.
- The FS will ask his Father in heaven any question.
- The SS will ask only what he thinks he is allowed to.
- The UBS never asks questions.
- The FS will plan ahead for many years to come.
- The SS will plan ahead only for a short time.
- The LS will not plan but will only live life day by day.
- The FS is ready for death at any time and still lives life to its fullest.
- The SS is not ready for death and needs more time to get ready.
- The UBS is not prepared for death but invites it daily.
- The FS will take the blame for a small matter.
- The SS will sometimes take the blame for small matters.
- The UBS will not take the blame for anything, even if it is small.
- The sleep of the FS will always be peaceful, because he is not troubled.
- The sleep of the SS will not always be peaceful, because he is sometimes troubled.
- The sleep of the UBS will always be disturbed, because he is always troubled.
- The FS hates his flesh but will always enjoy his life.
- The SS hates his flesh and does not always enjoy his life.
- The UBS loves his flesh and his life.
- The SS and the UBS think that they are the sum of their outer identity.
- The FS knows that he is the sum of his inner identity.
- The FS hears two inner voices, one from the Lord and one from Satan, and knows the difference between the two, because he tries the spirit by the Spirit.

- The SS will hear two inner voices and think that both are the same and not know which to choose.
- The UBS will hear both inner voices and always choose the wrong one.
- The FS knows how to eat and drink spiritually.
- The SS somewhat knows how to eat and drink spiritually.
- The UBS only knows how to eat and drink naturally.
- The FS looks for what is right first in a matter and therefore sees the good first and then the bad.
- The SS looks for what is wrong first in a matter and therefore sees the bad first and may never see the good.
- The UBS doesn't look for what is wrong, only what he thinks is right.
- The FS loves to spend time in the Spirit and with the Father.
- The SS spends only a small amount of time in the Spirit and with the Father, usually on Sundays while in church.
- The UBS does not spend any time with his natural or heavenly Father.
- The FS has overcome himself and is spiritually not a part of this world.
- The SS is still struggling with himself and is naturally still part of this world.
- The UBS loves himself just as he is but hates the world as it is.

Spiritual Body Parts
(Ears)

- The FS hears the voice of the Holy Spirit and Satan and knows the difference.
- The SS hears the voice of the Holy Spirit and Satan and does not know the difference.
- The UBS thinks that the other two are crazy.
- The FS will be able to listen to the person he is talking to and at the same time hear the Holy Spirit advising them as to what to say immediately.
- The SS will listen to a person and when that person is finished say, "I will pray for you."
- The UBS will not even take the time out to listen.

- The FS will be able to hear the faults of a person when he or she speaks.
- The SS will only look for the faults of a person in his or her actions.
- The LS will never look for the faults in others, because he himself knows that he is so full of faults that he will not judge anyone.

Spiritual Body Parts
(Eyes)

- The eyes of the FS see what is right and wrong in the world.
- The eyes of the SS see only what is wrong with the world.
- The eyes of the UBS see only selfish desires.
- The eyes of the FS are clear and can see far.
- The eyes of the SS are somewhat hazy and cannot see far.
- The eyes of the UBS are blinded and cannot see at all.
- The eyes of the FS see spiritually and cannot be fooled by spiritual or natural things.
- The eyes of the SS see naturally and cannot be fooled by natural things.
- The eyes of the LS cannot see past his own ways.
- The veil has been removed from the eyes of the FS.
- The veil has not been removed from the SS.

Spiritual Body Parts
(Heart)

- The LS has said in his heart, "I know I'm going to hell," and keeps on going against the will of God.
- The SS has said in his heart, "I must stop what I am doing, or I will go to hell," and tries to do the will of God.
- The FS has said in his heart, "I have changed," and is following the will of God.
- The heart of the FS is like refined gold.
- The heart of the SS is like refined silver.
- The heart of the UBS is like iron and cannot be refined; heat won't melt it.
- The heart of the FS is like a diamond that was formed from extreme pressure.

- The heart of the SS is like coal, still under pressure to become a diamond.
- The heart of the UBS is under no pressure to become anything.
- The veil has been removed from over the FS's heart.
- The veil has not yet been removed from the SS's or the UBS's heart.
- The FS will help a person out of the goodness of his heart and not expect to receive a return.
- The SS will help a person out of the goodness of his heart and expect something in return.
- The UBS will not help anyone.
- The heart of the FS is filled with love.
- The heart of the UBS is filled with love and hate.
- The heart of the SS is only filled with hate.

Spiritual Body Parts
(Mouth)

- The FS will know another FS by the words that come out of his mouth.
- The SS will know another SS by the words that come out of his mouth.
- The UBS will know another UBS by the words that come out of his mouth.
- From the mouth of the FS, rivers of water shall flow.
- From the mouth of the SS, only drops of water shall fall.
- From the mouth of the UBS, there is only dust.
- The SS will ask another SS if he is saved and believe that SS if he says he is saved by word of mouth alone and not because of the fruit the person produces.
- The FS will know another person is saved not by asking but because of the fruit the person produces from his or her mouth.
- The UBS will know that he is talking to a saved person without asking as well because of the words that come out of the person's mouth, which he hates.
- The FS will not need to prepare what he will say in order to help someone spiritually.

- The SS will use only prepared words and prayers to help someone spiritually.
- The UBS will use prepared words also but only to help himself take advantage of someone else's problems.
- The FS will know when and when not to answer, and when he does answer, it will be an answer that is intended not to cause anger.
- The SS will not know when and when not to answer, and when he answers, it will not always be a soft answer that will attempt to remove anger.
- The UBS will find a way to avoid answering at all, or if he does, it will cause anger.
- The FS will know that the power of life and death is in his mouth, because it reveals what is in his heart.
- The SS thinks that the power of life and death is in his actions only and not in his mouth.
- The UBS thinks that the power of life and death is in strength of arms or the weapons he carries.
- The FS knows that he will be rewarded either good or bad for every word that proceeds out of his mouth.
- The SS and the UBS do not know this.
- The mouth of the FS will only bless you and not curse you.
- The mouth of the SS will both bless and curse you.
- The mouth of the LS will only curse you.

Spiritual Food

- The FS knows how to eat and drink spiritually.
- The SS knows how to eat and drink spiritually, somewhat.
- The LS only knows how to eat natural foods.
- The FS no longer hungers because he has received the meat of the Word, because what he has eaten continues to fill him up continuously.
- The SS still hungers for more, because he has only received the milk of the Word, and he will need to eat again and again and again.
- The FS will give you bread, meat, and water to eat in abundance, because this is what he was given.
- The SS will give you bread and milk to eat sparingly, because this is what he was given.

- The UBS will give you a stone, which is no food at all.

Spiritual Water

- The FS no longer thirsts for the knowledge, because he has drunk the water that causes him to never thirst again, because it continues to quench his thirst.
- The SS still thirsts for knowledge, because the water he drank cannot cure his thirst forever.
- The UBS only knows of natural water, and he will thirst again.
- The FS knows that this water is the understanding that comes from the Holy Spirit and the fire baptism.
- The SS thinks this water is the water that comes from the water baptism.
- The FS knows that the source of this water is the river of God; his people are mixed with the Holy Spirit.
- The SS thinks this water is made spiritual by many prayers.
- The FS knows that this water can come from his mouth and can be used for healing.
- The SS does not always use the water in his well this way.

Spiritual Weapons

- The FS knows how to use the armor of God.
- The SS only knows about the armor of God.
- The LS uses money for his armor.
- The FS knows how put the armor on and keep it on.
- The SS only knows about the armor of God.
- The UBS uses only man-made weapons to fight his battles.

What Each Son of God Will Say to Himself

- The FS knows the will of the Father in all situations, so he does not say, "If it be his will, let it be done."
- The SS, since he does not always know what the will of the Father is will say, "If it be your will, let it be done."
- The SS does not understand the actions of the FS and will say to him, "Why have thou forsaken the church?" However, what the SS does not know is that it is impossible for the FS to forsake the church because he carries the church with him wherever he goes.

- The SS does not understand the actions of the FS and will say to him, "Why do you not observe the traditions of the church?" He will say this because he does not see the FS doing the same things that he does, but what the SS does not know, is that Jesus came to get rid of all the traditions of man.

- The SS does not understand the actions of the FS and says to him, "You are wrong because you stand alone. The majority stands with me; therefore, I must be right. I would rather stand with the majority than by myself," but what the SS does not know is the FS is never alone, because the Holy Spirit is with him and gives him the strength to stand apart from the crowd.

- If the FS communes with the SS and the FS tells the SS something he has never heard before, the SS will say to the FS, "If you cannot prove it to me, I will not believe you," but what the SS does not know is that neither the FS nor the SS can prove anything that he believes, because both are supposed to live by faith, not by sight.

- The FS will see a person in need and say, "How can I help you?"

- The SS will see a person in need and say, "He is getting what he deserves," and "If you are not willing to repent, I will not help you."

- The UBS will see a person in need and say, "What a great opportunity for me to take advantage of this person."

- If the Lord says, "Pick up your bed and walk," to the FS, he will do it.

- If the Lord says, "Pick up your bed and walk," to the SS, he will say, "Only if you help me, Lord."

- If the Lord says, "Pick up your bed and walk," to the UBS, he will say, "Let me see you do it first, because I don't believe it can be done."

- The FS will set goals and watch them carefully to make sure they happen.

- The SS will set goals and say, "Whatever will be, will be. I'll pray about it."

- The UBS will never set goals.

- Ask the FS about God, and he will be happy to talk with you about him.

- Ask the SS about God, and he will say to you, "Church begins at 11:00 am on Sunday."
- Ask the UBS about God, and he will say, "What God?"
- The FS waits to hear from the Lord to make a decision.
- The SS does not wait long but makes his own decision quickly and says to himself, "This is what the Lord wants me to do."
- The UBS does not wait at all, for anything or anyone.

Chapter Seven

The Spiritual Dictionary of Symbolic Words

This is a spiritual dictionary, and I believe it is the first and only of its kind. This dictionary has taken many years to make and is still growing. I originally started compiling this dictionary as an aid only for myself, so that it would help me in the understanding of God's symbolic language while reading his Word. I needed this because I noticed that God was using spiritual words instead of speaking of exactly whom he was referring to. At first, I did not understand why he did this, but now I have come to understand that he was ensuring some things remained hidden from certain people. This is why the Bible calls it hidden manna, or hidden bread, Rev 2:17. Now with the writing of this dictionary, God has chosen the time to reveal his secrets to the world.

One of the ways to begin to understand the symbolic language is to know that God uses natural things to try to explain spiritual things, this is how the Bible is written, naturally so that a person would even have a chance at understanding spiritual things. He had no choice in this matter since we live in a natural world, but God does not. These natural words are an attempt to help us understand how the spiritual world operates, and at the same time, by showing us this, he is attempting to show us how the natural world should operate.

This dictionary has taken more than ten years to compile. It started with me taking note of words that seemed to be out of place, as I read the Bible. I simply could not understand why these words were used. At first, I thought that the author of the Bible had made mistakes in putting these words in the Bible. Then I thought maybe when the Bible was translated into English, they accidentally put them in the Bible. So I sought to record these words in order to find their true meaning, and that was what God wanted me to do all along. If a person were to look these words up in a regular dictionary to find their natural meaning and then cross-reference them with every place they are found in the Bible, he or she would get a true sense of how God is using the word. The more of these so-called misplaced words I accumulated, the more I understood, and finally after so many words had accumulated, I realized I was able to speak a new language. This language is called the symbolic language. This is the language God speaks to man, in order to hide his true meaning from those who hate him. This is a language only the chosen of God can speak. He gave them this language so that they could also keep it hidden. With the understanding of this language, all things the Bible has hidden are revealed to you. This is what I believe God wants me to share with my fellow brothers in Christ. He wants me to share the understanding of these words, which are the key to understanding the Bible, from a spiritual perspective.

The format I will be using to share the understanding of these words is to first give the natural definition as found in any English dictionary. Then I will redefine that same word spiritually, followed up by referencing that word in other places in the Bible in order to aid in bringing out the spiritual meaning of that word as well as by showing a relationship between that symbolic word and others found throughout the Bible. These words will found at the bottom of the defined word and will not be in any particular order. By connecting these words to the one defined another mystery that God has hidden from most will start to be revealed and that is the meaning of certain patterns that God uses. These patterns come in the form of numbers, words, and in the way God has chosen to name certain things. Understanding the symbolic language is the key to unraveling those mysteries. This language cannot be found in a standard biblical dictionary or any other dictionary of which I am aware of because a spiritual definition cannot be proven or quantified.

Remember, this language has been kept hidden simply because it was not time yet to reveal his plan; unfortunately, this also kept what God was doing behind the scenes from those who are babes in Christ. You might say to yourself, "Why would God hide anything from those he loves?" You must understand that Satan wants to know what God is doing also, so that he can stop God from doing his will. God asks us to live by faith, which is the evidence of things not seen and the substance of things hoped for. We are not supposed to need hard evidence of the things that he has done or is doing. Those of us who have come into spiritual maturity can both see and understand what God is showing us, only because he wanted some to know, but if we did not, we would have kept on living by faith. However, God has chosen this time for me to share the meaning of these spiritual words as well as how he is using them as found in the Bible with the rest of my brethren. I will share these words as the Holy Spirit has shared them with me, in the hopes that it might mature those of you whose destiny it is to become mature in the understanding of God's word and will.

The Symbolic Dictionary

adopted sons

natural—those taken into one's family through legal means and raised as one's own children.

spiritual—A legal way of gaining a son, made possible by the death of Christ, whose life was sacrificed for the payment of the world's sins, so that many people could be grafted into the family of God; those having become the son or daughter of a new father, through the blood of Christ; those who have become related spiritually, which means to be born again; those allowed to have the same privileges as a natural born son or heir, made possible by faith in Christ, through the Holy Spirit. This is the fulfillment of the second covenant of God, which is the promise made to Abraham by God that his seed would receive the Holy Spirit (Heb. 8:13). They who receive this seed are then called the children of promise, because of the promise God made to Abraham and to his seed (Rom. 9:8.) At that time, Abraham becomes our earthly father and God becomes our heavenly father; even though it is good to be adopted into the family of God by being born again (John 3:3) because that person will inherit the kingdom of God if he or she makes the right choice, which is to choose Christ, it is not the same as being a natural son that was born from the Father. They do not need to be born again because they are already born of God 1 John 3:9; this kind of son is called an heir (Rom. 8:17).

173

The inheritance of the kingdom was predestined for him or her to receive because he or she was born an heir (Eph. 1:11); not all people are predestined to be heirs, so in order for God to bring these people into the kingdom, He had to adopt them. Their adoption will depend on one choice, and that is whether or not they choose Christ (Gal. 4:5). (Ref. Prov. 29:21; Mal. 1:6; Matt. 20:16; Matt. 22:14; John 8:35; Rom. 8:15–23; Rom. 9:4–8; 1 Cor. 3:2; 1 Cor. 7:17–24; Gal. 4:5–7; Eph. 1:5; Heb. 5:13; 1 Pet. 2:2; Rev. 17:14.) See also **born-again**; **called**; **called son**; **servant son**; **heir**; **chosen son**; **free son**; **predestined son**; **promised son**; **children of promise**.

adult son

natural—A son who was once a child who has reached maturity in the natural sense; someone who can make natural decisions without help from anyone else or without supervision.

spiritual—A son who was once a child who has reached maturity in the spiritual sense; someone who can make spiritual decisions with the help of the Spirit because the Spirit gave him spiritual understanding. Now he lives by faith. This is the opposite of those who live by sight. They are called babies in Christ. (Ref. Gal. 4:4; 1 Cor. 2:6; 1 Cor. 8:1; Phil. 3:15.) See also **full son**; **heir**; **son**; **anointing**; **free son**; **mature**.

adulterous woman

natural—A woman caught in the act of cheating on her husband; a woman guilty of having a sexual relationship with one man while being married to another.

spiritual—A group of people who will be lost, whose names are not written in the book of life. They are people who have turned against God. They do not believe in God. They are haters of God. They are different from those who fornicate against God, because spiritual fornication can be forgiven but not spiritual adultery. This is because those who commit spiritual fornication are unaware that they are doing so, but those who commit spiritual adultery are aware of the choices they have made and therefore are not committing this sin in ignorance. (Ref. Jer. 29:23; Ezek. 16:1–63; Hosea 4:14; Matt. 5:25–32; Rev. 2:17–23.) See also **female**;

feminine; lost son; lost woman; chosen woman; fornicating woman; desolate woman; bramble tree; tares; fowl.

adultery

natural—Having a natural affair with another man or woman after having proclaimed your love for your husband or wife and having been found guilty of cheating on one's spouse; letting someone else come between you and your wife or husband.

spiritual—Having a spiritual affair with another God after having proclaimed your love for God the Father and having been found guilty by your God, the Father of Jesus Christ; having once believed in God, but doing so no longer; a person who has stopped believing in God and started believing in another god or no god at all; to give up on God; to lose faith in God; to be no longer satisfied with God, so you take another. Our God is a jealous God, and He will be very angry with those who have put another god in His place. Israel was once married to God before He gave them a letter of divorce because they started worshiping another god called Baal. He gave them a letter of divorce because of this; this is called spiritual adultery. If we are married to him, by believing in Him, then we belong to Him. He has a right to be jealous of those whom He loves. Whom He loves He calls His bride. This, however, is not the same as fornication, which means a person never stops believing in God, but constantly puts other things ahead of Him, which pushes Him away from them. (Ref. Exod. 20:14; Exod. 34:14; Deut. 4:24; Deut. 6:15; Prov. 6:32; Jer. 3:8; Jer. 5:7.) See also **married; divorced; fornication; idolatry; woman.**

air

natural—What all life on the planet needs to breathe in order to sustain life.

spiritual—God calls air the breath of life. The breath of life keeps all things that breathe alive. Air is one of the four basic elements of life, which are air, water, earth, and fire. Air is also a symbolic word for a group of people born with a certain gift of God. There are three other elements, four altogether, and each group sees and understands God from a different perspective. The people of the air element see and understand God from the aspect of their intelligence. (Ref. Gen. 2:7; Gen. 7:15; Job 33:4.) See also **breath of life; element, air.**

agape, love

> **natural**—Man's attempt at unconditional love through religion, which eventually becomes conditional and fails.
>
> **spiritual**—Man's attempt at unconditional love through the Holy Spirit, which remains unconditional and never fails. (Ref. Matt. 5:43; Matt. 19:19; Matt. 22:39; John 13:34; Rom. 13:10). See also **love; forgiveness; grace.**

Ancient of Days

> **natural**—N/A
>
> **spiritual**—Another spiritual name for Jesus Christ, who will pass judgment on the earth at the appointed time. (Ref. Isa. 7:9–22; Dan. 7:9, 13–22.) See also **Christ; judgment; son, the.**

angels of God

> **natural**—A messenger, created to be a servant son of God; a spiritual being who lives in heaven with God but is not an heir to the throne of God.
>
> **spiritual**—A formerly spiritual being who has yet to be born on earth through a woman or has been born, lived, died, and returned to the Father in heaven. The Bible says this in Revelation 19:10:

> And I fell at his feet to worship him. And he said unto me, See thou do it not: I am thy fellowservant, and of thy brethren that have the testimony of Jesus: worship God: for the testimony of Jesus is the spirit of prophecy ...

This is where our spirits come from. Our spirits have put on flesh and have become the spirit of the man, for the purpose of training or learning the difference between good and evil. This is the same thing that that the Bible says happened to Christ in order that he could save his brethren in Hebrews 2:7–11:

> Thou madest him a little lower than the angels; thou crownedst him with glory and honour, and didst set him over the works of thy hands: Thou hast put all things in subjection under his

feet. For in that he put all in subjection under him, he left nothing that is not put under him. But now we see not yet all things put under him. But we see Jesus, who was made a little lower than the angels for the suffering of death, crowned with glory and honour; that he by the grace of God should taste death for every man. For it became him, for whom are all things, and by whom are all things, in bringing many sons unto glory, to make the captain of their salvation perfect through sufferings. For both he that sanctifieth and they who are sanctified are all of one: for which cause he is not ashamed to call them brethren.

All this was done because with the experience we gain from being in this world, we would never again make the incorrect choice of whom to follow: God or Satan. Those angels who made the choice to follow the angel Lucifer and lost the war, became known as the fallen sons of God, or demons. That there was a war in heaven is the evidence that the angels were not perfect—at least in the understanding of who God was and what he stood for. This meant that the rest of the angels were in need of training. This is where God came up with the idea of remaking them in a form lower than that of an angel, in order to train them. In the beginning, all angels were servant sons of God, not heirs. This means they could not inherit the kingdom of God, and this is why the Bible says in Hebrews 1:5 that they were not heirs—heirs to the throne that is. Angels also didn't know what was going on or what God's plan was for them, because they were not heirs. In 1 Peter 1:12, it says,

Unto whom it was revealed, that not unto themselves, but unto us they did minister the things, which are now reported unto you by them that have preached the gospel unto you with the Holy Ghost sent down from heaven; which things the angels desire to look into; and if not heirs what was their fate since?

The Bible even says that they are not subject to the world to come. In Hebrews 2:5, it says, "For unto the angels hath he not put in subjection the world to come, whereof we speak." This was done because a servant cannot inherit the kingdom of God, so then we would need to become heirs, which is made possible by faith in Christ. This is how angels become greater than they were before, by being born again through the womb of a woman in order to have the opportunity to become an heir and not just a servant. We are them, and they are us—our spirits, that is, which exist within us. (Ref. Job 4:18; Ps. 85:8; Heb. 1:5, 13; Heb. 2:7; Rom. 8:14, 19; 1 Pet. 1:12.) See also **brother; brethren; sons; mature sons; full sons; man.**

anger

natural—A strong feeling of displeasure; losing one's temper; being upset; not being in good spirits.

spiritual—Having a lack of patience with a given situation. When anger sets in, it opens the door for Satan to come into the heart of a person. Satan wants to take over the heart because this is what God talks to us from. Taking over the heart cancels out all reasoning, which comes from God. By reasoning with us, God tries to talk to man. Anger also causes the Holy Spirit to leave your heart. If a person does this too often, the Holy Spirit will stop returning. This is how we grieve the Holy Spirit. He becomes grieved because he cannot reason with us. The Father has commanded us not to grieve the Holy Spirit. Anger is a temporary loss of faith in oneself and in God. Anger acts like cancer. It can eat away at the soul and spirit. This will cause the spiritual body and the physical body to die. (Ref. Ps. 37:8; Ps. 38:3; Prov. 15:18; Prov. 16:32; Eph. 4:31; Col. 3:8–21.) See also **armor; forgiveness; fruits.**

anger of God

natural—N/A

spiritual—The anger of God is shown through the natural elements of the earth, which are really the spiritual elements of the Holy Spirit. The natural elements as we know them are really different spiritual elemental forms of the Holy Spirit that manifest themselves into the natural elements. The natural elements, which are water, air, earth, and fire, are physical manifestations of the Holy Spirit, because they are the natural as well as the spiritual building blocks of life. God uses the natural manifestations of the Spirit to punish man in the form of these same elements when God chooses to show his anger. He uses water in the form of a flood. He uses air in the form of strong wind. He uses earth and causes earthquakes. He can also use fire in a destructive way as well. These same elements can be used to create as well as destroy, so when God is angry, he uses these elements in their destructive forms. His anger in the form of a flood appears in Genesis 6:17. His anger in the form of air or wind appears in Jeremiah 18:17, in the form of earth in Luke 21:11, and in the form of fire in Isaiah 5:24 and Revelation 20:9. (Ref. Gen. 6:17; Isa. 5:24; Jer. 18:17; Luke 21:11; Rev. 20:9.) See also **wrath of God; elements of God; chastise; Holy Spirit; God.**

anointing

natural—To rub or sprinkle on; to apply an unguent, ointment, or oily liquid to; to apply oil for a sacred right; the placing of sacred oil on one's head in order to appoint or cleanse.

spiritual—There is a physical anointing, and there is a spiritual anointing. The spiritual anointing is the receiving of God's Holy Spirit, which is also known as the seal. To be sealed is to be saved without the possibility of losing salvation. This anointing makes it possible for the proper communication between man and his creator. The anointing, or Holy Spirit, was given in order to teach man all things about the Father and Son. The anointing is also called the baptism by fire, because God is the only one who can give this kind of anointing or baptism. Man can only give the water baptism, which is a baptism unto repentance and not a baptism unto salvation. (Ref. Matt. 3:11; Mark 1:8; Luke 12:50; 1 John 2:27; John 3:33; Rom. 4:11; 1 Cor. 12:13; 2 Tim. 2:19.) See also **Holy Spirit; seal; blessings; baptism by fire; water; unction; salted by fire.**

Antichrist

natural—A man who will do the will of Satan from a natural standpoint, which is to kill, take power, and morally demean others.

spiritual—A man who will do the will of Satan from a spiritual standpoint, which is to try to cause spiritual death by forcing people not to believe in Christ. This man receives his power and will from Satan but is completely unaware he is serving Satan. There have been a total of four of these men in history. There are two more to come; the next will be part of the fifth kingdom, and the last will control the sixth kingdom that is to come. People will not recognize the last Antichrist, because he will begin to gain power by helping to bring peace on the earth, and he will be religious, although he does not believe in any God, good or evil. He simply wants power. (Ref. Dan. 7:22–Dan. 11:31; Rev. 17:1–14; Rev. 20:1–10.) See also **horns; beast; dragon; Assyrian, the.**

armor

natural—Any covering worn as a defense against weapons for defensive or offensive purposes; protects the body in a natural battle; it is put on naturally.

spiritual—Any covering worn as a defense against weapons of defensive or offensive purposes; protects the body in a spiritual battle. This armor protects the spiritual body in spiritual warfare. It is put on spiritually by understanding love, patience, kindness, wisdom, truth, and faith. (Ref. Eph. 6:11–17; Rom. 13:12; Thess. 5:8.) See also **weapons**.

asleep

natural—To be in a partial or total state of unconsciousness naturally, unaware of what is going on around you.

spiritual—To be in a partial or total state of unconsciousness spiritually; to be unaware of what is going on around you in a spiritual sense. In a spiritual sense, sleep mimics death. Spiritually, death and sleep are no different. In both cases, a person is completely unaware of anything that is going on around him or her. God can wake a person from it. This is why Jesus said that when we die, we sleep in the Lord. This type of sleep means to lie in your grave and wait to see the Lord's face. When we are awakened, we will have no memory of how much time has passed, just like we do in the natural sense. We have to look at a clock to tell how much time has passed. In either case, a person only wakes from sleep because the Father allows it. In the grave or during a spiritual sleep, a person's spirit becomes separated from his or her soul therefore fulfilling the scripture found in II Cor 5:6-8, which says, "absent from the body, present with the father." (Ref. Ps. 30:5; Dan. 12:2; John

11:12–13; Rom. 11:8; 1 Cor. 15:16–18, 51; 1 Thess. 4:14–18.) See also **dead in the Lord; death; drunken; spirit of slumber**.

Assyrian, the
    natural—N/A
    spiritual—The hidden spiritual name of Satan. God uses this name as a disguise, so that men will not know about whom the Lord is talking. Most people who read the scriptures that contain references to the Assyrian think that God is talking about a man, because a real man was used to carry out the punishments that God placed on his people, Israel. However in the spiritual sense, he is talking to the spirit that is in the man who was used to carry out the punishment upon his people, for their disobedience. Just as God operates through people, Satan does the same. (Ref. Isa. 10:1–34; Isa. 14:24–27; Isa. 19:23; Ezek. 31:1–18; Mic. 5:5.) See also **Satan; spirit of the Antichrist**.

atonement
    natural—Satisfaction or reparation for a wrong or injury; to make amends or to reconcile one's differences with another.
    spiritual—Satisfaction or reparation for our sins through the death of Christ; receiving the forgiveness of God through believing in his son. This is how we receive the forgiveness that only God can give, which is for the covering of our sins. (Ref. Rom. 5:11.) See also **forgiveness; grace; love**.

authority
    natural—The power to determine, adjudicate, or otherwise settle issues or disputes; jurisdiction; the right to control, command, or determine; a person or body of persons in whom authority is vested, as a governmental agency.
    spiritual—The side of God that cannot reproduce itself in man. It can only be given to man, or Christ for that matter. This is what is considered the masculine or male side of God, meaning that which cannot be reproduced. (Ref. Matt. 7:29; Matt. 21:24–27; Mark 1:27; Mark 13:34; Luke 4:36; Luke 9:1; 2 Cor. 10:8.) See also **male part of God; masculine part of God; power; glory; honor; righteousness; wrath; holiness**.

babe

natural—A child; not yet an adult.

spiritual—A beginner in the Christian faith; a new Christian; or anyone with only a little understanding of the Christian faith, the Bible, or the Father and his son Jesus. Because of his or her lack of understanding, according to Paul the apostle, this person only drinks the milk of the word. It is a comparison to a baby, because a baby cannot eat meat. It will make him or her sick, and Paul says it is the same for some who try to eat the meat of the Word. They will not be able to hold it in. So, because he or she can't stomach meat, which is to have a full understanding of the Lord's Word, this person settles for just enough to get saved, which is the milk of the Word. The milk is the understanding that Christ died for our sins. This is small in comparison to those who eat the meat of the Word. If you eat the meat, you are called a mature Christian. The mature Christian not only eats the meat but also the eats the bread and drinks the water. If a person eats and drinks spiritually, he or she will never hunger or thirst again. The babe in Christ is in need of the bread, meat, and water, in order for them to never thirst or hunger again, but because he or she doesn't eat or drink, they hunger and they thirst. (Ref. Heb. 5:13–14; 1 Cor. 3:2; 1 Pet. 2:2.) See also **milk; religion; servant; child son; bread; meat; water**.

baptism by fire

natural—N/A

spiritual—This is the baptism that can only be given by God. It is called the anointing. Since God chooses whom he anoints, there is nothing a person can do to get this baptism. Only God knows the heart, and by this, he knows who has the faith for which he is looking. This baptism will cause a person show the fruit of the spirit, because God is literally living inside the person in the form of the Holy Spirit. The Holy Spirit will instruct, guide, teach, direct, and train these people in the ways of the Lord therefore transforming them in the image of Christ by bringing them into full understanding of the mind of Christ. Such people do not need to have the baptism by water, which is unto repentance, because they have already been forgiven of their sins. There is no need to repent. If they do, it is because they don't fully understand yet. They also do not need to receive the baptism of water in order to receive the baptism by fire. It can be done by God alone and not by the works of man. An example would be the thief on the cross and the people at the house of Cornelius; the thief on the cross received salvation simply by having faith in Christ while on the cross. He did not receive a water baptism but a fire baptism, which is through faith in Christ. The people at Cornelius's house who received the Holy Spirit without a water baptism also received a fire baptism, because they had faith when Peter preached to them. (Ref. Matt. 3:11; Matt. 20:22–23; Matt. 21:25; Mark 1:4, 8; Mark 9:49; Mark 10:38–39; John 1:26; Acts 10:43–48; Acts 11:1–18;Acts 19:3–4; Rom. 6:4; 1 Cor. 1:17; 1 Cor. 12:13; Col. 2:12; 1 Pet. 3:17–22.) See also **anointing**; **Holy Spirit**; **baptism of water**; **water**; **living water**; **cup**; **blood**; **salt**; **salted by fire**; **saved**; **born-again**; **chosen son**; **free son**; **unction**; **barren women**; **fire**; **kindled**.

baptism by water

    natural—An immersion into water; an act of dedication; an outward show of one's faith; this is also known as the baptism of repentance. Dipping people in water and raising them out of it is a symbolic representation of the death and resurrection of Christ, so that by submitting to this, one is saying one is willing to follow Christ into the grave by going underwater, and by faith, he will raise one from that grave.

    spiritual—The water symbolizes the death and burial of Christ; coming out of the water symbolizes the resurrection of Christ. It is a show of faith that saves the soul of man. Coming through the water symbolizes coming out of the grave, which is the equivalent of being born again through the Spirit. The water symbolically represents the Holy Spirit, who truly washes the sins of that person away. The water baptism does however bring salvation, but not by the washing away of sin, but by the showing of faith that also clears the conscience of a man, and brings that person into a relationship with God. This act, he is an open show of a person repenting from their sins. By this, God can grant forgiveness of sins. The latter part is up to God but not the beginning process. Only through the baptism by fire can a man or woman be forgiven of his or her sins outright. God has already decided to whom he would give this type of baptism before he or she was born. He has already decided to give that person forgiveness, even before that person asked for it. This is what it means to be chosen. (Ref. Matt. 3:11; Matt. 20:22–23; Matt. 21:25; Mark 1:4, 8; Mark 10:38–39; John 1:26; Acts 19:3–4; Rom. 6:4; 1 Cor. 1:17; 1 Pet. 3:17–22; Col. 2:12.) See also **circumcised; saved; water; born-again; chosen; called**.

barren woman

natural—A woman who cannot produce offspring naturally.

spiritual—A woman who cannot produce offspring spiritually because this woman is one of the three spiritual women the Bible speaks of who already has a set number of children from before the foundation of the world. They number 288,000, consisting of the first and the second 144,000. They are the chosen of God. She is not a literal woman but is called a woman, because of the nature of the spirit that is in her, meaning she can reproduce sons by the hearing of the word. She is a group of people who make up the bride. She is the bride of Christ, which consists of the first and second 144,000. The first 144,000 are of Israel, as mentioned in Revelation 7:1; the second 144,000 are from the Gentiles, as mentioned in Revelation 14:1. All chosen were born from the womb of earthly women whose wombs were previously barren, or from a women who were virgins, because there is no difference between a barren or virgin woman in God's eyes because both have never given birth before. According to the Bible, if a woman is a virgin or barren, God places the chosen in her womb, because the chosen are born from the will of God, not by the will of man, because they are predestined to know the will of God. However, before they learned his will, they first learned the will of themselves as well as man's will, which are both against God. While they were children, they did not know they were chosen and lived as servants of God, until the appointed time when God was ready for them to come into the understanding they were meant to come into, which is the understanding of his will. (Ref. Gen. 11:30; Gen. 25:21; Gen. 29:31; Judg. 13:2; Isa. 2:5; Ps. 113:9; Isa. 54:1; Luke 1:7; Luke 23–29; Gal. 4:26.) See also **chosen; chosen woman; female; elect; seed; firstfruit; wheat; fig tree, second; virgin; virgin, woman; baptism of fire; promised son; rain; rain former; rain latter**.

bear

> **natural**—A carnivore that eats flesh; that kills its enemy with one blow or one bite.
>
> **spiritual**—Symbolizes a type of government that in war delivers a very fast, crushing blow to its enemy; the second of the first four beasts that were destined to rule the earth for a time; the kingdom of Media and Persia. This beast or government is headed by a type of Antichrist, because it is the second of the six beasts that must rule until Christ comes. (Ref. Dan. 7:5–7.) See also **beast; lion; leopard; dragon; dragon, two-headed; dragon, seven-headed; dragon, combined; horns; horns, ten.**

beast

> **natural**—A carnivore that eats flesh.
>
> **spiritual**—A carnivorous type of government that spiritually eats the flesh of its citizens. This is done by making them follow its will instead of the will of God. Any form of government that is ruled by Satan, through the embodiment of a man or in biblical terms a type of Antichrist. This form of government thinks it is capable of self rule, without the aid of God. This is also why God calls this type of government a beast, because it will not follow his will. All governments should follow God's will; if not, they will be destroyed by God. (Ref. Dan. 7:5–7, 11, 19, 23; Rev. 13:1–18. See also **government; bear.**

beget

> **natural**—To bring into existence naturally; to give birth to naturally; to bring back; to produce; to make; to claim what is yours; to redeem or to retrieve what was lost.
>
> **spiritual**—To bring into existence spiritually; to give birth spiritually; to recover what has been lost; to cause to live again after its death; to be brought into the family of God; to be grafted in; to be adopted into the family of God; to send the Holy Spirit to retrieve. (Ref. John 1:14, 18; John 3:16; Acts 13:33; 1 Cor. 4:15; Heb. 1:5; Heb. 5:5; 1 Pet. 1:3; 1 John 5:1, 18; Rev. 1:5.) See also **son; Jesus; firstborn; female; firstfruits; elects.**

believers, three kinds

natural—All people who believe in God.

spiritual—According to the parable of the sower, the seed was the word of God that fell on four different kinds of people with four different kinds of hearts, or soils. Only three types of people believed when they heard the Word of God, but of those three, only one pleased God. Only one received the Word the way God intended—the one for whom the seed fell upon good ground. When this person received the Word, the root grew and he or she produced fruit. This person is spiritually called a chosen son of God, or free son. The believer who received the word in his heart but his heart was stony is a servant son or called son of God; however, the stony part of this person's heart caused the seed to grow fast, but when the sun came up, it quickly dried up, because the seed could not take root, meaning this person was easily turned away from Christ. The believer who received the Word of God but has thorns on his heart is a believer and a servant son of God; however, because he has a heart that is full of thorns, he doesn't seem to be a believer, because he seems to care for material things of the world more than the Word of God. Thorns choke the Word of God, because Christ demands that we help the poor, but they that have thorns hold on to their possessions too tightly to give to the poor; therefore, the word of God does not grow in them. Nevertheless, they are saved, but they will never truly enjoy the Word of God or the fruits of the Spirit of God, because their hearts are not tender soil or good ground, but ground that is unkept according to the Word of God. Before the servant son, or called son, is ready to come into the kingdom of God, the soil in his heart must be cultivated and made more fertile. God uses different methods to soften this soil. This is also why there are different harvest times for the different types of sons of God. God also calls this chastising. (Ref. Prov. 29:21; John 8:35; Gal. 4:1–7; Matt. 13:1, 18.) See also **chosen son; called son; servant son; female; tribulations; trials; rapture; Zion; women, three kinds.**

believing

natural—Trusting in or accepting something as the truth.

spiritual—Trusting in Christ; accepting that he is your savior, which is the key to salvation. Belief leads to faith; one must believe before he or she can have faith. However, belief is not faith; not even strong belief is faith. Belief is turned into faith once it is acted upon, because belief not acted upon remains belief. Although salvation does come from just believing, one does not obtain righteousness until that belief is acted upon. The spiritual meaning of believing is eating, because one must eat the bread that is Jesus, if one wants salvation. The Bible is also called bread. One must read it, which means to eat it, for one's spirit to be fed. So to believe is to eat the bread that came down from heaven, which is Jesus Christ. Another way to understand that believing is also called eating is to look at it this way: before a person eats something, he or she has to trust that it will not harm his or her body and that it would be good for nourishment. This is the same way we must trust in the word of God. We must trust that it will nourish our spirits when we take it into our bodies. We have to trust that it is good for nourishing the spiritual body before swallowing it spiritually; so to read is to eat, and to eat is to trust in what you believe. (Ref. Matt. 26:26; John 6:50–58; Rom. 3:3, 22; Gal. 3:22; Eph. 2:8–9; 1 Thess. 4:14; Heb. 11:6; James 2:19; Rev. 2:7, 17.) See also **faith**; **saved**; **works**; **eating**; **belly**; **mouth**.

belly

> **natural**—The stomach of a man where natural foods are processed and sent throughout the body to nourish the natural body.
>
> **spiritual**—It is the soul of a man where spiritual foods are processed and sent throughout the spiritual body to nourish it; the soul is a man's personality, which makes him unique. His uniqueness is his character or his ego. All natural foods please the natural body and in turn please the soul of a man. This is the same way in which spiritual foods work, if the man would eat spiritual foods. If a man only eats to feed his natural body, his spirit suffers, and this will lead to depression. If a person eats to feed both his or her natural and spiritual body, then the person will be healthy both spiritually and naturally. Whichever a man feeds the most, the natural or the spiritual body, is the one that will be stronger. God wants us to feed our spirits, so that we may be stronger spiritually, and he wants to feed us with his Word. It is up to us as to whether or not we eat, which means to study his Word. (Ref. Job 15:2; Job 20:10–29; Ps. 31:9; Ps. 44:25: Prov. 13:25; Prov.

18:20; Matt. 15:17–20; John 7:38; Rom. 16:18; 1 Cor. 6:13; Phil. 3:19.) See also **ego**; **soul**; **ground**; **will**; **eating**.

Bible

natural—A book written by man, inspired by God, about his sons.

spiritual—A book written by man, inspired by God, about the works of his sons; in order to teach his sons who he is and how much he is willing to go through in order to save them. The Bible teaches that our heavenly father is the creator of the Word of God, who is his Son, who created all other things. We should love the Son, because he created us. The Bible also teaches that we should love one another and warns us of what will happen if we do not love one another as well as the Father and the Son. The spelling of the word Bible is an abbreviation which stands for **B**asic **i**nstructions **b**efore **l**eaving **e**arth. It contains the Gospel which means the truth, or God's words which are the source of true enlightenment written through men, through the Holy Spirit. (Ref. Prov. 30:5; Matt. 28:19; Acts 6:7; John 1:1; John 3:16; John 14:26; Rom. 10:17; 2 Tim 3:16.) See also **Gospel**; **truth**; **word of God**.

birds of the air

natural—A flying animal with feathers; some can eat seed as their main diet.

spiritual—The spiritual name for a bird is fowl. God calls them fowl because they are the spirits of the fallen angels, whose mission is to fly around from person to person in an attempt to enter into them so that they may cause turmoil and wreak havoc in that person's life. They mainly do so by preventing the Word of God from taking hold in the person's life, as spoken of in the parable of the sower. They take away the seed planted by another believer in that person's heart. They cause despair by causing that person to feel sadness and a sense of hopelessness, and this is what their main purpose is. The Gospel is designed to kick out these spirits from a person's heart, by offering them a sense of hope and assurance, through the spirit that is also in the world called the Holy Spirit, which helps the seed that is planted to grow. (Ref. Job 35:9–13; Ps. 79:1–5; Jer. 5:27; Matt. 13:1–10; 1 Cor. 15–39.)

See also **unbelievers; demons; fowl of the air; creeping things; cattle; man; fish.**

blasphemy

> **natural**—To speak against God; to take the Lord's name in vain.
>
> **spiritual**—To teach that God does not exist when the person knows within himself or herself that he does exist. This can only be done by a person who knows that God exists and not by a person who is ignorant of his existence. This is the one and only unforgivable sin. (Ref. Mark 3:28–29.) See also **sin; unbelief.**

blessings

> **natural**—Having good luck.
>
> **spiritual**—God's rewards for acts of faithfulness; God's way of showing a person that he is in his or her life; God answering our prayers; God giving us peace of mind; God giving us joy. (Ref. Matt. 5:1–12.) See also **reward; faith; works.**

blind

> **natural**—A person who cannot see naturally.
>
> **spiritual**—A person who cannot see spiritually; a person who has little or no knowledge of Christ and does not care to receive more. Where there is no vision, people perish. Those who are blind cannot see the kingdom of God, nor can they hear the Word of God. God has blinded most people, because of their unbelief. (Ref. Prov. 29:19; John 12:40; Rom. 11:7; 2 Cor. 4:4–6.) See also **drunken; death; veil; flesh; sight; vision; eye.**

blood of Jesus

> **natural**—N/A.
>
> **spiritual**—The only acceptable payment for our sins; if you are covered by the blood of Jesus, it is what God sees when he see your sins. Because Christ gave his blood, we have forgiveness for our sins; it is the only sacrifice that was pure enough or valuable enough for God to except as payment for the forgiveness of all sins, past, present, and future. His son was the ultimate sacrifice, because it was as if God himself was sacrificed since they share the same spirit. (Ref. Col. 1:9–14; Rom. 3:20–31; Rom. 5:9; 1

Pet. 1:19.) See also **wine; Holy Spirit; living water; forgiveness; grace; payment; Christ; judgment; third part.**

body of Christ

natural—N/A

spiritual—All who believe in Christ. They are called the church. They are also called the bride of Christ. Each individual member of the church is a part of the body of Christ—the spiritual body, that is. Each person is given gifts of the spirit to use, in order to support the body of Christ; for example, some function as the head. This is a pastor or father who is head of the family. Some are eyes. These are people who have the gift of discerning prophecy, as God reveals it to them. (Ref. 1 Cor. 15:34–43; 1 Cor. 12:12.) See also **church; bride, the; Christ; temple; vessel; container.**

body, new

natural—N/A

spiritual—The body that will be given to all who are resurrected; it is incorruptible, indestructible, and everlasting; the reward for belief in Christ. (Ref. 1 Cor. 3:16; 1 Cor. 15:35–55; 2 Cor. 5:1–21; 1 Pet. 1:19.) See also **reward; resurrection; spiritual body.**

body, old

natural—Your present body; the body of flesh.

spiritual—Your present body which is called a temporary house; weak; fragile; corruptible; destructible; full of sin; a temporary place to house the spirit in order to unite it with a soul. The earthly body is an example of heaven and earth coming together, because the body and soul are both earthly and the spirit is from heaven. (Ref. James 2:26.) See also **house; flesh; body, new; spirit, man's; soul.**

bondage

natural—Being held against your will naturally; being enslaved; being bound to something or someone.

spiritual—Being held against your will spiritually; being enslaved because of the lack of understanding of how the death of Christ has the power to save anyone who believes in him as his or her savior. Knowledge of who our savior is and why he died for our sins gives us the power to be free from sin, death, fear, and the law. If a person were to be free from the worry of these things, they would no longer be in bondage to them. (Ref. Isa. 13:4; John 8:31–37; Rom. 8:15–21; Gal. 3:1–29; Gal. 4:3–9, 24; Gal. 5:1–5; Heb. 2:15; 2 Pet. 2:18–22.) See also **knowledge**; **fear**; **veil**; **darkness**.

born again
natural—N/A
spiritual—Getting a second chance. Those whom the Lord will resurrect in the millennium, who will have a new purpose for living. They are resurrected in order to have an opportunity to drink from the fountains of living water. This water is the spiritual knowledge of who the Father, Son, and Holy Spirit are as well as what their purpose is for creating man in the first place. This water will save them from eternal damnation; it will cause the renewal of hope, through the renewing of the mind with the knowledge of Christ through the Holy Spirit. This water will change one's way of thinking and cause a person to pass from the darkness, which is not understanding God, into the light, which is the understanding of God. To be born again is to receive the water and bread, which cause a man to never hunger again, to change one's will toward God, or to do his will. Man cannot cause himself to be born again. This is up to God. This is what Jesus told Nicodemus. This is what happens to those who come to believe in Christ. They get a second chance. This is not the same for those who are not in need of being born again, because they were born of God from the beginning of their lives. Those who are born of God are called heirs and joint heirs with Christ. (Ref. John 1:13; John 3:1–16; Rom. 9:11; 2 Cor. 5:17; Gal. 4:1–7; 1 Pet. 1:23; 1 John 3:9; 1 John 5:1–7.) See also **saved**; **confess**; **believe**; **fire**; **fire baptism**; **called**; **called son**; **servant son**; **fire**; **refining process**.

born of God
natural—N/A
spiritual—Born from God, not by the will of man; born saved; chosen; no sin can be held against them because God will not count it against them; they are born with the Holy Spirit in them. They are sinless because according to 1 John 3:9, the seed remains in them, and they will not be held accountable for their sins;

predestined to be conformed into the image of Christ. They are heirs and joint heirs with Christ. (Ref. John 1:13; Rom. 8:29; Rom. 9:11; 1 Pet. 1:23; 1 John 3:9; 1 John 4:7; 1 John 5:4, 18; Rev. 7:4; Rev. 14:1–5.) See also **chosen**; **sealed**; **free son**; **heirs**; **seed**.

bowl

natural—A man-made container used for holding natural food or water; can be made of fragile material and easily broken.

spiritual—A God-made container used for holding spiritual food or water; this container is the heart or the soul of the man. The heart and soul were made to receive and contain the Word of God. They were also created to receive knowledge and understanding. If people fail to receive these things from God, God calls them broken vessels. The heart and soul can easily be broken if mishandled. This container is designed to hold spiritual water. Spiritual water is also known as the Holy Spirit; this container is also designed to let water flow out of it, which means to teach the Word of God. (Ref. Eccles. 12:6; Rom. 9:20–23.) See also **cistern**; **vessel**; **spirit**; **heart**; **water**; **lamp**; **light**; **food**; **cup**; **container**; **temple**.

branches, grafted in

natural—An extension of a tree, which grows leaves that collect sunlight in order to process their food.

spiritual—An extension of the tree of life, which is God. They grow when they have collected light that comes from the knowledge and understanding that only comes from the Holy Spirit. The Gentile Christian nation is the branch that was grafted in; the branch is an extension of the tree of life. The main branch is his son, called Jesus; people are also branches off of the main branch that is Jesus. When the proper nutrients are given, from the Word of God, along with the proper light and water, which are understanding mixed with the Holy Spirit, the branch will grow. If the branch refuses to receive nutrients, water, and light, it will not grow and it will be cut off. The branch that refuses to be nourished will dry up and become fuel for the fire. This fire is called hell, and it will burn forever. (Ref. Hosea 14:6; John 15:5; Rom. 11:15–25; Zech. 4:12; John 15:5.) See also **judgment**; **tree**; **vine**; **palm leaves**; **wheat**; **green things**; **Gentiles**.

brass

natural—A yellowish alloy of copper and zinc, sometimes including small amounts of other metals, but usually 67 percent copper and 33 percent zinc.

spiritual—A group of people who are the last to be saved by God. The other two groups, which are first and second, are gold and silver. They are also known as the chosen son, servant son, and the faithful son. The term *brass* is a symbolic way to describe a group of people based on the value of the metal. There are two other metals according to God that are more precious than brass; the difference in value of these metals is also an indication of the condition of the heart of the people in each of these groups. One group loves God more than the other and therefore is more willing to do his will and has proven it by their works. Only God determines the value of one's heart. The metal brass is also used as a symbolic representation of the third kingdom that controlled the known world. That kingdom was Greece. (Ref. Num. 31:21–24; Jer. 6:28; Ezek. 22:18–20; Dan. 2:32–45.) See also **gold**; **silver**; **heart**; **lost woman**; **fornication**; **woman**; **chosen woman**; **woman, three**.

bread

natural—Food for man, it nourishes the natural body; it is made from wheat. In biblical times, it was the staple of most diets.

spiritual—Food for man, it nourishes the spiritual body. This bread is the belief and knowledge of Christ, found in the Bible. To eat this bread, one must believe in the word of Christ. This is why Jesus said he was the bread of life: if a man followed his teachings, he would give eternal life to this person. Christ, who is the bread, can only be eaten by believing in him, but Jesus himself said that man cannot live by bread alone. This means that it is not enough for us to simply know of Christ's teachings; we must do them as well. This is what Jesus meant when he said that it is not good just to be a hearer of the Word; one must be a hearer and a doer. The Bible is also called bread. This is why in the Lord's Prayer, we start by saying, "Give us our daily bread," which means to give us daily understanding of his word. (Ref. Matt. 6:11; Matt. 16:11; John 6:31–58; 1 Cor. 10:17; 2 Cor. 9:10; 2 Thess. 3:12.) See also **hearing**; **eating**; **Christ**; **understanding**; **knowledge**; **spiritual food**; **bread of life**.

bread, leavened

> **natural**—Bread that has an agent added to it so that it will rise.
>
> **spiritual**—This is the bread that Jesus warns those who love him about; this bread is known as man's own understanding of the Word of God, which will not lead to the kingdom of God. This bread comes from those who say they follow God and whose intentions may even be good but who do not practice what they preach. Jesus referred to this bread as religion; in fact, they are often the first to turn to violence if their religion is discredited in any way. It refers to those with puffed-up knowledge who honor only themselves, those with only a little understanding of God's words, which have become mixed with the understanding of the world, which acts as an agent and puffs up the person who teaches it. This causes those who would otherwise follow all of Christ's teachings to only follow a few of Christ's teachings. They accomplish this by only pulling out what scriptures they think are relevant and getting rid of scriptures they think are not. These people teach the word of God for selfish reasons and are not truly inspired by God. (Ref. Exod. 12:15; Matt. 8:15; Matt. 13:33; 1 Cor. 5:6–8; Luke 13:18; Gal. 5:9.) See also **knowledge; servant son; milk; yeast.**

bread of life

> **natural**—N/A
>
> **spiritual**—The spiritual meaning of bread is knowledge, food for the spirit of a man. Bread is one of three known spiritual foods. The other three are the meat and the water, which are given to us by the Spirit of God. Another name for bread is Christ. Christ is the bread of life, meaning, if we listen and believe in him, we will live and not suffer the second death. The understanding of his life is as important to us as natural bread is to our physical bodies. This is what the Bible meant when it gave us the Lord's Prayer, where it says, "Give us our daily bread," meaning a daily understanding of his Word. If a person eats the bread or the Word of God and gets the understanding that God intended for the person to get, then God rewards that person with everlasting life. The bread also causes a person to never hunger again, meaning they stop seeking spiritual food from any other source because they have found what

they were looking for and are fully satisfied with the taste and content of the Word of God. This is how the bread causes a person to never hunger again. (Ref. Prov. 12:11; Prov. 20:17; Eccles. 11:1; Matt. 6:11; John 6:31–58; 1 Cor. 10:17; 2 Thess. 3:12.) See also **bread; Bible; Word of God; Christ; faith**.

bread, unleavened

natural—Bread that does not rise, because it has no agent in it; bread without yeast.

spiritual—This bread is the knowledge that comes from Christ, who is the bread of life. This bread does not puff a person up to make him or her believe that he or she is better or greater than another person. This bread is eaten by those with the belief and knowledge of Christ, who do not turn to violence when agitated and are not puffed up with worldly knowledge. They do not walk after the flesh. Those who eat this bread become firstfruits. It is also another name for Jesus. In the Jewish culture, they have a day called the feast of the unleavened bread. (Ref. Exod. 12:15; Mark 14:12; Luke 22:1; 1 Cor. 5:7–8.) See also **Jesus Christ; free son; knowledge; understanding; firstfruits**.

breath of life

natural—The air we breathe; oxygen.

spiritual—It is the air that God breathed into Adam in order to bring him to life. It is the same as air; there is no difference. (Ref. Gen. 2:7; Gen. 7:15; Job 33:4.) See also **air; spirit; life; element, air**.

brethren

natural—A kinsman; a relative; a fellow man; a fellow servant; a close friend.

spiritual—A kinsman; a relative; a fellow man; a fellow servant; a close friend; a brethren in the spiritual sense; a person whom the Holy Spirit lives in. This person is not just a believer in Christ, because believers don't necessarily have the Holy Spirit in them. It may only rest upon them in the form of the Holy Ghost, which caused them to just believe. (Ref. Matt. 12:46–50; Matt. 18:15; Rom. 7:1–25; Rom. 8:29; 1 Cor. 1:10; Gal. 4:21–31; Gal. 5:13;

Heb. 2:11–17; James 2:5; Rev. 6:11; Rev. 12:10; Rev. 19:10; Rev. 22:9.) See also **brother; angel; Holy Spirit; Holy Ghost.**

bride, new

natural—A natural woman who is just been married.

spiritual—A spiritual woman who is about to be married. This woman consists of many people. These people are called the chosen of God. They are also represented by the five virgins who had oil in their lamps. They are not just the believers in Christ; they are those who have been found faithful. The bride and the bridegroom are one. This woman is only called a woman because she has the Holy Spirit within her, which makes it possible for her to spiritually give birth to other sons of God. This is made possible by teaching them what the Holy Spirit has taught them. Other names for this woman are the chosen woman, the barren woman, the elect woman, the elects, those who have the seal, and the first and second 144,000. (Ref. 2 Kings 19:31; Isa. 49:18; Isa. 65:5; John 3:29; Gal. 4:26; Rev. 21:1–9; Rev. 22:17.) See also **fig tree, second; spiritual body; elects; chosen; sealed; predestined, the; Zion; Sion; hundred and forty-four thousand, first; hundred and forty-four thousand, second; bridegroom; sun; moon; stars.**

bride, old

natural—A woman who has been divorced.

spiritual—The house of Israel and Judah. They were issued a bill of divorce by God; however, they will be remarried when they accept Christ as their savior. (Ref. Jer. 3:1–8; Jer. 4:1; Ezek. 37:1–28.) See also **Jerusalem; Zion; whore of Babylon; crown.**

bridegroom

natural—The man who is about to be married.

spiritual—Jesus is the bridegroom, and the chosen are his bride. The chosen are those whom the Father chose to become the Son's bride before the foundation of the world. This is one of the reasons they were predestined; this is because they are the first to be conformed to the image of Christ, meaning ready to be his bride. (Ref. Matt. 25:1–19; John 3:29; Rom. 8:29; Rev. 21:9; Rev. 22:17.) See also **Jesus; wedding; marriage; bride; chosen; husbandman; body of Christ.**

brother

> **natural**—Relation by blood or by adoption; having either the same mother or father.
>
> **spiritual**—Relation by blood or by adoption; having the same father. They who believe in the son are related by the blood of Christ, because this causes them to have the same father. You receive the covering of the blood through faith in Jesus, because Jesus said whoever does the will of his Father is his sister or his brother and whoever Christ is in, in the form of the Holy Spirit, is our brother or sister. (Ref. Matt. 12:50; Matt. 18:15, 21; Rom. 14:1–21; Mark 3:31–35; Philem. 1:16; 1 John 2:9–11; 1 John 3:10.) See also **brethren; blood, son, Christ.**

buy oil

> **natural**—This oil has been blessed and made holy and is used for religious purposes, such as anointing, baptizing, or blessing.
>
> **spiritual**—This is another spiritual name for the Holy Spirit, which is the anointing that causes a person to be saved; this oil can be purchased, but not by earthly money, only by heavenly money, a person's works of faith stored in heaven by God. By giving to the poor or by helping someone in need, by learning and understanding the Word of God, you are buying oil. This is what the five virgins were instructing the other five virgins to do when they told them to go and buy oil in the parable of the ten virgins. The five virgins also told them to buy this oil from those who sold oil. To sell oil means to freely give to the person asking the knowledge and understanding of the Word of God. Put simply, buying is accomplished by helping others and selling is accomplished by giving the oil you have to others who seek to buy it. This is all accomplished spiritually, with heavenly money, called treasure. (Ref. Exod. 27:20; Exod. 30:22–24; Neh. 10:31; Prov. 11:26; Prov. 21:20; Prov. 23:23; Isa. 61:3; Zech. 4:12; Matt. 25:1–13; Luke 12:33; John 4:36; Heb. 1:9; Rev. 3:13–18; Rev. 13:17.) See also **sell; wisdom; Holy Spirit; oil of gladness; oil; clothed; treasure.**

called son

> **natural**—Someone invited; someone asked to attend something.
>
> **spiritual**—Someone invited; someone asked to attend something. The Bible tells us in Mat 22:14 that "many are called, but few are

chosen"; the son that is called is also called a servant. What most people don't realize is that they are being called to a wedding. Those who are called will be guests at the wedding, but those who are chosen will be the bride. The servant sons or the called are asked to spread the word of God so that all may attend the wedding. The reason that the called son is not the bride is that they lack the full understanding of God's love and mercy toward all men; those who are called have too many divisions between them. The Spirit of God does not cause these divisions, for the Spirit is one; so those who are called think only of themselves or of a group of people that are like them. For this reason they were called but not chosen, and for this reason, they have to go through the tribulations, which are designed to cause them to have brotherly love. This will be accomplished because the tribulations will cause all men to have a common cause, which will be their spiritual survival, regardless of race, color, or creed. Only the chosen son has fulfilled the second covenant of God, which is summed up by loving one's neighbor as oneself. Christ loves all men because he created them, but the servant, or the called, love only those who are like them. This attitude is not limited to one religion; it is within all religions. The tribulations will remove this obstacle, so that they may attend the wedding. (Ref. Prov. 29:21; Mal. 1:6; Matt. 20:16; Matt. 22:14; John 8:35; 1 Cor. 7:17–24; Gal. 4:7.) See also **servant son; heir son; chosen son; milk.**

called woman
> **natural**—Someone who is invited to something.
> **spiritual**—Some who is invited to a wedding; according to the Bible, many are called or invited, but few are chosen to be the bride. But they that are called are people who have accepted Christ; accepting Christ gets you a seat at the wedding. Those who do not accept this invitation are lost to God and his son. The called are people who are saved but were not chosen. (Ref. Prov. 29:21; Mal. 1:6; Matt. 20:16; Matt. 22:14; John. 8:35; 1 Cor. 3:2; 1 Cor. 7:17–24; Gal. 4:7; Heb. 5:13; 1 Pet. 2:2; Rev. 17:14.) See also **female; feminine; servant son; olive tree; wedding guest; believers; chosen woman; adulterous woman; fornicating woman; desolate woman.**

candlestick

natural—A source of light.

spiritual—A source of light, which is the spirit of the man; a man is a candlestick if the light that is in him is the Holy Spirit, because he can contain light. Light is the understanding that comes from God. This understanding cannot be hidden; it will show when the man talks, if the other person recognizes light. (Ref. Prov. 20:27; Prov. 24:20; Matt. 5:15; Mark 4:21; Luke 11:36; Rev. 2:5; Rev. 18:23.) See also **spirit**; **lamp**; **lampstand**; **light**; **word, understanding, the**.

carnal-minded

natural—To be human; to be natural, or naturally minded; to do what feels natural; to not be spiritually minded.

spiritual—To be human; to be natural, or naturally minded; to not to allow the Spirit of God to lead you; to continue to defy God on a spiritual level, even when something inside you tells you that you are not doing what is right; to lean toward one's own understanding, which is influenced heavily by the flesh, which has selfish desires; to be led by the flesh, which is flawed by nature. (Ref. Matt. 26:41; John 3:6; Rom. 7:14; Rom. 8:1–13; 1 Cor. 3:1–4; 2 Cor. 10:4; Heb. 7:16.) See also **flesh**; **veil**.

cattle

natural—Domesticated animals, used for food and man's consumption.

spiritual—Domesticated people, who are supposed to be used for the will of God; *disparaging* human beings, who are not following the true will of God; a kind of beast, but a tame one. This beast is prey for other beasts who are not tame; in other words, these people fall prey to other people who are following the will of Satan. (Ref. Ezek. 34:17–22; Joel 1:18.) See also **beast**; **man**; **fowl**; **creeping things**; **fish**; **fowl of the air**; **prey**.

cedars of Lebanon

natural—A tree that has horizontally spreading branches.

spiritual—This is the hidden spiritual name for Israel. A cedar is a type of tree that grows very tall and strong and is supposed to stay green, even in winter. A cedar is also a fruitless tree. The height of a tree is a symbolic representation of closeness to God. The height is affected by the amount of water it is given. This water is the Holy Spirit. If a tree does not follow God, it will be cut down, and out of the stump, another tree from the same root will grow. This is a symbolic representation of starting over with God after a fall from grace. Israel also goes by the name of another tree, which is the fig tree, but since the first fig tree did not produce fruit, this tree was withered; then the Lord planted a second fig tree, the Gentiles. (Ref. Judg. 9:15; Ps. 29:5; Ps. 104:16; Is. 2:13; Isa. 14:8; Isa. 37:24; Zech. 11:1.) See also **Jerusalem**; **trees**; **branches**; **bramble tree**; **fire**; **kindled**; **cut down**.

chastising

natural—Punishment received for something that was done that was in another person's eyes wrong or contrary to the will of another; punishment is given in order to correct a person's actions or way of thinking.

spiritual—Punishment received for something that was done that in God's eyes was wrong; this punishment serves a good purpose. This punishment is intended to bring a person back to God by changing the way that person thinks. God only chastises or punishes those whom He loves. If you do not suffer, you are not his son. (Ref. Prov. 13:24; Heb. 12:1–11; Eph. 6:4.) See also **babe**; **child**, **sons**; **heirs**; **love**; **suffering**; **trials**; **tribulations**.

child, son

natural—The offspring of one or more parents; an infant; a baby; an immature son who still drinks milk in order to grow.

spiritual—The offspring of God; a babe in Christ until his or her appointed time. These people still drink the milk only because they have not yet found out that they were chosen to became mature sons of God. The child stage is a stage that all chosen sons must go through, just as the servant. The only difference is that the servant never matures. The Bible says that the "the child is not different from the servant" if he doesn't know who he is; the child eventually stops drinking milk, which religion teaches, and learns to eat strong meat, which means to be taught by the Holy Spirit. Milk is the symbolic word used for a person who has only a little understanding of God's word. This person is a child or babe. This person is unskilled in the use of God's word and does not know how to properly apply it to his or her life. This person is a follower and not a leader, a sheep and not a shepherd. Through many trials, the child matures spiritually, never forgetting the things the spirit taught him or her during the trials. The trials of these people are more severe, because God chastises them more than others, because he wants them to mature. They will be hated, cast out, condemned, different, unique, and never understood. The world will reject them, and it will not love them; to the child, these are called growing pains. We were all babes in Christ at one time, but the child will not remain a babe. (Ref. Prov. 20:11; Prov. 22:6; Prov. 23:13; Prov. 29:15, 21; 1 Cor. 13:11; Gal. 4:1.) See also **heir; servant; milk; meat; babe; sons; goats; sheep**.

chosen, son

natural—A son that is favored over another son; he is usually the firstborn son.

spiritual—A son that is favored over the other son, because the heart of this son is more pure than the heart of the other son; because of the pureness of his or her heart, this son was chosen to perform a special mission for God. This son was elected to be conformed into the image of Christ first. The son who is the servant son will be conformed at a later time. He is also a free son; unlike the servant son who is in bondage to the law, this son is free from the law. The chosen son was chosen before time began. He was not chosen because of his works, because the election was decided before the foundation of the world. This son's life will be predestined, according to Romans 8:29. The chosen are also called his firstfruits; the chosen sons are also called the children of promise, because they carry the seed of promise, which is the Holy Spirit. (Ref. Isa. 43:19–21; Matt. 20:16; Matt. 13:20; John 6:70; John 15:16–19; Acts 9:15; Rom. 8:29–39; Eph. 1:3–11; 2 Thess. 2:12–17; 2 Tim. 1:7–10; Rev. 17:14.) See also **firstfruits; elect son; free son; predestined son; promised son; born again; baptism by fire; female; water; rain, former; rain, latter**.

chosen woman

natural—One selected from a number of possibilities; picked by preference.

spiritual—The bride of Christ; those who were predestined to receive the Holy Spirit before they were born; those who are spiritually called the fig tree. They are those whom Romans 8:29 says are the first to be conformed into the image of Christ. They are also called firstfruits, firstborn, figs, or chosen sons. (Ref. Matt. 22:14; Mark 13:20; John 13:18; John 15:16–19; Rom. 8:29; Eph. 1:4; Gal. 4:26; 2 Thess. 2:13; Rev. 17:14.) See also **female; feminine; chosen son; barren woman; fig tree; elects; living waters; fornicating woman; adulterous woman.**

Christ, Jesus
natural—The Messiah; the son of God.
spiritual—The Word of God. Before he became Christ, he was the Word of God. The Word was the Spirit of God, also known as the Holy Ghost at that time. According to John 1:1, the Word became flesh. This person became known to us as Jesus Christ. He was fully man and fully God but without the power of God. He did not need his power because he relied upon his Father through faith and therefore had access to power from the Father. He did not use his own power, because he wanted to show us an example of how we are to rely on the Father. This is the same way in which we have access to the power of God through faith. (Ref. Matt. 1:18; John 1:1.) See also **Word, the; Holy Ghost; Holy Spirit; Son of God; Ancient of Days.**

Christian
natural—A man or woman of different religions that believe in Christ.
spiritual—A person who believes that Christ died for his or her sins and that he or she will be resurrected because of this belief in Christ; a person who believes that Christ is the Lord and mediator between himself or herself and God the Father; a person who believes in the resurrection of Christ as well as himself or herself, meaning he or she will also be raised from the dead if he or she believes in Christ. (Ref. Acts 11:26; Rom. 15:1–7; 1 Cor. 5:6–13; 1 Cor. 6:1–4; 1 Pet. 2:9–10; 2 Pet. 1:14.) See also **believing; sons; doer of the word; son, free.**

Christianity

natural—A religion whose followers believe in the Son of God and who worship God in a traditional way, usually through the letter of the law.

spiritual—A faith or belief, not a religion. This faith or belief becomes a religion only when a denomination is added to it. True Christianity does not worship God in traditional or in an organized way, but by following the Golden Rule, which is to love one's neighbor as oneself. If a person follows this commandment, he or she is fulfilling all that is required by Christ. Love is the key to having a spiritual relationship with God, because love does not require a religion. (Ref. Prov. 8:17; Matt. 5:43–48; Matt. 19:19; Matt. 22:34–40; John 13:34–35; John 14:21–31; Rom. 7:1–25; Rom. 13:10; Gal. 5:14–26.) See also **love; faith; believing; traditions**.

church, the

natural—A place; a building; a gathering place for Christians; a house of worship where Christians worship God; where believers in Christ receive the word of God; where unbelievers are converted into believers.

spiritual—A particular group of people who make up the body of Christ, which is not a building or a place but a people. The church is also known as the bride of Christ. The church at the moment is divided into many different bodies. Every church on every corner is a different body operating independently, but all are destined to be one body operating with a single mind. At present, different denominations of Christianity do not agree with each other, but there is only one Christ, one Father, and one Spirit, and they agree in one. This division will remain until the return of Christ. Christ will end the division that is within the body of Christ, because he is the head, and the body must follow the head; therefore, we will all be in agreement and the body will be whole. When this happens, the church that is to come will assemble for the first time. (Ref. Matt. 16:18; Acts 11:26; 1 Cor. 5:7; 1 Cor. 12:27; 1 Cor. 14:12; Eph. 1:22; Eph. 5:27.) See also **bride; bridegroom; Zion; body of Christ; spiritual body of Christ**.

circumcision

    natural—An outward show of one's faith in God by having the foreskin removed from the man's private parts as a symbol of his faith in God.

    spiritual—An inward show of one's faith in God by having the veil or blinders removed from a person's heart, so that a man can see spiritually, caused by the acceptance of Christ, which leads to faith. This circumcision cannot be seen with the naked eye; only the person of faith whose heart is already circumcised can recognize another person with a circumcised heart. (Ref. Rom 2–9.) See also **righteousness; faith; Holy Spirit; veil; baptism by fire**.

cistern

    natural—Container for holding natural water.

    spiritual—Container for holding spiritual water, which is the heart of man. This spiritual water is the Word of God; this water is released when a man speaks the word of God to another person. This is also the fulfillment of a certain biblical scripture, found in John 7:38, which says, "… out of his belly shall flow rivers of living water." God said he would give us this water, and this was fulfilled by Jesus when He died on the cross. By dying on the cross, he gave us the Holy Spirit, which is the living water. (Ref. Isa. 44:3–6; John 4:7–21; John 7:37–39.) See also **container; heart; bowl; water; river; cup; vessel; potter**.

city of God

    natural—Old Jerusalem

    spiritual—New Jerusalem; the bride of Christ; the city where all people must come in order to receive the water of life. (Ref. Ps. 48:8; Heb. 12:22; Rev. 3:12; Rev. 21:2.) See also **Zion; Sion; Jerusalem, New; bride of Christ**.

clay

    natural—A natural earthy material that can be made into any shape when wet, used for making bricks, pottery, etc; this material is regarded as the material that God used to make man.

    spiritual—*Clay* is a symbolic word meaning flesh; this is what God made man out of. It is also a word that means man in his natural form, that which he made him from. Clay represents the weakness of man and is the opposite of metal, which is what God is trying to transform us into, metal tried by fire. Clay is also a representation of the fifth kingdom that is to come, which is the feet of the statue, from the dream that King Nebuchadnezzar had. Clay can be formed, shaped, and molded into whatever God wants it to be. This is why clay is used as a representation of what we are made out of; we should let him mold and shape us. (Ref. Job 10:9; Job 13:12; Job 33:6; Isa. 29:16; Dan. 2:33–45; Rom. 9:21.) See also **potter; vessels; vessels of wrath; vessels of honor; cistern; cup**.

clothed

natural—Wearing natural clothing for protection from natural elements, made from natural materials, such as cotton or leather.

spiritual—Wearing spiritual clothing for protection from spiritual elements, placed on by following the Word of God; having been found with faith causes a person to receive their white robes. One's white robes are the righteous acts one will perform in one's lifetime, because one is a faithful son of God and so will receive the clothing that will make one shine. One's unrighteousness causes the opposite effect, making one naked, in a spiritual sense; God can see a person's righteousness or his or her nakedness. Being naked means a person has lost his or her faith in God or thinks that his or her own self-righteous works are good enough for him or her to be accepted by God. Being clothed means Christ's bright nature has covered the person's imperfections, and as a result, he or she becomes clothed with immortality. The words *white linen* also refer to righteous works or having been found faithful and therefore faultless or spotless. On top of this, a person can also put on the armor of God. (Ref. Rom. 13:12; Eph. 6:11–17; 2 Cor. 5:1–7; Rev. 3:5, 18; Rev. 19:7–9; Rev. 12:1; Rev. 18:16; Rev. 19:14.) See also **armor; buy; naked; white robes; clothing color; garments; righteousness**.

clothing color

natural—Wearing different colors usually indicates individualism or a sense of style; distinction.

spiritual—Wearing the same colors usually indicates unity or a sense of oneness; the color white indicates purity, freedom from sin, righteousness, or being forgiven of all sin. Spots on one's white garments represents sins that have not been forgiven yet; these spots are washed by the blood of Jesus and made white as snow. Wearing other colors, such as purple, gold, or scarlet, indicates rank and royalty. (Ref. Exod. 28:5; Mark 15:17; Zech. 3:3; Zech. 14:14; Rev. 17:4; Rev. 18:12–16; Rev. 19:8–14.) See also **clothes, filthy**; **clothed**; **garments**; **naked**; **white linen**; **blood of Jesus**; **righteousness**.

clothes, filthy
> **natural**—Clothing that is unfit to wear, soiled, dirty, or unclean.
>
> **spiritual**—This clothing is our flesh; it is unfit, full of sin, soiled, dirty, unclean, because a person is guilty of many sins and is in need of being washed clean, which means to be forgiven of sins by God. If the person is forgiven, the filthy clothes will be removed and replaced with clean garments. In other words, this is what the Bible means when it says, "mortality has been swallowed up by immortality," (2 Cor. 5:4). This means to be transformed or given the new body as a reward for your faithfulness. This new body is referred to as being clothed with white linen. This white linen symbolically represents a person who has been washed in the blood of the lamb and forgiven of all sins. (Ref. Isa. 52:1; Isa. 59:6; Isa. 61:10; Isa. 64:6; Zech. 3:3–4; 2 Cor. 5:4; Rev. 3:4; Rev. 16:14.) See also **flesh**; **clothed**; **white linen**; **self-righteousness**.

cold
> **natural**—Having a relatively low temperature; having little or no warmth; lacking in passion, emotion, enthusiasm, ardor; dispassionate.
>
> **spiritual**—A person who lacks the love that God wants us all to have; a person who will not fulfill the second covenant of God, which was to love your neighbor as yourself. (Ref. Matt. 24:12; Rev. 3:15–16.) See also **winter**; **unbelief**; **unbeliever**; **lost son**; **heart, evil**.

commandment
> **natural**—A written order; a law that must be followed. If it is not, the offending person has to follow the consequences of not following

the law. Without law, there can be no order; without order, there can be no punishment for disobedience or sin. Commandments are given to man in order to conform his behavior to the will of God. Ten were originally given; they spell out how man must act toward other men.

spiritual—An unwritten order or spiritual command to love one another. The spiritual law shows grace; the written law shows punishment. The spiritual law surpasses the written or natural law, which is the Ten Commandments. Because he knew we would not be able to keep the written law, he made a law that would override the written law, by allowing forgiveness for breaking the written one. This is how Jesus fulfilled the law without removing it. He was simply trying to tell us of a law that surpasses the law of sin, which pertains to the flesh, and trying to make us focus on the law of love, which pertains to the spirit. By this law, not the written law, which convicts us, we are saved. (Ref. Prov. 6:23; Exod. 20:1–17; Deut. 5:1–22; John 15:8–19; Col. 2:11–16; 1 Tim. 1:5–10.) See also law; new law; new commandment; love.

condemnation

natural—To condemn to death naturally.

spiritual—To condemn to death spiritually; the only people who will be condemned spiritually are those who will not repent of their sins. By refusing, they are showing their unbelief in the Son of God. For this, they will be condemned and face the judgment of God. (Ref. Matt. 12:33–37; 1 Cor. 6:9; Heb. 3:14–19; Rom. 8:1; Rev. 20:5–13.) See also evil; evil heart; unsaved; unbelief; tares.

confession

natural—An acknowledgement of guilt; telling the truth; admitting.

spiritual—Admitting you are a sinner; this leads to forgiveness from God, which leads to salvation. This is how a man can be saved. (Ref. Prov. 28:13; Rom. 10:9; Rom. 14:11; 1 John 4:15; 2 John 1:7.) See also sins; saved.

container

natural—Something used to hold a liquid, to store something valuable.

spiritual—The heart of man, used to house the Holy Spirit, or the body of man, used as a temple of God; where the second covenant is written. (Ref. Prov. 5:15; Prov. 20:5; Heb. 8:7–13. See also **cistern; vessel; heart; cup; bowl; house; temple; covenant, second.**

corn of God

natural—The grain, seeds, or kernels of this plant, used for human food.

spiritual—Food for the Spirit; God's corn is his Word. Corn refers to a type of corn bread or manna, found in Psalm 78:24. A man will need this corn in order to grow; corn are the people of God whom he grew and taught his word. They are those of the element earth, which learned the love of God through many trials and tribulations. This corn will teach the rest of man the ways of God. (Ref. Gen. 27–28; Neh. 10:39; Neh. 13:5; Ps. 72:6; Ezek. 36:29; Hosea 2:2–23; Hosea 7:14; Joel 2:19; Amos 8:1–14; Matt. 13:33; Mark 4:26–29; 1 Tim. 5:18.) See also **manna; meal; wine; oil; Holy Spirit; element earth; treasure; buy; sell.**

covenant

natural—A promise; an agreement; law.

spiritual—A promise between God and man; God never breaks his promises. God made a promise to Abraham, Moses, and David and to the seed that would come from them. That promise was that their seed would inherit the kingdom. The first covenant with man was when man was given the written law; the second covenant with man was when God brought salvation to man by grace. Grace was made possible by the death of Christ. This covenant made it possible for God to share his Holy Spirit with the believers who are in Christ therefore giving them the power to become the sons of God, joint heirs with Christ. (Ref. Exod. 20:1–17.) See also **promise; promised seed; law; covenant, first; covenant, second.**

covenant, first

natural—A promise between God and man.

spiritual—A promise between God and man; that covenant was a promise that God would always bless the man who could keep the law. The problem is that no one can keep the law, and under this covenant, there is no forgiveness. If anyone breaks these laws, death or separation from God will be the punishment. The Ten Commandments were given to man in this covenant. The law was given but never designed to save a man. It was only given to convict the man and make him realize that he could not save himself because he in and of himself was too weak. The law was designed to make man realize he needed God all along. This is what Christ came to remind us of. This is what Christ came to die for, so that there might be a way for man to be saved. The law was given to Israel, but the Gentiles were never supposed to live under the first covenant; they were supposed to live under the second covenant, which is grace. The first covenant was established by the blood of animals; the second was established by blood that was more precious, the blood of Christ. (Ref. Deut. 9:11; Deut. 31:25–26; Rom. 3:19–22; Rom. 7:1–6; 2 Cor. 3:1–17; Gal. 3:24; Eph. 2:12–22; Heb. 10:1–9; Tim. 1:9–10; 1 Tim. 1:5–10.) See also **law; covenant.**

covenant, second

natural—A new promise between God and man.

spiritual—A new promise between God and man, which means the old covenant is done away with. Under the new covenant, there is forgiveness for sins; this is what grace means, forgiveness without merit. This is the power of the blood of Christ. The new covenant is by grace and not law; it is by love and not force. (Ref. 2 Cor. 3:1–18; Heb. 8:6–13; Heb. 9:1–15; Rom. 3:31; Rom. 13:8–10; Gal. 5:14.) See also **new law; law fulfilled; love.**

covered head

natural—To put protection from natural elements on your head.

spiritual—To put protection from spiritual elements on your head. A covered head is a symbolic representation of having the protection of God, because he has found you faithful. God is the cover for Christ; Christ is the cover for man's head; the man is the cover for the woman's head; the woman is the cover for her child's head. God wants us to put Christ in our lives and let him be the head of our lives, and then he becomes our protection and covers our heads. To a woman, this means to have a godly man in her life, one who has Christ as the head of his life. (Ref. Ps. 140:7; Ps. 32:1; Ps. 139:13; Isa. 51:16; Isa. 61:10; Rom. 4:7; 1 Cor. 11:1–16; Eph. 5:23; Col. 1:18.) See also **uncovered head; son; man.**

creeping things
natural—Insects
spiritual—People who act like insects to God, meaning they will not follow his will. They are those people who are lost to God. They do the will of Satan. They are also called tares, meaning the seed of Satan. (Ref. 1 Kings 4:33; Ps. 104:25; Hosea 2:18; Hab. 1:14.) See also **tares; beast; man; fowl; cattle.**

crown of stars
natural—N/A
spiritual—This is a spiritual crown, a crown that shows the righteousness of the people who wear it; this crown is worn by an entire body of people. This crown is also a symbolic representation of a group of people; that group is Israel, the first 144,000. The woman who is crowned with this crown is the chosen woman, the bride of Christ; she is the second 144,000. The crown of stars is on the head of the woman who is clothed with the sun in Revelation 12:1. This crown was taken off of the woman who sits on the beast in Revelation 17:1–5. This woman used to be the bride of the Father, before she committed fornication with the beast she sits on. (Ref. Deut. 1:10; Isa. 62:3; Ezek. 16:2–12; Ezek. 21:24–27; Zech. 9:16; Rev. 12:1.) See also **elects; elects, first; elects, second; bride; sun; moon; stars; Israel; Zion; Sion.**

cup
natural—A container, designed to hold different things, usually holding water for drinking. It comes in different sizes for different purposes.
spiritual—A container, which is the heart, designed to hold the Holy Spirit for drinking. It comes in different sizes for different

purposes; the size of the cup depends on the mission you have been given by God. To drink of your cup would be to accept the mission that God has given you. There are two kinds of cups; they are the cup of blessings and the cup or bowl of wrath. The cup of wrath is to be poured on all who do not believe. (Ref. Ps. 16:5; Ps. 23:5; Ps. 116:13; Jer. 15:7; Zech. 12:2; Matt. 10:42; Matt. 20:22–23; Luke 22:17–20; 1 Cor. 10:16–21; Rev. 14:10; Rev. 16:19; Rev. 17:4; Rev. 18:6.) See also **cistern**; **spirit**; **drinking**; **water**; **hearing**; **heart**.

cut down

natural—To lower, reduce, prune, or divide.

spiritual—Spiritually, we are all trees or branches of one type or another. There are many types of trees; some trees know the will of God, and some trees do not. When we are but twigs, none of us know the will of God, and so we must be cut down in order that we may learn the will of God. When we are without understanding, we don't produce fruit, but once a tree is cut down, it can later produce fruit. All fruitless trees are cut down. Fruit refers to good works unto God. To be cut is to be made humble; being cut down is also equivalent to being chastised by God, and God only chastises those whom he loves. (Ref. Isa. 9:10; Isa. 10:30–34; Isa. 18:5; Isa. 37:24; Dan. 4:10–29; Luke 13:9.) See also **trees**; **fruit trees**; **cedars of Lebanon**; **fire**.

darkness

natural—A place void of light or with low visibility that one cannot see into.

spiritual—A man void of light, which means that he or she is void of the knowledge of Christ, which is the true light. This light reveals God's plan for man, that light is Jesus Christ. Jesus brought us the light. Darkness is also called lack of understanding. This is a person who is unwilling to accept Christ. Darkness also means blindness; to be blind is to live in darkness. Darkness is evil; it is the opposite of light. Jesus came that we might have light and come out of the darkness. (Ref. Matt. 5:13–16; John 1:1–14; 2 Cor. 4:4.) See also **unsaved**; **evil**; **unbeliever**; **heart**; **unbelief**; **knowledge, the lack of**.

dark place

> **natural**—A place void of light.
>
> **spiritual**—A heart that has only hatred in it, no forgiveness or compassion for others. We are children of the light. Our hearts should be full of light or love as well as understanding toward one another. (Ref. 2 Pet. 1:19; 1 Thess. 5:4–9.) See also **heart; darkness; evil.**

day

> **natural**—Twenty-four hours of time; measured by the earth revolving around the sun.
>
> **spiritual**—The equivalent in God's eyes of around one thousand of earth's years, since God is really not affected by time. God gave us this in order to have something to measure the approximate time when his Son would return. (Ref. 2 Pet. 3:8.) See also **time; day of the Lord, the; millennium.**

day, the great day of the Lord

> **natural**—N/A
>
> **spiritual**—This day is a spiritual day, not a literal day, because this day will last one thousand years. It is called the Sabbath day. During this time, the Lord will set up his government and he will rule along with his saints forever and ever. This thousand years has a purpose, which is to teach man the right way he should learn to worship the Father as well as the right way to love his fellow man. (Ref. Lev. 23:3–5; Ps. 118:24; Zech. 2:11; Zech. 13:2; Zech. 14:1–21; Mal. 4:5; Matt. 7:22; Matt. 24:20; Acts 2:20; 1 Cor. 1:1–8; 2 Tim. 4:8; 2 Pet. 3:8–10.) See also **day; time; millennium; harvest.**

day when the Lord comes as a thief in the night

> **natural**—A twenty-four-hour period of time.
>
> **spiritual**—The day when the Lord will come as a thief in the night; this is a literal day of twenty-four hours. This will be the day on which those who are his chosen will disappear, along with all who have died in Christ. This will happen just before the tribulations. They will meet him in the air, the dead in Christ as well as those he lives in who are alive and have not fallen asleep. (Ref. Joel 3:31;

Zeph. 1:10; Acts 2:20; 1 Cor. 15:47–57; 1 Thess. 5:2; 2 Thess. 4:14–18; 2 Pet. 3:8–10.) See also **harvest; tribulations; time.**

dead

natural—No longer physically alive; not able to breathe, move, or think; absent in mind from anything in the world.

spiritual—A spirit cannot die; death in the spirit means separation from God. Because of the sin of Adam, we were all born dead, or separated from God; however, the sin of Adam is removed, along with our own sins when we accept Christ as our savior. Then we have freedom from sin, if we died in Christ. Those who died out of Christ no longer have the ability to redeem themselves; this is also called the second death. (Ref. Rom. 6:4–7; Rom. 8:10–11; 2 Cor. 5:1–8; Eph. 2:5; Col. 2:20; Col. 3:3; 1 Thess. 4:16; Rev. 1:5.) See also **carnal; unbelief; sleep; death, second.**

dead in Christ

natural—A person who died a believer in Christ.

spiritual—A person who has died physically but is not dead spiritually and therefore will live again because of the faith he or she has in Christ. These people are the redeemed. Christ called this death or sleep and said these people are asleep and they just need to be awakened. They will be awakened or raised from the dead when Christ returns, as the thief in the night. (Ref. 1 Cor. 15:15, 29; 1 Thess. 4:16; Rev. 14:13.) See also **asleep; first resurrection; reborn; firstfruits; saved; sons.**

dead not in Christ

natural—A person who died not a believer in Christ.

spiritual—A person who died not a believer in Christ and as a result is also dead spiritually. These people will suffer the second death. They will not be raised again until the end of the millennium, because they are those who refused to believe no matter what, no matter how many times they were forgiven by God or anyone else. (Ref. Rev. 2:11; Rev. 20:1–14; Rev. 21:8.) See also **death, second; evil heart; lost son; unbeliever.**

dead works

> **natural**—N/A
>
> **spiritual**—Any work toward one's salvation after the person has accepted Christ. The reason for this is that salvation is assured once a person is covered by the blood of Christ. All work should be directed toward spreading the word of God by the examples we set, not toward our own salvation, which has just been assured. We are supposed to live by faith from that point, because salvation is by grace, which is a free gift, and is not to be worked for. Working for one's salvation after it has been received is an indication of a lack of understanding of that for which Christ died. If believers do not have a full understanding of the power of the blood of Christ, they will think that they have lost their salvation every time they commit what they call a sin, even though their sins have been forgiven. This is how they are brought back into bondage. Once again, this comes from the lack of understanding. Lack of understanding of the purpose of the law is another thing that keeps the babe in Christ in bondage to the law. This also happens because people do not have a full understanding of their own baptism, which symbolizes the putting to death of the old man inside. Once you realize your sins have caused you death, you are dead also to sin. A dead man cannot sin. We have no power to resurrect the dead man that is in us; therefore, we wait on Christ to resurrect us. Again, because we believe in Christ at present, the baptism symbolizes that the flesh has been put away and that we are spiritually dead, and since all are dead spiritually and have died in our sins, we are not to think that we live now, symbolically speaking that is, but should understand that we will live again when Christ returns and then we will truly begin to have life. (Ref. Heb. 6:1–2; Heb. 9:14; James 2:15–18.) See also **faith with works; works; baptism.**

death, second

> **natural**—N/A
>
> **spiritual**—Some will suffer the second death. They are those who hate God. They are in two groups: those who have died since the first time Christ came and those who will still refuse to believe in Christ even after he has come back the second time. The number of people who will suffer the second death will drop when Christ

returns, because during the one-thousand-year rule of Christ, Christ will have Satan bound so that he alone can influence people to believe in him, and those who are left behind or not raptured will have a thousand years to decide to follow Christ. Shortly before the thousand years are up, Satan will be let loose again to see whom he can still get to follow him. Those who do will suffer the second death. (Ref. Rev. 2:11; Rev. 20:1–14; Rev. 21:8.) See also **resurrection; salvation; harvest, first; harvest, second**.

demons
    natural—A fallen angel;
    spiritual—A former angel; a being void of light; evil; intent on the destruction of man; a follower of Satan; beings who chose not to be born of woman or born again, so that they might receive the salvation of Christ. They chose not to be born through a woman because it meant losing what they already had, which was their power and their position. Because of this, they are now enemies of God, trying to stop his plan of salvation for those of their brothers who were born through this earth, who decided to follow Satan. This means that they are also man's enemy. They manipulate men into doing their will, while not revealing themselves to the man, in order to stop or delay the plan that God has for us; they do this by bringing the following things into the life of a person: distractions, enemies, and women or men. Their greatest weapon is confusion and the fear of death, followed by loneliness, riches, and power. This is how people let themselves be controlled by demons. Another way people allow themselves to be controlled by demons is by anger and hatred. This is why God commands us not to do these things and to love one another. They have the ability to control a person without that person realizing it, and this is accomplished by getting that person to think that it is his or her own decision that he or she is making. They simply offer us, in our minds, suggestions, thoughts, and alternatives, and we tend to follow whatever seems best. What always seems best is that which comes naturally to us. This is the same method God uses to influence us; however, God is spiritual and his suggestions appeal to our spirit and not the flesh. Therefore, since we are unfamiliar with our spiritual needs, we tend to ignore the suggestions that he puts in our conscience. In this way, demons have the advantage,

because they appeal to the flesh, which is something with which we are very familiar. (Ref. Luke 8:2; Acts 19:13–19; Eph. 4:25–27; 1 Tim. 4:1–5.) See also **dry place**; **fallen angels**; **tares**; **birds**; **fowls**.

desolate

natural—Barren

spiritual—Those who do not have the Holy Spirit within them at this time. (Ref. Ezek. 15:8; Ezek. 20:26; Gal. 4:27.) See also **servant son**; **lost son**; **desolate woman**.

desolate woman

natural—A woman who does not have children.

spiritual—A woman who has many children; her children outnumber those of the woman who is barren. The desolate woman is a symbolic name for the servant woman who produces servant sons of God. God, however, does not want his sons to be servants. He wants heirs. The barren woman does not have children because the number of children she will have has already been numbered and she cannot have any more children; her children are numbered because they were chosen. The number of her children are 288,000, and they are composed of the first and second 144,000. The number of children belonging to the desolate woman is a number that no one but God can count. She is only desolate because she does not yet have the Holy Spirit dwelling in her and her children; she is also the woman riding on the back of the beast in the book of Revelation. She is referred to as a she only because the spirit that is in her has the ability to reproduce sons like herself. The pronoun *she* is given to her because of her ability to spiritually reproduce; however, this woman is really many people of different nations and tongues. She is the sister of the barren woman, who is the chosen of God composed of a small number of chosen people. (Ref. 1 Sam. 2:5; Gal. 4:27; 1 Tim. 5:5; Rev. 17:16; Rev. 18:19.) See also **female**; **feminine**; **servant son**; **silver**; **cedar tree**; **barren woman**; **lost woman**; **adulterous woman**.

dew

> **natural**—Moisture in small drops on a surface, as tears or perspiration.
>
> **spiritual**—Blessings from God; small favors; small blessings, as apposed to rain, which is a larger blessing from God. (Ref. Gen. 27:28; Num. 11:9; Prov. 19:12; Hosea 14:5; Mic. 5:7; Hag. 1:10; Zech. 8:12.) See also **rain; water; river; Zion; Sion; blessings; rewards; dry place; ground, good.**

dipper

> **natural**—An instrument used to extract water from a container.
>
> **spiritual**—An instrument called understanding; with understanding, a man can dip into his heart and pull out wisdom. The Word of God is the water; man's understanding is the dipper. The container for this water is the heart. Before we can give this water to another, we must first drink of it ourselves, and according to John 4:7–21, if we drink this water, we will never thirst again. This means once you have been enlightened, you will want to share it with others. If you dip into this water, you will find all the answers you have sought from the Holy Spirit and you will not need to look anywhere else for answers except inside yourself, inside your heart, that is. This is the fulfillment of the second covenant of God, in which God promised to write his laws on the heart of man. (Ref. Prov. 20:5; John 4:7–21.) See also **drinking; understanding; water; living water; container; bowl; cup; heart; Holy Spirit.**

discern

> **natural**—To detect, perceive, or to understand natural things.
>
> **spiritual**—To detect, perceive, or to understand spiritual things; to see what is invisible to the naked eye; a gift of the Holy Spirit; to know and understand the difference between what is good and bad; to tell the difference between good and evil spirits; to see spiritually; to see evil spirits within other people; to perceive their intentions; to know if someone means good or bad toward you; to know the outcome of something ahead of time; to see the works of the devil; to see how someone is being manipulated by Satan or to see how a person is being used by God. (Ref. 1 Kings

3:9–11; Mal. 3:18; Luke 12:54; Heb. 5:14.) See also **knowledge**; **wisdom**; **gifts**.

divorce

natural—To end or dissolve a marriage legally; to separate from or to cut off naturally.

spiritual—To end or dissolve a marriage spiritually; to separate from or to cut off spiritually. God divorced Israel because Israel stopped following God (Jer. 3:8). Israel is called a she, and she committed spiritual adultery with stones and rocks, which means the making and following of other gods. Those who commit this sin are guilty of spiritual adultery. This is not the same as spiritual fornication, which means to idolize worldly things without realizing it. (Ref. Jer. 3:8–9; Jer. 5:7–19; Prov. 6:32; Rev. 2:18–23.) See also **adultery**; **unbelief**; **fornication**.

doctrine

natural—Rules and regulations presented for belief by any religion that is taught and establishes precedent for any religion.

spiritual—Rules and regulations presented for belief by Christ; that rule is to love and forgive one another. This is the doctrine of Christ. This doctrine need not be enforced because love has a will of its own. Love wants to love and be loved; love begets love. The doctrine of love and forgiveness is not followed very often by those who say they love God. (Ref. Eph. 4:14; Col. 2:14–23; Matt. 22:33; Mark 4:2; John 7:17; Heb. 6:1–2; 2 John 1:9–10.) See also **love**; **second covenant**; **new commandment**.

doer of the Word

natural—One who acts on his or her belief.

spiritual—One who acts in accordance with his or her belief, which then turns into faith. This is different from just hearing the Word of God, which does not mean that the person acted upon his or her beliefs. To act upon one's belief symbolically represents eating the meat of God. To be a doer is to eat, and to eat is to do the will of God. They are those who are found with faith. The hearers and doers have faith and works. There are those who only hear the Word of God and do not do it. They are known as the believers of God. The believers have faith without works. There are those who do not hear and do not do the will of God, but Christ has said blessed is the one who when he returns, he finds him doing, because he will be made ruler of all that he has. So there are three kinds of believers, those who hear and do, those who hear and do not do, and those who do not hear and do not know. (Ref. Luke 12:42–51; James 1:23.) See also **believers, three kinds**; **eating**; **drinking**; **hearing**; **meat**; **bread**; **chosen**; **predestined**; **free son**; **watch, to.**

dragon

natural—A myth; a dinosaur-like creature; a large reptile.

spiritual—The term *dragon* symbolically represents Satan. Satan is the being who gives power to all beasts; beasts are governmental bodies that rule over people. According to the Bible, there will be seven of these beasts or seven kingdoms that unknowingly are controlled by the dragon. The man who carries out the will of the dragon is called an Antichrist, or a horn on the beast, which is controlled by the dragon. (Ref. Rev. 12:3–17; Rev. 13:1–11; Rev. 20:2.) See also **Satan**; **beast**; **horn**; **tare seed**; **Antichrist**; **unbeliever**; **government**; **bear.**

dreams

natural—Random unconscious thoughts, seemingly without pattern or form; manifestations of a person's fears, hopes, and desires.

spiritual—Not random thoughts, because they are based on what is happening in our lives at present or are from our past. Dreams are also another form of communication from God. God can use dreams to warn us of a future event. However, His messages are called visions, and visions have a pattern and form. This is the main difference between a vision and a dream. Regular dreams are often misunderstood because they are symbolic. One would have to know the symbolic language to understand the meaning of dreams, which is one of the gifts of the spirit. Angels often spoke to people throughout the Bible through dreams. (Ref. Gen. 31:11; Gen. 37:5; Gen. 41:1; Eccles. 5:3; Jer. 23:28; Dan. 2:3; Matt. 2:19; Acts 2:17.) See also **gifts**; **spiritual gifts**; **tongues**; **symbolic speaking.**

drinking, spiritually

natural—To satisfy your thirst naturally by consuming water.

spiritual—Drinking spiritually means to hear the voice of the Holy Spirit and to interpret the words properly. This is what Jesus meant when he said rivers of water shall flow from the mouths of those who love him. He gave them the water and taught them how to drink of that water. The water is wisdom. Wisdom comes into a man's heart. That water is then brought out by a man's understanding, and then the water will flow from the man's lips. This is why the ability to listen to the Holy Spirit is symbolically called drinking water. This water is also called living water, which causes a man to never thirst again, spiritually that is, meaning he or she will not continue searching for the truth because he or she has found it. (Ref. Prov. 5:1–23; Isa. 43:20; Zech. 7:1–7; Matt. 10:42; Matt. 11:19; Matt. 20:23; Matt. 25:42; Mark 9:41; Mark 10:38–39; Luke 7:34; Luke 22:30; John 4:7; John 6:53; John 7:37–39; John 14:17–22; 1 Cor. 9:4; 1 Cor. 10:4, 21; 1 Cor. 11:25–28; 1 Cor. 12:13; Rev. 14:8–10.) See also **wine; hearing; water; living water; Word, the; words; dipper; well; element, water.**

dross

natural—A waste product taken off molten metal during smelting, essentially metallic in character.

spiritual—A person whom the Lord has given up on and will throw into the lake of fire after the third resurrection. This is a kind of person who will not repent. This is why these people are lost or called dross. (Ref. Ezek. 22:18; Prov. 25:4; Isa. 1:25.) See also **fire; reprobated silver; reprobated mind; melting; refining process; metals of God.**

drunken

natural—Drinking in excess, to the point of becoming unaware of what is going on around you naturally.

spiritual—To be unaware of God's will; having drunk the wrong kind of drink; having drunk the wine that the world has to offer, which will make a person unaware of God's true will. There are several kinds of wines that the world offers. Some come in the form of hatred, violence, vengeance, money, and power. Other wine is the power that comes from religion, which is the ability to control people who are weak in spirit; in other words, this wine takes advantage of the person's spiritual needs. Wine takes the place of water, and water is wisdom. Wine can also simply be the distractions of the world or anything that takes your mind off of Christ. Wine keeps a person's mind distracted by worldly problems. This is what it means to be spiritually drunk, so that you forget about God and how he can help you. This wine teaches you how you can solve all your problems. Solving your own problems with the aid of God means the same as drinking your own water or eating your own fruit. All fruit, water, and meat, as well as other spiritual foods, should come from God. Another definition of drunkenness is false religion, which has blinded some people. Another definition of drunkenness is to not believe at all, which means this person does not believe at all, and only believes what he or she taught himself or herself. Drunken is the opposite of sober, and to be sober is to have the ability to hear the word of God. (Ref. Jer. 13:12; Jer. 23:9; Jer. 25:27; Jer. 49:12: Jer. 51:7; Hab. 2:15; 1 Thess. 5:5–17; Rev. 17:6.) See also **wine**; **death**; **unbelief**; **vision**; **sober**.

dry place

    natural—A place void of water.

    spiritual—A place void of water, which symbolically means void of the Holy Spirit. The place void of water can be a place, person, or thing. A dry place also means soil that is void of water. Water is needed to grow seed, seed being the word of God. If any man does not have good soil, water, and light in his heart, the seed cannot grow. (Ref. Ps. 105:41; Ps. 107:33; Isa. 44:3, 27; Hosea 10:12; 2 Pet. 1:19.) See also **drunken**; **darkness**; **demons**; **ground**; **unbelievers**; **unsaved**; **unfaithful**; **water**; **rain**; **dew**.

dry soil

    natural—Soil that won't grow anything because it lacks water.

    spiritual—Soil that won't grow the Word of God, because it lacks water, which is the Holy Spirit. This is a spiritual soil that is within a person's heart. The heart is supposed to be a container for holding water, spiritual water, and from this container, or cistern, water should flow, meaning the wisdom of God should come from this person's mouth. But in this person's heart, there is no water, so the soil is dry like a desert. This person is very far from God. This person can be saved, but he or she will have to allow God to water the ground, because this person is very thirsty for the Word. Ref. Ps. 107:33–35; Isa. 44:3.) See also **wet place; ground, good; ground, stony; ground, thorny; dry place; Holy Spirit; water; dew; rain; seed.**

eagle

natural—A large bird of prey.

spiritual—A symbolic representation of both Christ and Satan, found in the parable of the eagle; one eagle wanted to destroy Israel, the other eagle wanted to save it. (Ref. Ezek. 17:1–24.) See also **Christ; Satan.**

earth

natural—The place man calls home; the ground we stand on.

spiritual—Earth represents all things that are natural, which is where all of man comes from. Earth is the opposite of sea, which is where all things spiritual come from. Both the earth and sea have good and bad things in them. The good in the earth are the people who follow the Word of God; the evil in the earth are those who follow the ways of the world. The good in the sea is the Holy Spirit; the bad in the sea is Satan. According to the Bible, beasts come from the earth and sea, but the difference between these beasts is that the beast that comes from the earth is a natural man and the beast that comes from the sea is a symbolic representation of an evil spirit that gets its power from Satan. (Ref. Ps. 69:34; Matt. 5:5; 1 Cor. 15:47–49; James 3:15; 1 John 5:8; Rev. 7:2–3; Rev. 10:2; Rev. 12:16; Rev. 13:11; Rev. 14:18–19; Rev. 17:1–18; Rev. 18:1–24; Rev. 19:19.) See also **servant son; flesh.**

eating

natural—Satisfying a hunger naturally; nourishing the natural body; the body needs sustenance in order to be sustained.

spiritual—Satisfying a hunger spiritually; nourishing the spiritual body; the spiritual body needs sustenance in order to do the will of God; to believe wholeheartedly what is heard; to believe what is read; to believe the Bible. By the reading of the Bible, a man is symbolically eating the Word of God. If one believes in what

Jesus has said, then that person is eating the bread. If a person believes what the Holy Spirit has told him or her, then he or she is drinking water. If a person does the will of God, then that person is eating meat. If a person believes the Word of God but does not completely understand it and because of this, doesn't always follow the Word of God, then that person is drinking the milk of the Word, because he or she is a babe. The Bible says if your meat offends others, then do not give it to them, which in spiritual terms means not to force your beliefs on another person. (Ref. Matt. 11:19; Luke 7:34; Rom. 14:1–23; 1 Cor. 8:8–12; 1 Cor. 11:20–34.) See also **meat**; **bread**; **water**; **milk**; **drinking**; **hearing**; **religion**; **doer of the Word**.

ego

natural—A man's unique personality; that which makes one feel superior to another; self-image; self-importance.
spiritual—This spiritually represents a person's pride; the symbolic word used instead of this word is *belly*. The Bible says that evil men serve not God but their bellies, which is to say themselves. Pride is a deadly sin, originated by the selfish thoughts of the flesh. (Ref. Ps. 44:25; Prov. 13:25; Prov. 18:8, 20; Matt. 15:17–20; John 7:38; Rom. 16:18; 1 Cor. 6:13; Phil. 3:19.) See also **belly**; **will**; **heart**; **soul**; **mind**.

elect son

natural—A person nominated or appointed for a specific task by another person.
spiritual—A person nominated or appointed for a specific task by God; predestined or chosen before birth; those who are chastised by God, because they are loved; because of the chastisement, they will at their appointed time come into the understanding that the Father wanted them to come into. They are the firstfruits. They are the first to be conformed into the image of Christ. They are equipped with great knowledge, wisdom, and faith combined with love in order to carry out the missions God has given to them. An elect would be Paul who wrote most of the New Testament; an example of an elect from the Old Testament would be Moses who wrote most of the Old Testament. Not everyone is elected or predestined, only a few. They were predestined to be witnesses,

judges of their fellow man, and for a future mission, which is to help teach man during the one-thousand-year reign of Christ. This was made possible because they are the children of the promise. They received the seed of promise, which is the Holy Spirit. They are taught only by the Holy Spirit. The elects come in two groups of 144,000. The first 144,000 are 12,000 from each of the tribes of Israel (Rev 7:1); the second 144,000 are from the Gentile nations (Rev. 14:1). They make up the bride of Christ. The rest of the people who believe in Christ are servant sons, and the servant sons become wedding guests and will be in the kingdom. The elects have symbolic names. The first of these names is the fig tree, then the barren woman, the fruit tree, the tree in the middle of the river, the fish in the river, sheep, gold tried in fire, remnant, free son, or wheat. (Ref. Col. 3:10; Rom. 8:29–39; Rom. 11:1–17; Eph. 1:11; 2 Thess. 2:13–14; 2 Tim. 1:7–10; Rev. 14:1.) See also **fig tree; predestined; chosen; barren woman; free son; firstborn; firstfruits; gold.**

elements of God

natural—A component or constituent of a whole or one of the parts into which a whole may be resolved by analysis; one of the substances, usually earth, water, air, or fire, formerly regarded as constituting the material universe; any group of people singled out within a larger group by identifiable behavior patterns, common interests, or ethnic similarities; a fundamental, essential, or irreducible constituent of a composite entity; an environment naturally suited to or associated with an individual; a distinct group within a larger community.

spiritual—The word *element* in the spiritual sense means a type of personality, and there are four elements, but each of these elements has three personalities or zodiac signs within them. This means that since each element has three distinct personalities within them, there are a total of twelve; we know these twelve distinct personalities as the zodiac signs. This is what the Bible refers to in Revelation 22:2, when it says,

> In the midst of the street of it, and on either side of the river, was there the tree of life, which bare twelve manner of fruits,

and yielded her fruit every month: and the leaves of the tree were for the healing of the nations ...

These fruit that are yielded each month are the different personalities or zodiac signs born each month; each person that is born under a certain zodiac sign has a uniqueness about him or her. This uniqueness is in the way that person sees God or the perspective from which he or she sees God. People see God as they see themselves. God can be all things and all men, at least from an elemental point of view, when the zodiac signs are grouped by their elements. When the zodiac signs are grouped by the element—water, fire, earth, and air—they resemble the life forces that are with God. These life forces are the building blocks of life itself, which is what the zodiac signs in their elements represent. The elements are part of a whole. As long as they remain separated, they are weak, but it was necessary to separate them so that they could be judged. The elements were always meant to be brought back together. They will be brought together again upon Christ's return. This is why the Bible says that Christ will bring fire with him upon his return. This fire will cause the elements to melt together. In 2 Peter 3:10, it says,

> But the day of the Lord will come as a thief in the night; in the which the heavens shall pass away with a great noise, and the elements shall melt with fervent heat, the earth also and the works that are therein shall be burned up ...

This type of melting is not for destruction; it is for the bringing of them together, this will cause them to be greater than they were originally when separated. Each element is here to learn about the other elements and also to learn to get along with them. This can only be accomplished by love; at present, the elements don't all get along with each other. This is because they don't recognize that different elements exist. For the most part, each element thinks it is the only element that exists and therefore does not tolerate other elements, which in the real sense means an individual with his or her personality wishes that everyone else would be more like himself or herself, believing that then everything would be solved. In reality, God wants all the elements to recognize each other for what they are capable of doing, because all are unique and all are needed. God's final solution to the problems between the elements is to melt them with a spiritual fire and bring them together, or in a literal sense, he will cause them to get along and love one another. This will be done by fire, not a literal fire, but a spiritual fire, known as the Holy Spirit. The Holy Spirit will cause people's hearts and minds to change and cause them to love their neighbor, therefore causing them to blend or melt together. This will produce new elements that do not exist at this time. This is God's ultimate goal. In one sense, the principles of the Bible speak of this goal, when God will melt the elements together. This can be found in 2 Peter 3:10: "The elements shall be dissolved." In other parts of the Bible, Galatians 4:3–9 and Colossians 2:8 and 20, the expressions, "elements of the world," or "weak and beggarly elements," refer to a state of religious knowledge existing among the people of the world before the coming of Christ and the rudiments of religious teachings. The Bible is referring to these people as people who are "of the world," meaning this type of thinking on such a small level appeals more to the masses of people who are of the world than the truth. This is why the Bible calls these people or these elements "weak" or insufficient and "beggarly" or "poor." They are dry without water, water being the Holy Spirit, so in other words, to make an element stronger, we need the understanding that only the Holy Spirit can give us. (Ref. Gal. 4:3–9; Col. 2:8, 20; 2 Pet. 3:10–12; Rev. 22:2.) See also **sons, three kinds; women, three kinds; refining process; metals of God; gold; silver; brass; zodiac signs; trees of God.**

element, air

natural—A mixture of nitrogen, oxygen, and minute amounts of other gases that surrounds the earth and forms its atmosphere.

spiritual—A spiritual word for a group of people who are born under this element; they are the Gemini, Libra, and Aquarius. This element is one of four other elements. People who are born under this element are primarily blessed with knowledge and intellect, as well as the ability to communicate. God uses these people in this way; most of them become ministers and priests. They are also the seers of the four elements. The group of people who are air are also a type of tree. This tree is called an olive tree. They are called an olive tree, which is a fruit-producing tree, but its fruit is bitter. Their fruits are bitter because these people are closely associated with the law. These people tend to lean toward the law of God rather than the freedom in God, which falls under another tree, the palm tree, or the water element. (Ref. Gen 2:7; Gen. 6:17; Job 33:4; Neh. 8:15; Isa. 41:19; Acts 17:25.) See also **breath of life; olive tree; trees of God; wind.**

element, earth
> **natural**—The solid matter of this planet; dry land; ground.
> **spiritual**—A spiritual word for the people who are born under this element. They are the Taurus, Virgo, and Capricorn. This element's people are primarily blessed with the ability to stabilize things, because they like order. They are the standards because they like to follow rules and provide for others. They are the nurturers of the other elements. They lay the foundation, the solid ground needed for all other elements or people to stand on. They are down-to-earth, meaning practical, simplistic, and determined to finish anything they start. This element is a type of tree as well. It is called the myrtle tree. The myrtle tree is a type of tree found in the Bible. This tree is referred to in Zechariah 1:8–11 as the tree that reports back to Christ what is going on in the earth. They can do this because they are people who follow standards; therefore, they know what is right and what is wrong. (Ref. Neh. 8:15; Isa. 41:19; Isa. 55:13; Zech. 1:8–11.) See also **myrtle tree; trees of God; ground, good; ground, bad; corn.**

element, fire
> **natural**—A state, process, or instance of combustion in which fuel or other material is ignited and combined with oxygen, giving off light, heat, and flame; burning passion; excitement or enthusiasm; ardor or liveliness of imagination.
> **spiritual**—A spiritual word for a group of people born under the fire element. They are the Aries, Leo, and Sagittarius. This element's people are blessed with the ability to be the leaders of the free world; unfortunately, they are also the warriors of the world, and so they like war and to conquer. Because they like war, God punishes them. But if they do follow after God, they make very good leaders for God, because they are full of life, creative,

straightforward, and goal-oriented people. Fire is an element that has the ability to destroy everything it touches, and so it can be very destructive if not controlled; however, if controlled, fire can be used to change the composition of all things into useful materials. Fire is an element that changes things. The fire element's people are a type of tree as well. The fire element is called a cedar tree. A cedar tree is a fruitless tree that is simply tall and strong. It grows well in the winter as well as other times of the year under many different conditions because it is strong. The people who are cedars are strong. This strength, however, works against them. This is because it is easy for them to become self-righteous, and therefore, God cannot use them or their abilities. This tree will receive the most punishment from God. In fact, the majority of these people are in danger of being lost or thrown into the lake of fire, to suffer the second death. (Ref. Neh. 8:15; Isa. 9:10; Isa. 14:8; Isa. 41:19; Isa. 44:14; Jer. 22:7–15; Ezek. 17:3–23; Ezek. 31:3–8; Zech. 11:1–2.) See also **cedar tree**; **trees of God**; **Satan**; **tree**, **unfruitful**.

element, water

natural—A clear, colorless, odorless, and tasteless liquid, H_2O. It is essential for most plant and animal life and the most widely used of all solvents. A distinct group within a larger community.

spiritual—A spiritual word for the people who are born under the water element. They are the Cancer, Scorpio, and Pisces. Water is one of four elements. Water, in the spiritual sense, represents life or heart. It is one of the most essential elements of life; just as your natural heart is to the body, so is the water to your spirit. Without water, there can be no life, just as without a heart you cannot live. God gave some people who are born under the water element the ability to heal others because they have this form of life or love in them. This form of life is the ability to love. Water in a spiritual sense means heart or love. This is the gift of the people born under this element. The people to whom God has given this ability have heart or compassion for others. Since they are born with this compassion for others within them, they have the ability to bring people together. This brings about love, thereby healing them of the pain that this world has brought upon them. Much water will be needed to bring the amount of love that God wants to bring to this world or in another sense to bring it back to life.

This is the reason why Christ's first miracle was to turn water into wine. The element water, since it has heart, means to care or to love, and this heart has compassion for its fellow man. This means that they will be the first to be transformed into wine. The word *wine* is a symbolic word for the blood of Christ, meaning these people will be the first to be transformed into wine by the receiving of the Holy Spirit, which transforms all who receive it into wine. There is a reference to water being this way in the Bible. This is what Revelation 8:8–10 refers to when it says, "And the second angel sounded, and as it were a great mountain burning with fire was cast into the sea: and the third part of the sea became blood." This blood is the blood of Christ, so this means that they were transformed into blood or wine. This was the same as Christ's first miracle, turning water into wine, and here, in the book of Revelation, he has turned people into this same wine. The word *water* is also used to mean witness. This can be found in 1 John 5:6–8. Water is referred to as a witness. This is one of the missions those who are of the water element will undertake. Since they have the love of Christ in their hearts, which has been turned into wine, they act as witnesses. Water represents the Holy Spirit itself, which flows from the throne of God. So quite naturally and spiritually speaking, those who are of water will be the first to be transformed by water, since they have more in common with water. With water being the Holy Spirit which is love, they have love already in their hearts. This is something the other elements lack, but they have other things that are essential to the body of Christ. This is one of four elements that will be needed when the body of Christ is brought together. It must have heart, but only in a spiritual sense, meaning the ability to love. The other gifts that the water group were born with is the ability to do the will of God, to serve, and temperance which means the ability to remain calm in very stressful situations. This is how God uses this group of people. The water element is the most flexible of all elements. It has the ability to become like any of the other four elements. These people adapt to their surroundings; they blend in, in order to relate to whomever they are associated with, so as to eventually bring peace through understanding. Once the people of the water have walked in the shoes of those whom they seek to understand, they can relate to them and have a good chance at bringing peace. The element water is also a type of tree; this tree is called a palm tree, which is a fruit-producing tree, that produces sweet fruit. A palm tree also represents the water element people, because it is a tree the grows under hot conditions, meaning this tree was made to handle stressful situations. The palm tree is symbolic of peace, and peace leads to love, and love is the grace side of God. The law is the wrath side of God, which is what the air element or the olive tree is more closely associated with. (Ref. Neh. 8:15; Ps. 92:12; Isa. 41:18; John 2:1–9; John 3:5; John 4:10–14; John 7:38; 1 John 5:6–8; Rev. 7:17; Rev. 8:10; Rev. 14:7; Rev. 16:4; Rev. 22:1, 17.) See also **elements**; **element, air**; **element, earth**; **element, fire**; **water**; **living water**; **well**; **fountain**; **drinking**; **hearing**; **understanding**; **Holy Spirit**; **heart**; **love**; **palm tree**; **wine**.

Emanuel

natural—Another name for Christ.

spiritual—Another name for Jesus Christ, which means "God with us." This is only one of his many names. Names are simply attributes. (Ref. Matt. 1:23.) See also **names**; **Jesus**; **tree**; **son**; **rock**; **stone**.

end

natural—To finish something started.

spiritual—When God sets up his new government on earth; this happens when the Gospel has been preached all around the world, when the prophecy of the abomination of desolation is fulfilled, as well as the falling away. (Ref. Matt. 13:39–49; Matt. 24:6, 13–14; Mark 13:17; 1 Cor. 15:24; Rev. 21:1–2.) See also **rapture**; **time**.

end of written law

natural—N/A

spiritual—Christ is the end of the written law and the beginning of the unwritten law, which is the law of love. This law is the second covenant with man, which says God will write his laws upon the hearts of man. This law is fulfilled by loving our neighbors as ourselves. This is the last commandment by Christ. (Ref. Rom. 10:1–13; Col. 2:13–14; Eph. 2:12–22; Heb. 7:12–19; Gal. 3:6–14.) See also **law**; **love**; **saved**; **redeemed**.

Enoch

    natural—Father of Methuselah who never saw death but was translated.

    spiritual—One of the original men of God. He was the seventh man from Adam. He is also one of three persons who have never died a natural death yet. His mission is to record the names and works of people in the book of life. He was translated or transfigured, which means to be transformed into a spiritual being without having to die. Jesus showed us this type of body when he was transformed on the top of a mountain. (Ref. Matt. 17:1–3; Heb. 11:5.) See also **predestined; translated; elect.**

evil

    natural—Morally wrong or bad; immoral; wicked.

    spiritual—Spiritually evil means to not believe that there is a God. Unbelief is the only true evil, because unbelief is behind all unrighteous acts. Evil is an unrepentant heart. Evil is a person who will not forgive another. Evil is a person who does not have love. Evil is a person who hates. Evil is a person who will not listen to the Word of God. (Ref. 2 Cor. 12:21; Heb. 3:7–12; Rev. 9:20; Rev. 16:11.) See also **condemned; hatred; anger; strife; darkness; void of light.**

evil deed

    natural—Deeds that are contrary to the culture of a community.

    spiritual—The actions of a person that show unbelief toward God. (Ref. Heb. 3:7–12; Matt. 24:42–51; James 4:13–17; 2 Pet. 2:13–22; Luke 6:43–45; Gal. 5:19–26.) See also **evil; unbeliever; heart.**

evildoers

    natural—People who do harm to others and enjoy it.

    spiritual—People who do harm to others and enjoy it; they are aware that what they are doing is wrong and do not care. These people are without excuse; they will not escape God's wrath. (Ref. Rom. 1:16–32; Luke 6:43–45; Gal. 5:19–26.) See also **unbelievers; evil; evil heart; lost son.**

evil heart

> **natural**—A person who does not forgive, who is incapable of love.

> **spiritual**—A person who does not forgive, who is incapable of love, full of hatred, and will not ask for forgiveness. (Ref. 1 Tim. 1:1–2; Heb. 3:7–12.) See also **evil; condemnation; unbelief; hatred; lost son; rest**.

expedient

> **natural**—Fit for suitable use; used to build or improve oneself.

> **spiritual**—Gaining Godly knowledge and wisdom and use for a better lifestyle. The knowledge of Christ frees a person from the bondage of this world. Paul the apostle said in I Cor 6:12, "... all things lawful, but not expedient," meaning even if it is spiritually lawful for you to do things that seem contrary to the law, it may not good for you to do so. (Ref. 1 Cor. 6:12; 1 Cor. 9:22–23.) See also **wisdom; understanding; faith**.

eye, spiritual

> **natural**—Allows a man to see naturally.

> **spiritual**—Allows a man to see spiritually; it is also the light of the body. This light is the showing or the outward manifestation of God or goodness within the man. The eye is the light of body, the window to the soul. If the eye is full of light, then whole body is full of light, light being the knowledge of Christ and the eye being the willingness to see spiritually. The Bible in Matt 6:22 says, "Where there is no vision, people perish." (Ref. Prov. 29:19; Matt. 6:22–34; Luke 11:33–36.) See also **sight; vision; blind; veil; prophesy**.

faith

> **natural**—Faith in the natural sense is defined as strong belief; confidence; belief not based on proof.

> **spiritual**—Faith in the spiritual sense is defined as acting upon your belief. Faith and belief are two different things. Belief is something in the hearts and minds of people who believe. Until they act upon that belief, it does not become faith. Faith is an action, not a belief. Faith comes by hearing, not with natural ears, but with the ears that are part of your spirit. We all have the ability

to hear spiritually. According to the Bible, "the definition of faith is the substance of things hoped for and the evidence of things not seen". The things hoped for are your beliefs; the evidence of things not seen are our actions upon those beliefs. Also, according to the Bible, it is impossible to please God without it. This is because your faith is evidence of your belief. Another way to understand faith is through another biblical reference, found in James 2:18, which says, "Faith without works is dead" or "Works without faith are dead." These scriptures focus on two things working together. The word *work* means action or to take action; in other words, these scriptures are saying if you don't act on what you have faith in, it's dead and vice versa, if you act without truly having faith in what you believe in, it is dead also. (Ref. Rom. 10:17; Heb. 11:1–6; James 2:18–26.) See also **believer; love; saved; salvation.**

faith without works

natural—N/A

spiritual—Faith without works is the same as believing in something without acting on it. Faith without works, remains belief, because it remains in the mind of the person and does not manifest itself outside of that person. The Bible has concluded that this faith is dead. This works the same way if a person has done the work of the Lord but does not have faith in what he or she has done. This is dead as well. The only way to have our works count as faith is to act on what we believe in, which is the Word of God. (Ref. Rom. 3:26–31; Gal. 2:16; Heb. 6:1; James 2:14–26.) See also **dead works; belief; believers; servant sons.**

faithful, the

natural—Someone who believes in a cause and is not easily dissuaded.

spiritual—The faithful are a group of people who have only faith and not works toward their salvation. They are only called faithful because of their one act of faith that caused them to be saved. An example would be the thief on the cross, who was crucified with Christ. According to John 1:12, "But as many as received him, to them gave he power to become the sons of God, even to them that believe on his name." If you break this scripture down into two parts, you will see that the first part is referring to those who received Christ. Those who received Christ he gave the power to become the sons of God. These are the chosen. The second part of this scripture is another group of people altogether. They are those who did not receive Christ, but believe on his name alone. They are those who become the faithful. They believe but have no works because Christ is not in them to cause them to do works that please God. They are saved though, because they believe. This is the power of God, because God counts this as faith and faith saves a person. The evidence that this group exists is found in the book of Revelation. The three groups are the called, the chosen, and the faithful (Rev. 17:14). So a person who is called faithful is someone who has not been chosen or called by God or Christ but who through faith and determination makes it into the kingdom of God. The examples are the thief on the cross, the woman who begged for bread from Jesus's table, the centurion who asked Jesus to heal his servant, and all of the others who through the witnessing of others come to believe without having done the work of a Christian. These are those who are saved by the name of Jesus alone, having no works to speak of. (Ref. Ps. 31:23; Ps. 10:16; Luke 16:10; John 1:12; John 3:16–18; 1 Cor. 7:15; Rev. 17:14–15.) See also **saved**; **faith**; **Zion**; **called son**; **chosen son**.

fallen angels

    natural—Those who turned against God and fought against God, in heaven.

    spiritual—Those angels who fought against God. They fought against God because they found out that they would not inherit the kingdom of God in the state that they were in. The only way to have a chance to inherit the kingdom is to choose to be born again, through the womb of a woman and receive a second chance to prove their faith in God. The Bible tells us this in Romans 8:20, where it says, "For the creature was made subject to vanity, not willingly, but by reason of him who hath subjected the same in hope." The fact that this scripture says that the creature was not willing tells us that the creature, or the angel, wanted a say-so in his future. The scripture about what caused the rebellion in the first place can be found in Hebrews 2:5–8, which says,

For unto the angels hath he not put in subjection the world to come, whereof we speak. But one in a certain place testified, saying, What is man, that thou art mindful of him? or the son of man that thou visitest him? Thou madest him a little lower than the angels; thou crownedst him with glory and honour, and didst set him over the works of thy hands: Thou hast put all things in subjection under his feet. For in that he put all in subjection under him, he left nothing that is not put under him. But now we see not yet all things put under him …

These are the scriptures that the angels did not understand and therefore caused the war. The war that caused these angels to fall was started because God told them that the Son of man along with man, would inherit the kingdom. (Ref. Rom. 8:20; Heb. 2:5–8; Rev. 12:7.) See also **demons**; **fowl**; **dry places**; **enemy**; **evil**; **evil heart**.

family, the

natural—The center or core in all societies, typically consisting of one or two parents, natural parents or guardians, and their children; people who share the same goals or values.

spiritual—The center or core in God's society, consisting of our heavenly parents, the father and the Son, as well as our guardian the Holy Spirit, along with their children consisting of all who believe. This family consists of people who share the same goals or values. This represents the oneness of God, that he and his Son Christ share. The family represents the oneness of God, if they share the same values. God intended that man's destiny is to be in his family, which means to be one with him. The Bible has concluded that there is one God, one Spirit, one Lord, one body, which consists of those who believe in him, also called the church. The church consists of many members, from all over the world of all backgrounds. They are one, because if they fulfill the last commandment of Christ, which is to love one another, then they all have the same values and goals. Love makes us a family. Love treats everyone the same. Love is the glue that holds the family together. Love is the key to oneness, because love causes all to think, act, see, and hear alike. Love is universal and cannot be changed. Love makes us all a family. God is love, and God chastises those whom he loves in order to bring them into his family. (Ref. Matt. 3:31–34; Matt. 5:43–48; John 13:35; John 15:12; Gal. 5:13–18; Eph. 3:14; 1 John 2:5; 1 John 3:1; 1 John 4:8–21; 1 John 5:1.) See also **love; God; trinity; oneness; sons; Holy Spirit; body of Christ; church; chastise.**

famine

natural—For the natural body to starve from the lack of natural food, by which the natural body is nourished and is sustained.

spiritual—For the spiritual body to starve from the lack of spiritual food, which comes from the hearing and understanding of God's Word, from which the spiritual body is nourished and is sustained. (Ref. Ezek. 5:16–17; Ezek. 12:16; Ezek. 14:12–23; Amos 8:11.) See also **Word, the; lack of knowledge; drunken; blind; dry place; meat; water; bread.**

farmer

natural—A person who farms; a person who operates a farm or cultivates land.

spiritual—Another name for husbandman; a person who grows a vineyard. Man is the fruit growing in the vineyard. Someone who cultivates the soil; however, this soil is in our hearts. (Ref. Gen. 9:20; John 15:1; James 5:7.) See also **husbandman; God the Father; vineyard; grapes; olives; figs.**

fat

natural—Being overweight; weight not in proportion to height.

spiritual—Being overly blessed by God; blessed in abundance; rich in the Lord, having heavenly treasure; rich in faith; the opposite of famine. (Ref. Prov. 11:25; Prov. 28:35; Hab. 1:16; James 1:10; 2 Cor. 8:2.) See also **blessings; riches; feast.**

Father, the

natural—Our earthly parent; someone who gave physical life to a son or a daughter.

spiritual—Our heavenly parent; someone who gave spiritual life to a son or a daughter. He is also the father of Jesus Christ; the Lord of Host; the Alpha and Omega; the beginning and the ending; the giver of spirits; the Father of Lights; the Almighty; Jehovah; the witness of Jesus; the Meat; the tree of life; power; authority; the part in the trinity that is the soul of the Godhead; the I AM. (Ref. John 4:24; 2 Cor. 3:17; Gal. 1:1–3; Rom. 2:55; Heb. 11:13–16; Heb. 12:22–23; 1 John 4:7–21; Isa. 45:6.) See also **trinity**; **Godhead**; **God**; **names**.

feeding

natural—To eat naturally; to consume food for the natural body.

spiritual—To teach the word of God to those who are hungry for understanding so that the spirit of the person is satisfied; enlightening people; making the Word of God known or understood. This is the opposite of a spiritual famine. (Ref. John 21:15–17; Acts 20:28; 1 Pet. 5:2; Rev. 7:17.) See also **expedient**; **spiritual food**; **eating**; **drinking**.

fear

natural—An unpleasant emotion; to be in distress; to be afraid of something; to feel one's life is in danger.

spiritual—Fear of God means having respect for him or believing that he exists. This type of fear is the beginning of knowledge. Fear is the beginning of knowledge toward God, but we were never to stay in fear. We are supposed to move toward love once we understand what he has done for us. There are other kinds of fear. To fear the devil is to fear death. Fear of death is the greatest weapon the devil has. Fear can be used to stop faith, which is not the kind of fear God wants us to have toward him. To fear death is contrary to faith, because Christ has already conquered death, so we as Christians should not fear a physical death. Another kind of fear is doubt. Doubt is another killer of faith. To doubt one's salvation is to live in fear of losing one's salvation. Such a person cannot use his or her faith because he or she lives in doubt of his or her salvation. (Ref. Prov. 1:7; Prov. 8:13; 2 Cor. 5:6; 1 John 4:17–20.) See also **blind**; **veil**.

feast

natural—A large, elaborately prepared meal; usually accompanied by entertainment; a banquet.

spiritual—A large, elaborately prepared spiritual meal from God prepared for many people. This will take place in the millennium, during the Lord's day, the Sabbath day that will last one thousand years. This will take place after the famine, which is also called the great tribulations. The feast is a time when Christ and his chosen will begin to teach all of mankind the true understanding of who their heavenly Father is, what he has done for them, as well as anything else any man who believes wants to know. (Ref. Exod. 13:6; Luke 22:1; John 6:4; Judg. 1:12.) See also **gathering**; **harvest**; **millennium**; **fat**; **eating**; **meat**; **drinking**.

female aspect of God

natural—The opposite of male; the opposite of masculine, which is feminine; having the ability to reproduce.

spiritual—The opposite of male. Male in the spiritual sense means things that cannot be reproduced, only given to another. Female in the spiritual sense means the ability to reproduce sons. The Word of God, through the Holy Spirit, has the ability to reproduce sons. The Holy Spirit is the feminine part of God, which reproduces sons. What makes the Holy Spirit feminine is the fact that God does reproduce sons, which is a quality reserved for females. Yet the Holy Spirit does this. The Holy Spirit reproduces sons by causing spiritual things to grow and reproduce themselves inside of a person, things such as knowledge, wisdom, patience, and most of all, love. These attributes are feminine in nature because they reproduce and cause two or more people to be alike. For example, when God refers to making someone pregnant with the Holy Spirit, the Bible uses the phrase *planting a seed*; so when a seed is implanted in a person, meaning the Holy Spirit, that person is not pregnant. The seed will grow within that person. For a woman to get pregnant in the natural sense, a man has to place his sperm in her. The man's sperm is called his seed. His seed then travels through a woman's reproductive system where it finds the egg and fuses with it. This produces offspring. The seed of God does the exact same thing only spiritually. When the Word of God or seed is introduced, it first enters into the mind, through the hearing of it, and then it must travel down to the very core of a person, which is the heart. This is when it fuses with the man. If the heart of the person is fertile, the seed will grow. If the person does not have a fertile heart, the seed will not grow. However, if the seed does grow, it will change the person and cause that person to realize that he or she is born again, or become a new person. This new person will then want to share what he or she has learned from being impregnated with the Holy Spirit. He or she will now want to share this with others, and the process will be passed on to another, therefore starting the process all over again. We become feminine in nature even if we are males the instant we have the ability to impregnate others with the Word of God. A male can be considered female if he produces sons using the Word of God, because he is causing people to be born again. This is what it means to be female in the spirit. This has nothing to do with the fact that a man is male or that God is considered male. In fact, because of the ability to reproduce sons, God is female, but he is also male, which means that he is neither male nor female, since he can be both. You could also say he is all male and all female, but it is easier to just say he is neither. This is how Christ can call all who belong to him his bride, because all who belong to him have the Holy Spirit within them, so this makes them feminine in nature, even though they may be male physically. (Ref. Prov. 1:20; Prov. 2:3; Prov. 3:13–17; John 1:14; John 3:16; 1 Cor. 4:15; 1 John 5:1, 18; James 1:4.) See also **feminine; seed; Holy Spirit; bride; trinity of man; wisdom; love; patience; kindness; gentleness; forgiveness; long-suffering; happiness; joy; peace; fruits; seed; Word of God; begotten; woman; masculine; male,**

feminine aspects of God

natural—Having qualities traditionally ascribed to women, such as sensitivity or gentleness.

spiritual—Having the attributes of a female or the ability to reproduce spiritually. This type of reproduction is spiritual, reproducing likeness or people who think alike or are of the same mind or have the same culture. All children will in some way inherit traits of their parents. The word *feminine* is related to the culture of a people. Whatever culture we grow up in has the ability to affect the way we think, act, learn, and relate to the world. In many ways, we are all subject to culture. Culture teaches without intention, without purpose; therefore, our culture is feminine. It is feminine because it reproduces children who are part of that culture, and the culture has the ability to shape the thoughts and lifestyle of the person who belongs to that particular culture, but not in all cases. (Ref. Prov. 1:20; Prov. 2:3; Prov. 3:13–17; Amos 8:11; John 1:14; John 3:16; 1 Cor. 4:15; 1 John 5:1, 18; James 1:4.) See also **likeness; image; God; trinity; begotten; woman; masculine; male.**

fig

natural—Fleshy self-fertile fruits.

spiritual—A spiritual name for good works, works of faith; the fruit that the Lord wants us to produce; the fruit of the Spirit, which causes others to multiply their fruit. These fruits are not works of labor but of faith and cannot be seen visually. They are works of love. (Ref. Judg. 9:10–20; Prov. 27:18; Song of Sol. 2:11–17; Isa. 34:4; Zech. 3:10; Mic. 4:4; Matt. 21:21; Matt. 24:32; Luke 6: 44; Luke 13:6–9; Luke 21:29; Rev. 6:13.) See also **female; feminine; love; faith; fig tree; fig tree, second; grapes; olives; chosen; farmer; husbandman.**

fig tree, first

natural—A fruit-bearing tree. Fig trees are all self-fertile and very productive. One fruit of this tree can produce many seeds.

spiritual—Another name for Israel, they are his firstfruits. They were supposed to be producing fruit when he first came to this world, but they were not so he caused the tree to wither. The fruit on this tree are the people who were supposed to have known and recognized the Messiah when he came to them, but they did not recognize him; therefore, they could not produce any fruit, meaning faith. Faith was the fruit that Jesus was looking for when he came to them. (Ref. Judg. 9:8–20; Prov. 27:18; Isa. 36:16; Jer. 5:17; Jer. 8:13; Hosea 2:12; Hosea 9:10; Joel 1:7–12; Mic. 4:4; Hab. 3:17; Matt. 21:19–21; Luke 6:44.) See also **Israel; Zion; tree; olive tree; Jerusalem; servant son; bondswoman; female; ground, stony.**

fig tree, second

natural—A fruit-bearing tree. Fig trees are all self-fertile and very productive; one fruit of this tree can produce many seeds.

spiritual—Another name for the bride of Christ. The fruits off the fig tree are the people who believe in him. They all have seed in them, and they are very productive. One fruit off of this tree can produce many seeds, which would have fulfilled the promise that God made to Abraham, when he said that his seed would be like the sand by the sea, if Israel had believed in him. (Ref. Judg. 9:10–20; Prov. 27:18; Song of Sol. 2:11–17; Isa. 34:4; Zech. 3:10; Mic. 4:4; Matt. 21:21; Matt. 24:32; Luke 6:44; Luke 13:6–9; Luke 21:29; Rev. 6:13.) See also **bride; female; fruit; firstfruits; Word, the; words; Christians; Christ; Sion; chosen son; free son; living waters; good ground; feminine.**

fire

natural—A natural element that will change the composition of almost any other element with which it comes in contact. This element has shaped our world more than any other; two other elements have shaped our world as well. They are water and good soil.

spiritual—Another spiritual name for the Holy Ghost; this fire is the Father at work in a person's life. This fire causes repentance, which leads to the receiving of the water, water being the Holy Spirit or the Son of God. Fire causes a person to go through rough times. Without rough times, people will not think that they are doing anything wrong and therefore will not see a need to change. When burned with this spiritual fire, a person's natural composition is changed. This burning is the preparation for the receiving of the Holy Spirit. Before people receive the Spirit of God, a burning away of all the evil thoughts in their hearts starts to take place; the evidence of this burning or change will manifest itself by a noticeable difference in these people's behavior, intentions, or actions. This burning is also called the fire baptism; another name found in the Bible that describes this burning is kindling. To kindle with fire means to change the will of the person to correspond to the will of God. This person is then ready to follow Christ. Some men and women receive this type of burning before Christ returns. These are the men and women who will be ready to receive him upon his return. They will be called the chosen of God. This is the same fire that will rain down from heaven as described in the book of Revelation, during the tribulations, which begins the process of changing the will of all men and women by eventually causing them to believe in Christ. The book of Revelation also talks about fire coming from heaven, but what most don't understand is that this is not a natural fire. Therefore, it is not meant to destroy them but to save them by bringing about repentance first and then leading them to water, which means forgiveness. First, they must be burned with the fire of repentance which is the Father leading them to his Son. This fire will renew the mind of the person who is burned with it; this fire will bring about salvation and make it assured. (Ref. Hosea 8:14; Isa. 10:17; Isa. 24:15; Isa. 43:2; Isa. 50:11; Ezek. 20:47; Ezek. 39:6; Zech. 3:2; Zech. 9:4; Zech. 13:9; Matt. 3:10–12; Matt. 20:22–23; Luke 12:49–50; Acts 10:44–48; 1 Cor. 3:13–15; 2 Thess. 1:8; Heb. 12:29; 1 Pet. 1:7; 2 Pet. 3:7; Jude 1:23; Rev. 8:5–8; Rev. 9:18; Rev. 15:2, 8; Rev. 18:8.) See also **Holy Spirit; baptism by fire; judgment; born again; saved; refining process; third part; kindled by fire; melting; metals of God; gold; silver; brass; iron; tin; lead; dross; chastise.**

firstborn

natural—The first person born in a family; the eldest. It is usually customary for the firstborn son to inherit his father's wealth.

spiritual—The first to be brought back into the kingdom of God; the first of three resurrections. They are those who receive Christ in the from of the Holy Spirit. They were predestined to receive the seed or Spirit of God. They are called the chosen of God. They are the bride of Christ. They are also called firstfruits, which fall off the fig tree. This is why they are part of the first resurrection. They are also called the begotten of God. Jesus was the first to be begotten, but he will not always be the only begotten son of God, because he will be followed by those who are also firstborn sons of God. (Ref. John 1:14; John 3:16; Rom. 8:29; Col. 1:15–18; Heb. 12:23; 1 Pet. 1:3; 1 John 5:1, 18; Rev. 1:5.) See also **chosen; saved; mature son; firstfruits; fire; bride; living waters; feminine.**

firstfruits

natural—The firstfruits are the first to ripen on the vine and to be harvested.

spiritual—The first to receive Christ. They will be harvested or resurrected first, upon his second coming. They are those who believe by faith and not by sight. They are hearers and doers of the will of God. This will be the difference between the firstfruits and the second and third fruits. The second fruits are they who only hear the Word of God. This is why they are second fruits because they are not ripe yet, and so they will be harvested later. This is known as the second harvest. This is why Christ said in Matt 20:16, "the last shall be first and the first shall be last." The firstfruits are ready because they are ripe, or in other words, the Holy Spirit is in them and has removed all their unrighteousness. The fruits that are last are last because they refused many times to repent, as the second fruits did before them. The third fruits will have to be burned with fire before they will repent, so that they can be saved. The third fruits are people who were previously lost to God but believed at the last minute, like the thief on the cross. They are those who believe on his name only and have no works, works meaning good fruit, to present to the Lord upon his return. (Ref. Exod. 23:16; Exod. 34:22; Matt. 20:1–16; Rom. 8:23; 1 Cor. 15:20–23; James 1:18; Rev. 14:4.) See also **firstborn; harvest; predestined; chosen; elect; mature son; living waters; feminine.**

fish

    natural—Any of various cold-blooded, aquatic vertebrates, having gills, commonly fins, and typically an elongated body covered with scales.

    spiritual—Fish is a symbolic word for people, who are swimming in the sea; the sea is the world. The world is a sea, and there is a leviathan in the sea swimming with the small fish, and the fish are unaware of his presence. The leviathan is a devourer of fish. The fish are saved by a net cast by fishermen trained to fish and sent by the Lord. (Ref. Eccles. 9:12; Jer. 16:16; Ezek. 29:4; Ezek. 38:20; Zeph. 1:3; Matt. 4:18–19; 1 Cor. 15:39.) See also **net; man; fisherman; sea; river; beasts; fowl; creeping things; birds of the air; fowl of the air; cattle; leviathan; whale; prey.**

fisherman

    natural—A person who catches natural fish, either with a net or with a pole.

    spiritual—A person who catches spiritual fish, which means people, with a spiritual net, which is the Word of God. (Ref. Ps.

8:8; Eccles. 9:12; Isa. 19:8; Jer. 16:16; Ezek. 47:9–10; Matt. 4:19; 1 Cor 15:39.) See also **net; fish; sea; river.**

flesh

natural—What the human body is made of; that which is natural; the physical or carnal nature of humankind.

spiritual—A way of thinking or type of behavior, animalistic in nature. To be fleshly is to say, "I am only human," which from a human standpoint means I am flawed because I am human. This means to accept that we as humans are limited and therefore can never be made perfect. Our flesh, which is limited, has an influence on how much we can believe God. Because God is not flesh and humans are, they tend to think God thinks as they do. This kind of thinking to God is called thinking with one's flesh and not his spirit, which is not limited. Another word associated with flesh is the word *natural*. Being natural is the opposite of being spiritual. If a man is naturally minded, according to the Bible, he is an enemy to God, because he is a lover of the world. To be fleshly or naturally minded is also, according to the Bible, called being carnally minded. A carnally minded person is a person who continually has selfish thoughts, thoughts about lust, envy, strife, hatred, jealousy, etc. These thoughts become the acts of a person, and these acts are spiritually called works of the flesh. Works of the flesh will cause a person not to believe in Christ; too much thinking in the flesh and not having one's mind on heavenly things, such as Christ, will cause a person not to enjoy the life that he or she has been given. This is because the natural side of man can never be satisfied. It is insatiable, all consuming. The part of us that is spirit can be satisfied. It can be satisfied by the Word of God. (Ref. Rom. 3:20; Rom. 7:5, 18; Rom. 8:1–13; Phil. 3:3.) See also **carnal-minded; veil; man.**

flood

natural—A great flowing or overflowing of water, especially over land; to overwhelm with an abundance of something.

spiritual—Ungodly men. (Ref. 2 Sam. 22:5; Ps. 18:4; Ps. 29:10; Jer. 46:7–8; Dan. 11:22; Matt. 24:39; Luke 6:48; Rev. 12:15–16.) See also **unbelievers; adult.**

fool

> **natural**—A person without understanding; someone who doesn't listen to instructions.
>
> **spiritual**—A person who will not listen to spiritual instructions; someone who has rejected the Word of God. (Ref. Prov. 12:15; Prov. 15:5; Prov. 18:2.) See also **dry place; unbelief; fornication.**

fool, spiritual

> **natural**—Someone who appears to be unwise in the eyes of the world when it comes to the Word of God; someone who does not conform to tradition; does not go along with the crowd; speaks of the Lord too often.
>
> **spiritual**—Someone who has learned to speak the spiritual language of God. This is a person who speaks of foolish things to those who are of the world. The Bible says that God has used the foolish things of this world to confound the wise. These foolish things are what come out of the mouths of those who are wise in God's eyes. (Ref. 1 Cor. 1:27; 1 Cor. 3:18; 2 Cor. 12:11.) See also **chosen; predestined; called.**

forgiveness

> **natural**—The act of pardoning someone for something they did to you.
>
> **spiritual**—The act of pardoning anyone who believes of their sins; the power of God that allows a man to be cleansed of his sins; the power of God that causes a person to be made righteous, justified, and then brought into the house of the Lord by accepting; all caused by accepting Jesus Christ as one's savior. (Ref. Acts 26:18; Eph. 1:7; Col. 1:14; Rom. 3:24; Rom. 5:21; Eph. 4:17.) See also **love; grace; atonement.**

fornication

> **natural**—Having sex before marriage.
>
> **spiritual**—Putting something before God without realizing it totally; not truly following the ways of Christ but not giving up on him; having an idol in your life without realizing that you are idol worshiping. This form of idol worshiping acts as a distraction and keeps one's focus off of Christ. This is different from spiritual adultery, in which a person turns his or her back on God for some

reason and totally gives up on God. Spiritual fornication is called idolatry. Fornication and adultery are almost the same, except that in a spiritual sense, most people today do not know they are committing spiritual idolatry. God will forgive them for this, but they will suffer punishment. The form of spiritual fornication most people commit and are unaware of is accomplished when a person cares too much for the world and the worldly things in it. Worldly things choke the Word of God out of a person, but these same people are believers and will be saved based on that belief; however, for this reason, they are not the bride and become guests at the wedding. (Ref. Ezek. 16:26; Matt. 5:32; John 8:41; Acts 15:29; 1 Cor. 6:20; Rev. 2:17–23; Rev. 17:1–18.) See also **idolatry**; **adultery**.

fornicating woman

natural—A female who has sex before marriage.

spiritual—A person who worships God through religion and not in the Spirit. Religion causes a person not to love as he or she should. Religion divides and judges unto condemnation people who are not like them. God is the God of all people, whether they be good or bad, bond or free, black or white. God judges all people from the content of their hearts. The fornication occurs when the person listens to the voice of someone else rather than Christ. God is a jealous god, and he wants to teach us, but most people are not willing to listen to their hearts. The heart is where the Father and Son speak to us from. Fears of all sorts prevent people from listening. The fear of hearing from the Father on one's own is too great for most, and so they listen to another out of fear and weakness. If the Spirit of God is in the person that they believe in, God will allow it, but if the Spirit of God is not in the person they have chosen to listen to, that person is committing spiritual fornication. (Ref. Jer. 29:23; Ezek. 16:1–63; Hosea 1:14; Matt. 5:25–32; Rev. 2:17–23.) See also **fornication**; **servant son**; **called son**; **wedding guest**; **idolatry**; **adulterous woman**; **chosen woman**; **olive tree**.

fountain of life

natural—N/A

spiritual—Water or rain from God. This water heals. This water is the Holy Spirit, which forgives a person of his or her sins. This water causes a person to forgive others. This water causes all men to love one another. This water is the love of God. If a man drinks, he will never thirst again. (Ref. Ps. 36:9; Prov. 5:26; Prov. 13:14; Isa. 41:18; Jer. 2:13; Rev. 7:17; Rev. 21:16.) See also **water; living water; element, water; Word of God; understanding; rain; rain, former; rain, latter.**

fowl of the air

natural—Any bird.

spiritual—Any evil Spirit, which can influence a man to do its will. They are called fowls because they fly around from person to person seeking people in whom they can live in order to get them to become disobedient toward the Word of God. (Ref. Job 35:9–13; Ps. 79:1–5; Jer. 5:27; Matt. 13:1–10; 1 Cor. 15–39; Eph. 2:2.) See also **birds; cattle; creeping things; beast; fish; man.**

freedom

natural—Not being bound by anything; doing as you will.

spiritual—Accepting Christ as your savior; free from sin; not fearing death; enjoying life in Christ. It is made possible by grace. Grace is the key to freedom. The law has not made anyone free. The law is bondage to any man who tries to keep it, because it is impossible to keep. Christ died for us to be brought from under the law, so that we might enjoy the freedom that comes through love. The Bible says that whomever Christ frees is free indeed. This is why the Bible says we who accept Christ are no longer under law. Under law, there is no forgiveness; therefore, there is no freedom. Whoever tries to follow the law and fails will be chained to the law forever once it is broken. Freedom is found under grace, freedom from condemnation, and freedom from the second death. (Ref. Rom. 6:14–22; Rom. 8:21; 1 Cor. 8:5–13; 2 Cor. 3:16–17; Gal. 5:1, 13; James 1:25; 2 Pet. 2:19.) See also **grace; heir son; love; covenant, second; forgiveness.**

free son

natural—Not bound by anything.

spiritual—Not bound by law; not in bondage to the law; not in bondage to the world; made free by grace, which is the new covenant, which Christ died for. Faith in the new covenant frees a man from the old covenant. The old covenant did not have forgiveness because the law had no forgiveness. This freedom is simply the understanding that his salvation cannot be lost and that he is sealed and nothing can take that away, because nothing can overcome the power of the blood of Jesus Christ, except unbelief. Since he or she will never stop believing, his or her salvation can never be lost. The free son has discovered that salvation cannot be earned. A free son has discovered that salvation is a free gift from God, to all who believe, regardless of a person's faults and shortcomings. The free son has discovered the true love that God has toward him and that nothing can separate him from that love. The free son has discovered that he is an heir, a joint heir with Christ. A free son looks past the faults of others, as God looks past his, and loves his fellow brothers, and because of this, he has pleased his father by fulfilling the second and last commandment, which was simply to love. (Ref. Gal. 4:1–26; 1 Cor. 7:17–24; 1 Cor. 8:5–13; 1 Cor. 3:16–17; John 3:13–16.) See also **grace**; **love**; **freedom**; **chosen**; **elect**; **heir son**; **living waters**.

fruits

natural—The edible part of a plant developed from a flower; food that grows from trees or from a vine that is good for a person to eat.

spiritual—The actions of a person, whether good or bad, that give away the character of that person. Fruits of the Spirit are love, peace, joy, kindness, long-suffering, etc. The fruits of the flesh are anger, strife, hatred, violence, etc. If we are in Christ, we are to produce good fruit. The Bible says that you will know a tree by its fruit. Since man is a type of tree, he should produce good fruit. The best fruit of all is love. If we love our neighbors, we will fulfill all the commandments of God. Fruit gets its nourishment from the vine that it grows on. That vine is Christ. The water needed to grow the fruit comes from the Holy Spirit. (Ref. Matt. 7:16–20; Luke 6:43–45; Gal. 5:22–26.) See also **works**; **love**; **heart**; **tongue**; **Holy Spirit**.

fruits of the flesh
natural—N/A
spiritual—The works of a man that lead to his destruction. They are the works of a carnal-minded person; the actions of a person that the Bible calls bad works. These fruits or works are hate, anger, strife, jealousy, envy, adultery, fornication, uncleanness, idolatry, witchcraft, rumors, murder, lying, drunkenness, or anything that does not show faith toward God. (Ref. Deut. 28:50–53; Rom. 7:5; Gal. 5:19–21; Phil. 1:22.) See also **spiritual food; blessings; works; gifts.**

fruits of the spirit
natural—N/A
spiritual—The works of a man that lead to his salvation; the actions of a spiritually minded person; the actions of a person that the Bible calls good works. The fruits of a spiritual man are the outward showing of his love toward his fellow man. These works are joy, peace, happiness, love, patience, meekness, long-suffering, kindness, knowledge, honor, mercy, humility, truth, and honesty. (Ref. Gal. 5:22–26; Eph. 5:9–20.) See also **works; love; heart; tongue; Holy Spirit; spiritual food; wine.**

garments
natural—Clothing worn by people in order to protect them from the elements or to hide their nakedness.
spiritual—Symbolically speaking, the garments that we all have on now are our flesh. We are supposed to desire the garments or white robes that God desires to give us all, which is a new body, a body without sin. Spotted or filthy garments are sins attached to the flesh. The symbolic meaning of clean or white robes is a body without sin. Those who receive Christ have the garments washed, or in other words, they have their sins forgiven. When God resurrects his people, he will give them new garments. (Ref. Isa. 52:1; Isa. 59:6, 17; Isa. 61:10; Ezek. 42:14; Ezek. 44:19; Zech. 3:2–5; Matt. 23:5; Luke 24:4; James 5:2; Rev. 3:4; Rev. 16:15.) See also **clothing; clothing, filthy; clothing color; righteousness; white robes; naked; glory; buy; sell.**

Gentile

natural—Any non-Jewish nation or person.

spiritual—Any nation or anyone who was spiritually unable to put off sin because he or she did not receive the law; the first to accept Christ and salvation through the preaching of the cross. (Ref. Gal. 2:2; Eph. 3:8; 1 Tim. 2:7; 2 Tim. 1:11) See also **called**; **branches, grafted in; Sion.**

ghost

natural—The spirit of a dead person. According to myth, a ghost is someone with unfinished business that keeps him or her connected to the world.

spiritual—In the spiritual sense, there is no such thing as a ghost. There is only the spirit. A man does have a soul, but the soul is connected to the spirit. The spirit of the man gives the soul life. Without the spirit, the soul has no life. The spirit of a man belongs to God; therefore, God is in charge of what happens to the spirit. A man has no power to do what he wants to do after death. Since no man has life in himself, he cannot resurrect himself from the grave. To define the term *ghost* spiritually, we would have to say that it would have to be something that operated outside the will of God. This is the only way that a ghost, which is not a spirit, could be defined. Since this is not possible, there can be no such thing as a ghost. Whenever the word *ghost* is used in the Bible, it is referring to the spirit of a man. See also **death; dead; spirit.**

gifts of the spirit

natural—Something given voluntarily without expectation of payment in return; the act of giving; to be given something of value. This act usually makes one happy or feel loved.

spiritual—Something given voluntarily without payment in return. These are called blessings from God. They are used to carry out missions for God, which help others as well as the giver. Gifts aid in the production of fruit, fruit that God is pleased with. All gifts come from one main gift: the Holy Spirit. From the Holy Spirit come all other gifts. The main gift from the Holy Spirit is salvation. From salvation, we get to use other lesser gifts. The Holy Spirit is the one who helps us use the other gifts that come along with the gift of the Holy Spirit. There are many gifts that come from the Spirit. Examples of some of the gifts and fruits are wisdom, knowledge, faith, healing, the working of miracles, prophesying, the discerning of spirits, speaking in tongues, the interpretation of tongues. All of these are individual gifts. Gifts can come in the form of people, who are sent to us. In the past, they have come in the form of prophets, apostles, and teachers. Presently, they can come in the form of the ministry, teachers of the Word of God, or anyone whom God has sent to help someone with a problem. Gifts can be used to help us stay in the Spirit. The Spirit gives us foresight, which can be used to warn us of danger or tell us of blessings to come. The Spirit gives us the ability to discern between good and evil so that we may stay in right standing with God. The Spirit gives us the ability to judge but not to the condemnation of anyone. This type of judgment helps us to make good decisions, decisions that are based on clearly thinking something through. The Spirit gives us the ability to understand and expound on scripture. The Spirit of God allows us to see the hidden meanings of the Bible. There are many more things I would like to add, but the greatest of these gifts that the Spirit gives are the ability to worship God in the Spirit and the ability to walk with him in the Spirit. Those of us who are in Christ benefit from these gifts, if we use them, by having peace, joy, happiness, and love in our lives. (Ref. 1 Cor. 12:1–13, 27–29; Rom. 12:6–8; Gal. 5:22.) See also **fruits**; **blessings**; **rewards**; **works**.

glory of God

    natural—To be held in high esteem; to have great honor.

    spiritual—A respect and honor that is bestowed upon a person by God, based on one's faith in him. The glory and honor that are given to people are not based on their works, even though their faith will cause them to do great works. It will be the person's faith that God honors. This will vary based on the amount of faith each person has and uses, because God is no respecter of persons; he is only a respecter of faith. (Ref. Exod. 33:12–22; Exod. 40:35; Isa. 8:7; Ezek. 43:1; Ps. 19:1; Isa. 62:3; Matt. 19:28; Matt. 24:30; Eph. 1:17; 2 Pet. 1:17.) See also **faith**; **blessings**; **reward**; **works**.

goats

natural—A horned animal related to the antelope, domesticated by man.

spiritual—Someone who is somewhat disobedient to the Word of God; not always found to be faithful but believes in God. His or her punishment is to be a goat instead of a sheep. Both are flocks of the true shepherd, but sheep are favored over goats, because sheep have more faith than goats. Goats, however, are favored over cattle, because goats have more faith and works than cattle. (Ref. Ezek. 34:17; Zech. 10:3; Matt. 25:32–33.) See also **believers; belief; faith; called; servant sons; chosen sons; sheep; cattle; creeping things; prey.**

God the Father

natural—A being of divine omnipotent power; the creator of the universe.

spiritual—The father of Jesus; the Godhead; the father of the word and Christ; the head of the trinity. He gives life to all. He is the father of love, the father of light, the father of life, the father of all spirits, the father of hope, and the father of all things. God the Father brought the Word into existence. John 1:1 reads, "In the beginning was the Word, and the Word was God, and the Word was with God." God is both male and female at the same time. This is because he can reproduce sons, and anything that can reproduce is female in nature. The part of him that can reproduce is the Holy Spirit. The Holy Spirit impregnates men and women with the Word of God. This Word is called a seed. This seed grows, and as it grows, it changes the person it is within. Once that seed is fully mature, the person is a completely different person. This person has been remade into the image of God. This is a spiritual explanation of how God reproduces sons. God is also a trinity and a oneness at the same time. He exists in a trinity, because there is a Father, a Son, and a Holy Spirit. There is a oneness because these three work as one with one accord, with one goal, and with no disagreement. These three can be independent of one another but also have the ability to be one by occupying the same body, a spiritual body known as the body of Christ. This body is a spiritual body, which literally consists of a group of people who believe in him. He inhabits them in spirit, causing all of them to think alike, therefore, causing a oneness of mind. A type of Trinity is present within this oneness or body, because at the same time, each individual within this spiritual body will have the ability to think independently. This is because of free will. The love of God allows man to think independently. The only reason the man will want to be a part of the oneness is because of the love he will have for his spiritual father and the love the Father will have and show toward him. (Ref. John 1:1; John 5:18–26; Rom. 1:19–20; Rom. 15:5; 2 Cor. 1:1–3; 1 Tim. 6:13; Gal. 1:1–3; Gal. 4:6–8; Heb. 12:11; 1 John 1:5–6; 1 John 4:8–13; James 1:17.) See also **trinity, the; oneness, the; Father, the; Godhead; tree of life; meat, the.**

Godhead, the
natural—N/A

spiritual—A position of authority; above all; in charge of all; everything bows to it; also means the head of all things; the head of all power; the royal family; the king and prince; Father, Son, Holy Spirit, and the bride. (Ref. Acts 17:29; Rom. 1:20; Gal. 1:1–3; Col. 2:9.) See also **trinity; oneness; God the Father; Father God.**

gold
natural—The most valuable metal on earth.

spiritual—The most valuable metal to God; gold is a symbolic name for those whom God loves the most, because they have shown great faith toward him. People who are called gold have great honor in God's eyes. People who are gold use God's wisdom; they use kindness and compassion toward their fellow brothers, because their love has been perfected. They are people who have overcome the world through this ability to love along with their faith. Their faith in Christ has been refined by the pressures of the world through trials and tribulations; these trials have refined them as fire refines gold. Gold is more precious than silver. Silver represents those people who love God as well but who have shown less faith. Brass is another metal that God has saved. These are people who believed at the last minute and were saved by God. (Ref. Num. 31:21–24; Prov. 8:10; Ezek. 22:20–22; Isa. 13:12; Zech. 13:8–9; Mal. 3:3; 1 Tim. 2:20; 1 Pet. 1:7; Rev. 3:18.) See also **elect; mature son; chosen son; fig tree; living waters; bride; Sion; silver; refining process; melting.**

golden cup
natural—Something of great value.
spiritual—The holy city of God, New Jerusalem; the people of God make up this city; this city contains the wine, the wine being the Holy Spirit of God. (Ref. Jer. 13:12; Jer. 49:12; Jer. 51:7; Rev. 17:1–6.) See also **new city; New Jerusalem; Zion; Sion; holy mountain; wine.**

Good News
natural—Information that brings happiness to the listener.
spiritual—The Gospel; the truth about salvation; the truth about love and the power of God; good news is water to the thirsty soul of man. (Ref. Prov. 25:25.) See also **Gospel; water; food.**

good soil
natural—Soil that is good for growing all kinds of plants.
spiritual—Soil that is good for growing all kinds of plants that produce fruit, God's fruit, which are works of faith. God plants seeds. These seeds are his Word, and He expects his Word to reproduce and multiply. Good ground is a person with a good heart. (Ref. Gen. 2:9; Deut. 28:11; Ezek. 17:8; Matt. 13:8; Luke 8:15.) See also **ground, good; dew; rain; heart; love; gold.**

goodness
natural—Showing acts of kindness.
spiritual—Showing the will of God; treating your neighbor as yourself; showing good virtues; the favoritism the Lord shows toward those who believe in him; being blessed. (Ref. Hosea 3:5; Gal. 5:22; Eph. 5:9.) See also **heart; light; works; faith; love; blessings.**

Gospel
natural—The truth; reliable.
spiritual—The Word of God; the truth about God, his son, and the Holy Spirit; reliable. (Ref. Matt. 9:35; Matt. 24:14; Rom. 1:1.) See also **truth, the; good news; hearing; listening; drinking.**

government

> **natural**—The governing body of people in a state or community; the form or system of rule by which a state or community controls a society; man's attempt at self-rule; a system put in place to rule a nation, country, or state by man.

> **spiritual**—The governing body ruling over man known as the Godhead, which is composed of the Father, the Son, and the Holy Spirit; an organized Godly rule over man. All of man's attempts at governing himself are shadows of God's government. Man cannot rule himself, because man has too many flaws. God is allowing man to try to rule himself for a time in order to prove to man that he cannot rule himself, but man has to find that out for himself. There are no perfect societies on earth, but God will create a perfect society one day, one that only he can create. According to God, all of man's governments are a form of beast; they differ only by their nature. Their nature is either to bring war or to bring peace, to destroy their neighbor or to have peace with their neighbor. God's government will bring peace to the entire world. No earthly government has ever been able to accomplish this. This is because in the past, all earthly governments have tried to bring peace through war, but God's government will bring peace through love, something no earthly government has ever been able to do or is capable of bringing to the entire world. (Ref. Dan. 7:5–23; Rev. 19:19.) See also **beast**; **kingdom of God**.

grace

> **natural**—Mercy; clemency; pardon; an honor; a manifestation of favor.

> **spiritual**—To freely forgive all debts; to bless without merit; to love regardless of faults; forgiveness made possible because of the blood of Christ; freedom from the law of God. The law condemned us all; grace forgave us for the transgressions of the law. Grace is compassion. Grace means favor. Grace is unconditional love. (Ref. Gen. 6:8; Gen. 19:19; Acts 15:11; Rom. 3:19–31; Rom. 4:4–16; Rom. 5:20; Rom. 11:6; Gal. 5:4.) See also **love**; **atonement**; **forgiveness**; **gift**; **mercy**.

grapes

natural—The edible, pulpy, smooth-skinned berry or fruit that grows in clusters on vines and from which wine is made.

spiritual—Another name for the people of God. These people spiritually live in the vine, the vine being Christ. Wine is made from grapes, both in the natural and spiritual sense. Wine is a spiritual name for the Holy Spirit. This is why people who are grapes produce wine, or works of the Spirit. The wine can also be called the blood of Christ. (Ref. Isa. 5:2–4; Isa. 17:6; Isa. 24:13; Jer. 8:13; Jer. 25:30; Hosea 9:10; Matt. 7:16; Luke 6:44; Rev. 14:18.) See also **wine**; **vineyard**; **vine tree**; **figs**; **Holy Spirit**; **blood of Christ**; **forgiveness**; **farmer**; **husbandman**.

grass

natural—The most numerous of all plant species; will grow under extreme conditions but will not grow without the sun, water, and good soil.

spiritual—The most important of all species on earth: man; will grow under extreme conditions but will not grow without the son, water, and someone to till the soil: the Son, the Holy Spirit, and the Father. They will not grow spiritually, that is, and some may even die. Without the Son, they will never learn of the Father. The Bible has concluded that all flesh is the same as grass, meaning without the sun, it will not grow but will perish. (Ref. Isa. 40:6; 1 Pet. 1:24; Rev. 8:7; Rev. 9:4.) See also **wheat**; **green things**; **man**.

grave

natural—Where family members place the body of their loved ones; where the body is placed back into the earth, where it came from, which is an earthly custom; where the physical body can be found after a physical death.

spiritual—The place where the soul and body rest while they are separated from the spirit that God placed in the body of man. This is how the scripture that says, "whilst we are at home in the body, we are absent from the Lord" (2 Cor. 5:6) can be true. The grave is a symbolic word for death. This is a physical death to the Lord; therefore, it is not the end. This is why this type of death is called sleep. Only a spiritual death is the end, and it is called the second death. During this sleep, the soul is unaware of anything that is going on, and time passes without the person being aware until he or she is resurrected. Those who are resurrected fulfill the scripture spoken by Jesus in John 11:26, "he that believe in me shall never die," which means if you are asleep, you never truly died. This is why Christ calls the physical death sleep; where that person lies while asleep is the grave. (Ref. Dan. 12:2; Eccles. 9:1–6; Luke 8:52; John 11:11–26; Eph. 5:14; 1 Thess. 4:14; 1 Thess. 5:10; Heb. 10:27.) See also **sleep; death; second death; judgment; resurrection**.

green things

natural—Vegetation, such as plant life; the greenness of the plant indicates the life that is in the plant, and dry or brown represents death.

spiritual—Any person who believes in Christ is green, which means he or she has life in him or her and is not dead. (Ref. Job 39:8; Ps. 37:2; Ps. 52:8; Isa. 15:6; Ezek. 17:24; Luke 23:31; Rev. 9:4.) See also **grass; judgments; millennium; tree; vine; palm leaves; branches; wheat**.

ground, good

natural—Soil that contains all the right nutrients for growing any seed; used for growing organic foods, such as vegetables and fruits, in order to sustain natural life.

spiritual—A believing and faithful heart; a heart that listens to the Spirit; an obedient heart, which is vital for growing in the Word, which at first is just a seed but will grow into a fig tree in order to sustain that person's spiritual life. Good ground is a person who, after he hears the Word of God, he or she never forgets it and never stops practicing or doing the Word of God, which is different from people who have stony and thorny ground in their hearts. The person with the good ground will be mocked but will endure it. The person with the stony ground will not endure much mocking before he or she will quit. The person with the good ground in his or her heart will not be liked by the world but will endure it. The person with the stony ground will be liked by the world and will not have to endure rejection. The person with the good ground in his or her heart will not be politically correct but will endure it and still enjoy the peace and comfort of the Word of God. The person with the stony ground in his or her heart will seek to be politically correct, in order to be more accepted by the world. (Ref. Matt. 13:18–30; Matt. 13:32.) See also **fig tree; Christian; hearing; chosen; sons; Word of God; seed; ground, stony; ground, thorny; dry soil.**

ground, stony

natural—Ground that contains only a little of the nutrients for growing a seed.

spiritual—Ground that contains only a little of the nutrients for growing a seed, which is the Word of God. This seed is planted in a person's heart as soon as this person hears the Word. According to the parable of the sower, people with stony ground in their hearts are people who receive the Word of God, but the Word cannot take root. When trials and tribulations come, these people let go of the Word of God, in favor of the way the world does things. This is mainly because they cannot endure much mocking by their friends for believing in something they cannot prove. These people, however, are saved because they do believe, but they do not practice the Word of God very often. However, they will always be confused and will never be able to put their faith in action because of fear. They will also not be able to enjoy the true peace that the Word of God brings until Christ returns. God calls these people lukewarm, because they are neither hot nor cold. (Ref. Matt. 13:18–23.) See also **sons; servant son; seed; word of God; ground, good; ground, thorny; dry soil; lukewarm.**

ground, thorny

natural—Ground that contains only a little of the nutrients for growing seed.

spiritual—This is a person who receives the Word of God and the cares of this world at the same time. This happens because the person is trying to change who he or she is and draw closer to God but is also trying to live by the ways of the world. This causes confusion and conflict within the person, because these two ways of living conflict with one another. The Bible says that we cannot serve two masters, which the Bible calls man and manna—manna being the bread from heaven or how we should live according to

God and man meaning how the world thinks people should live their lives. The person with the thorns in his or her heart or the ways of the world, as long as he or she remains a believer, will be saved but will not have the true peace that the Word of God brings, because he or she tries to please the world as well as God. This is why God calls these people lukewarm, because they are neither hot nor cold. (Ref. Matt. 13:18–23.) See also **sons; servant son; called son; called woman; lukewarm.**

harvest, first

> **natural**—Gathering of planted goods in due season; reaping a bounty that was planted.

> **spiritual**—Gathering of God's people, who were planted in this world, who are spiritually called wheat, and taking them to be with him, in order to reward them for their faith. The first harvest takes place before the period of tribulations. This harvest is also known as a rapture. The harvest is plenteous, meaning all the people who believe in God and Christ, but the laborers are few, meaning the people who will be used to bring them to Christ. They are also called the chosen. The chosen are people whom the Lord predestined to be the first to receive the Holy Spirit so that it may live in them. During the time of planting, Satan planted tares in with the wheat, in the hopes that it would prevent the harvest. Tares are Satan's seed, or people who hate God. According to the parable of the tares and wheat, the tares will be gathered together and thrown into the lake of fire, and the wheat will be brought into the barn. The barn is God's house or kingdom. (Ref. Isa. 18:5; Matt. 3:12; Matt. 9:35–39; Matt. 13:25–30; Mark 4:29; Luke 3:17; Luke 10:2; Rev. 14:15–16.) See also **rapture; new city; resurrection; harvest, second; harvest, third; laborer; seed; wheat; tares.**

harvest, second

> **natural**—The gleaning of the fields or picking up what was left behind from the first harvest.

> **spiritual**—The gathering together of those who were not ready for the first rapture; this takes place directly after the tribulations or some time during the millennium. They will be ready because they will come to have full faith in the Word of God. The millennium

is for people who deserve a second chance to get to know Christ. When their faith has matured, he will perform the second harvest. There is also a third harvest, but this harvest is for those who will be thrown into the lake of fire. (Ref. Isa. 18:5; Jer. 5:24; Matt. 9:38; Matt. 13:25–39; Matt. 24:29–31; Mark 4:29; Rev. 14:17–18.) See also **rapture**; **new city**; **Judgment Day**; **end**; **second death**; **resurrection, first**; **resurrection, second**.

harvest, third
natural—N/A
spiritual—This is for people who refused to believe in the Lord. They would not repent, even after they had seen the Lord. This is called the third harvest, the harvest of the tares. Tares are people who have been planted by Satan. They are the haters of God. They have the spirit of the world within them or the spirit of the Antichrist. These are the people whom the Lord allowed to live among the wheat, so that they might teach the wheat the difference between good and evil, so that they might remain wheat in order to be harvested. (Ref. Jer. 50:16.) See also **tares**; **unbelievers**; **heart, evil**; **cold**; **lost son**; **lost woman**; **cedar tree**; **tree, fruitless**.

hearing
natural—Physically distinguishing sounds.
spiritual—Spiritually distinguishing the Lord's voice from one's own; receiving revelation on the inside or knowing that the Lord is trying to tell you something; knowing by faith and acting upon it; being aware of something spiritually because the Lord has spoken to you in your spirit; knowing when you are doing the will of the Father. Hearing spiritually is also called drinking. It is called drinking because the Spirit of God is symbolically called water. This water is placed in a person's heart, which is symbolically called a cistern. If your cistern is not cracked, it can hold this water. This water is symbolically called living water, or the Holy Spirit. This water was placed there based on the man's ability to hear the Word of God. This is why Jesus would begin his parables with, "Let them that hear, hear and let them that see, see." These are spiritual ears and spiritual eyes that Jesus is referring to. The Father is the only one who gives a person these types of ears and eyes to

hear and see with. (Ref. Matt. 13:14–16; John 12:44–50; John 10:1–16; Prov. 8:1–10; Heb. 3:1–19.) See also **believing; chosen; called; drinking; listening; cistern; cup; water.**

heart

natural—The most valuable organ in the body; the organ that pumps the life-giving blood and oxygen around the body as well as nourishment to the body so that it can have mobility.

spiritual—The soul of man; this is because the heart has a mind of its own. The heart will be used for the judgment of man. It will either condemn or excuse a person based on its intent. The heart is where love and hate originate. The heart is the dwelling place of the Holy Spirit. If a man has good ground or soil in his heart, the heart is where the second covenant of God has established the new covenant or, in other words, where he wrote his laws so that a man could not forget them. It is where understanding and fear of God starts. Where a man's heart is so is his treasure. It is where light is placed, where water flows out of the mouth from, and a container for the holy spirit or living water. (Ref. Prov. 10:8; Prov. 16:23; Prov. 20:25; Luke 12:34; Rom. 2:29; Rom. 8:10; Rom. 10:10; 2 Cor. 1:20–22; 2 Cor. 3:1–18; 2 Cor. 4:1–7.) See also **soul; mind; saved; treasure; kingdom; Holy Spirit; light; container; cistern; water.**

heir, son

natural—A son who is first in line to succeed his father; due a great inheritance; related to the one who can will the inheritance by blood.

spiritual—A son who is to receive an inheritance from his father. The inheritance is to become part of the Godhead. This is made possible because it is the birthright of the sons of God, because they were born from him. All heirs are born from God and are related not just by the blood of Christ, but by birthright as well. Being born again by accepting Christ causes a person to become an adopted son, but the heir was not born again. He or she was born from God, and God has known him or her since he or she was born. This is what Rom 8:29 refers to when it says, "for those whom he foreknew he also predestinated." He knew them because they came from him, as Adam did. This is not the same as the angels, who were beings he created from outside of himself. Their spirits are created, but the heir's spirit came from God and has always been a part of his spirit. The heir's spirit is one with God, just as his son Jesus Christ's spirit is one with God; otherwise, the heir would not be an heir. The heir is related to God because God is his father literally. The heir is the seed of God on earth, and God has planted him. They that are heirs are also called joint heirs with Christ. This is because they are brothers, not just because they have accepted him as others have done, but because they were born that way. According to Galatians 4:1, it says, "that the heir, as long as he is a child differeth nothing from a servant though he be lord of all." This is because the heirs didn't know who they were, because there was no one to tell them, until God was ready for them to know. They are different from all other people in the world, because they are the chosen, and they were chosen to change this world alongside Christ when the appointed time comes. Until that time, they are in training, under the elements of the world. They are not servants. They are the children of God. John 1:13 says that they are not born by the will of flesh, not by the will of man, but by that of God. Romans 9:11 says, "For the children being not yet born, neither having done any good or evil, that the purpose of God according to election might stand, not of works, but of him that calleth." In 1 John 3:9, it says, "Whosoever is born of God doth not commit sin; for his seed remaineth in him: and he cannot sin, because he is born of God." These scriptures confirm where the heirs come from and that they cannot be lost because they were predestined, chosen, because they are born from God. (Ref. Matt. 21:33–40; John 1:13; Rom. 4:13; Rom. 8:17; Rom. 9:11; Gal. 4:1–7, 30; Heb. 1:2; Heb. 6:17; Heb. 11:7.) See also **chosen; free son; predestined; adult son; Holy Spirit.**

holiness of God

natural—Regarded with or worthy of worship or veneration; revered; something that is hallowed and has been made worthy to be worshiped.

spiritual—A sacred right of God that can only be given to another by him, and since it cannot be reproduced, it is therefore part of the masculine side of God. (Ref. Ps. 47:8; Ps. 48:1; Rom. 1:4; Rom.

6:22; 2 Cor. 7:1.) See also **masculine side of God; male side of God; power; glory; righteousness; honor; authority; wrath.**

Holy Ghost
natural—N/A
spiritual—God in the form of his Spirit, but not the Son, the actual Father. The Holy Ghost was active in the Old Testament, unlike the Holy Spirit, who is active under the New Testament. The Holy Ghost is different from the Holy Spirit in that the one convicts us of our sins and the other frees us from our sins. The Holy Ghost must come before the Holy Spirit. The law must come before grace. The Holy Ghost and the Holy Spirit are the same spirit, because the Father and the Son share the same spirit. This is what makes them one literally. The only difference is in which one is with you at the present time. The Holy Ghost only rests upon a person, while the Holy Spirit resides inside a person. If the Holy Ghost only rests upon a person, change will occur within that person and he or she will believe, but this change will not be as significant as the change that occurs when the Holy Spirit resides forever within a person. There were a few cases when God said his Spirit the Holy Ghost was placed within a person. Even still, it did not stay permanently. One exception was Mary, the mother of Jesus. The Holy Ghost was inside of her, in order for Jesus to be born. The Holy Ghost became flesh and became known to us as Christ. If the Holy Spirit resides inside a person, much change will occur within that person, because God has chosen that person to receive his Spirit. The Bible uses the word *Spirit* as a name for both the Holy Ghost and the Holy Spirit. One way to know if it is the Father or the Son is to figure out the action being performed, and if the action is of conviction, wrath, or prophesying, then it is the Father. If the action is forgiveness, change, or revelation, this is the Spirit in the form of the Son, the Holy Spirit. (Ref. Gen. 1:2; Gen. 6:3; 1 Sam. 10:6; Isa. 11:2; Isa. 61:1; Ezek. 11:5.) See also **Father; God the Father; Godhead; Lord of Host; Law.**

Holy Spirit
natural—N/A
spiritual—God in the form of the Spirit, but in reference to the Son of God, not the Father; the name of the second person in the

trinity; also known as the Word of God before he became known as Christ. Technically speaking, only half of the Word became known as the man called Christ, because he did not reunite with his Spirit until he was baptized. The Holy Spirit is Christ in the Spirit. The same Spirit is also the Spirit of God. This is technically how they are one. They share the same Spirit. The Spirit gives those who believe in Christ the ability to become the sons of God. This is the reason Jesus died on the cross. He died in order to make it possible for his Father to place the Spirit in the hearts of those whom he had chosen. He gives us access to the power of God by faith. The Spirit gives the believers in Christ the ability to become overcomers of the world. The trinity of God exists in three forms, the soul, the spirit, and the body of Christ. The soul is the part that is the Father (Matthew 12:18.) The Spirit, which is his spirit, called the Holy Spirit, he shares with his son (Matthew 12:18). He has a body, just as we do. After all, he did create us in his own image. The body refers to Christ (John 1:14.) The Bible says, "and the Word was made flesh." These are the three manifestations of God. This is just like our bodies in that very same image. The trinity of man is a combination of body, spirit, and soul, and these three are one. The Holy Spirit is also known as the Comforter, the Teacher of man, the Seal, and the part of the Godhead that dwells in those who have received the Spirit of God. The Holy Spirit gives man all the gifts he needs to fulfill the destiny of the church, gifts, such as speaking in tongues, interpreting tongues, the laying on of hands, discerning between good and bad spirits, the gift of faith, the gift of wisdom, and the gift of knowledge, etc. This is but a little of who the Holy Spirit is and what he does for man. The Holy Spirit comes to men in different forms. There are seven manifestations of the Holy Spirit, and only one man has ever possessed all seven, and that is Christ. The seven manifestations of the Spirit are wisdom, understanding, knowledge, fear or wrath, power, counseling, and love. These are the seven ways a man can receive the Holy Spirit. Each element receives the Holy Spirit in a certain way. The water element people receive the Holy Spirit in the form of wisdom and understanding; the air element people receive the Holy Spirit in the form of knowledge; the earth element people receive the Holy Spirit in the form of counseling and love; the fire element people receive the Holy Spirit in the form of fear or the wrath of God. The different ways in which the Holy Spirit can manifest himself to people and dwell in them is found in 1 Corinthians 12:1–14. (Ref. Prov. 16:9; John 1:1–14; John 14:26; John 15:26–27; John 16:13–14; 1 Cor. 2:9–16; 1 Cor. 12:1–14; Eph. 1:17; Eph. 4:30; 1 John 5:6.) See also **son; God the son; seal; word, the; Jesus; Christ; Godhead; trinity; Holy Spirit; grace; wisdom; knowledge; understanding; elements God; element water; element air; element earth; element fire; gold; silver; brass; chosen son; servant son; faithful son; wine; corn; oil; bride of Christ.**

honor of God

natural—A source of credit or distinction; high respect, as for worth, merits, or rank.

spiritual—A sacred right of God. It can only be given to another by him, and since it cannot be reproduced, it is therefore part of the masculine side of God. (Ref. Ps. 104:1; 2 Pet. 1:17; Rev. 7:12.) See also **masculine, side of God; male side of God; power; glory; righteousness; holiness; authority; wrath.**

hope

natural—To desire something with all expectation; to never give up on something; to wait on and expect something to happen.

spiritual—To never lose one's belief in Christ; to never lose the belief in one's salvation; to not lose the belief in the resurrection upon the day of Christ's return; to never give up on one's goals spiritually; to never give up trying to find God; to be assured of something; the substance of things not seen; key to man's salvation; hope removes doubt. (Ref. Rom. 5:1–5; Rom. 8:24–25; Rom. 15:4–13.) See also **faith; saved; joy; word, the.**

horns of God

natural—N/A

spiritual—These are mentioned in the book of Daniel, in the vision of the goat and the ram. The horns on the ram are a symbolic representation of God's power. The horns represent the two groups of God's people. The two horns are also known as the two brides. The first bride was Israel, spiritually called Zion. The second bride is the Gentiles, spiritually called Sion or those who have accepted

Christ. He lives in the form of the Holy Spirit. (Ref. Dan. 7:8–21; Dan. 8:8–21; 1 Sam. 2:10; Mic. 4:13; Luke 1:69.) See also **bride of Christ; Zion; Sion; Power.**

horns of Satan
natural—N/A
spiritual—These horns are mentioned in the book of Daniel, in the vision of the goat and the ram. The horn on the goat represents the person who was used, who is in a position of authority and power of the beast that it is attached to, the beast being a form of government that existed at that time. The type of beast depends on the nature of the beast that is used to attack the people of God. All horns attached to the beast are types of Antichrist, who get their power from Satan. The one large horn on the head of the goat, in the book of Daniel, is a symbolic representation of Alexander the Great, who conquered the Babylonians who had conquered Israel. Since Israel had been captured by the Babylonians and taken to Babylon, God considered Babylon the home of his people at that time; therefore, the goat was attacking the ram, which represented his people. The goat is a symbolic representation of Satan's people. This horn broke, and when this horn broke, it broke up into four pieces or kingdoms, controlled by four little horns, or Alexander's four generals. They controlled Greece, Asia Minor, and Egypt, along with Arabia. According to the Bible, there are ten more horns that will rise in order to form a fifth kingdom. That fifth kingdom will be controlled by ten horns or ten kings. These ten horns will give their power to the one horn that will rise, who is more powerful than all the other horns. This last horn is someone we have been warned is coming, known as the future Antichrist. According to the Bible, he will control the world, just as all previous horns have done. (Ref. Dan. 7:1–21; Dan. 8:1–21; Zech. 1:21.) See also **goat; power; Antichrist.**

hot
natural—Having or giving off heat; having a high temperature; having a strong enthusiasm; eager; fervent.
spiritual—A person who is following the will of God; a person who listens to God; a person who has received the baptism by fire and has the Holy Spirit within him or her; a person who has been

kindled by the fire of the Lord. (Ref. Rev. 3:15–16.) See also **faith; fire; kindled; love; works; hearing; gold; chosen son; heir; ground, good; lukewarm; cold.**

house
natural—The dwelling place of man; something that provides shelter.
spiritual—A house is a spiritual representation of your body. It is also known as the temple of God and a dwelling place of the Holy Spirit. The body also goes by other symbolic names, such as garments or filthy garments, our first house, or old tabernacle. This is the opposite of a new house or white robes, which is our new body or spiritual body that God will give us to replace the flesh we now live in. (Ref. Matt. 7:24–27; Luke 11:24; 2 Cor. 5:1; 1 Pet. 2:4–5.) See also **body; garments; white robes; container; cistern; cup; bowl.**

hundred and forty-four thousand, first
natural—N/A
spiritual—This number represents the number of people God chose out of the Old Testament time to be used in the building of his new kingdom to be used in the millennium, the one-thousand-year rule of Christ, starting from the time of his second return. The chosen from the Old Testament are the ones who will teach those who have been resurrected from the Old Testament times, because they have to be taught by someone who understands what they have gone through. The former rain, or first 144,000, understand God's law better than anyone else and are therefore more equipped to bring those who were born under law, or before Christ died, out from under it and teach them what grace truly means. The elects were chosen before they were born to endure the hardships of this world and to overcome it by the power of God. Those who were chosen before Christ died on the cross, received the Holy Ghost in a greater measure than anyone else. This is the only way they would be able to overcome the world in order to do God's will. Another name for the first and second 144,000 is the living waters. They are called living waters, because they have drunk the water that if a man drinks he will never thirst again. This water is called living water, or the Holy Spirit. They are called living waters in

Zechariah 14:8. This scripture also tells us what their mission is and how God will use them, which is what I have stated before. Half of the chosen will go to the people born under law or before Christ died on the cross, and the other half will be sent to those born after the death of Christ in order to teach them the love and forgiveness of God. (Ref. Deut. 11:14; Zech. 10:1; James 5:7; Matt. 24:22; Rom. 9:11; 2 Tim. 2:10; Rev. 7:4; 1 John 5:1–6; Rev. 2:7, 11, 17, 26; Rev. 3:5, 12–21; Rev. 14:1; Rev. 21:7.) See also **former rain; latter rain; chosen; elects; fig tree; chosen woman; wine; free son; overcomers of the world; living waters.**

hundred and forty-four thousand, second
natural—N/A
spiritual—This number represents the number of people God chose out of the New Testament times to be used in the building of his new kingdom during the millennium, the one-thousand-year rule of Christ upon his return. The second group, the latter rain, or second group of 144,000, will teach those who are born after Christ died what grace truly means. The elects were chosen before they were born to endure the hardships of this world and to overcome it by the power of God. Those who were chosen after Christ died on the cross received the Holy Spirit in a greater measure than anyone else. This is how it was made possible for them to become overcomers of the world in order to be useful to God. Another name for the first and second 144,000, is the *living waters*. They are called living waters because they have drunk the water that if a man drinks he will never thirst again. This water is called living water, or the Holy Spirit. They are called living waters in Zechariah 14:8. This scripture also tells us what their mission is and how God will use them, which is what I have stated before. Half of the chosen will go to the people born under law, or before Christ died on the cross, and the other half will be sent to those born after the death of Christ in order to teach them the love and forgiveness of God. (Ref. Deut. 11:14; Zech. 10:1; James 5:7; Matt. 24:22; Rom. 9:11; 2 Tim. 2:10; 1 John 5:1–6; Rev. 2:7, 11, 17, 26; Rev. 3:5, 12, 21; Rev. 14:1; Rev. 21:7.) See also **former rain; latter rain; chosen; elects; fig tree; chosen woman; wine; free son; overcomers of the world; living waters.**

hunger

natural—The painful sensation or state of weakness caused by the need for food.

spiritual—The sensation or state of being weak spiritually due to a lack of spiritual food. People lack spiritual food because they don't ask questions, which leads to the receiving of spiritual food. Reading and listening to the Word of God is another way to receive spiritual food. Hunger is the drive behind how much food or understanding a person receives. How hungry a person is, can determine how much knowledge he or she receives. Hunger causes a person to want to gain knowledge, but understanding is determined by how much thirst a person has. (Ref. Isa. 49:14; Matt. 5:6; John 6:35; Rev. 7:16.) See also **spiritual food; eating; bread; corn; manna; drinking; water; wine; milk.**

husbandman

natural—A natural farmer; the act or practice of cultivating crops and breeding and raising livestock; agriculture.

spiritual—A spiritual farmer; the act or practice of cultivating people symbolically called crops and livestock. Man is referred to as crops, sometimes wheat, corn, grass, tares, trees, or fruit trees. When God refers to man as livestock, he refers to them as cattle, sheep, goats, or fish. God is cultivating or farming us so that we will be ready to enter into his new kingdom. (Ref. Gen. 9:20; John 15:1; 2 Tim. 2:6; James 5:7.) See also **Jesus; farmer; vineyard; wheat; corn; grass; tares; trees; trees, fruit; cattle; sheep; goats; fish.**

I AM

natural—It means to exist.

spiritual—It means that he is everything and that he is in everything. There is nothing that exists without him. All things are made by him and nothing that is made is without him. "I Am" is a way of saying, "I am everything, and everything is me." Since everything is made by him, it would do no good to say that he is any one thing, or for that matter to try to describe him with a thousand names. There is no one name that can describe him. This is why God told Moses, "I AM." (Ref. Exod. 3:14.) See also **Jehovah; trinity; God; Godhead; Father, the; tree of life.**

image of

natural—A physical likeness or representation of a person, animal, or thing, photographed, painted, sculptured, or otherwise made visible.

spiritual—God made man in his own image. The word *image* spiritually means an exact copy of. This is different from the word *likeness*, which spiritually means to resemble but not quite be a complete copy. Jesus was made in the image of his father. This is why Jesus said to his disciples in John 14:9, "If you have seen me, you have seen the Father." According to Rom 8:29, we are in a process that will transform us into the image of God. (Ref. Gen. 1:26–27; Gen. 5:3; Rom. 8:29; 1 Cor. 11:7; 1 Cor. 15:49; 2 Cor. 3:18; Col. 1:15; Col. 3:10; Heb. 1:3; Rev. 14:9; Rev. 16:2; Rev. 19:20; Rev. 20:4.) See also **Christ; female; feminine; likeness; trinity; oneness; God; living waters.**

impute

natural—To put in; to apply; to hold accountable.

spiritual—To apply a person's sins against him or her. The Bible says in Psalm 32:2, "Blessed is the man unto whom the LORD imputeth not iniquity, and in whose spirit there is no guile." This scripture means that this person's sins were not held against him or her. This essentially means that this person is without sin; therefore, this person has never sinned in his life, not that he or she didn't do anything that wasn't contrary to the Word of God but simply God chose not to count it against him or her. (Ref. Ps. 32:2; Rom. 4:1–8, 11, 22–23.) See also **forgiveness; grace; sins.**

iron

natural—An alloy found in the earth, used for construction and other building materials.

spiritual—A symbolic word for people who have not chosen to follow God. This is why God calls them iron, because they are a hard metal and need more heat in the fire to soften. There are softer metals, such as silver and gold, which have a lower melting point, or in other words, they don't need as much heat from God's furnace in order to be refined so that they can do his will. There are other metals, such as tin and lead. These are words God uses to describe the kinds of hearts that people have, as well as the melting point, gold being the softest metal of all. This is why these people are so precious to God. (Ref. Num. 31:21–24; Deut. 4:20; Deut. 28:23; Isa. 60:17; Jer. 6:28; Ezek. 22:18; Dan. 2:35.) See also **metals; gold; silver; brass; tin; refining process; kindled with fire.**

Israel

natural—The descendents of Jacob; the Hebrew people, past, present, and future, regarded as the chosen people of God by virtue of the covenant of Jacob.

spiritual—The spiritual name for Israel is the olive tree, the tree that produces bitter fruit. This is because they rejected Christ. Although this fruit is useful, it cannot be readily eaten like the fruit of a fig tree, which is what God wanted Israel to be. When Christ found that there was no fruit on the fig tree, he withered it. The withering of the fig tree symbolically represented the changing of Israel into an olive tree. The fruit on this tree is also bitter, because this tree represents the law and therefore will be bitter to men. The tree that represents grace is the fig tree, which is sweet. The tree that became a fig tree was the Gentile nation, because they accepted Christ. God said this in Romans 2:13–15,

(For not the hearers of the law are just before God, but the doers of the law shall be justified. For when the Gentiles, which have not the law, do by nature the things contained in the law, these, having not the law, are a law unto themselves: Which shew the work of the law written in their hearts, their conscience also bearing witness, and their thoughts the mean while accusing or else excusing one another) …

This is how the Gentile nations gained the opportunity to become the fig tree or bride of Christ, by the falling of Israel. However, God will save some, a remnant, in order to become the crown on the head of the bride. Israel is also spiritually called the cedars of Lebanon or Jacob. (Ref. Judg. 9:8–15; Ps. 52:8; Isa. 17:6; Isa. 24:13; Hosea 14:6; Hab. 3:17; Rom. 2:13; Rom. 11:24; James 3:12.) See also **olive tree; Zion; law; fig tree, first; stars; cedars of Lebanon; crown of stars.**

Jehovah

natural—The name of God the Father.

spiritual—This name means "I AM," meaning everything; "My will be done"; "all judgment is Mine"; everlasting strength. (Ref. Exod. 6:3; Ps. 83:18; Isa. 26:4.) See also **God; father.**

Jerusalem, New

natural—N/A

spiritual—The new city that will descend from heaven, where the people who are found faithful will dwell with God. This is also another name for the bride of Christ. (Ref. Gal. 4:26; Rev. 21:2.) See also **Zion; new city; bride; bridegroom.**

Jesus

natural—A prophet of God.

spiritual—God in the flesh; Jesus was known as the Word of God before he came to earth; Jesus himself was just a man; after he was baptized, he became the Christ, which is a combination of a man and the Holy Spirit. This made him God and man at the same time, and because he was part man, he was also the Son of man and because his spirit came from God, he was the Son of God. He is now God the son, the only begotten son of God, meaning firstborn of all and the first to return to the Father after having conquered death, the first to be resurrected. Jesus is the one who shed his blood for us, so that the Father would have a way to forgive us of our sins. His blood is so valuable to God that if a man believes in him, he receives forgiveness. This is why Christ is the mediator or advocate for man, because of his sacrifice and obedience to the Father. He was anointed the king of glory, meaning no one else could have greater honor than he. He is the express image of God, equal with God, because this was the reward that God bestowed upon him; however, he is still subject to the Father because he knows that he was not first. He was born from the Father. A good son would not try to take his father's place. He is the Word of God, meaning a being that is another manifestation of God, the third person in the Godhead or order of things. He is God in bodily form, the light of the world, the way, the truth. He is also symbolically called the bread of life. If a man eats this bread, meaning receives the understanding that Jesus brought to this world, he will never hunger again or seek another savior. He is also called the branch, a branch off the tree of life, his father. He is also a tree, the vine tree, and we are branches off of him if we believe, but if someone stops believing in him, that branch would be cut off. He is also the bridegroom, and we who have received him are his bride. His blood, which was used for the forgiveness of sins, is symbolically called wine. If a man drinks this wine, he will receive the Holy Spirit, or Christ in the spirit form; Christ in the spirit would then live in the man, in order to begin the process of changing the man or transforming the man to become Christlike. This process takes time. It is not a short or easy process, since a man's nature is contrary to God's nature. Even if a man does not receive the Holy Spirit in his heart, he can still be saved by just believing in the name and blood of Christ. (Ref. John 1:1–15; 1 Cor. 15:17; Col. 1:9–22; Gal. 4:23–31; Phil. 2:5–11; Rev. 19:11–16.) See also **son of God, the; Word, the; Yahweh; Holy Spirit, the; trinity, the; oneness, the; tree, vine; wine, the; eagle, the; mediator, the; bread, the; Christ; lamb, the.**

joy

natural—A feeling of great happiness; a product of happiness.

spiritual—A gift from God, given by the Holy Spirit; one of the fruits of the Holy Spirit. This great feeling of happiness comes from the knowledge that one has been saved from death and that nothing can change that. This joy comes from knowing you have been forgiven for your sins. (Ref. James 1:1–5.) See also **Holy Spirit; peace; gifts; fruit.**

judgment

natural—A verdict, a decision, or condemnation based on evidence.

spiritual—Knowledge of the difference between good and evil; knowing what is righteous and unrighteous based on the Word of God. Man has been given the right to judge but told only to not judge a man unto condemnation, which means to try to determine if he is going to heaven or hell. This is the only judgment God asks man not to determine. This was based on the fact that man cannot determine this; only God can make this determination. However, man is allowed to judge between good and evil works. This type of judgment must be used in conjunction with the Holy Spirit. If the judgment is to be right in God's eyes, a man will be judged by his works. He will be judged by the faith or lack of faith in his heart. A man's works are simply the proof that he or she believes. They are not used to determine salvation; works are used to determine the amount of reward a person will receive after he or she has become saved. If a person is found to be a believer in Christ, only his good works or green works will count toward his reward. That same man also has bad works or dry works; these works will not count against his salvation; they will simply not add to his reward. If a man is not a believer in Christ, his bad works will be used against him, because he does not have the blood of Christ to cover his sins. Therefore, the unrighteous works that this man has done will condemn him. (Ref. Matt. 7:1; 1 Cor. 2:9–16.) See also **works**; **condemnation**; **forgiveness**; **gifts**; **fruits**; **blessings**; **Holy Spirit**.

justified

natural—To be found innocent of any wrongdoing.

spiritual—To be forgiven for all sins; caused by faith proven by works. (Ref. Rom. 3:19–31; Matt. 12:33–37; Gal. 2:15–16; Gal. 3:22.) See also **righteousness**; **saved**; **works**; **faith**; **heart**; **mature son**; **predestined**; **impute**.

key

natural—A tool for unlocking things, such as doors or safes.

spiritual—A tool used for unlocking the mysteries of God. This key is the knowledge that Christ gives, which leads to the understanding of his father in heaven. This key or knowledge leads to belief, which opens up the gates to heaven as well as all mysteries found in the Bible. This key leads to the Holy Spirit, who teaches a man how to use it. (Ref. Luke 11:52.) See also **knowledge**; **wisdom**; **belief**; **faith**.

kindle with fire

natural—To set fire to.

spiritual—To set fire to, only this is a spiritual fire. This fire is meant to bring about change. To kindle also means to anger God, so that his wrath falls upon a person, but his wrath does not always destroy; it sometimes rebuilds. (Ref. Jer. 11:16; Hosea 8:14; Isa. 10:17; Isa. 24:15; Isa. 43:2; Isa. 50:11; Ezek. 20:47; Ezek. 39:6; Zech. 3:2; Zech. 9:4; Zech. 13:9; Matt. 3:10–12; Matt. 20:22–23; Luke 12:49–50; Acts 10:44–48; 1 Cor. 3:13–15; 2 Thess. 1:8; Heb. 12:29; 1 Pet. 1:7; 2 Pet. 3:7; Jude 1:23; Rev. 8:5–8; Rev. 9:18; Rev. 15:2, 8; Rev. 18:8.) See also **fire**; **saved**; **chosen**; **baptism by fire**; **refining process**.

kingdom

natural—That which is possessed by an earthly king.
spiritual—That which is possessed by a heavenly king; where God dwells and where all men will eventually dwell with God and his son. (Ref. Luke 17:20–21.) See also **heaven**; **heart**; **faith**.

knowledge

natural—A state of knowing; fact; the perception of fact or truth; clear and certain mental apprehension; awareness, as of a fact or circumstance.
spiritual—The key to unlocking the gates of heaven. It brings salvation. Knowledge is the truth about Jesus as to who he is, where he came from, and what his death accomplished. The Bible has concluded that we die from lack of knowledge. It leads to belief, belief leads to faith, and faith leads to salvation. This is how knowledge works. The symbolic word for knowledge is bread. This is what we must eat in order to live. This bread or knowledge comes from Christ; however, Christ told Satan, man should not live by bread alone. This means that it is not enough to just know of something, we need to do it as well. Symbolically speaking, there are two types of bread in this world, leavened bread and unleavened bread. The bread that is leavened is the knowledge that the world teaches. The bread that is unleavened is the knowledge that Christ teaches. One will puff a person up because it is filled with leaven or yeast. The other will cause a person to be humble, because it has no leaven in it. If a man eats the bread that is leavened, he will hunger again. If a man eats the bread that is unleavened, he will never hunger again, meaning he will never be unsure that he has found Christ. (Ref. Hosea 4:6; Matt. 13:11; Rom. 1:16–20; 1 Cor. 2:9–16; Eph. 1:23–29; Col. 2:1–6; I Pet

1:1-9; 2 Pet. 1:1–2.) See also **bread; wisdom; hearing; eating; drinking; seeing; faith; light.**

laborer

natural—A person who works for another man to make a living.

spiritual—A person who works for Christ. (Ref. Matt. 9:37–38; Luke 10:7; 1 Cor. 3:9; 1 Tim. 5:18.) See also **Christian; chosen; called; faithful.**

lamb

natural—A harmless animal; related to the goat, domesticated for wool, milk, and meat.

spiritual—A harmless person; related to God; his name is Jesus; another name for Jesus. Even though he was harmless, he was seen as a threat to society. He was called a lamb because he did not fight back and willingly made the ultimate sacrifice in order for man to receive forgiveness for sins. There is only one condition to receiving this forgiveness: you have to believe that Jesus is your savior, the Son of God, and that he truly died for your sins. If you do not have faith in this but still believe in God, you will then place yourself under the Ten Commandments, and these commandments will only convict a person of his or her sins and make him or her live in guilt all his or her life. This would negate the purpose of the sacrifice of the lamb, "the lamb slain from the foundation of the world," (Rev. 13:8). People who follow after Christ are also called sheep. Sheep is another word for lamb. Lamb is also a symbolic word for people who are slaughtered like sheep, helpless animals, for their beliefs. (Ref. Ps. 44:22; Acts 8:32; 1 Pet. 1:19; Rev. 5:6–13; Rev. 6:16; Rev. 7:10, 14; Rev. 12:11; Rev. 13:8; Rev. 17:14.) See also **Jesus; Word, the; sheep; child of God; blood.**

lamp

natural—Something that holds or contains a source of light.

spiritual—A person's spirit. The Spirit of Christ is a lamp. A lamp is a container that holds oil, and this oil is used to give light. A person is a lamp, and the oil is wisdom which comes from the Holy Spirit. If man receives this oil in his lamp or body, according to the Bible, he will shine and not be able to hide the light that will come from him. This light is the wisdom of God that will come through his mouth. This is how you let your light shine, or in other words, share it with others as the Holy Spirit shares it with them. Another word for lamp is *candlestick*. A church is a candlestick that gives light as well. Seven candlesticks are supposed to shine the light of Christ throughout the world by keeping the Lord's last commandment, which was to love one's neighbor as oneself. We would be keeping the light in our hearts. If we tried to follow law, then we would not be shining our light, because the law does not have forgiveness in it. Therefore, we would not be forgiving our brother when he trespassed against us. The Spirit of God helps us to do this, and the Spirit that is within the church is the light of the church, which helps the world. (Ref. Exod. 27:20; 2 Sam. 22:29; Ps. 119:105; Prov. 6:23; Prov. 120:20; Prov. 20:27; Isa. 62:1.) See also **light; candle; candlestick; spirit; lampstand; man; spirit; cup; container; light; knowledge.**

law

natural—Made for the punishment of crimes; to deter wrongdoing.

spiritual—Law is the knowledge of sin, the Ten Commandments. It was given so that we as men would know what is right and what is wrong. Before there was law, no one could have been found guilty of doing any wrong. Law is the power or enforcement behind sin, meaning without law, sin has no power. The law is the extent of punishment for sinning against God. The law, however, only punishes those who are under law. It is for the lawless. Law is not for those who are found faithful by God, because of their faith, they are no longer under the law. This was made possible by the death of Christ; upon his death, the law, according to the Bible, was nailed to the cross, meaning it died with Christ, and we were made free from it. If it had remained, then no one would ever have the possibility of salvation because no one has the ability to keep the law. The law was replaced by grace once Jesus died for our sins, whereby a man is saved by faith, not the deeds of the law; under grace, there are only two requirements: believe in Christ and love your neighbor as yourself. The law was the forerunner to grace. It was never meant to save anyone. It was only meant to convict us of our sins, so that we would know that we could not save ourselves and that we would need a savior; his name is Christ. (Ref. 2 Cor. 3:1–18; Heb. 8:6–13; Heb. 9:1–15; Rom. 3:19–31; Rom. 7:1–35; Rom. 13:8–10; Gal. 5:14; Col. 2:13–14.) See also **commandments; covenants; love; faith.**

law, end

natural—N/A

spiritual—Love is the end of all law, because love can do no evil. Love is the fulfillment of all law. Love forgives all, and since the law had no forgiveness, love is the end of law. Christ is the end of law as well, because he is love. (Ref. Rom. 10:4; Rom. 3:19–31; Rom. 7:1–6; Rom. 13:10; Gal. 5:13–14; Col. 2:24; Eph. 2:12–22; 1 Pet. 4:8.) See also **love; covenant, second; grace.**

lead

natural—A type of metal; not high in value.

spiritual—Those who are wicked in the sight of God; when God tries to use the refining process on these people, they do not change. (Ref. Jer. 6:29; Ezek. 22:18; Ezek. 27:12.) See also **metals of God; gold; silver; brass; iron; tin; refining process; fire.**

leaven

natural—An agent, such as yeast, that when added to bread causes it to rise. Leavened bread is bread mixed with yeast, an agent that causes it to rise.

spiritual—An agent that when added to the knowledge causes a man's ego to rise. This agent can be self-righteousness, pride in works, or anger. This leaven or ego gets in the way of God's message when too much attention is placed on the individual who is delivering the message, when too much attention is placed on the messenger instead of the message. This also happens when one leans toward his or her own understanding and adds it to the Word of God. This is symbolically the same as mixing yeast with bread. Another type of mixing is when a person accepts Christ but still cares for the things of the world. This can be found in the parable of the sower, which tells us not to mix faith with worldly knowledge, because it will cause a person to be puffed up with pride. (Ref. Matt. 16:6–12; 1 Cor. 5:6–8; Gal. 5:9.) See also **unleavened bread; bread; dead works; self-righteousness.**

life

natural—Awareness; existence; the quality of being alive; the physical and mental state of a being.

spiritual—A free gift from God; the chance to choose and have everlasting life; making choices; an opportunity to learn about the one who created you; knowing the difference between good and evil. (Ref. Gen. 9:4; Prov. 8:35; John 1:4; John 3:15; John 5:24–26; John 6:47–48; John 12:25.) See also **gifts; spirit, man's**.

light

natural—Something that allows a person to see by day and night; natural sunlight; other forms of light are called artificial light, which can be produced by man.

spiritual—The knowledge of Christ that leads to the understanding of the father, which in turn leads to salvation. Light is also called the way. Light is understanding. Light can be goodness that is shown toward a fellow man. Light can also mean the revelations of God. The Bible says that God is light. Light is the opposite of darkness, which means the lack of knowledge of God. (Ref. Prov. 20:27; John 1:1–9; Matt. 5:15–16; Luke 11:36; 2 Cor. 4, 5; 1 John 1:5.) See also **truth; goodness; wisdom; understanding; knowledge; Word of God, the; Holy Spirit, the; candlestick**.

likeness of

natural—The semblance or appearance of something; guise.

spiritual—The semblance or appearance of something in the spiritual sense. God made men in his image and likeness; the difference between the two is that the image means an exact copy while likeness only means something that is similar but not quite the same. All men bear the likeness of God, but some are born in his image, and the people who are born to bear his image are called chosen sons, free sons, or heirs. Those who bear his likeness are called servant sons or adopted sons. The likeness of and the image of are not the same thing. (Ref. Gen 1:26; Gen. 5:1–3; Ps. 17:15; Rom. 6:5; Rom. 8:3; Phil. 2:7.) See also **Christ; God; image; female; feminine; man; trinity**.

lion, young

natural—A large carnivorous feline mammal; a very brave person.

spiritual—A large group of people or a person willing to do the Lord's will as opposed to an old lion who is not so ready to do the Lord's will. (Ref. Job 4:10–11; Ps. 34:10; Ps. 104:10–21; Is. 5:29; Is. 31:4; Ezek. 41:19; Hosea 5:14; Mic. 5:7–8.) See also **old lion**; **chosen**.

lion, old

natural—A large carnivorous feline mammal; a very brave person.

spiritual—A large group of people or a person who has become weary or old and not so willing to do the Lord's will, either because he or she lacks faith or does not completely understand the will of the Lord. (Ref. Gen. 49:9; Job 4:11.) See also **young lion**; **chosen**.

listen

natural—To hear with natural ears an audible sound; to pay attention to; to understand what is being said by someone.

spiritual—To hear with spiritual ears or have the ability to hear an inaudible voice; to pay attention to what the Holy Spirit has to say; to understand what is being said by the Holy Spirit; to do what came by revelation; to know what the Lord wants you to do. (Ref. Prov. 8:1–10; James 1:21–25; John 7:15–17; John 8:43–47; Heb. 3:1–19.) See also **hearing**; **drinking**; **water**; **Gospel**; **Holy Spirit**; **gifts of the spirit**.

little flock

natural—A group of animals that live, travel, or feed together.

spiritual—Those who will be ready when Christ returns; they are called the chosen of God. (Ref. Luke 12:32–36.) See also **chosen**; **heir**; **sheep**; **goats**.

living water

natural—N/A

spiritual—Another name for the Holy Spirit; Jesus tells us that if we drink this water, we shall never thirst again. This water is given by Jesus alone. This water teaches a person everything he or she need to know about the Father, the Son, and the Holy Spirit. This water purges a person of all sins by causing him or her to love one another therefore fulfilling the commandments of God. This water washes the person as white as snow by causing him or her to love, which therefore causes God to forgive that person. This is also the water that flows from the throne of God, which God will use for the healing of the nations (Rev. 22:1); only by the drinking of this water can a man enter into the city of God (Rev. 22:17). (Ref. Prov. 11:25; Prov. 20:5; Ezek. 36:24–27; Jer. 2:13; Matt. 10:40–42; John 4:10–11; John 7:38; 1 Pet. 3:20; Rev. 22:1.) See also **river; water; hearing; drinking; dipper; understanding; Holy Spirit; elements; element, water.**

living waters
natural—N/A
spiritual—Another name for the people who have drunk the living water and are now ready to give this water to anyone who will listen. Those who have drunk this living water are those who are filled with the Holy Spirit. These people are the people whom the Bible describes as having rivers of water flowing from their mouths (John 7:38); since they have drunk this water, they have become living water themselves and are called the living waters. This is found in Zechariah 14:8 and Revelation 7:17. This means that these people are filled with the Holy Spirit. This has caused them to be transformed into the image of Christ, and this is found in Romans 8:29. (Ref. Zech. 14:6–9; 2 Cor. 3:18; Rev. 22:1.) See also **image; elects; chosen; free son; chosen woman; bride; fig tree; gold; river; female; feminine; water; living water.**

Lord, the
natural—Someone who is in a position of authority or power; royalty.
spiritual—Someone who is in position of authority or power; royalty; Jesus Christ, savior of man, forgiver of sins. (Ref. Exod. 6:2; Isa. 43:11; Ezek. 38:23; Rev. 1:8.) See also **Jesus; Lord; vine tree; trinity.**

Lord of hosts

    natural—N/A

    spiritual—God the Father; the head of the Godhead. (Ref. 2 Chron. 16:8; Isa. 13:4.)

    See also **trinity; Godhead; tree of life; father of spirits; father of lights**.

lost son

    natural—Someone who cannot find his way home or his destination; someone who has forgotten who he is naturally.

    spiritual—Someone who cannot find his way home or his destination; someone who has forgotten who he is spiritually; someone who does not believe in God or Christ; someone whose love has been replaced with hate in his heart and who cannot forgive or repent; someone who hates authority, leadership, organization, or order. (Ref. Heb. 3:7–19; 2 Pet. 2:1–22; 2 Cor. 4:4; Mark 11:25–26; 1 John 4:1–21; Luke 13:3–5; Rev. 2:22; Rev. 3:19.) See also **lost woman; unbelief; unbeliever; evil; evil deeds; heart; evil heart; condemnation**.

lost woman

    natural—A female who is lost and cannot find her way home or her destination.

    spiritual—A group of people who agree that there is no God; a group of people who refuse to repent even though God has tried to change their minds many times within their lifetime. They are called a woman because spiritually they reproduce children like themselves. They reproduce sons like themselves because they either teach them directly or indirectly by their actions, by their way of life, or by their hatred for others. The inability to love or to come to Christ is spiritually called adultery, which is to not believe, since we all have the ability to reproduce sons who believe or believe not. So the sons of God who refuse to believe are spiritually called an adulterous woman. This is what God called Israel in Hosea 3:1. This kind of adultery applies to anyone who refuses to believe in Christ, since all people were called to be married to Christ. Those who don't come to the wedding are committing spiritual adultery. This is different from spiritual fornication because in this the person comes back to Christ after he or she finds out that he or she was doing something wrong. But the person committing adultery doesn't care and doesn't want to return to him and be remarried. Because of this, his or her fate is to receive the second death. These people are also the ones who will be the last to be raised from death. They will be raised in the third resurrection to receive the death sentence. This death is to be separated from God forever. This is the second death. (Ref. Hosea 3:1; Mark 11:25–26; Luke 13:3–5; 2 Cor. 4:4; Heb. 3:7–19; 2 Pet. 2:1–22; 1 John 4:1–21; Rev. 2:22; Rev. 3:19.) See also **female; adulterous woman; lost son; unbelief; unbeliever; evil; evil deeds; heart; evil heart; condemnation; second death; cedar tree; fornicating woman.**

love

natural—Strong affection; to cherish; to have passion; to show compassion; the opposite of hate.

spiritual—The fulfillment of the law; eraser of sins; to do unto others as you would have them do unto you, which is the fulfillment of the law. God shows us unconditional love by allowing us to live under grace, instead of the law. Love is the greatest power of God, even greater than faith. (Ref. Rom. 13:10; 1 Pet. 4:8; Gal. 5:22–26.) See also **works; grace; atonement; forgiveness; fruit; God.**

lukewarm

natural—Moderately warm; having or showing little ardor, zeal, or enthusiasm; indifferent.

spiritual—A person who is not overly enthusiastic about following the ways of Christ; a person who has little faith; a person who only worships God in the body and not the spirit; a person who does not understand the God he or she worships; a person who believes in the Father, Son, and Holy Spirit, but the Lord has trouble getting him or her to do his will. These people are not hot, meaning doing the will of God as often as possible; neither are they cold, which means they never do the will of God. (Ref. Matt. 24:12; Rev. 3:15–16.) See also **believers; servant son; called son; called woman; olive tree; hot; cold; ground, thorny.**

male side of God

    natural—N/A

    spiritual—The part of God that doesn't reproduce. These are gifts that can only be given to another. They are power, honor, glory, holiness; righteousness; authority; and wrath. These aspects of God are different from the aspects of the Holy Spirit, which reproduce. The Holy Spirit when given reproduces sons by causing them to produce virtues called the fruits of the Spirit. These fruits, which are reproduced in us, are called love, peace, happiness, joy, kindness, forgiveness, etc. This is why these are feminine in nature. Those things that do not reproduce are masculine in nature. (Ref. Matt. 5:48; Matt. 21:24; John 5:26–27; 2 Pet. 1:17.) See also **masculine side of God; God the Father; power; honor; glory; holiness; authority; wrath; righteousness.**

man

    natural—A human being; the highest form of animal on the earth, different in the fact that they have the ability to reason. The first man was Adam, and the first woman was Eve.

    spiritual—Man is a being that is the solution to a problem that began in heaven. The problem was that some of the angels rebelled against their creator. This was caused by the lack of understanding as to who their creator was and what his purpose was for creating them in the first place. This rebellion was born out of the fact that God gave the angels free will. This meant that an angel could choose to follow or not follow God. Those who chose not to follow him did so out of not knowing the difference between what was good and what was evil, so God made it possible for all of them to find out what the difference between good and evil was. He did this by placing the spirit of the angel in an earthly body and calling him man. Man was made in the image of God, both literally and naturally as well as spiritually. Man is God's greatest source of accomplishment and pain at the same time. We are his greatest source of joy when we choose to follow him, and when we don't, we are his greatest source of anger. Man is a combination of heaven and earth, meaning God made an earthly body, which has a soul, and joined it with a spirit. That spirit is the spirit of a former angel. The flesh is the only reason a man has become a little lower than an angel. The flesh causes man to not hear, see, or think spiritually. This is what we must learn to do again, and this is why God put us here for the purpose of learning the difference between good and evil. The understanding of this is what will make us more like God. This is why God said, in Genesis 3:22, "And the LORD God said, Behold, the man is become as one of us, to know good and evil." Man is also created in the image of Satan in the sense that he is ruled by his carnal desires. For this reason, man is torn between following God and following Satan. His spirit pulls him toward God, and his flesh pulls him toward Satan. This is a battle that goes on inside of every man and woman. Man was given free will to choose whichever of these two beings he wants to follow. The last commandment man was given by Jesus was simply to love his neighbor as himself. This will be the test as to whether man gets to spend eternity with God or eternity with Satan. There are twelve different kinds of men or twelve different kinds of personalities, and these personalities are based on the zodiac signs. Based on the month and day the person was born, they will have certain characteristics that can change over time, but nevertheless, they will start their journey toward God from the point on the calendar they were born. The zodiac signs are also grouped into four elements: water, air, earth, and fire. These elements are the types of personalities that guide these elements. Each of these elements has unique qualities, both good and bad. Each of these qualities are meant to be combined, and so the elements must mix. In the mixing of the elements, one element becomes stronger than it originally was. God is a combination of all of these elements, not just the four, but also the different combinations the four can make once they are mixed together. There are twelve possible elements that can be made from the different combinations, which is what God will ultimately achieve in man. The completion of all of these elements is life. (Ref. Gen. 11:1–9; Matt. 10:16–22; Mark 12:30; Acts 17:26; Rom. 7:14–25; 1 Cor. 15:39; 1 Pet. 2:1–5; 1 John 3:1–3.) See also **angel; servants; sons of God; mature sons; believers, three kinds; adopted sons; mature sons; child, sons; grass; wheat.**

manna of God

natural—Any sudden or unexpected help, advantage, or aid to success.

spiritual—The knowledge of God; bread is Christ who came down from heaven. (Ref. Gen. 27:28; Ps. 78:23–25; Hosea 2:8–22; Joel 2:19; Matt. 13:33; John 7:35.) See also **corn**; **meal**; **bread**; **knowledge**.

mark of God

natural—N/A

spiritual—This mark cannot be seen by the naked eye. The Bible has said that this mark is on the foreheads of those whom God has chosen. The mark is also called a seal, and this seal can be on the forehead or the heart, or both at the same time. If the mark is on their foreheads, this means that they retain God in their thoughts, this can only be identified by the way a person lives their life. It can also be identified by what these people are passionate about in their speech. This is because these people think about God every day and therefore have a great desire to tell someone about their Father in heaven. If a person wonders about God every day, they become more like God, because their curiosity leads them to answers. God sends his Holy Spirit to reveal answers to these kinds of people. If the mark is on their hearts and minds, this person will in turn show that he or she has the mark by his or her actions, which are based on the understanding of God's Word. The mark will be shown in a person's actions, which will show the will of Christ in the form of fruits this person produces. The mark is also called a seal. A seal means that this person cannot be lost. This seal is also known as the Holy Spirit. The Holy Spirit is the force behind causing people to show that they have the mark, which will produce fruit. These fruits are known as love, peace, joy, happiness, kindness, gentleness, faith, etc. Anyone not having the seal will be lost to God. This is found in Revelation 9:4. (Ref. Matt. 7:16–20; Luke 6:43–45; John 3:33; Gal. 5:22–26; 2 Tim. 2:19; Rev 7:1-3; Rev. 9:4.) See also **Holy Spirit**; **seal**; **fruits**; **born-again**.

mark of the beast

natural—Love of money

spiritual—This mark cannot be seen by the naked eye. It is within the forehead, which is to say, in or on the mind of the person who has a love for money and power. People with this mark on their foreheads will show a lack of concern for the Word or the people of God. People with this mark in their hearts and minds will show it by their actions, by showing the opposite of love. Because of a love of money people will show the the fruits of the flesh which are idolatry, adultery, fornication, uncleanness, hatred, strife, murder, etc. The people who have this mark and produce these fruits are not necessarily lost. God knows that these people are unaware of the mark and is willing to give these people a chance to repent. He will remove the mark of the beast and place his mark upon them. (Ref. Gal. 5:20–21; Rev. 13:17; Rev. 14:11; Rev. 15:2; Rev. 16:2; Rev. 19:20; Rev. 20:4.) See also **fruits of man; anger; lost son; fornicating woman; adulterous woman; cedar trees; element, fire.**

marriage, the

natural—A union between a woman and man.

spiritual—A joining of body, mind, and spirit with God through Christ. This joining will be called his church or his bride. This marriage will take place during the tribulations, which is the three and a half years that the world will be experiencing its most troubled times. This marriage is a spiritual marriage, in which those who were chosen from the beginning of the world, will finally get to be united with Christ in mind, body, and Spirit through the Holy Spirit of God. These people in turn will then be ready to go out into the world to bring about salvation to other men in the world, during the millennium, the one-thousand-year rule of Christ. (Ref. Rom. 9:9–21; Rev. 19:9.) See also **church; head of the body; bridegroom.**

masculine side of God

natural—The Father of all.

spiritual—The masculine aspects of God are those things that cannot reproduce. They can only be given. They are power, authority, righteousness, honor, glory, holiness, and his wrath.

These are the sides of God that make him the Father of all or greater than all, because these things make him sovereign over all, and nothing can take these things away from him. Since these aspects or characteristics of God do not reproduce themselves, the only way that his Son gained them or became equal with him is by the Father bestowing these things upon him. They were Christ's rewards for his faith. (Ref. Ps. 48:1; Matt. 5:48; Matt. 9:6; Matt. 21:24; John 5:26–27; Rom. 1:4, 18; Rom. 4:5; Rom. 8:10; Rom. 9:22; 2 Pet. 1:17.) See also **power of God**; **authority**; **righteousness**; **honor**; **glory**; **holiness**; **wrath**; **God**; **trinity**; **feminine part of God**; **male part of God**.

mature son

natural—Someone who is no longer a child and has reached the adulthood part of his life and is able to make decisions on his own.

spiritual—Someone who is no longer a babe or child of God. This person no longer drinks the milk of the Word of God. He or she eats the meat of God, which means he or she is able to understand spiritual things. By eating strong meat, he or she is able to rightfully discern the Word of God. By eating meat, this person knows that he or she is no longer under the law of God. By eating meat, this person knows that he or she is free from all bondage. By eating meat, this person has found favor in the eyes of God and is able to utilize God's power through faith. (Ref. 1 Cor. 2:6; 1 Cor. 8:1; Phil. 3:15; Heb. 5:14.) See also **sons, the**; **overcomer**; **meat**; **firstfruits**; **firstborn**; **born again**.

meal, the corn of God

natural—The food miraculously supplied to the Israelites in the wilderness.

spiritual—Bread from heaven or the knowledge of the Father. (Ref. Gen. 27:28; Exod. 16:14–36; Ps. 78:23–25; Hosea 2:8–22; Joel 2:19; Matt. 13:33; John 7:35.) See also **manna**; **bread**; **knowledge**.

meat of God

natural—The edible flesh of animals, especially that of mammals as opposed to that of fish or poultry; the edible part, as of a piece of fruit or a nut; protein, which sustains the body; sustenance from the flesh of animals that keeps a person alive.

spiritual—The will of God, which is food for the spirit of man. This spiritual food can cause a man to live forever. To eat the Father's meat is to do his will. A man's meat is to follow his own will or the will of another man, which will not please God. Only the mature son knows how to the eat the meat of God and not to eat the meat or bread of another man. (Ref. Matt. 24:45; Luke 12:42; John 4:32–34; John 6:27, 55; Heb. 5:14; Heb. 13:9.) See also **will of God; doers; spiritual food; doing**.

meditate

natural—To look into one's subconscious; to concentrate very hard on something.

spiritual—This is how the people of God access the Spirit of God, in order to gain the understanding of God. This means to consider something with your spirit by the Spirit or to try a spirit by the Spirit. This also means to concentrate on the will or the Word of God. To meditate means to hear and to listen with your spirit in order to learn to develop a type of communication with God through the Spirit of God. This is how we all should worship God in the spirit, because God is looking for such a person. To meditate is to commune with him in spirit. To meditate is to learn to hear an inner voice, which is God speaking to us through the Holy Spirit. (Ref. Ps. 1:2; Ps. 119:15; Ps. 143:5; 1 Titus 4:15.) See also **hearing; mind; heart**.

meek

natural—A weak person; poor person; someone easily imposed upon; someone easily taken advantage of.

spiritual—A visibly weak person but a spiritually strong person in the eyes of God. These person are strong in the eyes of God because these people resist temptations that other people cannot. So to be meek in this world is to remain humble, and to remain humble in this world, a person has to gain control of himself or herself. To gain control of himself or herself, a person has to gain the wisdom of God and then turn around and use that wisdom on himself or herself in order to remain meek. These people are the ones who the Bible says will inherit (Matthew 5:5). (Ref. Matt.

5:5; Matt. 11:20–30; 2 Cor. 6:14; Gal. 5:1; 1 Tim. 6:1.) See also **marriage; heirs; chosen son; bride of Christ.**

melting
> **natural**—Becoming liquefied by warmth or heat, as ice, snow, butter, or metal.
>
> **spiritual**—Bringing affliction upon a person so that he or she will learn to fear God. Once the fear of God has come, through trials and tribulations, the person will seek refuge from the fire. That refuge will be the Father or the Son. This melting is the punishment of God that leads to salvation. This melting causes the elements or people of God in their original form to blend together with other elements or other people of God, and the end result will be love for one another. This is necessary because each element or each group of people thinks that their element or those that are like them are greater than everyone else and that everyone else should be like them. The melting removes impurities from the element, impurities such as, strife, anger, hatred, lust, envy, and inequality. (Ref. Dan. 2:34–35; Jer. 9:7; Ezek. 22:20; Mal. 3:3; 2 Pet. 3:10.) See also **fire; metals of God; refining process; gold; silver; brass; iron; tin; lead; dross; chastise.**

metals of God
> **natural**—Something with a metallic surface; can conduct electricity; can be alloyed or bonded with other types of metal; used as a monetary standard or unit of measure; a good conductor of electricity; examples are gold, silver, copper, or platinum, etc.
>
> **spiritual**—Someone who is valuable in the eyes of God; the most valuable metal in the eyes of God is gold; the next is silver and then brass, iron, lead, and tin. This analogy can be found in the statue of precious metals found in Daniel 3. According to the Bible, this statue had a head of gold, a chest and arms of silver, and an abdomen of brass. The legs were iron, and the feet where iron mixed with clay. These metals indicate how God valued each of the nations. It was also an indication of the types of hearts that were in the leaders of these nations, which went from gold in the eyes of God to clay, not even a metal at all. This statue started out as gold because at the time, this was where the beloved nation of Israel was taken, and God converted King Nebuchadnezzar so that

he believed in him. The next most precious metal is silver, which is what the arms and upper body were made out of. This is an indication of his people falling away from him, as demonstrated by the drop in value from gold to silver. The next metal was brass, which again indicates his people falling further away from him, as indicated by brass. The next is iron, which again indicates an even further distance that people have fallen away from him. Lastly is clay, which is not even a metal. It indicates people not caring about him at all. This the time that we are in now; it indicates the last days. Since clay is not even precious in the eyes of God, neither are the people of this time. It is not that he won't save them, but that their value is so low. We are all living in those times today, in the feet of the statue, which is iron mixed with clay. The type of metal also indicates the hardening of the heart. Gold is soft. Silver is a little harder. Brass is still harder, and iron is the hardest metal of that time. The harder the metal, the harder it is to get these people to believe. The type of metal also indicated the strength of the kingdom: the harder, the metal the stronger the kingdom; the stronger the kingdom, the more the people trust in weapons of mass destruction and not God, who can never be matched in destructive or creative power. (Ref. Num. 31:21–24; Dan. 2:34–35; Prov. 27:21; Is. 48:9–10; Jer. 6:27–30; Ezek. 22:18–20; Mal. 3:3; Zech. 13:8–9; 1 Tim. 2:20; 1 Pet. 1:7; Rev. 3:18.) See also **refining process; elements; gold; silver; brass; fire.**

milk

natural—An animal by-product; used to feed its offspring; also used in the early developmental stages of children in order to help develop their bodies.

spiritual—Those who have a very limited understanding of God; they are called newborns or babes in Christ. It can also mean a weak delivery of God's message, so that the people who listen believe but never grow. To drink milk means that a person is not that interested in the full understanding of God's will but is satisfied with just a little understanding of God's Word. Milk is the natural understanding of God's Word as opposed to the meat, which is the spiritual understanding of God's Word. Milk supports a religious understanding, while meat is more of a spiritual understanding. Bread is the knowledge of Christ; it can lead to either the milk of the Word or the meat of the Word. (Ref. Heb. 5:13–14; 1 Cor. 3:2; 1 Pet. 2:2.) See also **religion; tradition; unleavened bread.**

millennium, the
natural—A measure of time, usually consisting of one thousand years.
spiritual—A one-thousand-year period of time of peace that will follow the return of Christ. During this time, Christ and his chosen will teach mankind the ways of God. All who are thirsty will eventually see Christ and seek after the water that they must drink in order to enter the city of God that will come down from heaven. During this time, almost all will come to believe because they will see with their eyes the proof they need in order to believe. (Ref. Matt. 24:29–31; Mark 13:26–27; Rev. 20:1–15; Rev. 21:1–27; Rev. 22:1–21.) See also **rapture; tribulations; Zion; great day of the Lord, the.**

mind
natural—The human consciousness that originates in the brain and is manifested especially in thought, perception, emotion, will, memory, and imagination.
spiritual—The human consciousness that originates in the brain is our spirit or our consciousness. Our consciousness is our spirit. The heart is another consciousness, which is our soul. This is why there is a war between our brain and our heart. This war is what God is trying to help us win, since we are at a disadvantage. That disadvantage is that most men are unaware that they even have a spirit within them that could help them in their decision making. The soul is the center of our consciousness, but the mind, which is where the spirit resides, is trying to influence us from the outside. The heart has a mind or will of its own. It can choose to do evil or good. The mind or spirit gives the person character, and character is who he or she is, which makes him or her different from everyone else. Therefore, you truly are who you think you are. Identity is in the mind or the spirit of the person. (Ref. Prov. 16:23; Rom. 8:5–11.) See also **spirit; heart; Holy Spirit; will; soul; oneness of God.**

minister

> **natural**—Someone who renders aid to another; helps another; someone of much humility.
>
> **spiritual**—Someone God uses to render aid in the form of the Word of God to others in need; someone who preaches to those who are desperate for relief from the pressures of the world; someone who leads others to Christ. Christ set the example of what a minister should be like. A minister is supposed to be someone who desires to be the least, which is what is really supposed to make him or her great in the eyes of God. Christ demonstrated this by washing the feet of the apostles, and in doing so, he was showing what it would take to be the least in the kingdom of God, which in turn would really make him the greatest. This means to seek the kingdom in humility in all things. A minister is not to seek the kingdom of God by exalting himself or herself based on the amount of work he or she does for God as some do today. Ministers who have done right in the eyes of God will receive a special reward from Christ upon his return. (Ref. Matt. 11:11; Luke 7:28; Luke 9:48; Luke 16:10.) See also **ox**; **shepherd**; **laborer**; **servant**; **called**; **chosen**.

moon

> **natural**—A natural satellite revolving around a planet.
>
> **spiritual**—A part of the bride of Christ. The bride of Christ consists of a third, a third, and a third. Another analogy would be the sun, the moon, and the stars. These symbolic words represent three small groups of people who make up the bride of Christ (Rev. 12:1). God calls them the sun, moon, and stars, because this is a perfect analogy to show the difference between the status with him. Each of these three groups of people have a different amount of light or glory with the Lord. This is why they have different names but have become one. Even though all were chosen to be the bride of Christ, the people who are of the sun have shown more faith than the people who are of the moon, and the people of the moon have shown more faith than the people of the stars. Their symbolic names are also represented in a natural sense by the amount of light that is given by the real sun, moon, and stars. Since the light of the sun is greater than the light of the moon and the moon has greater light than the stars, people who are symbolically called the sun, moon, and stars are called by these

names. These people will be used to help bring people to Christ during the millennium, the one-thousand-year rule of Christ. Another name for these people is firstfruits, because they are the first to be conformed into the image of Christ (Rom. 8:29). The people of the sun, moon, and stars are the same sun, moon, and stars who will not give their light during the tribulations and shortly after the tribulations, which means that they will not be found. Christ will remove them during the most terrible times on the earth, so that they will not have to face the Antichrist. Shortly afterward though, Christ will release them to go out and change the world. (Ref. Gen. 37:9; Ps. 148:3; Isa. 13:10; Isa. 30:26; Isa. 60:20; Matt. 24:29; Mark 13:25; Luke 21:25; Acts 2:20; 1 Cor. 15:41; Rev. 8:12; Rev. 12:1; Rev. 21:23.) See also **bride of Christ; sun; stars; first fruits; hundred and forty-four thousand, first; hundred and forty-four thousand, second.**

mother

natural—A woman who conceives, gives birth to, or raises and nurtures a child; a woman who creates, originates, or founds something; a creative source; an origin.

spiritual—The spirit who brought us all into the world; the spirit that nurtures us all and causes us to become spiritual sons of God. This spirit is known to the world as the Holy Spirit. He is our mother, because he gave birth to us through the Word of God, who is our Father. (Ref. Isa. 50:1–2; Isa. 66:6–13; Ezek. 19:1–10; Ezek. 23:1–49; John 1:1–16; Gal. 4:22–31; Eph. 6:2; Rev. 17:5.) See also **Word of God, the; seed; Jesus; Holy Spirit; female; feminine; woman; bride; chosen, woman; called, woman; lost, woman.**

mountain

natural—Earth that rises above land; can be seen above land and sea.

spiritual—Earth that rises above land and sea. A mountain is symbolic of God's throne. Height represents something that is righteous, pure, and clean. Depth or a valley represents something that is sinful, impure, and unclean. This is why the Bible says that the world is the valley of the shadow of death (Psalm 23:4). The seven continents of the world are also mountains. They are mountains because they rise up from the sea. These are the seven mountains that the woman sits upon, mentioned in Revelation 17:9. This means all the world. A mountain is spoken of as a place of refuge, a place of authority, heavenly or divine, and symbolizes a throne. (Ref. Ezek. 11:23; Ezek. 20:40; Joel 3:17; 8:3; Mark 6:46; John 4:21; Rev. 6:14; Rev. 21:10.) See also **Zion**; **new city**; **New Jerusalem.**

myrtle, tree
natural—Any of several evergreen shrubs or trees of the genus Myrtus.
spiritual—A spiritual name for a group of people known as the prophets of God. Those who are a standard for other men to be like, because naturally, this tree is used as a hedge plant. To hedge naturally means to form a fence around something. This is why this tree spiritually represents God hedging all of man. This tree also symbolically represents the element earth. There are four elements altogether, which represent all of man. There are also four trees that symbolically represent all of man. They are the palm tree, the olive tree, the myrtle tree, and the cedar tree. (Ref. Neh. 8:15; Job 1:10; Job 3:23; Isa. 5:5; Isa. 41:19; Isa. 55:13; Zech. 1:8–11.) See also **earth**; **prophet**; **trees of God.**

naked
natural—Having no natural clothing on; no protection from natural elements.
spiritual—Having no spiritual clothing on; being found a nonbeliever, not believing in God or Christ; being found a believer but committing the acts of a nonbeliever; a believer's acts can be found to be naked, or without God's approval; all naked acts will be exposed. Naked is the opposite of clothed, which means to be following the will of God. (Ref. Ezek. 16:8; Ezek 23:29; Hab. 2:15; Matt. 25:36, 43; Rom. 8:5; 2 Cor. 5:1–7.) See also **uncovered**; **clothed**; **white robes**; **armor**; **judgment**; **drunken.**

net
natural—Anything serving to catch or ensnare.
spiritual—There are two kinds of nets: the net of the wicked and the net of God. The wicked use trickery and deceit to try to enslave

other men. Satan uses this to further his goals. The Word of God is a net that catches men and brings them out of the sea, or the culture that enslaved them. For this reason, God made certain men fishermen to catch other men (Matt. 4:19). Jesus spoke a parable in Matthew 13:47–50:

> Again, the kingdom of heaven is like unto a net, that was cast into the sea, and gathered of every kind: Which, when it was full, they drew to shore, and sat down, and gathered the good into vessels, but cast the bad away. So shall it be at the end of the world: the angels shall come forth, and sever the wicked from among the just, And shall cast them into the furnace of fire: there shall be wailing and gnashing of teeth ...

God will use a net when Christ returns, meaning the Spirit of God, along with the Word of God to catch all people or to draw all people to him. God will also use a net to catch Satan and destroy him according to Ezekiel 32:3–9:

> Thus saith the Lord GOD; I will therefore spread out my net over thee with a company of many people; and they shall bring thee up in my net. Then will I leave thee upon the land, I will cast thee forth upon the open field, and will cause all the fowls of the heaven to remain upon thee, and I will fill the beasts of the whole earth with thee. And I will lay thy flesh upon the mountains, and fill the valleys with thy height. I will also water with thy blood the land wherein thou swimmest, even to the mountains; and the rivers shall be full of thee. And when I shall put thee out, I will cover the heaven, and make the stars thereof dark; I will cover the sun with a cloud, and the moon shall not give her light. All the bright lights of heaven will I make dark over thee, and set darkness upon thy land, saith the Lord GOD. I will also vex the hearts of many people, when I shall bring thy destruction among the nations, into the countries which thou hast not known.

(Ref. Ps. 141:10; Prov. 12:12; Prov. 29:5; Eccles. 9:12; Ezek. 9:12; Ezek. 32:3–9; Matt. 13:47.) See also **fish**; **whale**; **sea**; **world culture**; **fisherman**.

new body

natural—N/A

spiritual—A new life and a new body given as a reward for having been found faithful in Christ; given a new body because the Bible has concluded that flesh cannot inherit the kingdom of God; translated or changed in a twinkling of an eye; changed by being given a spiritual body, not a natural body as we have now. (Ref. Is. 26:29; Luke 20:35–36; John 5:29; John 11:25; Rom. 1:4; Rom. 8:10–23; 1 Cor. 15:44, 51–52; 2 Cor. 3:18; Phil. 3:21; 1 Thess. 5:23; Heb. 4:12; Heb. 11:35; James 2:26; Rev. 20:5–6.) See also **translated; resurrection.**

new city

natural—New home.

spiritual—Zion; New Jerusalem; belongs to those who believe in Christ regardless of race; will be set on Mount Olive. (Ref. Isa. 60:19–22; Isa. 61:11; Isa. 65:17–25; Rev. 9:4; Rev. 20:1–14.) See also **rapture; end; time; Jerusalem, New; Zion.**

new creature

natural—A previously undiscovered creature found on the earth.

spiritual—New person in Christ; when someone comes into a new understanding of spiritual things; a mind that has been renewed. (Ref. 2 Cor. 5:17–19; Eph. 4:22–32; Col. 3:9–17.) See also **born again.**

new commandment

natural—New orders

spiritual—The new commandment by Christ is to love one another as ourselves. This is the second covenant, given to us by Jesus. (Ref. John 15:8–19.) See also **love; commandment; new covenant.**

new heaven and earth

natural—N/A

spiritual—Created at the end of the seventh day or the end of the one-thousand-year reign of Christ called the millennium, just before the eighth day when all who are saved will live with the

Father and His Son, and we shall all be changed because all things will be created new. (Ref. 2 Pet. 3:13; Rev. 21:1–8, 27.) See also **eighth day; time; end; judgment.**

New Jerusalem

natural—N/A

spiritual—The new city that will descend from heaven; where the people who are found faithful will dwell with God; this is also another name for the bride of Christ. (Ref. Gal. 4:26; Rev. 21:2.) See also **bride; Jerusalem; chosen son; barren woman; city of God.**

New Testament

natural—An eyewitness account of someone's life; the testimony of Christ.

spiritual—Grace, or a new beginning for man. Began with the death of Jesus on the Cross. His death or blood made it possible for the introduction of the Holy Spirit into a person's life. It showed the man how he could be forgiven for his sins as well as how to forgive others; those who receive the Holy Spirit are called the church. The church is one body, regardless of what earthly church people attend and regardless of where they are in the world or what religion they have, if any at all. (Ref. Matt. 26:28; Mark 14:24; Luke 22:20; 1 Cor. 11:25; 2 Cor. 3:6; Heb. 7:22; Heb. 9:15–20.) See also **blood; Jesus; new covenant.**

numbers

natural—A numeral or series of numerals used for reference or identification; one of a series of symbols of unique meaning in a fixed order that can be derived by counting.

spiritual—A numeral or series of numerals used for reference or identification; one of a series of symbols of unique meaning in a fixed order that can be derived by counting. God uses numbers to establish all things and to bring all things to an end. There are certain numbers that God uses, and each of these numbers represents something.

Example of Numbers

1—This number represents the oneness of God. The term *God* when used properly refers to the trinity as one or as a whole. It also means the beginning or unity.

2—This number represents Christ. He is the second in the trinity that is God. The number also represents a true witness, which is what Christ is. It also represents the minimum number of witnesses needed by the law of the Old and New Testament in order to establish a thing to be true.

3—This number represents the Trinity of God. This also represents completeness in the sense of wholeness. It represents wholeness by bringing three things together in one, which is the body, soul, and spirit within a person. This number also represents the family, the Father, the Mother, and the offspring, the circle of life.

4—This number represents the four seasons, the four elements, and the four main trees of man. The four seasons are summer, spring, fall, and winter. The four trees are trees whose seasons are summer (the palm tree); spring (the olive tree); fall (the myrtle tree); winter (the cedar tree). The four elements are water, air, earth, and fire. The four elements and the four trees are a symbolic way to describe the four groups of people.

5—This number represents the number of senses within man. They are our ability to see, hear, touch, taste, and smell. These same five sense are also present within our spirit. Our spirit has the ability to see, hear, touch, taste, and smell as well.

6—This number represents man. It also represents the number of days allowed for work. God worked six days and rested on the seventh, and he wanted man to follow the same example. The number 666 represents three different things: a seal, the Antichrist, and the Antichrist's kingdom. The first six represents the opening of six seals, in which the sixth seal gives the Antichrist the authority to rule for three and a half years. The second number represents Satan's time or the six thousand years God gave man and Satan to complete their work. The last six represents the last kingdom that will exist before the seventh kingdom, or Christ's kingdom.

7—This number represents perfection and conformation. God finished his creating upon the earth in seven days, not seven twenty-four-hour days but seven thousand earth years. We have seven days that complete a week. The seventh day of the week is the Sabbath, and the seven-thousandth year is also a Sabbath day. It is also called the Lord's day, and it will last for one thousand years. The Lord's number is also the number seven, and the complete representation of his number is 777. The number 777 represents a seal, Christ, and Christ's kingdom. The first represents the opening of the seventh seal. The second seven represents the beginning of the seventh day, Christ's time or his one-thousand-year rule on the earth. The last seven represents the number of the kingdom that will exist during that time, which is the final kingdom. Seven represents the seven churches which form one. Seven represents the seven spirits that surround the throne of God, which are one, because they are the seven virtues of the Holy Spirit.

8—This number represents a new beginning. This is when God will create a new heaven and a new earth, when he himself will make his dwelling place on the earth and live with man. The eighth day is also the day when Israel circumcises its children, just as God will circumcise the world.

12—This number represents a complete cycle. There are twelve months in a year. There are twelve tribes of Israel. There are twelve hours in a day. There are twelve zodiac signs, which are the twelve manners of fruit that are produced on the tree of life every month (Rev. 22:1).

24—This number represents a combination of the Old and New Testament elders who sit around the throne of God. Twelve are from the tribes of Israel, and the other twelve are the apostles. (Ref. throughout the Bible.) See also **God**; **Christ**; **Trinity**; **Holy Spirit**; **trials**; **man**; **day**; **time**.

oil

natural—Used to make things run smoothly without friction; used in lamps as fuel or a source of light; used in cooking.

spiritual—Another name for the Holy Spirit. The Holy Spirit in this form means source of knowledge. Another meaning of oil is a source of light. Spiritual oil teaches. Spiritual oil testifies of Jesus. This is the same oil that was in the lamps in the parable of the ten virgins. This oil was the knowledge of who Christ really is. Oil is the way in which knowledge comes to the people of the air element or olive tree. If oil is within a group of people, they have become oil, and God will use oil to teach other people to use their oil, which is the spirit of knowledge. (Ref. Exod. 35:6; Exod. 29:7; Matt. 25:1–12; Rev. 6:6.) See also **Holy Spirit; olive tree; olive berries; element air; treasure; buy; sell.**

olive, berries
natural—Any small, usually stone-less, juicy fruit, irrespective of botanical structure, such as the huckleberry, strawberry, or hackberry.
spiritual—Any person who is found faithful after God does the shaking of Israel by his East Wind. (Ref. Isa. 17:6; James 3:12.) See also **figs; grapes; olive tree; fig tree; Israel.**

olive tree
natural—A plant native to the Middle East.
spiritual—Another name for Israel; or people who were given the law. (Ref. Jer. 11:16; Hosea 14:1–9; Zech. 4:3, 11–14; Rom. 11:16–24; Rev. 11:4.) See also **Israel; fig tree, first; anointed; candlesticks.**

oneness of God
natural—When the Trinity of God works as one. The trinity is the Father, Son, and Holy Spirit working as one. They have one goal and are in agreement at all times, because they are of the same mind, body, and spirit.
spiritual—The goal of the trinity is that we all be as one, as they are, which means that we as men first learn to have the same mind, body, and spirit and later learn to share in the oneness of the trinity as well, which is to be in agreement with the Father, Son, and Holy Spirit. (Ref. Matt. 19:1–8; John 14:1–12; John 17:1–26; Rom. 6:16–19; Rom. 12:3–6; Rom. 15:1–6; 1 Cor. 1:1–11; 1 Cor. 6:15–17; Phil. 2:1–15; 2 Pet. 1:19–20.) See also **body; mind; spirit.**

outcast

natural—Someone who does not belong; society deems guilty.

spiritual—Someone who does not belong in this world; seen by the world as nonconforming. This is because this person is not of the world. He or she is of God. (Ref. Isa. 56:7; John 1:10; John 8:23; John 15:19; John 17:16.) See also **sons**; **meek**; **believer**; **overcomer**.

overcomer of the world

natural—Someone who triumphs; one who has obtained victory; someone who puts forth great effort.

spiritual—Someone who was predestined to receive the Holy Spirit; someone born of God or by water and blood; someone who has endured all manner of hardships of this world, learned of Christ, become a believer in Christ, learned of the faith of Christ, learned to have faith, drunk of the living water who is the Holy Spirit, ate the bread which is Christ, and learned to eat the meat of the Father; someone capable of great love; someone who is capable of loving all people. (Ref. 1 John 3:9; 1 John 5:1–8; Rev. 2:7, 11, 17, 26; Rev. 3:5, 12, 21; Rev. 21:7.) See also **sons**; **born of God**; **Christian**; **believer**; **saved**; **doer**; **wheat**; **rewards**.

ox

natural—a beast of burden; used for manual labor; used for man's purpose.

spiritual—a man of great burden, used for spiritual labor; a minister of God; a pastor or teacher who is used for God's purpose to give bread, meat, and water to the needy. He or she deserves and will receive much prosperity, but the people who employ this person do not want him or her to have more prosperity than they do, so they begin to hate him or her or become jealous. (Ref. Deut. 25:4; Prov. 14:4; Isa. 1:3; 1 Cor. 9:9; 1 Tim. 5:18.) See also **teacher**; **minister**; **gifts**.

palm, leaves

natural—The branches from the palm tree.

spiritual—The men of God who will go out to teach the nations after the tribulations and after the millennium. These are the leaves from the tree that will be for the healing of the nations.

This is because they are leaves off of the palm tree, which is Christ. (Ref. Rev. 7:9; Rev. 22:1–3.) See also **palm tree**; **chosen**; **full son**; **adult son**.

palm tree

natural—Any of numerous plants of the family Palmae, most species being tall, un-branched trees surmounted by a crown of large pinnate or palmately cleft leaves.

spiritual—This tree is a symbolic representation of victory. This is why it is also a symbolic representation of Christ. Those who have been found faithful in Christ will have one of these branches in their hands in the Lord's day. This tree is also represented by the element water. (Ref. Ps. 92:10–12; Ps. 104:16; Jer. 10:5; Ezek 40:16; Rev. 7:9.) See also **trees of God**; **palm, leaves**.

perfection

natural—A perfect embodiment or example of something.

spiritual—A perfect embodiment of Christ, who is a perfect embodiment of his Father. Our Father is a perfect embodiment of love, and this is the direction our Father in heaven is taking us. He will cause this to happen to those who love him. This kind of perfection is not a perfection of the body or of our ways, but of our understanding, faith, and love. These are the things that God is trying to perfect in us. (Ref. Matt. 5:48; Luke 6:40; Luke 8:14; John 17:23; Rom. 12:2; 1 Cor. 2:6; 2 Cor. 7:1; 2 Cor. 13:9; Eph. 4:12–13; Heb. 6:1; Heb. 10:14; Heb. 12:23; 2 Tim. 3:17; 1 John 2:5; 1 John 4:12–18; 1 Pet. 5:10.) See also **love**; **forgiveness**; **faith**; **will of God**.

potter

natural—A person who makes pottery.

spiritual—Spiritually speaking, God the Father is our potter, or he who made us. We are the clay. The potter has power over the clay and does as he wills with the clay, making some vessels honorable and some not honorable. (Ref. Isa. 64:8; Jer. 18:6; Jer. 19:1; Rom. 9:21; Rev. 2:27.) See also **clay**; **vessels**; **cistern**.

power of God

> **natural**—The ability to act; to produce an effect or force; to utilize energy to do work.
>
> **spiritual**—To have the legal right, ability, and the authority to decide man's fate; to have dominion over; to be in a position to decide one's fate. The power of God is within his spoken word. It is activated by speaking it. This is why the Bible says that God spoke everything into existence. Power is also masculine in nature. It is not something God is trying to reproduce in man. It is something God is trying to give man. Power cannot be reproduced; it can only be granted or given, and therefore, it is masculine in nature. (Ref. Matt. 9:6; Matt. 10:1; Matt. 26:64; Matt. 28:18; John 17:2–10; Acts 1:18; Acts 8:19; Rom. 7:1; Rom. 13:1; Rom. 15:19; 1 Cor. 4:20; 1 Cor. 6:14; 1 Cor. 8:1; 1 Cor. 15:43; Col. 1:13; Heb. 7:16; Rev. 9:19.) See also **faith; Holy Spirit; masculine side of God; male side of God; authority; honor; glory; righteousness; holiness; wrath of God.**

prayer

> **natural**—Giving acknowledgement to a higher being.
>
> **spiritual**—Communication with God; asking for something in Jesus's name; thanking him; asking for forgiveness; showing respect; showing loyalty; most of all, simply communing with him and offering up praise. We should pray in secret, not in public so that we don't make the mistake of doing it for show. (Ref. Luke 15:1–17; Matt. 6:5–8; Matt. 14:29–31.) See also **asking; forgiveness; communication.**

predestined son

> **natural**—N/A
>
> **spiritual**—Those who were chosen to be the first to be conformed into the image of Christ, because they were predestined to perform a specific mission. They were chosen before the foundation of the world, before they had done any good or evil. They are also known as God's elects. There are 288,000 altogether, half from the Old Testament and half from the New Testament. (Ref. Rom. 8:29–39; Eph. 1:1–11; 2 Thess. 2:13–14; 2 Tim. 1:7–10.) See also **chosen; free son; born of God; gold; silver; brass; bride of Christ; elects.**

prey

natural—An animal hunted or seized for food, especially by a carnivorous animal; a person or thing that is the victim of an enemy, a swindler, a disease, etc.

spiritual—A spiritual name for those who love Christ but fall victim to the beasts of the world. (Ref. Isa. 42:22; Ezek. 43:8–22.) See also **sheep; cattle; goats; fish; beast; whale.**

promised, son

natural—Someone who has an inheritance.

spiritual—Someone who has been chosen by God to fulfill his destiny because he was promised to receive the Holy Spirit, who would in turn ensure that he fulfilled his destiny; one who is predestined also to fulfill the Lord's will; one who has been given the Holy Spirit from birth and is therefore born saved. This person is also known as an elect, because he was elected to perform a mission. (Ref. Gal. 4:26–31; Acts 2:33; John 16:1; Rom. 9:9; Gal. 3:14, 29; Gal. 4:23; Eph. 1:13; Eph. 3:6; Rev. 7:1; Rev. 14:1.) See also **predestined; chosen; free son; bride, of Christ; hundred and forty-four thousand, first; hundred and forty-four thousand, second.**

prophecy

natural—Predicting what the future holds.

spiritual—People predicting what the future holds, because the Father has revealed it to them; only given by divine inspiration. To have truly prophesied, God's Word must come true or the person who said these things would be a liar. The Bible is the most proven book of prophecy that there is. (Ref. 2 Titus 3:16.) See also **Bible; word of God.**

rain

natural—Water that is condensed from the aqueous vapor in the atmosphere and falls to earth in drops.

spiritual—Blessings from God; blessings in the form of revelation, prosperity, or spiritual awareness; favor from the Lord; deliverance by the Lord. This rain can also come in the form of a person, who has already received the water from the Holy Spirit and has learned to give this water to others. (Ref. Lev. 25:4; Deut. 11:17; Isa.

55:10; Ezek. 22:24; Hosea 6:3; Joel 2:23; Zech. 14:17; Acts 14:17; Heb. 6:7; James 5:7.) See also **dew; water; Holy Spirit; blessings; rewards; living water.**

rain, former
natural—N/A
spiritual—The first group of chosen people. They are from Jerusalem. They were the prophets and all whom God used before the New Testament. They were under the law. They are called rain because they were mixed with water. Water is a spiritual name for the Spirit of God. The opposite of water is desert, which means a place where there is no spirit; it is desolate. Rain in the natural sense brings life to anyplace it falls on. Where there is no rain, there is no life. All things earthly need water, so this carries the same meaning spiritually. (Ref. Deut. 11:14; Job 29:23; Prov. 16:15; Jer. 3:3; Jer. 5:24; Hosea 6:3; Joel 2:23; Zech. 10:1; James 5:7; Rev. 7:4; Rev. 14:1–5.) See also **hundred and forty-four thousand, first; hundred and forty-four thousand, second; chosen; free son; bride of Christ.**

rain, latter
natural—N/A
spiritual—The people whom Christ has chosen to do his will; they are predestined. They are called rain because they are full of water, the fountain of life. Christ gave them the ability to give this water to anyone who thirsts. They are wellsprings or fountains, which means they are full of the Holy Spirit and seek only to share it with others. Their time to give this water is in the millennium, the thousand-year reign of Christ. The former rain, or the first 144,000, will be present as well, because God would have resurrected all those who deserve a second chance who died under the law in the Old Testament. The former rain will minister to them, while the latter rain will minister those who died and are resurrected under the New Testament or grace. The former and latter are also referred to as a former sea and a latter sea. This can be found in Zechariah 14:8. (Ref. Deut. 11:14; Job 29:23; Prov. 16:15; Jer. 3:3; Jer. 5:24; Hosea 6:3; Joel 2:23; Zech. 10:1; Zech. 14:8; James 5:7; Rev. 7:4; Rev. 14:1–5.) See also **hundred and**

forty-four thousand, first; hundred and forty-four thousand, second; chosen; free son; sea.

rapture
natural—The day when Jesus returns.
spiritual—Return of Christ; the literal day when Jesus returns to gather the chosen. This will be the beginning of the seventh day, which is also called the millennium or the spiritual day, which will last one thousand years. This occurs before the tribulations; this day is also referred to as the day when Jesus returns as the thief in the night. The only ones who will know he has come are his chosen and the dead in Christ. The rest of mankind will go on as if nothing has changed. The reason is because the chosen are so few in number that the world will not miss them. The chosen or elect are the only ones spared from the tribulations. The called sons of God have to go through the tribulations. (Ref. 1 Thess. 5:2; 2 Pet. 3:10.) See also **tribulations; seventh day; end; time; gathering; harvest; chosen son; called sons.**

reborn
natural—N/A
spiritual—To become a new person. This takes place only when the Holy Spirit has joined with a person. This causes a renewal of one's hope and understanding. (Ref. Luke 22:31–32; John 3:3; 2 Cor. 5:17; 1 John 3:1–21; 1 John 5:1.) See also **born-again; saved.**

refining, process
natural—To bring to a fine or a pure state; free from impurities; *to refine metal, sugar, or petroleum;* to bring to a finer state or form by purifying.
spiritual—This process is God's way of making a person ready to receive the Holy Spirit. This process is caused by bringing a person through many trials, tribulations, and afflictions. Another way this is said in the Bible found in Heb 12:8 is, God chastises those whom he loves. Chastisement was never meant to be a pleasant thing. The Bible refers to refining when it is referring to people as precious metals. (Ref. Isa. 48:10; Hag. 2:8; Zech. 13:8–9; Mal. 3:2–3; Heb 12:8.) See also **fire; metals of God; gold; silver; brass;**

elements, the; sons, three kinds; third part; kindled; chastise; gold; silver; brass; iron; lead; tin.

religion

natural—An outward show of one's faith; a traditional way of worship; a systematic and institutionalized way of worship; a formal way of worship; duty toward God, under law.

spiritual—N/A (Ref. Acts 26:5; Matt. 15:1–9; Gal. 1:13–14; Col. 2:6–23; James 1:26–27.) See also **tradition; worship; leavened bread; unleavened bread; bread; milk.**

reprobate, person

natural—A depraved, unprincipled, or wicked person; *a drunken reprobate;* rejected by God and beyond hope of salvation.

spiritual—A person who has rejected God; a person who refuses to repent. This is a person whom God has given up on or turned over to a reprobated mind. The Bible also calls these people reprobated silver that he has melted in vain. The refining process does not work on these people, neither does chastisement or punishment. Nothing will work on these people to bring them back into him. (Ref. Jer. 6:27–30; Rom. 1:28; 2 Cor. 13:5; 2 Tim. 3:8.) See also **dross; unbeliever; lost; tare; melting; fire; refining process.**

resurrection

natural—N/A

spiritual—Being raised from the grave or sleep; being given a second chance at life. This will happen at the beginning of the millennium for all people who have died not sure of who Christ is and the reason he came into this world. When the resurrection takes place, some will be resurrected in the flesh again, because they are not yet worthy. This is so that they can receive a better resurrection. Some who are resurrected will receive a new body, because they are worthy. They will be given a new spiritual body, an incorruptible body, because God has chosen them. The last group to be resurrected will not be resurrected until the end of the millennium, because God has judged them never to be worthy to come into his kingdom. They are raised only to be judged and thrown into the lake of fire, because they refuse to repent and to believe in Christ. (Ref. Isa. 26:29; Luke 20:35–36; John 5:29; John

11:25; Acts 24:14–16; Rom. 1:4; Rom. 8:10–23; 1 Cor. 15:44; 1 Cor. 15:51–52; 2 Cor. 3:18; Phil. 3:21; 1 Thess. 4:16; 1 Thess. 5:23; Heb. 4:12; Heb. 11:35; 2 Pet. 3:10; James 2:26; Rev. 20:5–6.) See also **dead in Christ; dead not in Christ; grave; born-again; translated; new body.**

resurrection, first
natural—N/A
spiritual—Those whom the Lord has chosen, who are alive, who will be received by Christ immediately upon his return as well as those who have died in Christ. The Bible says that the dead in Christ shall rise first and shall be with him and shall reign with him one thousand years. Some of those who are raised during the first resurrection will help the chosen of God to teach others and cause them to believe in Christ. This is why the Bible says in Revelation 20:5–6, "blessed and holy is he that will take part in the first resurrection." This will take place before the three-and-a-half-year period called the tribulations. (Ref. Matt. 9:37–38; Matt. 13:30–39; John 5:9; John 11:25; Acts 24:15; Rom. 6:5; 1 Thess. 4:16; 1 Thess. 5:2; Heb. 35:11; 2 Pet. 3:10; Rev. 14:14; Rev. 20:4–6.) See also **rapture; harvest; thief in the night; watch.**

resurrection, second
natural—N/A
spiritual—This is the second time those who are on the earth will get a second chance. This will take place at the beginning of the seventh day or the at the beginning of the millennium, right after tribulations. (Ref. Matt. 9:37–38; Matt. 13:30–39; John 5:29; John 11:24–25; Acts 24:15; Rom. 6:5; 1 Cor. 15:23; Heb. 11:35; 1 Pet 1:3; Rev. 14:14–19.) See also **harvest, second.**

resurrection, third
natural—N/A
spiritual—These are those who will not be raised from the grave until toward the end of the millennium, and they will only be raised to receive judgment. These are people who refused over and over again to believe in Christ and were given many chances within their lifetime but refused them all. These are the people who will continue to refuse to repent. This will take place at the end of the

one-thousand-year rule of Christ, called the millennium. (Ref. Acts 17:31; 1 Cor. 15:42; Rev. 20:5–6.) See also **unrepentant; second death; lost son; unbeliever.**

rest

natural—Means to relax; to sleep; or to stop working.

spiritual—Means to relax spiritually, which means this applies to the soul, based on one's understanding of the love of God toward him or her. The only way a person can find this kind of rest is to cease from all worries or, in other words, to truly rest is to have total faith that Christ will save one from one's sins, not because of the work he or she is doing, or not doing, but because of faith alone. One reason most people can't enjoy this type of rest is because they worry about the kind of work they are doing for the Lord. Work is the only way in which most people want to prove their faith in God; however, even though all who believe in him will work, it is not a means of salvation in and of itself. It is simply what one does as a result of belief. Works are a product of belief, which God turns into faith. If this were understood in this way, one could rest assured of his or her salvation. So based on this understanding, we could rest whether we work or not since it is not based on work in the first place. Jesus is at rest now because he finished his work. This is why he is sitting beside the Father now. This is also why when Christ returns, it will be called the true Sabbath day, a day of rest, or a one-thousand-year period of time when the world will be at rest. (Ref. Heb. 3:7–11; Heb. 4:1–11; Rev. 14:13.) See also **rapture; New Jerusalem; Zion; saved.**

righteousness

natural—Doing what a person feels is the right thing to do, based on his or her own understanding.

spiritual—Not leaning on one's own understanding but instead following the teaching of Christ, known as the Word of God; to be found to have faith in Christ. As a result, we are made righteous by God. This means that no man in and of himself can be righteous, because righteousness is something only God and Christ can bestow upon a person. (Ref. Acts 10:43; Matt. 12:33–37; Rom. 3:21–31; Rom. 10:4; Gal. 2:15–16; Gal. 3:22; James 2:14–26.) **See**

also forgiven; blessed; justified; firstfruits; born-again; Holy Spirit.

righteousness of God
natural—A quality or state of being just or rightful.
spiritual—A sacred right of God that can only be given to another by him, and since it cannot be reproduced, it is therefore part of the masculine side of God. (Ref. Ps. 9:8; Ps. 11:7; Mal. 4:2; Rom. 4:5; Rom. 8:10; Rom. 10:10; 1 Cor. 1:30; Gal 5:5; James 3:18.) See also **masculine side of God; male side of God; power; glory; honor; holiness; authority; wrath.**

righteousness, self-
natural—Thinking of oneself as better than others; thinking selfishly; looking down on others; thinking of oneself as an individual and not as a part of a whole; thinking that one is morally upright, without considering God's word.
spiritual—All of man's attempts to be like God, through religion, war, or worship, etc.; man's work that he deems good. The Bible has concluded that all of our works are as filthy rags to him. Self-righteousness is an attempt to be like God without truly ever understanding him. This is because God has not revealed himself to a lot of people. (Ref. Matt. 16:6–12; 1 Cor. 5:6–8; Gal. 5:9.) See also **leaven; yeast; filthy clothes; sins; dead works.**

riches
natural—Lots of money or material things.
spiritual—Lots of wisdom, patience, humility, and understanding of the Father through the Holy Spirit. This is the form of wealth the Bible refers to, which is not a physical type of wealth. Matthew 6:19–21 says,

> Lay not up for yourselves treasures upon earth, where moth and rust doth corrupt, and where thieves break through and steal: But lay up for yourselves treasures in heaven, where neither moth nor rust doth corrupt, and where thieves do not break through nor steal: for where your treasure is, there will your heart be also.

(Ref. Prov. 15:6; Isa. 33:6; Matt. 6:19; Matt. 12:35; Luke 12:21, 34; Luke 18:22.) See also **blessings; rewards; fat; buy; sell.**

river

natural—A place where running water flows.

spiritual—Another name for the Holy Spirit. This same river, which is the Holy Spirit, is also full of people who have become a part of the same spirit. They are within the river, so they are flowing with the river. Being a part of the river means being blessed in abundance with wisdom, knowledge, understanding, faith, counsel, power, and love. When this wisdom is spoken by a person, it is referred to as a river of water flowing from a person's mouth. John 7:38 says, "He that believeth on me, as the scripture hath said, out of his belly shall flow rivers of living water." Those who can only receive drops of water are called babies in Christ. Those who can receive much more water are called mature in Christ. Those who are mature are people capable of much water or truth flowing from their mouths. The Bible tells us that rivers of water flow from the throne and down the middle of the street in heaven, which spiritually means that truth and enlightenment will be flowing from God to the people. (Ref. Isa. 66:12; Exod. 47:1–23; John 4:7–21; John 7:34–39; Rev. 16:12; Rev. 22:1–2.) See also **Holy Spirit; wisdom; water; living water; drinking; fish; trees.**

salt

natural—Used to give food taste; used to preserve food; used to cure or purify it.

spiritual—God's people who are used to preserve life, used to pass his message on; the called; the chosen of God; the ones who will teach others about Christ during the one-thousand-year rule of Christ. (Ref. Matt. 5:13; Mark 9:49–50; Mark 11:49–50; Col. 4:6; James 3:12.) See also **Christians; laborers.**

salted by fire

natural—N/A

spiritual—To be given the Holy Spirit of promise so that a person is able to answer any question asked by another person concerning the word of God correctly using the wisdom of God. (Ref.

Matt. 5:13; Mark 9:49–50.) See also **salt; water; living water; Holy Spirit; baptism by fire; Christians; laborer; anointing; unction**.

Satan

natural—N/A

spiritual—The first to sin; a former angel called Lucifer; the principality behind all that is against God; cast down from heaven; the accuser of man; the hater of all that is good; the adversary; the dragon who gives power to the beast that was slain; our enemy; the prince of this world; the planter of bad seed called tares. The children of Satan are called tares, meaning weeds in the wheat field of God. God planted wheat, and Satan planted tares in order to choke the wheat and take its place. Satan is also symbolically called a cedar tree. There are other symbolic names by which God calls him. They are the leviathan, the whale, the spirit of deceit, the dragon, the beast, a lion, an eagle, a serpent, and a tree, the tree of the knowledge of good and evil. These are but a few of his spiritual names. (Ref. Job 1:6–12; Job 2:1–7; Zech. 3:1; 2 Cor. 11:14; Rev. 12:10.) See also **dragon; tares; whale; Leviathan; serpent; tree of the knowledge of good and evil**.

saved

natural—Rescued from danger; rescued from certain death.

spiritual—Rescued from danger; rescued from spiritual death. This is made possible by belief in Christ. This is accomplished by a confession with the mouth that you are a sinner and Christ is your only savior. We are saved from the second death, which means to be separated from God forever. (Ref. Acts 2:37–41; John 6:65; Rom. 1:16–17; Rom. 10:9–10; 1 Cor. 1:18–31; Eph. 2:5–9; Tim. 4:10; 2 John 3:1–3.) See also **faith; belief; Holy Spirit**.

Sea

natural—The saltwaters that cover the greater part of the earth's surface.

spiritual—A spiritual word to God, meaning the culture of the world, in which all people are caught. It is an invisible force that has in invisible influence on people in the way they think, which causes them to think more alike than they are aware of doing.

One common way of thinking is not to believe that there is a God or that Christ has come once in the flesh. Another way of thinking that is common to all men is war, hatred, division, power, distrust, violence, murder, depression, etc. We are all in a type of sea. According to the Bible, there are two types of spiritual seas: the one of the Old Testament and the one that exists now, under the New Testament. This is why the Bible calls all men fish. Habakkuk 1:14 says,

And makest men as the fishes of the sea, as the creeping things, that have no ruler over them? They take up all of them with the angle, they catch them in their net, and gather them in their drag: therefore they rejoice and are glad. Therefore they sacrifice unto their net, and burn incense unto their drag; because by them their portion is fat, and their meat plenteous. Shall they therefore empty their net, and not spare continually to slay the nations?

Because of this, God made some men fishers of other men to fish men out of the sea, which means to save men or to bring men out of the world. This is why Jesus said this to his disciples. Matthew 4:19 says, "And he saith unto them, Follow me, and I will make you fishers of men." This is because at one point or another, we were all in the sea or caught up in the world, which the Bible calls a sea. The Bible refers to this sea in Ezekiel 28:2. God tells one of his prophets to prophecy to the prince of Tyrus, who was filled with Satan and therefore became a symbolic representation of Satan.

Son of man, say unto the prince of Tyrus, Thus saith the Lord GOD; Because thine heart is lifted up, and thou hast said, I am a God, I sit in the seat of God, in the midst of the seas; yet thou art a man, and not God, though thou set thine heart as the heart of God.

The sea is where small fish and large whales swim. According to the Bible, we are fish and Satan is a whale or the leviathan of the sea among small fish. This is found in Ezekiel 32:2, which is where God told another prophet to prophecy to another person, the king of Egypt:

Son of man, take up a lamentation for Pharaoh king of Egypt, and say unto him, Thou art like a young lion of the nations, and thou art as a whale in the seas: and thou camest forth with thy rivers, and troubledst the waters with thy feet, and fouledst their rivers.

This is the language that God uses when he refers to the spiritual damage that Satan does to the culture of the world, which God initially intended to be good, but Satan stirs it up to be violent. (Ref. Gen. 1:21; Job 7:12; Ezek. 29:4–5; Ezek. 32:2; Ezek. 47:9; Job 41:1; Ps. 104:26; Isa. 21:1; Isa. 50:2.) See also **fish**; **fisherman**; **whale**; **leviathan**; **river**; **world culture**; **net**.

seal, the
natural—It encloses something; preserves something; protects something; marks something; gives authority to.
spiritual—The seal is the Holy Spirit, which preserves and protects. The seal is the mark of God. This mark cannot be seen by the naked eye of man. It can only be seen in the nature of the person who has it. Only by looking at a person's works can it be seen, and the only way to see a person's works is to have the ability to judge that person spiritually. Only the Father can give the seal to a person. The seal is not given to a person because he or she has done anything to deserve it. The seal is given to a person before he or she is born. This is because whoever receives the seal that person's life becomes predestined by God, and it means, once saved, always saved. The seal cannot be removed, or in other words, those whom God chooses cannot be lost. Those who have received the seal are called the chosen, the elects, the promised sons of God. They have received the Holy Spirit within them so that they may be among the first to be transformed into the image of Christ. This can be found in Romans 8:29. Those who have the seal eventually realize that they have the seal and are chosen of God. (Ref. Rom. 8:29; 2 Cor. 2:22; Eph. 1:9–23; Eph. 4:30; 1 John 3:22–24.) See also **Holy Spirit**; **water**; **seed of promise**.

seed of promise

natural—The fertilized, matured ovule of a flowering plant, containing an embryo or rudimentary plant; the first stage of a plant's life; a seed needs earth, sun, and water in order to grow.

spiritual—The Holy Spirit; the Word of God; the Gospel; the truth; the beginning of knowledge about Christ, who teaches us about the Father. Once it is planted in the person, it will grow, because the Father chose good ground for the seed to grow in. Good ground is a symbolic term for a person who loves to hear the Word of God. It also is symbolic of a person with a good heart or an obedient heart. The seed needs water to grow. Water is a symbolic word meaning the knowledge of God. The kind of knowledge needed for the seed to grow can only come from the Holy Spirit himself; the person in whom the seed was planted was chosen by God, before birth. This can be found in John 17:24 and Ephesians 1:4. Those who will see the kingdom of God are called the seed. This is said in Romans 9:8. (Ref. Matt. 13:18–23; Matt. 13:38; John 17:24; Eph. 1:4; Rom. 4:16; Rom. 9:8; 1 John 3:9.) See also **Holy Spirit**; **Word of God**; **fruit**; **good ground**; **female**; **seal**.

sell

natural—To persuade or induce (someone) to buy something; to persuade or induce someone to buy (something); to cause to be accepted, especially generally or widely.

spiritual—To persuade or induce someone to accept the Lord; to persuade people to accept something they have never believed in or heard of or to try to cause the world to accept a new understanding, something that will free them from the bondage of the world. This type of selling is not with money. It is done with the treasure God has given a man from heaven; in order to buy this treasure, a person must be willing to follow Christ and work the works that will earn him treasure in heaven. This work is the work of faith. The things that will be sold are wine, bread, and corn. These are symbolic representations of the knowledge of God from the aspect of his understanding, his forgiveness, and his love. These things are bought with faith toward the Father and the Son. (Ref. Neh. 10:31; Prov. 11:26; Prov. 23:23; Matt. 19:21; Matt. 25:9;

Luke 12:33; Rev. 13:17.) See also **buy; oil; corn; wine; wisdom; knowledge; love; treasure.**

servant son

> **natural**—Someone who works for another or is in the service of another; a person who owes or is in debt to another and serves to work off the indebtedness.
>
> **spiritual**—A person who believes in God or Christ or both but also believes he or she is still under law. This is the opposite of what the free son believes, which is that he or she is no longer under law. (Ref. 1 Cor. 3:2; 1 Cor. 7:19–24; Heb. 5:13; 1 Pet. 2:2; Rev. 17:14.) See also **laborer; called son; Christians; lamb; sheep; babe; tribulations.**

seven, seven, seven

> **natural**-N/A
>
> **spiritual**-The number 777 is a number that stands for a seal, a kingdom, and the number of Christ. The first seven is the last seal that will be opened on the seventh day or seventh thousandth year since creation, which gives the autority and power to the second seven, which is the seventh kingdom or the kingdom of Christ. The last seven is the number of the Son of God, Jesus Christ. (Ref. Rev 13:18; Rev 14:9; (Rev 6:1-17; Rev 7:2; Rev 8:1; Dan 2:1-10; Dan 7:1-28; Rev 17:1-10.) **See also 666; mark of God; mark of the beast; new Jerusalem**

shaking

> **natural**—Trembling with emotion; becoming dislodged and falling; causing to doubt or waver; weakening.
>
> **spiritual**—Bringing about the fear of the Lord by the showing of his power, usually accomplished by the falling of a nation and then the saving of that same nation. The shaking is done by the wind of God or in other words the Holy Spirit. The wind is how God shows his anger. (Ref. Isa. 17:6; Isa. 24:13; Ezek. 38:19.) See also **wind; wrath of God.**

sheep

> **natural**—A timid, defenseless creature; a timid, docile animal; easily influenced or led by a shepherd.

spiritual—A timid, defenseless person; a timid, docile person; easily influenced or led by Christ, who is the shepherd. The sheep hear the voice of the Lord. This means that those who are called sheep by Christ literally hear him in their hearts. (Ref. Jer. 23:1; Jer. 50:6–17; Ezek. 34:6; Matt. 9:36; Matt. 10:6, 16; Matt. 15:24; Matt. 25:33; Mark 6:34; John 10:1–18; 1 Pet. 2:25.) See also **servant; son; chosen; called; Christians; cattle; goats; beast; prey.**

shepherd

natural—A person who tends to his flock; a pastor; a priest; or a leader of people.

spiritual—A spiritual name for Jesus who is the shepherd of all who believe in Christ. (Ref. Ps. 23:1; John 10:1–11, 16; Heb. 13:20; 1 Pet. 2:25; 1 Pet. 5:4.) See also **Jesus; Word, the; vine, the; rock, the; palm tree; savoir, the.**

sight

natural—Seeing naturally; having vision.

spiritual—Seeing spiritually; seeing God's work; seeing beyond the obvious; being a true witness; having foreknowledge; knowing the future, which is a gift from God; seeing evil before it happens; seeing the soul of a person; knowing what someone is thinking, in his or her spirit. (Ref. 1 Cor. 2:9–16; 1 Cor. 8:1–3; Col. 1:9–14; 1 John 2:20–29.) See also **eye; vision; prophesy; gifts.**

silver

natural—This metal as a commodity or considered as a currency standard; a medal, traditionally of silver or silver in color, awarded to a person or team finishing second in a competition, meet, or tournament.

spiritual—This metal is the second closest metal to gold, gold being the most precious of metals. This means God loves this group of people more than the other groups. When these people went through the refining process, they became closer to God, but not as close as they could have come. It is because they lacked the ability to receive unconditional love. Their way of love remained somewhat conditional toward their fellow man, but their love is still greater than that of those who are brass. The Bible calls people silver as a way of determining their value to God. Silver is still more precious than brass, iron, lead, and tin, which are symbolic representations of the order of men according to their glory or closeness to God. (Ref. Num. 31:21–24; Prov. 27:21; Isa. 48:9–10; Jer. 6:27–30; Ezek. 22:20–22; Zech. 13:8–9; Mal. 3:3; 1 Tim. 2:20.) See also **servant son; called son; bondwoman; refining process; melting; fire.**

silver cord
natural—A precious metal, usually worn around the neck of a person.
spiritual—A man's spirit. (Ref. Eccles. 12:6.) See also **spirit; candle; candlestick; light.**

silver, reprobated
natural—N/A
spiritual—This is a type of person God has tried to redeem, but the person or people refuse to follow him. God has tried chastising and punishment, but these people still refuse to repent and follow him. So God calls them reprobated silver, which means he gave up on them, because the refining process did not work on them. (Ref. Jer. 6:27–30; Rom. 1:28; 2 Cor. 13:5; 2 Tim. 3:8.) See also **dross; reprobated person; lost person; unbeliever.**

six; six; six
natural-N/A
spiritual- It is the number that signifies when the Anti-Christ will rule. The number 666 is a number that is broken down into a series of events that will happen at the same time. The meaning of the first six is a seal which is opened on the sixth thousandth year from the day of creation. This six is a countdown, and at the end of it is the beginning of the seventh thousand year or the rule of 777, which stands for Christ. However before the seventh seal, or the seventh kingdom can rule the six seal is open so that the sixth kingdom can rule for three and half years. When this seal is broken, it give the next six it's power. The last six is simply the number man ruling, instead of seven ruling, which stands for God in particular Christ. This was because man was made on the sixth day of creation. (Ref. Rev 13:18; Rev 14:9; (Rev 6:1-17; Rev 7:2;

Rev 8:1; Dan 2:1-10; Dan 7:1-28; Rev 17:1-10.) **See also seven, seven, seven; mark of God; mark of the beast.**

sleep

natural—To be unaware of what is going on around you naturally; to be at ease, not prepared to fight; to be in a state of unconsciousness in order to revive the natural body. Sleep, however, is not rest, only the soul can rest. The body sleeps. Sleep gives us an idea of God's rest. In order for the body to rest, its conscience must be clear.

spiritual—To be unaware of what is going on around you spiritually; to be in a state of natural unconsciousness but at the same time spiritually conscious; to be in a state in which your spirit can interact with what is going on in the dream state. Sleep is one way that God can interact with man, by teaching, visions, or warnings. Asleep is also what the Bible calls a person when he or she has died in Christ, because the person is not truly dead but awaits the resurrection. The Bible also calls people asleep when they are unaware of his Word. He calls them drunken, which means not to have an understanding of God's Word or not to be prepared to fight spiritually for him. This is the opposite of sober, which means to be aware of God and have an understanding of his Word. (Ref. Prov. 20:25; 1 Cor. 15:6–18.) See also **death; drunken; unbelief; unsaved; grave; judgment; rest.**

sober

natural—To be not drunk; to not drink; to be fully aware of everything going on around you.

spiritual—To be not drunken or to be aware; to watch for and wait for Christ; to continue to do God's will and to be ever watchful; to be ready at all times in order to show love; this is the opposite of drunken or asleep, which means a person is unaware of the coming of the Lord. (Ref. 1 Thess. 5:5–10; 1 Pet. 1:13.) See also **saved; born-again; seeing; hearing; drinking; eating.**

soil

natural—What a seed is planted in. It is what nourishes vegetation.

spiritual—What a seed is planted in. It is what nourishes vegetation. The Bible calls man different types of plants, trees, flowers, grass, or fruits, and so we would then need good soil to grow in as well as water and sunlight. When the Bible uses a type of plant to describe man, God describes himself as the husbandman or farmer who tends to his garden. He waters with the Holy Spirit and gives light through his Son. He plants another seed in our hearts and depending on the type of ground within our hearts that seed will grow or it will not. That seed is the Word of God. If our hearts are the soil the seed grows in, depending on the condition of the soil, the seed will take root, meaning if there is enough love within that person's heart, the Word of God will remain in the person and that person will do the will of God and God will love that person. (Ref. Ezek. 17:8.) See also **ground**; **seed**; **water**; **sowing**; **heart**; **will of man**.

sons of God, different types
natural—All of mankind.
spiritual—All of mankind; however, there are different kinds of sons of God. There are many different ways to describe the sons of God, but the Bible uses these four names to describe the major divisions of the sons of God: the chosen, elect, or heir sons; the called or servant sons; the faithful or redeemed sons; and the lost, unbelieving, or unredeemed sons of God. The chosen sons are born of God or in other words born saved. The called or servant sons of God become saved upon accepting Christ and are born again; they have many works in the name of Christ. The faithful son or redeemed son is a son like the thief on the cross, a person who accepted Christ at the last minute through one faithful act and became saved but has no works to speak of. These are the previously lost. The last group of sons is composed of the ones who refuse to believe or repent and are thrown into the lake of fire. (Ref. Matt. 20:16; John 15:16; 2 Thess. 2:12–17; Eph. 1:3–11; Rom. 8:29–39; 2 Tim. 1:7–10.)
See also **chosen**; **elect**; **heir**; **free son**; **predestined son**; **promised son**; **servant son**; **called son**; **faithful son**; **unbelieving son**; **mature son**; **child son**; **lost son**.

soul, the

natural—The essence of an individual's life; the moral and emotional center of man.

spiritual—The personality of the man; his ego, talents, gifts, abilities, etc.; the things that make each individual unique. All souls are different from each other; like a fingerprint, it is unique to one person. Our flesh is an outward representation of the soul, meaning we express the condition of our soul through our emotions. Our emotional state of mind is determined by our ability to control our soul, so therefore we express our soul through our personality. The soul reacts to our environment through the five natural senses of a person. These natural senses were given so that the soul could learn from interacting with the world. The five senses are the ability to see, feel, hear, touch, and taste. Most people think the soul and spirit are the same thing; however, the soul is not the spirit. Although similar, the soul is different from the spirit for one main reason: the spirit is not capable of love, hate, or any emotion, because the spirit is pure logic. The soul is the opposite of logic. This is why the five senses originate from the soul, because the soul is what we learn to love, hate, or to become happy or sad with. The soul is our connection to this world. Without it, we would be no different from the angels, who do not have souls, because a soul is an earthly thing that only a man can gain. The soul is part of a man's trinity, which is the body, spirit, and soul. These three make up an individual, and an individual cannot be complete if one of these is missing. The soul is the neutral part of a man's trinity, meaning the body or flesh has a will of its own and is highly influenced by Satan. The spirit has a will of its own as well; it is highly influenced by God. The soul can get pulled in either of these directions. The direction cannot be determined, but depending on which one, a person will either be for or against God. There is a third position, which means that this person remains in the middle of these two. This person is called lukewarm, neither hot nor cold. The soul, however, will always be at the center of the battle between good and evil. The soul remains neutral until one of the major influences wins out in a person's life. (Ref. Prov. 13:35; Prov. 15:32; Mark 12:30; Acts 4:32; 1 Thess. 5:23–28; Heb. 4:12.) See also **body**; **mind**; **will**; **belly**; **ego**; **spirit**.

speaking

natural—Uttering words using one's voice naturally; conveying thoughts audibly or orally.

spiritual—Uttering words using one's voice spiritually; conveying thoughts audibly or orally with the authority of God; activating faith with one's mouth; utilizing the power of God with the mouth. God spoke everything into existence. To use the power of God, it must be activated by speaking it. For faith to be activated, it must be spoken; otherwise, it remains belief, and belief is not where the power lies. The mouth has been given the power of life and death. A man can speak words of life or death. Living water flows from the mouth of the person who has a well of water in his or her heart. (Ref. Prov. 18:4; Prov. 20:5; Prov. 16:24; Jer. 28:14; Matt. 12:33–37; Matt. 18:18; Eph. 4:15; Eph. 5:26.) See also **words; power; mouth; water; well; faith; tongue; faith; Word, the; Word of God**.

spirit, God's

natural—N/A

spiritual—Depending on the context in which this word is used, this could mean the Holy Ghost or the Holy Spirit. The Father's spirit is known as the Holy Ghost. God and his Son, Jesus Christ, share the same spirit. This is how it is made possible that they are one and the same or one with each other. This is the same way we who are in Christ will be made one and the same with God. The Father and Son have the same spirit but not the same body or soul. The spirit is the source of power for both the Father and the Son. However, there is a slight distinction between the spirit of the Father and the spirit of the Son. The spirit of the Son is known as the Holy Spirit and the same spirit is known as the Holy Ghost. There is no difference in the spirit; the difference is in what form the spirit comes to an individual. The Holy Ghost always precedes the Holy Spirit, because the Holy Ghost or the spirit of conviction must first bring about repentance before a person can be saved by the spirit of forgiveness or the Holy Spirit, because you cannot be ready for forgiveness unless you need a reason to ask for it. The Spirit of God in the form of the Holy Ghost goes by many names: the Spirit of Life, the Giver of Life, the Father of Light, the Spirit, the all-consuming fire, the right hand of the Father, the Spirit of Repentance, the Spirit of Fear, the Spirit of Burning. These names bring men into repentance, but the Holy Spirit which brings salvation to men is known as the Spirit of Adoption, the Spirit of Wisdom, the Spirit of Truth, and the Spirit of Love. There is one last major difference between the two: the Holy Spirit when he comes to a person will dwell within that person; the Holy Ghost when he comes to a person will only rest upon him or her. This difference is because this is how the Father makes some remain under law and some to come out from under law. This is God's decision to make. (Ref. Job 33:4; Rom. 8:2, 10; 2 Cor. 3:6; Rev. 11:11; Rev. 22:17.) See also **Holy Spirit; fire; water; Word of God; wine; power; trinity.**

spirit, man's

natural—The part of man that man thinks of as being a ghost or his or her conscience.

spiritual—The spirit is the consciousness of a person, that which gave him or her life. Without the spirit that God gave us, we would not be alive. Since most of us are not in touch with our spirits, we do not know God, because this is how God speaks to man through the spirit of a man because he is spirit. He does not speak to the flesh of a man or to the untrained spirit of a person. The closest he or she would come to understanding the spirit that is within him or her is realizing that his or her spirit is the same as his or her mind, or how the person thinks. However, since a man or a woman is made in the image of God, this makes him or her a trinity just as God is. Because of this, man can think from three different parts of himself. He can think with his mind, his flesh, and his soul. They all have minds and wills of their own. This is why there are battles within a person as to what he or she should do. This is what causes indecisiveness within a person. Everyone has a mind. Everyone has a body, but what makes a person is the soul or the character of that person. If the spirit is our consciousness, then the soul is our subconscious. The spirit which gives us life is what we were all first made in, but as a result of our ignorance toward God, God put us in the flesh so that he could teach us his will and love and give us the understanding of good and evil. The spirit has the ability to receive spiritual gifts from the Holy Spirit, such as faith, wisdom, understanding, knowledge, and power, as well as spiritual hearing, sight, smell, taste, and touch, the same five natural senses that the soul has. (Ref. Job 32:8; Job 34:14; Prov. 17:27; Prov. 18:14; Prov. 20:27; Eccles. 4:4; Matt. 6:22–24; 1 Cor. 2:11; Heb. 4:12; 1 Pet. 3:4.) See also **candle; life.**

spirit of bondage
natural—Slavery or involuntary servitude; serfdom; the state of being bound by or subjected to some external power or control.
spiritual—The world is in bondage or subjected to the control of the spirit of Satan until Christ comes a second time and brings all of man out from under the control of the spirit of bondage, because Christ is the spirit of freedom. The power that the spirit of bondage uses to keep people under control is ignorance. As long as a person is unaware of God's love for man, as well as what he is doing for man, which is found in the Bible, people will stay in bondage. This is also how Christ frees people. He causes them to understand, therefore opening their eyes, and when their eyes are opened, they repent and want to start living for the Father. (Ref. Isa. 14:3; Luke 11:32; Luke 11:46; Rom. 8:15; Gal. 4:3–9, 23–25.) See also **unbelief; spirit of deceit; Antichrist.**

spiritual
natural-N/A
spiritual- Unseen; not measureable; cannot be proven; the way in which God operates; can only be seen by your spirit, with the eyes of your heart; can only be measured by the faith one has; it is a way in which one thinks the is not of this world; to see, hear, and think spiritual means to see God the handy work of God. **(Ref. Jn. 4:23-24.) See also Holy Spirit; Christ; grace; faith**

spiritual, body of Christ
natural—N/A
spiritual—A symbolic representation of the oneness that is in Christ; composed of all the people who believe in him. This is made possible through the sacrifice and blood of Christ. They are brought in by having belief in this sacrifice and by having faith that it will save them from eternal damnation. (Ref. 1 Cor. 6:19; 1 Cor. 10:16; 1 Cor. 12:12–27; Eph. 4:4–16; Eph. 5:28–33.) See

also **Christ; Holy Spirit; grace; forgiveness; saved; sons of God; belief; faith.**

spiritual drink
natural—N/A
spiritual—What a person needs to drink is the living water of God. This is because to drink is to hear from God, and his Word is the water. All knowledge of the Father, Son, and Holy Spirit is called living water. How thirsty a person is determines how much water he or she will drink. The Father and Son want a person to drink so much that they will never thirst again. See also **drinking; hearing; understanding; water; living water; wine.**

spiritual food
natural—N/A
spiritual—Spiritual food is the Word of God, which contains knowledge of God. This food comes to us in different ways and in different types. The major categories of these foods are those that are eaten and those that are drunk. The Bible mentions several kinds of spiritual foods that we can eat or drink. For food, the Bible mentions bread, meat, corn, manna, fruit, and honey. For drink, the Bible mentions the living water, wine, and milk. Concerning food, this is food that our spirit needs in order to gain strength and power, because they increase our understanding of God. Therefore, all foods are a form of knowledge. There are different types of knowledge in God. The two major divisions of this knowledge are natural and spiritual. God is both natural and spiritual, so this is how the food is divided up as well. To receive the natural foods of God is to have only one half of the understanding needed to be complete. In order for one's understanding to be complete, he or she will need to drink. The Bible says this water is the spiritual understanding of who Christ is as opposed to the bread, which is the natural understanding of who Christ is. The Bible says that Jesus was the bread from heaven. For us to eat this bread, we must read the Bible; therefore, by reading, we are eating. When we hear the Word of God and believe what we hear, we are drinking, because this is how faith comes, through hearing the Word. Not all of us have drunk of the living water, because we are still drinking milk, which is only those of us who are babes in

Christ. Water is for those who are mature in Christ. Now getting back to the food of God that nourishes the spiritual body, they are as follows: bread, which comes from Christ, also known as the knowledge of God concerning the natural understanding of Christ and his Father—to eat this bread, one must read the word of God, which was brought to us by Christ (John 6:33); meat, which comes from God, also known as his will, to eat this meat is to do the will of God by following the example of Christ (Psalm 111:5; Ezek. 47:12; John 4:34); corn, which comes from God, also known as cornmeal or as manna from heaven, which is the knowledge of the love of the Father and the Son for man (Gen. 27:28; Ps. 78:23–25; Hosea 2:8–22; Joel 2:19; Matt. 13:33); manna, the bread of God, which is the same as the cornmeal of God, also the knowledge of God (Exod. 16:15; Ps. 78:24; Rev. 2:17); fruits, the natural works that reap a spiritual benefit—joy, peace, happiness, patience, kindness, meekness, love, etc. (Galatians 5:22); honey, these are pleasant words that are spoken to someone in desperate need of hearing them (Prov. 16:24; Exod. 16:19); milk, the Word of God in its most basic form, so that even a babe can understand it—when the milk is taught, it leads to salvation (1 Cor. 3:2; Heb. 5:12–13; 1 Pet. 2:2); water, which comes from the Holy Spirit, also known as living water—to drink this water, a person must listen to the words of the Father; this water causes a person to understand spiritual things (John 4:10; John 7:38; Rev. 7:17); wine, the spiritual knowledge of God (Prov. 9:5; Isa. 55:1; Mark 2:22). (Ref. Isa. 44:3–6; John 4:1–34; John 6:32–71; John 7:37–39; 1 Cor. 10:16; Gal. 5:19–23; James 3:8.) See also **eating**; **drinking**; **hearing**; **doing**; **bread**; **meat**; **water**; **milk**; **fruits**; **gifts**; **wine**; **honey**; **fruits of the spirit**.

spiritual gifts
   natural—N/A
   spiritual—Extraordinary talents given to someone by the Holy Spirit, in order to show God's presence within the person, so that they might cause others to become witnesses. (Ref. Eccles. 5:18; Matt. 7:11; Rom. 6:23; Rom. 11:29; Rom. 12:6; 1 Cor. 12:1–31; 1 Cor. 14:1, 12; Heb. 2:4–5; Heb. 6:4; 1 Tim. 4:14; 1 Pet. 4:10.) See also **gifts**; **fruits**; **fruits of the spirit**; **Holy Spirit**.

spiritual warfare

natural—N/A

spiritual—An eternal conflict that is fought in the mind, heart, soul, or spirit of an individual between what the world is trying to teach a person and what God through the Holy Spirit is trying to teach a person. The battle is mainly fought over the truth versus lies. These conflicts are fought using spiritual weapons, and they are the Word of God as found in the Bible and the Word of Satan as found in the world. The battles are fought over things, such as whether or not to continue to believe in God or to keep your faith in God, based on the fact that since a person came to believe, either good or bad things have happened to that person. Those who are babes in Christ believe that only good things should happen to them once they come to believe, but those who are mature understand that that is not the case. The battle that Satan tries to win is fought more fiercely at the beginning of a person's belief in God, because that person is more vulnerable and the main purpose is to snatch the seed of God away from the person by causing doubt. This doubt gets the opportunity to come in because the believer has asked God for something, and based on what it was, God will either do it quickly or not. If God does not do what that person asked for quickly, the person will need to develop trust and faith. This is where the battle begins, because a person does not know whether God will do something he or she has asked of him; things a person may have asked for in prayer include a house, a car, or a job. Sometimes, the outcome of the person's request will determine whose side that person will remain on, God's or Satan's. There are defensive and offensive weapons on both sides. The main objective of all battles is the possession of the souls, not the spirit, because the spirit will always be a part of God and belongs to him. The body will go back to the dust from where it came, but the soul will cause the spirit to either live eternally with God or with Satan. (Ref. 2 Cor. 10:1–5; Eph. 6:12–19; 1 Tim. 1:18; 1 Tim. 4:1–10; 1 Tim. 6:12; 2 Tim. 4:7; Heb. 10:32; 1 John 4:1–6.) See also **weapons; armor; gifts; mind; soul; spirit; Holy Spirit.**

stars

natural—Any of the celestial bodies visible at night from Earth as relatively stationary, usually twinkling points of light.

spiritual—A part of the bride of Christ. The bride of Christ consists of a third, a third, and a third. Another analogy would be the sun, the moon, and the stars. These symbolic words represent three small groups of people who make up the bride of Christ (Revelation 12:1). God calls them the sun, moon, and stars, because this is a perfect analogy to show the difference between their status with him. Each of these three groups of people have different amounts of light or glory with the Lord. This is why they have different names, but they have become one. Even though all were chosen to be the bride of Christ, the people who are the sun have shown more faith than the people who are of the moon, and the people of the moon have shown more faith than those of the stars. Their symbolic names are also represented in a natural sense by the amount of light that is given by the real sun, moon, and stars. The light of the sun is greater than the light of the moon, and the moon has greater light than the stars. This is why the people who are symbolically called the sun, moon, and stars are called by these names. These people will be used to help bring people to Christ during the millennium, the one-thousand-year rule of Christ. Another name for these people is firstfruits, because they are the first to be conformed into the image of Christ, as found in Romans 8:29. The people of the sun, moon, and stars are the same sun, moon, and stars who will not give their light during the tribulations and shortly after the tribulations, which means that they will not be found, because Christ will remove them during the most terrible times on the earth, so that they will not have to face the Antichrist. Shortly afterward though, Christ will release them to go out and change the world. (Ref. Gen. 37:9; Dan. 12:3; Ps. 148:3; Isa. 13:10; Isa. 30:26; Isa. 60:20; Matt. 24:29; Mark 13:25; Luke 21:25; Acts 2:20; 1 Cor. 15:41; Rev. 8:12; Rev. 12:1; Rev. 21:23.) See also **bride; chosen; sun; moon; crown of stars; Zion; hundred and forty-four thousand, first; hundred and forty-four thousand, second.**

stone

natural—A rock; hardened earth.

spiritual—Another name for Jesus; he called himself the stone the builders rejected; men are called lively stones or living stones.

(Ref. Dan. 2:34–45; Matt. 21:42–44; Acts 4:11; Eph. 2:20; 1 Pet. 2:4–8.) See also **Rock, the; Jesus.**

stony ground
natural—Soil that won't grow any type of seeds.
spiritual—Hard-hearted people; people who have trouble keeping their belief when times get hard. (Ref. Matt. 13:18–23.) See also **unbelief, tares.**

suffering
natural—To endure great hardships.
spiritual—Also known as trials; trials that come to make us stronger. God made us to suffer because of the sin in the world. God makes us endure great hardships in order to learn knowledge and wisdom, so that we can know the difference between good and evil and knowing this will lead to salvation. Suffering brings us into the understanding that we need to cease sinning. Since we all have to suffer whether we do right or wrong, logically, we should suffer for righteousness or God's sake, and not for Satan's sake, so that it may not all be in vain. (Ref. Rom. 8:16; 1 Cor. 4:1–15; 1 Cor. 6:1–12; 1 Pet. 3:1–22; 1 Pet. 4:1–19.) See also **chastise; trials; tribulations.**

summer
natural—The time of the year the sun is closest to the earth.
spiritual—A symbolic word for the trees that bloom during this time. This refers to one tree in particular, the fig tree. The palm tree is also known as a summer tree or a tree that does well in hot places. These trees are the spiritual names of the people whom Christ has chosen or predestined to be the firstfruits. They are the first to come into the kingdom of God, and summer is their season. Other trees have different seasons when they come into bloom, but summer refers to the parable of the fig tree, in which the end is near. (Ref. Prov. 30:25; Matt. 24:32; Luke 21:30.) See also **fig tree; palm tree; elements of God; trees of God.**

sun, the
natural—A star that is the center of a planetary system.

spiritual—A part of the bride of Christ; the bride of Christ consists of a third, a third, and a third. Another analogy would be the sun, the moon, and the stars. These symbolic words represent three small groups of people who make up the bride of Christ (Rev. 12:1). God calls them the sun, moon, and stars, because this is a perfect analogy to show the difference between their status with him. Each of these three groups of people have different amounts of light or glory with the Lord. This is why they have different names, but they have become one. Even though all were chosen to be the bride of Christ, the people who are of the sun have shown more faith than the people who are of the moon, and the people of the moon have shown more faith than those of the stars. Their symbolic names are also represented in a natural sense by the amount of light that is given by the real sun, moon, and stars. Since the light of the sun is greater than the light of the moon, and the moon has greater light than the stars. This is why the people who are symbolically called the sun, moon, and stars are called by these names. These people will be used to help bring people to Christ during the millennium, the one-thousand-year rule of Christ. Another name for these people is the firstfruits, because they are the first to be conformed into the image of Christ, as found in Romans 8:29. The people of the sun, moon, and stars are the same sun, moon, and stars who will not give their light during the tribulations and shortly after the tribulations, which means that they will not be found, because Christ will remove them during the tribulations, the most terrible times on the earth, so that they will not have to face the Antichrist. Shortly afterward though, Christ will release them to go out and change the world. (Ref. Gen. 37:9; Ps. 148:3; Isa. 13:10; Isa. 30:26; Isa. 60:20; Matt. 24:29; Mark 13:25; Luke 21:25; Acts 2:20; 1 Cor. 15:41; Rev. 8:12; Rev. 12:1; Rev. 21:23.) See also **chosen; predestined; mature son; moon; stars; hundred and forty-four thousand, first; hundred and forty-four thousand, second.**

symbolic speaking

natural—A language that uses symbols to communicate; an example would be how we use symbols to symbolize numeric meaning in mathematics.

spiritual—A language that uses symbols to communicate; by using everyday basic pictures of common-day life, God tries to get man to understand his way of thinking. The Bible is a perfect example when it uses parables. Parables are God's way of saying something about heaven using earthly terms. This how the Bible speaks to us in more than one way. The first meaning of a word can be translated literally, which will give a person at least a basic understanding of what God is trying to tell him or her. The second more hidden meaning is harder to find, but it is also embedded within the same scripture or word; however, only the Holy Spirit can reveal this meaning to a person. This is done so that a man can at least get saved, but if he wants to know more about God, it will not be because of the person's ability, but because God chose to reveal it to him. All the knowledge in the Bible is called bread, but another name for the deeper meaning is hidden manna or hidden bread. Bread can bring salvation to the one who at least believes, but understanding can cause more than just salvation, it can cause a person to be an overcomer of the world. To make people overcomers of the world is the real objective of God. However, being an overcomer does not mean a person does not still have problems in this world; it simply means that that person will overcome them through faith. They gained that faith through suffering, but if a person has been given the hidden manna, their faith will grow that much greater. This is because the meaning of their suffering will be made clear to them, however the meaning of hidden manna is only revealed to those whom God will use for special purposes. This person will understand all parables, all symbolic speaking, and any mystery in the Bible. According to Jesus, this understanding is only given to certain people. This is why Jesus said in Matthew 13:11: "He answered and said unto them, Because it is given unto you to know the mysteries of the kingdom of heaven, but to them it is not given." This language is used throughout the Bible. It is also known as speaking in tongues. (Ref. Isa. 28:11; John 6:51–63; 1 Cor. 13:1; 1 Cor. 14:16.) See also **tongues; mouth; dreams.**

tares
    natural—Any weed that grows in grain fields.

spiritual—The seed of God's enemy, the devil; they are people who will not repent or ever learn to love God. According to the parable of the tares, these seeds, when they are young, look exactly like the wheat when they are young, because neither person understands or loves God. This is why no one can tell the difference between either seed when they are young, so God lets them grow together until they reach maturity. After they reach maturity, it will be easy to tell the difference between the two. (Ref. Matt. 13:24–40; John 8:41–45.) See also **seeds; wheat; unbelief**.

third, part

natural—Being one of three equal parts.

spiritual—The number of people who were chosen from among each of the three divisions of man. The four divisions are the chosen sons, the called sons, the believing sons, and the lost sons of God; they are also divided by the four elements. Although there are four elements—earth, air, water, and fire—From these four elements, he chooses a third from each to place his Holy Spirit in from their birth, so that they would know his will, love, wrath, and knowledge. They were predestined so that they would be the first to be conformed into the image of Christ. This is found in Zechariah 13:8:

> And it shall come to pass, that in all the land, saith the LORD, two parts therein shall be cut off and die; but the third shall be left therein. And I will bring the third part through the fire, and will refine them as silver is refined, and will try them as gold is tried: they shall call on my name, and I will hear them: I will say, It is my people: and they shall say, The LORD is my God.

These are the same groups of people who in Revelation 8:7–12 are those who had life until wormwood fell upon them and they died to the world.

> The first angel sounded, and there followed hail and fire mingled with blood, and they were cast upon the earth: and the third part of trees was burnt up, and all green grass was burnt up. And the second angel sounded, and as it were a

great mountain burning with fire was cast into the sea: and the third part of the sea became blood; And the third part of the creatures which were in the sea, and had life, died; and the third part of the ships were destroyed. And the third angel sounded, and there fell a great star from heaven, burning as it were a lamp, and it fell upon the third part of the rivers, and upon the fountains of waters; And the name of the star is called Wormwood: and the third part of the waters became wormwood; and many men died of the waters, because they were made bitter. And the fourth angel sounded, and the third part of the sun was smitten, and the third part of the moon, and the third part of the stars; so as the third part of them was darkened, and the day shone not for a third part of it, and the night likewise.

(Ref. Zech. 13:8–9; Rev. 8:8–10.) See also **blood of Christ; wine; fire; refining process; chosen; elect; bride of Christ.**

thorns

natural—Something that wounds, annoys, or causes discomfort.

spiritual—A symbolic word used for the cares of the world. It is also a symbolic word used for people who believe in God, but whose cares are more for the world than God. This is why the Word that is preached to them gets choked up and does not grow within them. This is why the Bible says that God will send a fire to burn up the thorns that choke up the Word of God or prevent it from growing out of a person. (Ref. Isa. 10:17; Isa. 27:4; Isa. 33:12; Matt. 13:22; Heb. 6:8.) See also **tares.**

thorn tree

natural—Something that wounds, annoys, or causes discomfort.

spiritual—A symbolic tree name for Satan. A thorn tree is also called a briar tree or bush, or a bramble tree or bush. This tree is also known as the tree of the knowledge of good and evil. This tree tries to rule instead of the tree of life, which is God. (Ref. Judg. 9:8–15.) See also **trees of God; bramble tree.**

three women of the Bible
natural—N/A
spiritual—The three women of the Bible are really three groups of people who are influenced by a spirit differently than the others. They are the chosen sons of God, the servant sons of God, and the lost sons of God. The spirit that influences and teaches those who are chosen is the Holy Spirit. The spirit who teaches and influences those who are servants of God is the Holy Ghost. The spirit who influences and teaches the lost sons of God is Satan's spirit. The reason they are called women is because the spirit that is within each group can reproduce; therefore, they are feminine in nature. Each group reproduces more sons and daughters exactly like themselves, because God has chosen who will be in which group. Each group sees God from a different perspective. The chosen group sees the love and forgiveness of God; the group that is made of servants sees the lawful or unforgiving side of God, while the last group only sees the anger and wrath of God. Although each side is correct, neither of these groups will agree with each other. These three women are part of the bride divided into equal parts—a third, a third, and a third. These thirds who are chosen to be firstfruits will eventually help the two-thirds who are not chosen to become part of the kingdom of God. (Ref. Hosea 3:1; Matt. 20:16; Matt. 22:14; Mark 13:20: John 8:35; John 13:18; 1 Cor. 7:17–24; Heb. 3:7–19; 2 Pet. 2:1–22; Rev. 2:22; Rev. 17:4.) See also **female; feminine; chosen woman; called woman; lost woman; gold; silver; brass; palm tree; olive tree; myrtle tree; wisdom; knowledge; love; third, part.**

time
natural—The system of those sequential relations that any event has to any other, as past, present, or future; indefinite and continuous duration regarded as that in which events succeed one another.
spiritual—God is not affected by time, but because he wanted to limit man, he appointed times and seasons. God did, however, give man a clue to the way he measured time in 2 Peter 3:18. The Bible says that a day to the Lord is like one thousand years to a man. (Ref. 2 Pet. 3:8.) See also **end; rapture; day; day of the Lord; day, the great.**

tin

natural—A type of metal; mainly used to coat other metals to prevent rusting.

spiritual—A type of person whom God sees as wicked; a person who does not think about God. When the refining process is used on this person, no change occurs. (Ref. Num. 31:22; Isa. 1:25; Ezek. 22:18–20; Ezek. 27:12.) See also **metals; gold; silver; brass; iron; lead; fire; refining process**.

tongue, the

natural—Used in the mouth to create words; used to help swallow food.

spiritual—Used by God to create all life. The tongue has the power of life and death to use. A person can either speak words of faith or word of despair. We can either speak negatively or positively. We can either speak words of love or hatred. We will be judged by the words that come out of our mouths. (Ref. Prov. 15:4; James 3:8.) See also **mouth; power; speaking; death**.

tongues

natural—Different earthly languages.

spiritual—Symbolic speaking; our everyday language but it carries a different meaning. Only the Holy Spirit can teach us how to translate the meaning of these words. The gift is known as the gift of interpretations. This is how the Holy Spirit is able to translate the hidden manna to an individual. The Bible also says to let those who hear, hear. God is the one who gives the hearing, by the Word, not the spoken word, but the word that is known as Jesus. This means that the person will have the ability to both hear and speak in tongues, which is done by a second set of ears and a tongue that the Lord through the Holy Spirit gives. According to 1 Corinthians 14:22, tongues are not for the believer, but for the nonbeliever, so that he might believe. (Ref. 1 Cor. 12:10, 20; 1 Cor. 13:1; 1 Cor 14:1–40.) See also **speaking; hearing; mouth; gifts**.

tradition

natural—A set pattern, usually cultural or religious in nature.

spiritual—No definition; this is because Jesus was against all traditions because they lacked forgiveness and insight. (Ref. Job

15:14–17; Matt. 15:2–6; Mark 7:8–13; Col. 2:8; 2 Thess. 3:6; 1 Pet. 12:18.) See also **religion.**

translated

natural—Made known; seen or understood; interpreted.

spiritual—To be changed into something else after you die or to be changed into something else before you die so that you do not see death; to be transformed into light; to receive a glorified new body upon your resurrection. Two men in the Bible did not see death, because they were translated. These two people were Enoch and Elijah. Those who are translated after death and receive a new body are those whom God chose to receive it. Those who are not translated after they are resurrected have to gain faith in God in order to be translated or receive their new bodies. (Ref. Isa. 26:29; Matt. 17:1–2; Mark 9:2; Luke 20:35–36; John 5:29; John 11:25; Acts 24:14–16; Rom. 1:4; Rom. 8:10–23; 1 Cor. 15:34–54; 2 Cor. 3:18; Phil. 3:21; Col. 1:13; Heb. 11:5; 1 Thess. 4:16; 1 Thess. 5:23; Heb. 4:12; Heb. 11:35; 2 Pet. 3:10; James 2:26; Rev. 20:5–6.) See also **body, new; resurrection; reward.**

treasure

natural—Great wealth on earth; something known to be very valuable on earth.

spiritual—Great wealth in heaven; something valuable only to our Father in heaven. This treasure allows a person to purchase oil, wine, and corn or wisdom, knowledge, and love, which in turn causes a man to produce fruits. The fruits are faith, love, hope, forgiveness, understanding, kindness, gentleness, etc. When we produce these fruits, God stores our treasure or our rewards in heaven. (Ref. 1 Cor. 3:14; Col 2:1–3.) See also **works; faith; heart; wisdom; buy; oil; wine; corn.**

tree

natural—The largest plant on earth; helps cool the earth; creates oxygen for us to breathe; can also feed us and provide shelter; any of various shrubs, bushes, and plants, resembling a tree in form and size.

spiritual—Another name for God and the people of God. God the Father is known as the tree of life. The Bible calls people either branches off of that tree or trees themselves. There are several reasons why God calls himself a tree. This is because of what a tree does for the earth. A tree gives oxygen which allows everything to breathe. God does the same thing spiritually; he calls it the breath of life, which is our spirit. A tree can be cut up and used for shelter. God wants us to use him as our shelter. A tree can give us food. God wants to feed us as well. The Bible calls man a tree as well. This is because a man can provide all these things for his family, just like God. A tree also produces fruit; so are the works of a person called fruit. A person's fruits can be either good or bad, and this is why the Bible says in Matthew 12:33 that you shall know a tree by its fruit. Satan is also known as the tree of the knowledge of good and evil (Gen. 2:17). (Ref. Prov. 3:17–18; Prov. 15:4; Prov. 11:30; Joel 1:1–12; Zech. 4:11:14; Matt. 12:33; Matt. 15:20.) See also **God; father; man; fruit; elements of God; palm tree; olive tree; myrtle tree; bramble tree.**

tree, fruitful

natural—A tree bearing edible fruit.

spiritual—A tree is symbolic of a person, who is doing works of faith that please God. (Ref. Gen. 1:11–12; Jer. 17:8; Ezek. 36:30; Ezek. 47:12; Hosea 10:1; Matt. 7:17–19; Matt. 12:33; John 15:2–8; John 15:16; Gal. 5:22; Eph. 5:9; Col. 1:10.) See also **female; feminine; works.**

tree, fruitless

natural—A tree that bears no fruit.

spiritual—A person who bears no fruit, or is not following the will of God. The Bible calls these types of people cedar trees. Satan is called a cedar tree in Ezekiel 31:3–16 because he does not produce fruit for God. (Ref. Jer. 6:19; Jer. 20:7–15; Ezek. 31:3–16; Amos 2:9; Zeph. 2:14; Zech. 11:1–2.) See also **tree of the knowledge of good and evil; cedar tree; female; feminine.**

tree of life

natural—N/A

spiritual—The tree of life is a symbolic name God calls himself. This is because a tree represents God in many ways. It provides shelter, which is what God does when he offers his protection to us. A tree provides oxygen, which is what God does when he gives us the breath of life, which is what he blew into Adam when he made man. A tree provides shade, which is what God does with the clouds. A tree has deep roots, which is what God makes when he plants a seed in us. A tree holds the soil together, which is what God does within our hearts. He does this when the wind and rains or trials and tribulations come. He holds us together by causing us to keep our hope and faith. A tree holds water, which is what God does when he gives us his Holy Spirit, which is also known as living water. A tree can be used as material to make a building, which is why God calls us his building, temple, or vessel. A tree can produce natural food. God can produce spiritual food. Naturally speaking, the leaves on some trees can be used for medicine. This is the same analogy the Bible uses in Revelation 22:2, where it says these leaves are for the healing of the nations. These are the leaves off of God's tree, which are really the chosen people he is using to teach the world to have faith in him. Naturally speaking, if all the trees were gone from an area, the area would look barren. There would be no life. The soil would be poor, and there would be no water. This would be the same analogy the Bible would use if God were to leave an area. It would look barren. Without trees, the earth would die; (Ref. Prov. 15:4; Prov. 3:18; Prov. 11:30; Ps. 1:1; Isa. 47:12; Isa. 61:1–3; Dan. 4:9; Zech. 4:12; Matt. 7:15–20; Rom. 11:17–25; Rev. 22:2, 14.) See also **God; Father; trinity; wisdom; palm tree; olive tree; fig tree; fruits; female; feminine.**

tree of the knowledge of good and evil
natural—N/A
spiritual—The tree of the knowledge of good and evil is a symbolic name of Satan. This tree tries to mimic the tree of life, by offering man what only God can give, which is eternal life. This tree does have fruit on it, as does the tree of life; however, if a man eats its fruit, he will die and not live, because these fruits do not produce righteousness. They are the ways of man. The fruit off this tree is not Godly knowledge but worldly knowledge. This knowledge is contrary to the Word of God. This tree got its name because it was once good, or an angel, and then it was evil, or a fallen angel. This is why it is called the tree of the knowledge of good and evil, because at first, he knew only good, but now he knows only evil.

This fruit is only good for worldly things. God wants us to produce spiritual things. To do this, we must live in the spirit. This is the kind of fruit that pleases God. If men choose the wrong tree, which is what Adam and Eve did, they will make the choice of letting Satan be their mentor, rather than God. This is the same as choosing not to believe in God or Christ, because of the things the world has thought of a person. The world has blinded them, which is what Satan wants. (Ref. Gen. 2:9, 17; Gen. 3:1–14; Judg. 9:8–20; Ezek. 31:3:16; 2 Cor. 11:3; Rev. 12:9.) See also **cedar tree**; **bramble tree**; **Satan**; **dragon**; **evil**; **hate**; **fruit of man**.

trees of God
natural—All natural trees are made by God.
spiritual—All spiritual trees are made by God. God calls people trees because since there are so many different kinds of trees, a tree is a perfect analogy for people since there are so many different kinds of people. There are trees that produce fruit, and there are trees that don't. There are trees that grow best in one type of soil, and trees that grow best in another. There are trees that grow best in warm weather, and there are trees that don't. There are trees that can be used for building, and trees that can't. There are trees that are beautiful and trees that aren't. There are trees that are strong, and trees that are weak, etc. The Bible says in Ezekiel 17:24:

> And all the trees of the field shall know that I the LORD have brought down the high tree, have exalted the low tree, have dried up the green tree, and have made the dry tree to flourish: I the LORD have spoken and have done it.

The trees that have exalted themselves will be brought down low. These are people who look down on others, and the trees that have been looked down on all their lives will be lifted up. These are people who worship God and have been oppressed because of it. In Isaiah 55:12, the Bible says, "For ye shall go out with joy, and be led forth with peace: the mountains and the hills shall break forth before you into singing, and all the trees of the field shall clap their hands." These trees are people who are happy because they are in the presence of the Lord. Although there are many kinds of trees, all of them can be broken down into three categories.

Those categories are trees that produce spiritual fruit, trees that produce natural fruit, and trees that produce no fruit at all. In these three categories, the main trees the Bible speaks of are the palm tree, the olive tree, and the cedars. The palm tree produces spiritual fruit. The olive tree produces natural fruit, and the cedar tree produces no fruit at all. Palm trees are also called the water element. They are people who were born after the spirit. They that are born after the flesh, which is the olive tree, are people who do not agree with those born after the spirit (Galatians 4:29). This is not to say that those who are born after the olive tree are evil. It is just that God has two sides, both natural and spiritual; however, the people don't realize this and so they disagree over natural and spiritual things not realizing how they work together, but since they who are natural don't get along with they who are spiritual, the understanding on both sides never comes together to increase the other. Both natural and spiritual knowledge were meant to work together. This means that both natural and spiritual people were meant to work together. God will cause this to happen. This is why God is going to burn the trees and melt the elements. This can be found in Joel 1:19, where God talks about burning the trees up. In 2 Peter 3:12, God talks about melting the elements. These scriptures simply mean that God will use his heavenly fire, or the Holy Spirit, to cause these trees or elements to learn to work together. (Ref. Ps. 92:12; Ps. 104:16; Ps. 148:9; Isa. 9:10; Isa. 41:19; Isa. 44:14; Ezek. 17:1–24.) See also **female; feminine; elements of God; palm tree; olive tree; cedar tree; bramble tree; fig tree.**

trials

natural—The act of testing or trying of charges or claims against someone, in order to prove innocence or guilt.

spiritual—The act of testing or trying of charges or claims, in order to teach a person patience, faith, and love. God calls these trials chastisement, and the Bible says God only chastises those he loves. God does not give us the trials himself; instead, he simply lets the devil do his job. This is the only reason God has not destroyed Satan yet. God allows him to continue because the trials Satan puts us through bring us into the understanding that God wants us to have, which is knowing the difference between good and evil. Since God cannot teach the understanding of evil, because he has no evil in him to show us, he allows Satan to do it for him. Knowing and understanding evil is an essential part we must learn in order for us to move toward perfection. Satan, however, knows his days are numbered. As far as trials go, a trial does not begin until a person is being drawn toward God and away from the world or ungodly things. A trial begins when God starts to call a person toward him, and the world simply pulls back the other way. The harder God pulls, the harder the trial. All trials are hard, and all trials are necessary. This is why the Bible says in James 1:2, "count all things joy when temptation fall upon you." The only way a person can truly count all things joy is to know that a trial is for his or her own good and not for his or her destruction. (Ref. 2 Cor. 8:2; Heb. 11:36; James 1:1; 1 Pet. 1:7; 1 Pet. 4:12.) See also **temptation; chastise; tribulations; patience.**

tribulations
natural—Hard times; a stressful situation, which seems to have no end or any good purpose.
spiritual—There are two kinds of tribulations. The first is the kind everyone goes through, which basically refers to the hard times in a person's life. We must go through these tribulations in order to grow in Christ but not all people will have tribulations in their lives and certainly not all people will grow from their tribulations. This is why there is a need for the second kind of tribulations; the second kind of tribulations is a time in earth's future when God will cause the world to go through hard times in order to bring it closer to him. The tribulations that are to come will serve God's purpose, which is actually good. The tribulations through which a lot of people will have to go are not for the destruction of those people, because most of them will be people who believe in God, which is contrary to the belief of the church. This is because salvation is not the main goal of God; perfection is. This is why the tribulations are necessary, because they will bring believers who are now separated by religion into a oneness with Christ. One of the main reasons for the tribulations is to remove religion from the world. The tribulations only last three and half years, but what follows the tribulations is the time of teaching in which Christ, along with his chosen, will teach the true love of God. This will last for almost one thousand years, according to the Bible. The

purpose of the tribulations is to show some believers that they still lack something that they need, and that is the living water. This is something only they who have been chosen have drunk prior to the tribulations. At present, everyone of a different religion believes that everyone else is doomed for what they believe in, but the tribulations will answer that question once and for all, by showing that no religion is correct. Because of the tribulations, all will call out to Christ for forgiveness, then all will be of one accord and ready to be taught as to who Christ is and his importance to every man. The Bible says that the number of people who came through the tribulations was so great that no man could number them. This is found in Revelation 7:9. (Ref. Isa. 10:19; Rom. 5:3; Eph. 3:13; 2 Thess. 1:4; Rev. 7:9.) See also **trials; temptation; called sons; servant son; believers, three kinds; chastisement.**

trinity of God
natural—When three work together in unison.
spiritual—A belief that God is three persons and that these three are one. The trinity is represented in three manifestations: the Father, the Son, and the Holy Spirit. There are three that bear witness in heaven; these three are equal. The trinity works as follows. Jesus represents the body; the Holy Spirit represents the Spirit; and the Father represents the soul. The Father shares the same Spirit with Jesus, which is the Holy Spirit, which makes them one. Man is made in this exact same image; we have one body, and within that body is a soul and a spirit, thus completing a trinity of our own. Our body is also designed to make room for another spirit, the Holy Spirit, which will make us one with God. (Ref. Matt. 11:27; Matt. 12:17; Luke 20:42–43; John 5:18–19, 30–37; John 6:38; John 8:37–42; John 12:28–30; John 17:20–21; Phil. 2:5–8; 1 John 5:5–6.) See also **witness; oneness; Jesus; God; Holy Spirit; Spirit, God's.**

trinity of man
natural—N/A
spiritual—How man resembles the image and likeness of God. Man is divided into three parts, just as God is. God has a body, soul, and spirit, and man has a body, soul, and spirit. These three parts operate independently of one another if a person is not in

Christ. If a person is in Christ, he or she is made whole, meaning all of his or her parts work together, because they become united by Christ. If a person is not united in Christ, these three parts do not agree with each other and war against each other. The body, which is the flesh, will fight against the spirit, and the soul will not know which side to choose. The soul is connected to the flesh, and the heart is connected to the spirit of a person. If the soul does what the flesh tells it to do, a person's soul is in danger of being lost. If the soul does what the spirit tells it to do, the soul will be saved. The more the soul listens to the spirit, the closer the body is to being made whole, or in agreement with its parts. (Ref. Matt. 12:18; Matt. 14:36; Matt. 15:28; John 5:6–9; 1 Thess. 5:23; Heb. 4:12.) See also **soul**; **spirit, man's**; **trinity of God**; **family**; **Holy Spirit**.

understanding
natural—To comprehend; to agree with.
spiritual—To comprehend; to agree with; to be brought into the oneness with God; the wellspring of life; better than any treasure on earth. This understanding is done with the heart and not with the mind. To understand the things we need to understand from God, we must drink the water of life from God. The living water that he has to give us causes our understanding to grow. This living water is called spiritual knowledge. It is something that most of us do not have at this time and is something that the world needs. The knowledge that leads to this kind of understanding will cause a person to free himself or herself from the bondage of the world, and the only thing that can do that is the Holy Spirit, which is why he is called living water. We must drink of living water to increase our understanding. (Ref. Prov. 8:21–36; Prov. 16:22; Hosea 4:6; John 12:38–40; Col. 3:10.) See also **wisdom**; **knowledge**; **Holy Spirit**; **water**; **heart**; **eating**; **drinking**; **light**.

unbeliever
natural—A person who does not believe in something.
spiritual—A person who refuses to believe in Christ or the Father. Because of unbelief, these people will not repent, and because of their unrepentant hearts, they are lost, but not just because they don't believe. Believing or not believing can be changed when a

person has evidence or can see with his or her eyes; in fact, Christ is coming back to show most that he does exist. After most have seen, they will come to believe. The problem is that some will not come to Christ even after they have seen with their eyes. They will still refuse to repent and follow Christ, and these will be the only sons of God who will not enter into the kingdom of God. (Ref. 1 Tim. 1:1–12; Heb. 3:14–19.) See also **unsaved**; **tare**; **condemnation**; **veil**; **evil heart**; **unrepentant heart**; **unbelieving heart**; **void of light**.

uncovered head

natural—To not have protection from the elements upon your head.

spiritual—To not have protection from the elements upon your head, and those elements are the Father or Christ over your head. Only the Father and Son can protect a person from Satan. To not have Christ is to not have a covered head. To not have Christ is also to be found naked, and to be found naked is to live a life without knowing truly who Christ is. Not knowing means that you do not believe; you must believe in order to receive the robes that he has to cover you with or the crown that he has to place on your head, the crown of righteousness, which covers your head. (Ref. Lev. 18:17; Isa. 47:1–15; Ezek. 4:7; Ezek. 16:37; Hab. 2:4; 1 Cor. 11:7; Heb. 4:13; 1 Pet. 4:8; Rev. 3:18.) See also **naked**; **unbelief**; **covered head**.

unleavened bread

natural—Bread that does not rise when heat is applied.

spiritual—Unleavened bread is another symbolic name for Christ. He was unleavened, meaning not puffed up by the amount of knowledge that he possessed. A person who is full of wisdom and knowledge but remains humble and does not rise up or puff himself or herself up is also called unleavened bread. There is bread of this world that puffs up a person, and that bread is call leavened bread. This bread is the knowledge of the world, which will cause a man to become vain. Leavened bread can cause a person, when offended, to want to fight when things heat up. Unleavened bread or the Word of God, which calms the spirit, does not make one think that he or she is better than another. Therefore, it causes a person not to want to fight when he or she is put down. This is called humility. This is the character of Christ. (Ref. Exod. 23:15; Luke 22:1–7; 1 Cor. 5:8.) See also **humble; Jesus; bread; wine; oil; corn.**

unrepentant heart
natural—A person who will not admit he or she is guilty or wrong naturally and will not forgive others or himself or herself, so other people will not forgive him or her.
spiritual—A person who will not admit he or she is guilty or wrong spiritually and will not forgive others or himself or herself, so God will not forgive him or her. (Ref. 1 Tim. 1:1–12; Heb. 3:14–19.) See also **unbelief; evil; unforgiveness; lost son; unbelieving heart; unbeliever; void of light.**

veil
natural—Something that hides the face; something that cannot be seen through.
spiritual—Not being able to see spiritually because something is blinding you; something that hides the face of God from man. That something is the flesh. The flesh is something that interferes with spiritual sight. The flesh does not allow man to see, meaning understand, God, because it has a desire of its own. If flesh is to be satisfied, it must cause the man to hate God, because if a man follows the will of God, the flesh cannot do what it wants to do. This is how the flesh wars against the spirit and causes a man to be blind toward the will of God. The flesh does not forgive, and this is why God brought the law, because neither does the law forgive. So God wanted to show men who do not forgive how it feels not to be forgiven, so that they might turn from their ways and learn to forgive. According to the Bible, the same thing happens today when a person without understanding reads the Old Testament laws of Moses. The Old Testament can cause the veil to cover our hearts and so we do not forgive our brother. This is found in 2 Corinthians 3:18. If a person does not have a full understanding of the New Testament, which is the forgiveness of God that came after the law, then he or she has a veil over his or her heart. (Ref. 2 Cor. 3:1–18; Heb. 10:15–20.) See also **flesh; Old Testament; blindness; void of light; heart.**

virgin

    natural—An unmarried person; pure; unsullied; undefiled; without admixture, alloy, or modification; (of a metal) made directly from ore by smelting, rather than from scrap.

    spiritual—A person who is not mixed with sin or not mixed with the cares of the world; a person, according to Zechariah 13:9, who has been brought through the fire and been refined as silver or gold, this fire being trials and tribulations that have shaped and molded that person's life and conformed him or her into the image of Christ. (Ref. Isa. 7:14; Matt. 19:12; Matt. 25:1–11; 1 Cor. 7:25, 34; 2 Cor. 11:2; Rev. 14:4.) See also **barren woman; bride; chosen woman; sons; hundred and forty-four thousand, second.**

virgin, woman

    natural—An unmarried girl or woman; pure; unsullied; undefiled; without admixture, alloy, or modification; (of a metal) made directly from ore by smelting, rather than from scrap.

    spiritual—A group of people who have been chosen out of the world to be the first to be conformed into the image of Christ. They are called virgins because they have not been defiled by the world or religion. They have been set aside, sanctified, justified, and glorified by Christ. This is according to Romans 8:29. Spiritually speaking, there are three women of the Bible or three main groups of people. They are the virgin or chosen woman, the called or servant woman, and the woman who is called faithful because this group of people believed at the last minute and were saved by their faith alone. The called woman or those who have been called to the wedding are saved but have been defiled by women and the cares of the world, but because she was not chosen, this group will be the guest at the wedding. The Bible illustrates this in the parable of the ten virgins. Five of them had oil in their lamps and were allowed to enter. The other five were not allowed to enter because they had no oil. This oil is the wisdom of God that keeps a person from being defiled. This parable is found in Matthew 25:1. (Ref. Isa. 62:5; Matt. 22:14; Matt. 25:1; John 15:6, 19; Eph. 1:4; 2 Thess. 2:13; 1 Pet. 2:19; Rev. 17:14.) See also **bride; chosen woman; barren woman; Sion.**

virtuous woman

natural—A woman highly sought after by men; a woman of high status; a woman to be desired.

Spiritual—A woman who exhibits the will of Christ toward her husband; a woman who has all the virtues and qualities to be a good wife and a good mother; raises her children properly; is the strength behind her husband. (Ref. Prov. 12:54.) See also **Christian; saved; blessed; reward.**

vessel

natural—A container for natural food or water; a ship or aircraft or anything that carries precious cargo.

spiritual—A container for spiritual food or water; the heart of the person which carries the precious Word of God around in it. (Ref. Acts 9:15; 1 Thess. 4:4; 2 Titus 2:21; 1 Pet. 3:7.) See also **body; cup; bowl; cistern; church; lamp; light; container; heart; potter.**

vine, tree

natural—A plant that produces a variety of fruits and vegetables that sustain life on earth.

spiritual—A symbolic name for Jesus, who produces fruit on his vine; the fruits on his vine are those who believe in him. (Ref. Judg. 9:12; Ezek. 19:10; Zech. 3:10; Mark 14:25; John 15:1–5; Rev. 14:18–19.) See also **Christ; bridegroom; rock, the; Jesus; stone, the; husbandman.**

vision

natural—The ability to see naturally.

spiritual—The ability to see spiritually, to see God's handiwork; seeing God's plan in action or prophesying God's impending wrath. The Bible says that where there is no vision, people perish. (Ref. Prov. 29:19.) See also **eye; discern; prophesy; sight.**

void of light

natural—Having no light present; darkness; not easily seen; hidden from view.

spiritual—Having no light present, light meaning understanding of God. This is truly when a person is in darkness; the love of God is hidden from a person's view; having no knowledge of God or his Son; having not received the bread; not doing the will of the Father; not having the love of God in one's heart. (Ref. Prov. 11:12; Prov. 24:30; Eccles. 3:13; Isa. 5:20; Matt. 4:16; Matt. 25:30; Luke 11:35; John 3:19; John 12:46; 1 Thess. 5:5.) See also **darkness; knowledge; unbelief; unbelieving heart; evil.**

watch, a

natural—A watch is a certain time to be observed; looking or waiting expectantly; being ready for the unexpected or expected.

spiritual—It means looking for the Lord's return; continuing to do his will while waiting upon the return of Christ. All watches take place at certain hours. The first watch was from 12:00 AM until 3:00 AM; the second watch was from 3:00 AM until 6:00 AM. The third watch was from 6:00 AM until 9:00 AM, and the fourth watch was from 9:00 AM until 12:00 PM. Jesus said that he could return either the second or the third watch. If he comes at 3:00 AM, he is returning as a thief in the night, and he will take those who are ready. When he returns at 6:00 AM, which is by day, all eyes shall see him. He has said that since no man knows at which of these hours he will return, we should be ready for either time. If you are taken at 3:00 AM, you do not have to go through the tribulations. The three hours of darkness that fall between 3:00 AM and 6:00 AM are symbolic of the three years of darkness that will fall upon the earth during the tribulations. (Ref. Matt. 20:3; Luke 12:38.) See also **darkness; tribulations; rapture; harvest; harvest, second; harvest, third; harvest fourth.**

watch, to

natural—To keep looking for something; to wait for something; to anticipate; to expect something.

spiritual—To keep looking for the return of Christ; to wait on Christ; to expect his return; to continue to do His will while excepting to be rewarded by him and that reward is to be with him. (Ref. Matt. 24:42–51; Luke 12:38; 1 Thess. 5:6; Rev. 3:3). See also **servants; doer; patience; reward.**

water

> **natural**—A vital fluid needed by man to survive; needed to keep all bodily functions working properly; the major component of blood.
>
> **spiritual**—Another name for the Holy Spirit; needed to keep all spiritual bodily functions working properly. This water is the Word of God. If a man drinks, which means to listen to anyone else who has drunk this water and believes or accepts what that person has told him or her, then he or she will never thirst again or, in other words, he or she will not look for another Gospel. This water will cause a person to fully understand the forgiveness and love of God. This water will cause the person who drank it, which means to have faith, to realize the Father has forgiven him or her of his or her sins. The Bible can refer to this water in several forms; one form is rain, which means when the blessing of God comes down from heaven out of nowhere. This water can come in the form of a river, which means from the mouth of a person who has drunk this water and has many things to tell a person, so much that the person who is willing to listen won't be able to handle it all at one time. This water can come in the form of only one cup at a time, which means to only give a person just enough of the Word of God to keep him or her going. Water in the form of rain, naturally speaking, causes dry land to yield vegetation, thereby healing the land, causing the soil to become fertile. When it comes to man, God calls us trees or grass, and since we are plants to God, we need rain in order to make us grow. The soil in some of our hearts needs to be tilled so that the seed of God once planted can break the soil and take root. If the soil in our hearts is good soil, the seed will never stop growing. If the soil in our hearts is not good, the seed that has been planted in our hearts by the hearing of the Word will not grow very well. Fertile soil is a spiritual word for a man who has a good heart. This analogy for good soil being in the heart of man can be found in two places in the Bible. The first is Ezekiel 17:1–10 and the second, Matthew 13:1–9. (Ref. Isa. 43:19–21; Prov. 11:25; Prov. 20:5; Ezek. 36:24–27; Isa. 44:3–6; Matt. 10:40–42; John 4:7–21; John 7:37–39; Heb. 10:16–22; I Pet. 3:20.) See also **Holy Spirit; chosen; blood; drinking; hearing; trinity; baptism; baptism by fire; anointing; rain, former; rain, latter; living water; living waters.**

wedding

natural—The act or instance of blending or joining, especially opposite or contrasting elements; union.

spiritual—This is a period of time when they who are chosen of Christ will become one. This is the reward of those who were chosen. This wedding will take place while the tribulations are still going on in the earth. (Ref. Matt. 22:3–10; Luke 12:36; Rev. 19:7–9.) See also **marriage; bride; chosen**.

wedding garments

natural—Formal clothing set aside for a special day.

spiritual—The evidence of one having overcome the world; the reward for being found faithful; the evidence of having one's sins washed away. (Ref. Isa. 61:10; Zech. 3:4–5; Matt. 22:11–12; 2 Cor. 11:27; Rev. 3:18; Rev. 7:14; Rev. 16:15.) See also **white robes; white linen; righteousness; reward**.

wedding guests

natural—Those who attend a wedding.

spiritual—Those who were not chosen to be in the wedding but made it to the wedding of Christ; they are those who are of the two parts who were not chosen. (Ref. 1 Thess. 4:16.) See also **called son; servant son**.

well

natural—A place where water can be found in the earth.

spiritual—A place where water can be found. The water in this well is called the water of life. The well is our hearts. The water in the well comes from the Holy Spirit; only understanding the Word will draw it out of a person. (Ref. Prov. 10:11; Prov. 16:22; Prov. 20:5; Isa. 12:13; John 4:14; 2 Pet. 2:11–22; Rev. 2:6; Rev. 22:1, 17.) See also **water; Holy Spirit, the; understanding; Dipper; trees; grass; wheat**.

whale

natural—A large mammal that swims in the sea.

spiritual—Another name for Satan. This analogy is used when the Bible refers to men as living in a sea. Within that sea is Satan, and he is called a whale or leviathan. The Bible says that God will cast a net and catch Satan. This is said first in Ezekiel 29:4:

> Speak, and say, Thus saith the Lord GOD; Behold, I am against thee, Pharaoh king of Egypt, the great dragon that lieth in the midst of his rivers, which hath said, My river is mine own, and I have made it for myself. But I will put hooks in thy jaws, and I will cause the fish of thy rivers to stick unto thy scales, and I will bring thee up out of the midst of thy rivers, and all the fish of thy rivers shall stick unto thy scales. And I will leave thee thrown into the wilderness, thee and all the fish of thy rivers: thou shalt fall upon the open fields; thou shalt not be brought together, nor gathered: I have given thee for meat to the beasts of the field and to the fowls of the heaven. And all the inhabitants of Egypt shall know that I am the LORD, because they have been a staff of reed to the house of Israel.

Even though in the beginning of these scriptures, God is speaking to a man, he is really speaking to the spirit that is within the man. This same analogy is used in yet another place with this same book, Ezekiel 32:3–9 says,

> Thus saith the Lord GOD; I will therefore spread out my net over thee with a company of many people; and they shall bring thee up in my net. Then will I leave thee upon the land, I will cast thee forth upon the open field, and will cause all the fowls of the heaven to remain upon thee, and I will fill the beasts of the whole earth with thee. And I will lay thy flesh upon the mountains, and fill the valleys with thy height. I will also water with thy blood the land wherein thou swimmest, even to the mountains; and the rivers shall be full of thee. And when I shall put thee out, I will cover the heaven, and make the stars thereof dark; I will cover the sun with a cloud, and the moon shall not give her light. All the bright lights of heaven will I make dark over thee, and set darkness upon thy land, saith the Lord GOD. I will also vex the hearts of many people, when I shall bring thy destruction among the nations, into the countries which thou hast not known.

352

(Ref. Ezek. 32:2–9; Isa. 27:1; Ps. 104:26; Matt. 12:40.) See also **leviathan; fish; sea; serpent.**

white linen
natural—Clothing that does not have any spot on it.
spiritual—Clothing that does not have any spot on it, given by the Lord, as a symbol of one's righteousness, as a reward for having faith; shows that all sins have been forgiven. The opposite of this clothing is our flesh, which the Bible calls filthy garments. (Ref. Rev. 19:8–14.) See also **filthy clothes; clothed; clothing color; wedding garments; faith; armor; naked.**

whole, made
natural—Something that is put back into one piece.
spiritual—Having caused the three main parts that make up man, which is our body, spirit, and soul, to work together through faith. It is faith that makes the body, mind, and spirit come together and not work against one another. It is a feeling of great joy to not be in conflict with oneself or God. Only Christ through the Holy Spirit can cause this to happen; through one's belief in him, the body is made whole. (Ref. Matt. 14:36; Matt. 15:28; Matt. 22:37; Mark 10:52; Luke 8:48; John 5:6–9.) See also **oneness; faith; Holy Spirit.**

Whore of Babylon
natural—N/A
spiritual—These were the people of Israel during the time that they were captured and brought into Babylon. During that time, they lost hope in God and forgot him. Some chose other gods to follow. This is what God means by the word *whore,* those who turned away from him, those whom he loved and to whom he was married, who forgot about him. It was not until he converted the king of Babylon (Dan. 4:33–34) that he made his people remember him and they began to follow him again. The spirit of doubt that inhabited his people during that time is the same spirit that causes many people today to not believe in him. This means that the spirit of this woman still exists today. She causes people to become drunk with her wine, which means to doubt God. (Ref.

Rev. 17:1–18; Zech. 1:1–16; Ezek. 37:1–28.) See also **Jerusalem; old bride; olive tree; divorce.**

wilderness

natural—A wild and uncultivated region, as of forest or desert, uninhabited or inhabited only by wild animals; a tract of wasteland.

spiritual—A wild and uncultivated place that God does not care to dwell in. A wilderness is the opposite of a city, where God does care to live and dwell with his people. (Ref. Ps. 107:33–35; Isa. 14:12–21; Isa. 27:10; Isa. 64:10; Jer. 12:10; 1 Cor. 10:5.) See also **dry place; desolate.**

will of man

natural—To desire; to wish for; to want something; the ability to control one's own action.

spiritual—A man's personality, that which drives him. According to the Bible, a person's will is controlled by the heart, or in other words, a man's will comes from strength of heart or weakness of heart. According to the Bible, a man has two wills (Rom 7:18), one to do right and one to do wrong. One is controlled by the flesh, and the other is controlled by the spirit, with the heart stuck in the middle not knowing which to do. One will wants to follow God; the other will wants to follow its own desires. So man's will is in a state of confusion. Man's will is caught between the will of the flesh and the will of God. Whoever does the will of the Father is a brother to Jesus, and whoever does his or her own will is in danger of losing his or her soul, because the will of man is to conquer his fellow man. (Ref. Matt. 12:50; John 15:8–19; Rom. 7:14–25; Col. 1:21–23; Col. 1:9–14.) See also **ego; heart; mind; meat; soul.**

will of God

natural—That we all love one another.

spiritual—That we believe in his Son, Jesus Christ, as well as every word that comes out of the Father's mouth. If we were to believe and have faith in God, then this would be called eating the meat of God. If we only believe some of what God says that is found in the Bible, it is said that we only drink the milk of God. This is why milk is for those who are babies in Christ, but meat, being the will of God, is strong meat mentioned by Paul in 1 Corinthians 3:2. The Bible also tells us in John 4:34, that "Jesus saith unto them, My meat is to do the will of him that sent me, and to finish his work." That will is to show all mankind the love of the Father. (Ref. Mark 3:35; John 4:34; Rom. 8:27; Rom. 12:2; 1 Cor. 3:2; 1 Thess. 4:3; 1 Thess. 5:18; Heb. 5:12.) See also **meat**; **love**; **will of man**.

wind of God
natural—Air in natural motion, as that moving horizontally at any velocity along the earth's surface; any influential force; a gale; storm; hurricane.
spiritual—Wind is one of the four natural elements of God. The other three are water, earth, and fire. Wind is both a natural and a spiritual element, and since it is a natural and a spiritual element, it can be used to create or destroy as all the elements can. When used to create life, it is called the breath of life (Gen. 2:7) or wind (Ezek. 37:9). When it is used to destroy life, it is called a hurricane (Luke 12:55; Rev 6:13). The breath of life is the air we breathe every day in order to live. This is wind or air, one of the four natural elements of God, being used to sustain life. (Ref. Gen. 2:7; Gen. 7:22; Ps. 48:7; Ps, 78:26; Jer. 18:17; Hosea 13:15; Luke 12:55; Rev. 6:13: Rev. 7:1.) See also **air**; **breath of life**; **wrath**; **elements, of God**.

wine of God
natural—The fermented juice of grapes, made in many varieties, such as red, white, sweet, dry, still, and sparkling, for use as a beverage, in cooking, in religious rites, etc.; something that invigorates, cheers, or intoxicates like wine.
spiritual—Those who are of the water element who have been chosen by God and mixed with the blood of Christ and have been made into wine, or have been spiritually changed from water to wine. Wine is also a symbolic word for the blood of Christ. They who have been made into wine have been given the spiritual understanding of Christ. This is different from the air element, which are people who have been made into the oil of God by the blood of Christ and have the understanding of the natural side of Christ, because the Father and the Son are both natural and spiritual. How both the natural and the spiritual sides of God

work together in harmony is very difficult to comprehend for any man, and so God splits or divides these aspects of himself between different groups of people. He calls them the four elements: water, air, earth, and fire. The people of each group see God from a different perspective, and so those of the water see his spiritual side; those of the air see his natural side; those of the earth see the side that is love, and those who are of the fire element see the side that is called God's instincts, which are his wrath against all things that he dislikes. The wine of God or this group of people will be used during the millennium to teach other people the spiritual side of God, along with the group that is oil, love, and the wrath of God. (Ref. Prov. 4:17; Isa. 5:22; Isa. 24:9; Zech. 7:1–6; Rom. 14:17–22; Rev. 6:6; Rev. 14:10.) See also **blood of Christ; drinking; fountain; elements of God; water; hearing; heart; love; elects; chosen; element earth; element air; element fire; zodiac signs.**

wine of the world

natural—An alcoholic drink made from grapes; too much will cause a man to be drunk and not fully aware of what is going on around him.

spiritual—Wine has a double meaning; there are two kinds of spiritual wines: the wine of God and the wine of the world. The wine of the world leads to ignorance and hatred; the wine of God leads to love and forgiveness. The wine of God is the knowledge of why Christ had to died for all to become saved and the understanding of the importance of the blood of Christ, which covers our sins. If the wine of the world causes a man to become drunk or suffer for a lack of understanding, then the blood of Christ, which is another form of symbolic wine causes a man to be saved. This means that the lack of understanding God Word is what makes a man spiritually drunk. The wine of God or the life of Christ teaches man how to enter into the kingdom of God. The wine of the world, according to the Bible, is known to us as false religions or false teachings by false prophets; too much of this type of teaching will cause a person to be drunk or, in other words, unaware of the true nature and love of God. According to Revelation 17:2, the woman riding on the back of the beast causes the world to drink of her wine, the wine of fornication, which is spiritually translated into idolatry or the worship of the creation more than the creator. The woman sitting on the beast represents the ways of the world, and the beast represents the spirit of the Antichrist. The world has been made drunk by this wine, which means to not know God. (Ref. Matt 9:14:17; Mark 2:22; Luke 5:38; John 2:1–10; 1 Pet. 4:3; Rev. 14:8; Rev. 17:2.) See also **Blood of Christ; drunken; drinking; hearing.**

wisdom

natural—The ability to judge what the truth is; to discern right from wrong.

spiritual—Wisdom is the experience of something; having been exposed to something. This is unlike knowledge in that you do not have to experience it to learn, because knowledge is the knowledge of something; wisdom can only be given by the Holy Spirit. Otherwise, the hardships that we go though in life are looked on as bad luck. Wisdom is the evidence of the presence of the Holy Spirit; wisdom is also called the fruit of the Spirit. Wisdom is how we will learn to drink from the fountain of living water, which Christ will offer to all people, because wisdom is the spiritual knowledge of God. (Ref. Prov. 1:20–23; Prov. 2:1–13; Prov. 3:18; Prov. 4:22; Prov. 5:15; Matt. 7:24; 1 Cor. 2:7; 1 Cor. 12:8; Col. 2:3; Col. 4:5; James 1:5; James 3:13–17.) See also **oil; oil of gladness; understanding; meat; knowledge; gifts; bread; Holy Spirit; element water.**

witness

natural—A person who has firsthand knowledge of something; a person who has seen with his or her own eyes; only one is required on earth.

spiritual—A person who has firsthand knowledge of God's works; a person who has seen with his or her own eyes the work of God. According to Biblical law, there must be more than one witness to verify truth. In Deuteronomy 19:15, it says, "One witness shall not rise up against a man for any iniquity, or for any sin, in any sin that he sinneth: at the mouth of two witnesses, or at the mouth of three witnesses, shall the matter be established." The Bible says that there are at least three that bear record in heaven in 1 John 5:7. This is so that the truth is established. Jesus and the Holy Spirit are witnesses on our behalf to establish us. The Bible also speaks of another witness in 1 John 5:8: "And there are three that bear witness in earth, the Spirit, and the water, and the blood: and these three agree in one." These three are the Holy Spirit, the spiritual knowledge of God—to us from the Bible, which is confirmed by the Holy Spirit—and the blood of Christ. (Ref. Matt. 18:16; John 5:30–38; John 8:15–19; Rom. 2:14–15; 2 Cor. 13:1; Heb. 10:15–20; Heb. 12:1; 1 John 5:1–8.) See also **trinity**.

woman

natural—Female; feminine; capable of reproduction; opposite of male.

spiritual—Women came from God, and the word *woman* was given to the gender that could reproduce. God is able to reproduce. He reproduces sons, and the part of God that reproduces, or in other words causes him to gain sons, is the Holy Spirit. The Holy Spirit is the thing that God impregnates us with, and we then start to reproduce spiritual fruit in the form of love, peace, joy, kindness, happiness, gentleness, wisdom, faith, etc; these things are feminine because they reproduce in others if they see your fruit. This is the opposite of masculine things, which are things in God such as power, glory, strength, divinity and honor. These do not reproduce in us now, because they are not necessary for now. They are the rewards that God will give man later. The Bible says that when God first made man, he made him in his own image; therefore, God is both male and female, because this is what he said about himself in Genesis 1:27. Therefore, if he made man both male and female, it is because they came from him. The side of God that is feminine in nature is the Holy Spirit. (Ref. Prov. 14:1; Prov. 31:30–31.) See also **feminine; wife; love; wisdom; faith; joy; God; Holy Spirit; bride; male**.

women, four

natural—Feminine quality or aspect; a wife; more than one woman.

spiritual—Feminine qualities of three different groups of people; they are called women because they have the ability to reproduce sons and daughters like themselves. These three groups have come into Christ three different ways because they are of two different covenants. They are the chosen, the called, and the faithful. The chosen group were predestined by God and were never under law but grace (Gal. 4:24); the group that is called were previously under law but called out or redeemed from under law and have come into Christ. The group that is called faithful are those who were previously lost (Gal. 3:13 and Gal. 4:3) but came to believe only after they had seen and were saved, just like the thief on the cross. There is a fourth group, the group of people who are lost to God, because they would not repent (Revelation 9:20), but the first three are saved. (Ref. Rom. 8:29; 2 Cor. 4:3; Eph. 1:4; Gal. 3:13; Gal. 4:1, 23–24; Rev. 9:20.) See also **female; feminine; women.**

Word of God
> **natural**—God's voice; God's commandments.
> **spiritual**—Another name for Jesus Christ before he came to earth; he is the manifestation of God's words. Born from God, he was always a part of God but was brought out of God, which means to be born, when God the Father created him. In John 1:1, it says, "the Word was God and the Word was with God." This is showing us the birth of the Word. One minute, he was inside the Father, and the next, he was outside of the Father, next to him. Later, the Bible says the Word made everything that was made; this includes the angels and man. From the beginning, the Word knew that he would have to die for his creations, and so the Word accepted his mission and his fate and kept his faith in his father that he would resurrect him. The Word made himself a flesh body to dwell among men, and he was called Jesus, which became another manifestation of God but in bodily form. This is how Christ can be both God and man on earth. This is because his father is God, and his mother is Mary. Jesus Christ is part of the trinity through the Holy Spirit, and since God is whole or one, when Jesus died on the cross, it served the same purposes as the Father dying on the cross, because they share the same spirit. (Ref. John 1:1–13; Rev. 19:11–16.) See also **Jesus; bread; trinity; oneness; begotten son, the; son, the; Holy Spirit; seed; good ground; female.**

words

natural—A combination of sounds used to communicate.

spiritual—The power of God is located in his words and Word, and this power is activated by speaking the words in faith. These words are also known as spiritual water and have the power of life or death in them. Words can be used either in our defense or persecution, depending on if we believe. Words can be used to show love, hate, anger, happiness, joy, etc. We are judged by our words. A man is only as good as his word is. God is as good as his word is. God's words are so powerful that the Bible calls them a sword. (Ref. Prov. 20:5; Prov. 18:4; Matt. 12:33–37; Rom. 10:9–10; Eph. 5:26; Rev. 19:15.) See also **power; mouth; faith**.

works that can be seen

natural—The natural occupation of a person; physical labor.

spiritual—The natural duty of the church, which causes people to become saved; work that leads to salvation. These works include the ministry, the preaching of God's word, baptizing, feeding the hungry, taking care of the needy, etc; these are works that can be seen, and all of these types of work are designed to lead a person to the cross of Jesus. These are natural fruit that are produced from our belief in Christ. Although these works are good, they alone are not good enough. This is why the Bible says in James 2:18–26, "… faith without works is dead." (Ref. Matt. 16:27; John 14:12; Gal. 1:16; 2 Tim. 1:9; James 2:18–26; Rev. 2:23, 26.) See also **church**.

works that cannot be seen

natural—N/A

spiritual—The spiritual duty of an individual; works of faith; spiritual labor, which show the love of God from the inside; the spiritual fruit of a person; love in action. These types of fruit cannot be readily seen by another person; they are called the fruits of the Spirit. They are love, peace, happiness, joy, understanding, wisdom, and knowledge that increases our faith. The greatest of these kinds of works are our faith and our love for God as well as our fellow brothers in Christ. Although these works are good, without faith, they are dead as well. This is what the Bible says in

James 2:18–26: "Yea, a man may say, Thou hast faith, and I have works: shew me thy faith without thy works, and I will shew thee my faith by my works." This is because both types of works—those that can be seen and those that cannot be seen—plus our faith must be combined in order for us to be made perfect. (Ref. Rom. 3:27; Rom. 4:4–17; Rom. 11:6; 1 Cor. 3:13–15; Gal. 2:15–21; Gal. 3:5; Gal. 5:22; Eph. 2:5–9; Heb. 4:1–11; James 2:14–26.) See also **fruits**; **love**; **faith**.

world, culture
natural—N/A
spiritual—*Sea* is a symbolic word found in the Bible for world culture. A sea is the culture of the world in which many people have many things in common and don't realize it. They don't realize it because it is invisible, too large, and can only be revealed by the Holy Spirit to a person. The world is unaware of its influence. The Bible also calls this sea or culture the spirit of the Antichrist (1 John 4:3). Where cultures were developed from is a mystery to most men but not to God. Scientists try to prove how these things developed from a natural standpoint, but the Bible has concluded that these things developed from a spiritual standpoint. Over thousands of years, many small cultures have come and gone, but world culture, or the culture which stems from unbelief, has rarely ever changed. This is because a culture can only be changed by the collective agreement of the people as a whole, and since people rarely agree as a whole, large cultures never change. The Bible calls men fish in Habakkuk 1:14, and in Mark 1:17, Jesus tells his disciples that he will make them fishers of men. (Ref. Ezek 47:10; Hab. 1:14; Mark 1:17; 1 John 4:3.) See also **sea**; **man**; **fish**; **fisherman**; **net**.

worship
natural—To give reverence to someone having great authority.
spiritual—To give reverence to God; to worship God in the spirit. God wants all to worship him in the spirit, because God is a spirit. Those who love him should worship him in the spirit. (Ref. Exod. 24:1; John 4:22–24; Phil. 3:3.) See also **meditate**; **blessings**; **drinking**; **eating**; **meat**; **spirit of God**; **spirit**.

wrath of God

natural—Vengeance or punishment as the consequence of anger.

spiritual—A sacred right of God that can only be given to another by him, and since it cannot be reproduced, it is therefore part of the masculine side of God. (Ref. John 3:36; Rom. 1:18; Rev. 14:10, 19; Rev. 15:1.) See also **masculine side of God; male side of God; power; glory; honor; authority; holiness; righteousness**.

yeast

natural—Something added to bread; used to cause bread to rise; causes bread to be puffed up.

spiritual—Something added to the word of God or something someone adds from his or her own understanding in order to make himself or herself look good. This is called adding yeast. Yeast can cause the person who is using it to resort to anger quickly when someone does not believe him or her. Yeast causes the person to be puffed up or be self-righteous. Too much knowledge—not the knowledge of God but the knowledge of the world—is another form of yeast. (Ref. Matt. 13:33; 1 Cor. 5:6; Luke 13:18.) See also **bread; bread, one's own; Word, the; knowledge**.

yoked, evenly

natural—To be tied together; to work in union; to strive for a common cause.

spiritual—To join with someone who is also a believer in Christ or like-minded with a common goal. (Ref. Matt. 11:20–30; 2 Cor. 6:14; Gal. 5:1; 1 Tim. 6:1.) See also **marriage; oneness**.

yoked, unevenly

natural—To have two things pulling against one another; two things that do not have the same natural strength.

spiritual—To have two things pulling against one another, two things that do not have the same spiritual strength; to have one member carry the greater burden; to have two things pulling against one another; to marry someone who does not believe in the Father or Christ. (Ref. Jer. 28:14; Gal. 5:1.) See also **marriage; bondage**.

Zion

> **natural**—The name of the new city of God.
>
> **spiritual**—The name of the new city where the bride of Christ will be. This city will be divided into three parts. They are the inner court, middle court, and an outer courtyard. There are three divisions because there are three divisions of the sons of God. They are called the chosen, the called, and the faithful, or the first, second, and third fruits, by order. (Ref. Isa. 49:14; Zech. 1:1–16; Zech. 2:10; Zech. 9:9; Rev. 16:19; Rev. 17:14–15.) See also **bride**; **Sion**; **New Jerusalem**; **mountain**; **chosen**; **called**; **faithful, the**; **City of God**.

zodiac signs

> **natural**—In astrology, this band is divided into twelve equal parts called signs, each 30° wide, bearing the name of the constellation for which it was originally named but with which it no longer coincides owing to the precession of the equinoxes.
>
> **spiritual**—The term *zodiac signs* can be translated as elements of the world, or the twelve fruits on the tree of life. In the spiritual sense, a zodiac sign to God means a type of personality, and there are twelve distinct kinds. However, these twelve are grouped together, three each within the four elements, which are water, air, earth, and fire. This is what the Bible refers to in Revelation 22:2, when it says,

> In the midst of the street of it, and on either side of the river, was there the tree of life, which bare twelve manner of fruits, and yielded her fruit every month: and the leaves of the tree were for the healing of the nations …

These fruit that are yielded each month represent the different personalities or zodiac signs of those born each month. Each person that is born under a certain zodiac sign has a uniqueness about him/her. This uniqueness is in the way they see God or the perspective from which they see God. They see God as they see themselves. God can be all things and all men, or at least from an elemental point of view, when the zodiac signs are grouped by their elements. When the zodiac signs are grouped by the elements—water, fire, earth, and air—they resemble the life forces that are with God. These life forces are the building blocks of life itself, which is what the zodiac signs in their elements represent. The elements are part of a whole. As long as they remain separated, they are weak. It was necessary to separate them so that they could be judged, but the elements were always meant to be brought back together. They will be brought together again upon Christ's return. The Bible says that Christ will bring fire with him upon his return,; this fire will cause the elements to melt together. In 2 Peter 3:10, it says,

> But the day of the Lord will come as a thief in the night; in the which the heavens shall pass away with a great noise, and the elements shall melt with fervent heat, the earth also and the works that are therein shall be burned up.

This type of melting is not for destruction. It is for bringing them together. This will cause them to be greater than they were when they were separate. Each element is here to learn about its creator, God, and the other elements, its brethren, as well as to learn how to get along with them, meaning to love them. This can only be accomplished by love. At present, hardly anyone gets along, and love between the signs does not exist. This will all change when Christ shows us how to love one another and appreciate one another for our differences and uniqueness. (Ref. Gal. 4:3–9; Col. 2:8; Col 2:20; 2 Pet. 3:10–12; Rev. 22:2). See also **elements of God; element water; element air; element earth; element fire.**

SUMMARY

The message that this book is attempting to bring to the understanding of those who believe is that God is more active and loving than anyone can ever imagine. People are simply unaware of just how active God is in the lives of the average everyday person. What they are unaware of is that God has already predetermined all things so that he will have a particular outcome. This plan begins with the angels because it was the angels who sinned against God first and the evidence of this a war that took place in heaven led by one of his angels Lucifer. It was because of this war that God realized that his angels did not know his will, as a result of this God must have realized that he would first have to teach them the difference between good and evil. This meant that God would have to come up with an elaborate plan to teach his angels this, since he himself is not capable of evil this led to the plan called the Doctrine of predestination. This book, however, only deals with a small portion of that plan, called the Doctrine of Election, which means those whom God chose to know his will first and carry out whatever mission he had for them. Those who were chosen are called by many names found within the Bible. Some of those names are the elect, true witnesses, sons of gold, the fig trees, or the children of the chosen women, to name a few.

These witnesses will in turn make known this plan and eventually everyone will follow those witnesses. The problem is that people don't know this, and this is mainly because God has been hiding his plans from the world in plain site, within the pages of the Bible. It is hidden because most of this plan is written in the symbolic language, and cannot be understood except the Holy Spirit gives the translation. The main reason why God hid this plan is because he knows how the people of this world

365

think, in that if they knew how his plan worked, they would no longer think of him as a loving God. What is it that people would not like most about his plan? The answer is centered around choice. To the average Christian, choice means everything. We are taught that we must choose Christ in order to be save, and to not chose Christ will condemn us. This is true, the problem is that we needed help in making that choice. What those need to understand is that God loved us so much, he helps us to make that choice. Some have preached that that choice is one hundred percent yours, as if somehow that would make God more favorable towards that person. The people who teach this don't really realize the impact of what they are saying. To preach that the choice is one hundred percent yours is to say that we follow a God that just sits and waits on man to make choices. This means that the God that we follow does not really get involved in the affairs of man, unless man makes the right choices in which he is often shown the ability to do. This is not the God I serve, the God I serve is a very active God in the affairs of man, particularly when it comes to those who come to believe. The notion that a man decided on day that he would be saved, by confessing his believe in Jesus Christ, leaves out the fact that God had been calling that person long before that person confessed Christ. Just because the person can recall the day he got saved, doesn't mean that God wasn't active in that persons life long before that date. This brings me to the point that this book has been trying to make all along. The activity within a persons life long before he or she got saved, is predestination at work. What we all need to understand about predestination is that the main reason for it is to predetermine a certain outcome. So if God wants a certain amount of people saved in this world, then that means that he will be hard at work making sure it happens. So that means that that choice that the person eventually made, most of credit goes to the one who urged in into it, who is none other than God the Father, working with Jesus and the Holy Spirit. If you still don't understand how predestination works, let me ask you a question? Let's say you have two choices, choice A and B, and you can't decide which choice to make. Depending one which choice you make, life could end in disaster, or prosperity. Now because you don't know what to do, you seek help in making the right decision, and the person you sought help form, eventually helped you to make up you mind. Years later you finally realize that you made the right decision. The question is, was the final choice you made one hundred percent yours? Remember, without the person who helped you by giving you his or her advice you may not have made the right decision. Then the correct answer is that you cannot take one percent credit for that decision, and if you can't then your choice was not one hundred percent yours. This is how God's Holy Spirit works, he helps us to make the decisions that we make. This is how God remains active in our lives, this is how he guides us. When you think you just talking with yourself, you may be in counsel with God's Spirit and not realize it. This is why the Bible calls the Spirit, the Counselor. So then, if God is an active God, this is what he would be very busy doing, and not just waiting around to see what you or I will do. In this way he is in control, and it is in this way he can predetermine an outcome. He knows who will listen and He knows who will not, because he made the hearts that we all have.

Lastly, I know that this brings up a very important question, and that question is what about the people who don't listen, what about those who don't becomes saved? This brings me to another reason for the world not wanting to accepted predestination and that is the fact that not everyone is saved. People want to know why would God not save all mankind, why would he let anyone become lost? The answer to that is what the world is not ready to understand, but I will give you the answer that I believe my Father in heaven gave me when I asked this question of Him. The answer can be found in two places within the Bible.

Isaiah 45:5-7 (KJV)
I *am* the LORD, and *there is* none else, *there is* no God beside me: I girded thee, though thou hast not known me: 6 That they may know from the rising of the sun, and from the west, that *there is* none beside me. I *am* the LORD, and *there is* none else. 7 I form the light, and create darkness: I make peace, and create evil: I the LORD do all these *things*.

What these verses tell us in a what many people have always wanted to know but were afraid to ask, and that is did God create evil. The answer is yes, and the reason is why found in the book of Romans.

Romans 9:14-24 (KJV)

14 What shall we say then? *Is there* unrighteousness with God? God forbid. 15 For he saith to Moses, I will have mercy on whom I will have mercy, and I will have compassion on whom I will have compassion. 16 So then *it is* not of him that willeth, nor of him that runneth, but of God that

sheweth mercy. [17] For the scripture saith unto Pharaoh, Even for this same purpose have I raised thee up, that I might shew my power in thee, and that my name might be declared throughout all the earth. [18] Therefore hath he mercy on whom he will *have mercy*, and whom he will he hardeneth. [19] Thou wilt say then unto me, Why doth he yet find fault? For who hath resisted his will? [20] Nay but, O man, who art thou that repliest against God? Shall the thing formed say to him that formed *it*, Why hast thou made me thus? [21] not the potter power over the clay, of the same lump to make one vessel unto honour, and another unto dishonour? [22] *What* if God, willing to shew *his* wrath, and to make his power known, endured with much longsuffering the vessels of wrath fitted to destruction: [23] And that he might make known the riches of his glory on the vessels of mercy, which he had afore prepared unto glory, [24] Even us, whom he hath called, not of the Jews only, but also of the Gentiles?

If I summarize these verses as well as this book, what I would get is that God is trying to tell us is that He is all powerful and that no man of which he created can question him. However, if we take a closer look at these verse twenty three, the answer is there and that is to make known the richness of his glory. In other words, by creating evil, and showing us what is not good, it will eventually cause to understand what is good, and love the one who is Good. This is none other than God our Father. So in the process of showing us what we need to understand about what is good and what is bad, God had to create some who would do evil in this world, and subsequently they would never be able to come to him and be saved. This is what the Christian world has been unable to accept about God our Father. This is why he could not until now tell them of his plan, because they would not even until this day accept it.